C000244116

BORN A MUSLIM

Also By Ghazala Wahab

Dragon on Our Doorstep: Managing China Through Military Power
(with Pravin Sawhney)

BORN A MUSLIM

SOME TRUTHS ABOUT ISLAM IN INDIA

GHAZALA WAHAB

ALEPH

ALEPH BOOK COMPANY
An independent publishing firm
promoted by Rupa Publications India

First published in India in 2021
by Aleph Book Company
7/16 Ansari Road, Daryaganj
New Delhi 110 002

ISBN: 978-93-90652-16-7

3 5 7 9 10 8 6 4 2

Printed at Thomson Press India Ltd, Faridabad

To my parents,

Shabana and Wahab, with gratitude

And to my babies,

Eliza, Ayra, Zara, Arham, and Anayah, with hope

CONTENTS

INTRODUCTION

Sometime in the second decade of the last century, when my great-grandmother was a young bride, an unverified, supposedly paranormal, event gave birth to a family philosophy that has survived cynicism, pragmatism, agnosticism, and revisionist conservatism.

It was one of those moonless summer nights in large swathes of northern India when the breeze is held captive by the day's heat, making the courtyards of the houses only marginally more bearable than the rooms inside. In my great-grandfather's stone-and-mud house in the small settlement of sawyers adjacent to the Taj Mahal on the outskirts of Agra, each room had only one small token window that opened onto the courtyard. Though open to the sky, the size of the courtyard ensured that even as the heat rose from the freshly watered mud floor in the evening, the breeze seldom reached the rooms.

On that summer night, my great-grandmother could not fall asleep. It was not just the stifling heat, but the absence of breeze that greatly bothered her. But unlike the men of the house, who included her father-in-law, she couldn't sleep in the open. So once everyone had fallen asleep, she quietly dragged her charpoy to the doorway of her room. Striking a compromise between modesty and comfort, she placed it astride the threshold.

Close to midnight, just as she was drifting off, she felt her charpoy shaking violently. She woke up with a start. Sitting upright, clutching at the bamboo frame that held the cot together, she looked around. The night was quiet except for the snores coming from all around. Looking down, she noticed that her charpoy was now at an angle and, rather than halfway through the door, was mostly inside her room. One foot of the charpoy was touching her bedroom wall. It was as if somebody had pushed the charpoy aside so that they could go past it. She sat thinking about it for a long time. And, instead of the heat of the night, she felt a cold frisson of fear. Finally, she pulled her charpoy back inside her room.

Next morning, she narrated her experience to her husband. Finally, when word reached her father-in-law, he reportedly nodded meaningfully without saying a word. In the evening, when he returned home after his maghrib prayer,[1] he sat down on his daybed and asked my great-grandmother for a drink of water. As he took the copper bowl from her, he told her, 'You were in the way. You must always be considerate to others. After all, we are not the only ones living here. When they don't trouble us, why must we trouble them? He didn't harm you because he respects our family. You must respect him.' Later, at dinner, he instructed all his sons and daughters-in-law to ensure that the thresholds were never blocked and explained that one must always be clear which side one was on. Since then, thresholds became as sacrosanct as borders in my family. Their sanctity had to be maintained.

His was a Shaikh family. In the Sunni pecking order, this was just below the Sayyids, considered descendants of Prophet Muhammad through his grandsons, Imam Hasan and Imam Hussain, sons of his daughter Fatima. Even though Islam was envisaged as a classless and casteless religion, it could not overcome the human obsession with social hierarchy and power. Hence, amongst the tradition-bound Sunni Muslims of the Indian subcontinent, the top three communities—Sayyids, Shaikhs, and Pathans—were categorized as Ashrafs (high class). These communities could intermarry, but most Sayyids married other Sayyids or sometimes Shaikhs, Pathans being considered lower in the order. Shaikhs married both Sayyids and Pathans. This hierarchy, however, did not imply untouchability; and it was based neither on occupation nor education.

My family, for instance, was poor and illiterate, yet commanded respect because of their supposed high standing in the social hierarchy, overt piety, and generosity (sometimes even towards complete

[1]All five compulsory prayers or namaz that Muslims are required to perform daily are symbolic of the time of the day. Maghrib is read at dusk. Muslims refer to maghrib as the twilight hour, or that brief moment when day and night become one. In Muslim folklore, maghrib is also the time of day when djinns move around more freely, hence the time humans need to be mindful. The other four daily prayers are fajr (dawn), zuhar (afternoon), asr (evening), and isha (night).

strangers), which often stretched their economic means. In our extended family and community, generosity in those days was regarded as a very high virtue, on a par with piety and was indicative of a strong moral character. Perhaps this had to do with one of the sayings attributed to Prophet Muhammad. He apparently told one of his companions that the best Islam is 'feeding the hungry and spreading peace among those you know and those you do not know'.[2]

When my grandfather married into a Sayyid family, he further raised the family status, now referred to as Shaikh-Sayyid, though in terms of education and economic power there was only marginal improvement. My grandfather was illiterate, but my grandmother, owing to her Sayyid family background, had had a basic education. Her brothers were educated and most of them were in government jobs. Perhaps this fuelled my grandfather's ambition and as his children (he had eleven) started to grow up, he decided to move to Agra city from the settlement. Apart from the family, he brought with him his inheritance of piety, tolerance, benevolence, and respect for thresholds.

The piece of land that my grandfather bought in a Muslim mohalla of Agra came with a small room and a mazar, a shrine that suggested the presence of a noble spirit in that area. Over the years, as he slowly started to build a house, he remained conscious of the mazar and what it represented. Here, thresholds became even more important because the invisible resident would obviously be moving around. He understood that not all spirits were kind, and some were short-tempered; hence, care had to be taken to ensure that they were not hampered. The unseen cohabitant was periodically propitiated by the burning of incense and distribution of nukhtiyas (deep-fried chickpea flour drops soaked in sugar syrup) every Thursday evening to the neighbourhood children after the maghrib prayers. This was a routine that continued well into my adolescence.

I learnt about the importance of thresholds when, as a child, I once decided to run away from home. When it came to it, I couldn't

[2]Faith in Allah: Daily Hadith Online, available here: https://abuaminaelias.com/an-nawawi-on-spreading-peace-on-earth/

muster the courage to step out into the narrow lane outside. We had frequently been warned how dangerous that lane was—riddled with poverty, illiteracy, backwardness, and unthinkable danger—and the message had been ingrained in us. As kids we were discouraged from venturing out without an adult escort. Hence, I decided to register my protest by sitting in the doorway. One of my aunts, my father's younger sister, tried to persuade me to quit my post. When all else failed, she told me the story about my great-grandmother and convinced me of the perils of sitting in the doorway. I decided to go back inside.

Throughout my childhood, I never questioned the veracity of the story, though I realized that the details changed with every retelling. Subsequently, I added my own elements of drama to the story, even describing the appearance of the spirit.

Over the years, despite the story becoming increasingly fanciful, and hence dubious, thresholds continued to hold a special meaning for my family. Apart from instilling the importance of coexistence and tolerance (even with the unseen), they also marked the line between private and public. This line was extremely important because our home didn't leave much room for privacy. Even without intending to, everyone eavesdropped on everyone else, both within the house and outside it.

Loosely based on the traditional havelis, our home was built around a central courtyard. But since the area was small, the family large, and finances limited, my grandparents had to dispense with the inner courtyard which creates a buffer between the rooms and the central courtyard, lending a layer of privacy to the inhabitants. All rooms opened onto the central courtyard, which doubled up as a common family area. On the ground floor, even the windows of the rooms opened onto the courtyard for ventilation. The only other option would have been to have the windows open onto the lane outside. And that was not permissible.

The gully was canopied by crisscrossing electric wires. This gully represented everything that my grandparents and his children, especially my father, wanted changed in our lives. The neighbourhood we had chosen was of necessity not choice. Our neighbours were small-time traders, shopkeepers, artisans, and butchers. The narrow lanes around our home converged on a maidan-like small ground. At the edge of this ground, hemmed in by the houses, was a mosque. In front of the mosque was a handpump and, behind it, a partially covered drain. Along the drain, the lane sloped downwards to the shanties in which the so-called 'low-castes' (the sweepers, cobblers, etc.) lived.

Such was the confidence of the local administration in the civility of these two communities that a permanent police presence was maintained at the mouth of the main lane which led into this maze. About ten policemen lived in tents pitched on the open maidan outside the lane. Interestingly, a full-fledged police station was barely half a kilometre away.

Our home, built one room at a time as the income of the family grew, was an island in this labyrinth of lanes and over-peopled houses. It was as if my grandfather and his children (my parents, uncles, and aunts) knew that this would not be our permanent residence, that all of us would move on to better homes the moment we could afford it. Hence, as kids, we never socialized with the neighbourhood children. We could only see a sliver of the sky from the lane but from our terrace, it was an uninterrupted expanse. That's where we, the cousins, played—two storeys above the lanes where the other Muslim and the dispossessed kids played.

Early Lessons

My most vivid childhood memories pertaining to religion are of Ramzan, the month of fasting which culminates in the biggest festival of Muslims—Eid. For several years (from the time I was seven to eleven), Ramzan, or at least part of it, used to fall during my summer holidays.[3] As kids, while we were not allowed to fast, we were instructed to be good.

'This is the month when all good deeds are multiplied,' my mother used to tell me and my brothers. 'If you behave well, help others, and remain truthful it will be as good as fasting.'

The preparation for the fast would start in the evening, when my

[3]This is as per the Islamic calendar which is lunar, and hence fifteen days shorter than the Gregorian calendar. This is the reason all Muslim festivals in any given year occur fifteen days earlier than the year that preceded it.

mother and aunts began to cook the meal which would be eaten during sehri[4] at dawn. Usually, it was some mutton curry cooked with a seasonal vegetable accompanied by dal and a vegetable preparation. Sometimes the mutton curry was replaced with mince cooked either with potatoes or peas or even bitter gourd. The flour was kneaded and kept ready, so that fresh rotis could be made quickly in the morning.

Nearly two hours before the time for sehri expired, sehri-criers, a set of small drums tied to their waists, would walk down the lanes waking people up. Some sang devotional songs and some simply repeated a wake-up call, 'Haazareen sehri ka waqt ho chuka hai' (Gentle people, it is time for sehri) in a sing-song voice. The women of the family were the first to rise. It was their job to heat the food and make rotis for everyone. The kids were not woken up but with so much activity in the house, most of us usually got up, and were not forced back to bed because of the summer break. Honouring the commitment to help, I and some of my cousins used to help lay out the sehri spread—first we put down a thick dhurrie and then a white sheet on top. Across the middle would go the saffron, red, and brown printed dastarkhwan (a sort of table runner) on which we placed the plates and serving bowls. The adults would gather and eat the sehri meal.

About ten minutes before sehri ended, the criers would be back in the street, counting down. Finally, the azaan would crackle through the night from the mosque, announcing the end of feasting and the beginning of fasting.

The same routine was repeated when the day came to a close. In the late afternoon, all the women would start preparing for iftar (the evening meal). Kids were assigned small jobs like stirring the sugar in icy water used to make huge jugs of lemonade or crushing the ice added to the water or stirring the lemonade to make sure all the ingredients were properly blended. Special trays of iftar were prepared to be sent to the mosque so that travellers and those who couldn't afford a meal

[4]Sehri is the meal eaten before sunrise during the month of Ramzan. With sehri, the daily fast or roza commences. It concludes with iftar at sundown.

were also able to break their fast with good food. Delivery of these trays to the mosque was one of the duties entrusted to the kids. Carrying the trays to the mosque, we used to feel a sense of importance and pride. Not only were we carrying food for the less fortunate, our trays had more delectable offerings compared to the small plates which would come from the neighbouring houses.

My pride, however, was short-lived. When I mentioned this casually to my grandfather over iftar, thinking he would be pleased by my observation, he surprised me by saying, 'Now all your sawaab (the reward that Allah is meant to bestow for good deeds) is gone. When you do something good, it is not for you to decide it is good. It is for Allah mian to judge whether it is good. When you speak for him, he gets upset.'

My grandfather was the mildest and kindest person I remember. Amongst my fondest memories of him was watching him distribute clothes to the poor during Ramzan. In the last fortnight of Ramzan, every afternoon, my grandfather, Abba to me, would seat himself on a rickety wooden chair in the small passage that connected the main door facing the lane with the central courtyard of the house. This passage was almost like a room, the most public part of the house where visitors waited until invited inside. My grandfather would sit here, not only to keep the doorway unobstructed, but also to maintain a distance from the lane outside. Next to him, stacked neatly on a coarse white sheet laid out on the floor, would be bolts and bolts of fabric. Stiff white cotton meant for pyjamas to one side, colour block pastels in mulmul for kurtas next to them. On the other side were cheerful prints for women. Next to the white sheet was a plastic basket with faux georgette scarves or dupattas to complete the ensemble for women.

This was the zakat (charity) spread my grandfather used to lay out during Ramzan. It was not just the money spent (roughly 2.5 per cent of one's annual assets according to Quranic stipulation, though my illiterate grandfather had no way of doing the math), but the effort that made it noble, as he used to personally visit the market to select the fabric, including the prints for women. Everyone in the market knew him and the fabric used to be delivered home for distribution during the holy month. According to Abba, he was giving the poor a chance to wear new clothes on Eid.

Since he had been doing this for years, people knew about it and thronged our home; there was no signage outside and my grandfather always sat inside the house. He didn't want to make a public display of his charity. His elderly man Friday, who had been with him for years, would double up as a tailoring assistant, measuring the material according to the requirement and cutting it up. Most of the time my grandfather never questioned the supplicant; he believed her, whether she asked for clothes for two or five family members. Only in the cases of well-known offenders would he restrict the number.

For kids in the family, this was just one more reason to enjoy Ramzan. Stacked-up bolts of fabric were a new arena for play and once the distribution started in the late afternoon, watching the whole exercise was like a live entertainment show. Often, we would offer help by trying to match the dupattas with the suits.

Many years later, one of my flashier uncles assumed this responsibility after my grandfather's stroke; but with a difference. He crossed the threshold. With a skullcap perched on his head, he used to place his chair outside the house in the lane, frequently engaging passers-by in conversation so that nobody could fail to notice what he was doing. For good measure, he exhorted the receivers of zakat to pray for the family which was making their Eid joyous; the louder the expression of gratitude, the happier he was. All in public view.

After Abba's death, the practice was stopped, because good intentions had been replaced by 'exhibitionism'. Thereafter, like most Muslim families, we started sending zakat money to madrassas. It was both convenient and soul-satisfying because we believed that the money was being spent on poor children. Also, there was a feeling that since these children would be getting an Islamic education, they would grow up to serve the faith. Service to the faith was considered a noble job, something that ordinary Muslims, engaged in worldly pursuits, were not able to do.

I discovered these nuances much later in life. As a child, Islam came to me gently, and in driblets. There was no structured imparting of religious education at home. Learning to read namaz and the Quran was not considered necessary for children, though at my mother's insistence some half-hearted efforts were made to teach us the Quran—a few tutors were hired and fired. No maulana or hafiz[5] was ever recruited for the job, neither were we sent to the mosque as the neighbourhood kids were. This was another way of keeping us insulated from the larger Muslim community of our mohalla. I started to learn about Islam through proverbs and the stories that my mother and sometimes my father narrated to me.

This learning was supplemented by the questions that I asked of them about our faith. While some of these questions came from my own curiosity, quite a few of them were those that my school friends asked me. Their questions covered the entire gamut from genuine curiosity to inherited prejudice: 'Why do you fast during Ramzan?', 'Do you put meat in all your food?' Some questions stemmed from stereotyping: 'Why don't Muslims bathe every day?' And some were downright ridiculous: 'How many mothers do you have?'

These questions neither bothered me nor offended my parents. I always managed to get very sensible replies from them, which I dutifully conveyed to my friends. My school friends never appeared malicious to me, though I had fewer friends than others. Despite being the only Muslim girl in my class, I never sensed any prejudice. Even the reluctance to share my tiffin didn't bother me because at my convent school many girls usually ate only their own packed lunch. Maybe that is what they were taught at home. Or I was not perceptive enough to understand. Or maybe those were simpler times.

Gradually, I became aware that prejudice ran both ways. Since most of my friends were Sikhs, I was told at home not to eat non-vegetarian food in their homes because, 'it was not halal'[6]. So the first time I was

---

[5]Maulana is a salutation used for a learned person, especially one who has studied religion as a discipline, for example Maulana Abul Kalam Azad. It is not a qualification or a title. The word 'hafiz' on the other hand comes from hifz, which means 'to memorize'. Hence, a hafiz is a person who has memorized the Quran. This is the first level of learning which must be completed if one wants to be an Islamic scholar.

[6]Halal means permissible for Muslims to consume. It applies both to food items and

invited for lunch to a Sikh friend's home, I stuck to chhole bhature rather than chicken. However, when my Sikh friend came over to my house, she merrily tucked into several shami kebabs before whispering to me that her grandmother had forbidden her to eat non-vegetarian food at my house. Her defiance brought my own cowardice into sharp relief. Whatever excuses I had made to myself about convenience (I had justified abjuring the chicken by saying to myself it was easier to eat chhole than wrestle with a chicken drumstick), my mother's instructions had been echoing at the back of my mind!

Often the women in my family would ignorantly snigger about how impure Hindu or Sikh women were as they didn't clean themselves properly. Being semi-literate and having lived only among other Muslims, the worldview of the women in my family was extremely limited. This was something I was aware of right from my childhood, primarily because it was diametrically opposite to the views of my father and grandfather, who had several non-Muslim friends and business associates. Occasionally, they came to our house for meals and grand non-vegetarian feasts were prepared for them. But I noticed that the men came alone. Hence, the social interaction was essentially male-oriented.[7]

Abba's Indulgences

Growing up in a large family, among several aunts, uncles, and cousins ensured that I was never short of entertainment and playmates. It also meant that there were several figures of authority that I had to defer to in addition to my parents. Even as discipline came from several quarters, so did indulgence. Abba was our biggest source of indulgence. By the time we all came along, he was leading a semi-retired life. He used

---

the manner in which they must be prepared for consumption. In the case of meat, it refers to a particular way the animal must be slaughtered—cutting through the carotid artery, jugular vein, and windpipe in a single swipe. Thereafter, blood must be drained out of the animal.

[7]Several years later, when we moved out of the Muslim mohalla and shifted to a non-Muslim locality (it was a Hindu neighbourhood and ours was the only non-Hindu family), my parents made friends with several Hindu couples. Even now, all their friends are non-Muslims.

to go to my father's shoe factory for a few hours every morning and returned at lunch time, after which he rarely stepped out, except to the mosque next door. So, while I saw my mother infrequently during the day, busy as she used to be with housework, and my father briefly in the mornings and evenings, I saw Abba for most of the day after school.

Being a widower (my grandmother died a few months after I was born), he drew comfort from the pack of grandchildren running amok in his room. To keep us engaged, he would come up with several innovative ploys, most of which involved bribery. For instance, he would ask us to draw, and award the best drawing 50 paise (over the years it increased to two rupees). During winter, he used to shell pine nuts during the day so he could reward us with fistfuls of shelled nuts in the evening. He enjoyed being with the kids and it didn't matter if they interfered with his prayer time or messed with his prayer mat.

I was eleven when he decided to accompany his daughter and her husband to Ajmer. He wanted to visit the dargah of Khwaja Moinuddin Chishti. A couple of days prior to their departure he asked me, while I was playing in his room, if I wanted to accompany them. I readily agreed. It didn't occur to me to ask my parents first. Sure enough, there was a bit of a showdown at home. My parents thought it was inappropriate of Abba to ask me to come along without checking with them first, giving me the opportunity to nag my parents. Abba was clueless about the chain of command and couldn't understand what the fuss was about. Eventually, faced with two-pronged pressure across the age divide of nearly fifty years, my parents had to relent.

It was my first and only holiday with my grandfather. As my aunt and uncle had other engagements, I was left in Abba's care for nearly three days. We stayed in Zauki Manzil, one of the rest houses adjacent to the dargah, where a big room with an attached bathroom was the only luxury. The room had no pretensions to being even partially furnished—white sheets over dhurries was all it had. This was also my most Spartan holiday ever.

The owner of the rest house was a kind man. He allowed my grandfather to use one of his employees as a runner to fetch breakfast for us from one of the several shops that lined the lane to the dargah.

After eating breakfast, the two of us took a rickshaw or walked to the dargah. We would stay there for a few hours and return to our room for lunch and rest. In the late afternoon we trudged the same path again, returning to our room well past dusk for dinner, which my aunt and uncle brought for us.

Spending two full days at the dargah of Khwaja Moinuddin Chishti in Ajmer was the closest Islamic spiritual experience I had ever had. Even though in Agra we lived next to the mosque and I almost knew the muezzin's call by heart (because of hearing it many times a day ever since I was born), I had no real experience of religion. I had some theoretical and anecdotal knowledge through my parents and exposure to Ramzan charity through my grandfather but nothing beyond that as I was never given any structured religious education. I was never asked to say the namaz or read the Quran, except for fun when I would place an extra prayer mat (janamaz) next to my mother's during Ramzan and imitate her, repeating the first kalima over and over again. That was the only thing I knew by heart.

As kids, we were told that there were five fundamentals of Islam—kalima (there are a total of five kalimas or pledges which emphasize the oneness of Allah, and establish Muhammad as his Prophet), namaz (prayer), zakat (charity), roza (fasting) and hajj (annual pilgrimage)—adherence to which was sufficient to get through life as a Muslim. Since namaz and roza looked difficult to me, and hajj nearly impossible, I checked with my grandfather whether I could book my passage to paradise on the basis of kalima, zakat, and being kind to people. He assured me that it was possible because what really mattered was what was in one's heart. Being all-knowing and all-seeing, Allah would know my intent. That, in short, was my religion.

The Call from Beyond

In Ajmer, my experience of religion was different. I became acutely conscious of my surroundings there—the incessant chirping of the birds and their sudden quietude the moment the muezzin began his call. When my grandfather used to get up for his ablutions and prayers,

I felt no urge to follow suit. And he never asked me to join him. I used to sit and simply watch since I had the sense of being engaged by everything around me. It didn't bore me at all. We would spend a lot of time sitting in the open courtyard just outside the main shrine, soaking in the sounds and silences. There was a continuous stream of devotees, which increased in the evening, but there were no standing crowds. Everyone moved in their own bubble of peace. People could sit for hours without being disturbed.

And that is what we did. Sometimes we'd listen to the birds, noticing the variations in calls, from solo to chorus; sometimes a stranger would come and sit with us, striking up a conversation with my grandfather; sometimes, the conversation would involve me and I would become part of it; and sometimes we'd just stare into nothingness, lost in our own thoughts, often drifting in and out of slumber.

I noticed that my grandfather neither kneeled at the shrine nor offered the customary shroud, as many did. Whenever we (yes, I was allowed inside) went inside the shrine he always stood at the foot of the shrine and offered a prayer. And then we'd step out and resume our place in the courtyard—always unhurried. He did his own thing. And nobody told him otherwise.

A couple of years after this visit, I went to the Ajmer dargah again with my parents. This time we couldn't go inside. My father had an argument with one of the caretakers (khadim) who insisted that he wear a skullcap before entering. My father argued (and rightly so) that Islam doesn't insist on men covering their heads, that headgear for men was more cultural than religious. The caretaker didn't relent, neither did my father. So, we turned back at the threshold. I remember that visit only for its noisy ugliness. In a mere two years, the dargah had changed vastly.

I went to Ajmer for the third time a few years ago. I was in Jaipur for an assignment and, on an impulse, decided to drive to the dargah the next day instead of returning to Delhi. I shouldn't have. It ruined my childhood memory forever. Seeing it from an adult perspective, the dargah seemed dwarfed by the chaotic street that led to it and the milling crowd jostling to get inside. The khadims were omnipresent. I had not even climbed the stairs to the dargah when I was waylaid by one. Apparently, they are very good at spotting the occasional visitors to the dargah who are well-off and seem unsure of themselves, as opposed to regular visitors who are allowed to pass unhindered. Nobody bothers with the poor, regular or not. I clearly looked like a first-timer who wouldn't resist too much when asked to donate money for various causes championed by the dargah.

At first, I tried to brush off the khadim by telling him that I would manage on my own. But, by fawning over me and helping me jump the queue in which the women behind me were uncomfortably pushing against my back, he broke through my defences. Thereafter, it was a lost cause. He led me inside the dargah and towards the shrine, weaving his way through an unimaginable throng of people (it was not even a Thursday, which is considered special). Inside the shrine, he took the small basket of rose petals, incense sticks, and sugar candy from my hands and went behind the lattice partition to make the offering on my behalf. Coming out, he handed the incense sticks and the candies back to me, the former to be lit and placed in one of the several incense holders all around and the latter to be carried home as tabarrukh or prasad (blessed sweets).

His job done, he gestured me towards the exit. I shook my head. 'I want to sit here for a while,' I told him coldly, looking around. His gaze followed mine. There was wonder in his tone when he asked me, 'Where?'

Where, indeed? There was no place to sit. There were people everywhere, sitting, prostrating, or simply resting. This was not the courtyard from my childhood, there were no birds to be heard and certainly no calm. In fact, the atmosphere at the dargah was the opposite of calm. It was frenzied. The ambient noise was deafening. For the second time in fifteen minutes I conceded defeat.

The khadim was graceful in victory. He led me out of that melee and into a tiny office near the exit. Picking up a register he asked me how much I would like to donate to which cause. The register had entries like dargah's maintenance, community kitchen, madrassa, etc. Finally, he escorted me out of the complex. After this five-star service, I got back in the car; my wallet was lighter, my heart heavy. I felt sad and cheated. But there was a lesson too. Memories should be left alone.

Before my last visit to Ajmer, I had convinced myself that, like my grandfather, I was inclined towards Sufism—I am the kind of person who would find a connection to Islam in the flexible religious practice of dargahs, where everyone is allowed to do their own thing, as opposed to the regimentation of the daily namaz and annual rozas. This self-belief partly grew out of our Sunday family picnics to the fort at Fatehpur Sikri, about 45 kilometres from Agra, led by my grandfather.

Our first stop always used to be the dargah of Hazrat Salim Chishti, which is part of the fort complex. My grandfather used to spend a good part of his Sunday morning in the marble courtyard of the dargah which, because of sparse footfall, was extremely quiet. The main shrine was surrounded by a few dozen unknown graves. As kids, we often played there under the benign gaze of Abba and a few of the dargah minders who used to hang around my grandfather, having known him for many years. Sometimes, tired of playing in the hot sun, or after a fight with my siblings, I would retreat to the dargah and stretch out on the cool marble floor smoothened by centuries of wear. Here, I always felt at home. Over the years, I realized that it was the isolation and quietness of the dargah which used to fill me with an inexplicable contentment. My conducted tour of the Ajmer dargah had shattered that.

This change between my first visit to the Ajmer dargah and the subsequent ones is indicative of the way Islam has changed over the past few decades. Today, it has very little space (and tolerance) for personal faith. Everything, right down to the degree to which one has to bend when offering namaz, is dictated by the ulema who claim a better understanding of the religion and its practice than ordinary people. To ensure their complete control over worshippers, they have laid down military-like standard operating procedures for the practice of Islam. Any deviation from this invites rebuke and, in some cases, threats of excommunication, as I have pointed out in later chapters.

Family Heritage

In my immediate family, as well as the extended one, we didn't police each other's faith. We had some extremely devout family members who never missed a namaz even if it meant missing work, while some remembered prayers only every Friday. Most of my immediate family was content with the annual Eid prayer. Nobody was forced to do anything and nobody was admonished for not doing certain things. The guiding principal was that Allah was keeping record so we didn't need to record-keep for each other. The common thread that bound everyone, irrespective of their devotion, was complete disdain for the mullah[8]. A mullah was viewed as a half-learned man, one who was more likely to mislead than guide. A common refrain was: neem hakeem khatraan jaan—a half-doctor is a danger to one's life. Needless to say, mullahs were not welcome in our home.

In 1983, we finally left the narrow lanes of the mohalla behind. My immediate family—my parents, my two younger brothers (my younger sister was born a few years later), one of my younger uncles—and I moved into the house my father had been building over a few years in a neighbourhood inhabited by Brahmins and Baniyas; we were the only Muslims there. Our new home had a lawn on three sides with a fence lined with creeping bougainvillea. At the corner of the lawn were cycas plants and on the side overlooking the porch were leafy bottle palm trees. Each bedroom had thematic furniture ordered especially from Delhi; but our lives were completely changed by the attached bathrooms fitted with washbasins, WCs, and bathtubs—luxuries we had not even imagined as kids. In the house that we had left behind, each floor had just one Indian style toilet and one bathroom—these faced each other; in addition, at the end of the terrace there was a washbasin, which was often used by several people at the same time, especially in the morning.

Abba didn't move with us. As my father's older brother had made this transition a couple of years earlier, Abba said that he now had three homes and would spend time equally in all three. He was not ready to

[8]A religious leader, most likely a hafiz, someone who has memorized the Quran and leads the prayers at the local mosque.

break ties with the mohalla because his two middle sons still lived there.

Perhaps it was the waning influence of my grandfather or the exit of the older brothers, but after we left the old house, its walls and the door became increasingly less impregnable. My uncles who stayed in the mohalla became more friendly with the neighbours, including the kids that we had stayed away from. And just as this physical breach happened in our old house, the mental and aspirational distance between our families started to grow.

And then the unthinkable happened. The mullah, a hafiz from the mosque next door, was invited through the doors that had always been shut to him. My grandfather suffered a stroke which paralysed one side of his body, impairing his speech. For a person who had always started his day with a long, leisurely walk along the Yamuna River, this inability to move or talk was hugely traumatic. He became irritable and short-tempered and was no longer pleasant company for the children. With the adults busy with their lives, his days became long and lonely. The male nurse hired to take care of him only served to irritate him further, as a constant reminder of his debilitated state. Finally, it was decided that if a hafiz visited him twice a day to recite the Quran it would calm him down and give him something to look forward to. The idea worked and the hafiz, respectfully addressed as hafizji, became a daily visitor.

Since he was poor and had a large family which could barely survive on his income as the leader of the prayer in the mosque, he started to linger in our house so that he could eat with Abba and take food home. Gradually, he became a full-time companion of my grandfather. When Abba came to stay with us, hafizji came too. And slowly he became a permanent fixture in our family, so much so that we stopped noticing his presence. Sometimes, his opinion was sought and at others he offered it even without being asked. He was a benign person without firm convictions and believed in not stressing his benefactors. So, his opinions were flexible enough to be modified to suit their requirements.

Now that hafizji was spending so much time at home, one of my uncles, who still lived in the mohalla, decided to use him to educate his sons in the ways of Islam. In a first, my cousins started to read the Quran with the help of a religious teacher. On days when hafizji couldn't find time for my cousins, as he was accompanying Abba to our house or to my eldest uncle's house, the boys started going to the mosque next door so that their education was not interrupted.

My grandfather died in 1986. The family unanimously decided to observe the full mourning period of forty days. It was partly out of love for him and partly because he had touched so many lives that strangers continued to drop into our new home (which is where he breathed his last) to share anecdotes of him or to just sit quietly for a while with his family members. For months, his funeral was the subject of awestruck discussions as an unimaginable number of people, irrespective of religion, had turned up to walk with his bier on his journey to the graveyard. So many people wanted to be his pallbearers that his own sons barely got the chance to carry the coffin for a minute or two.

Hafizji was amongst the mourners who remained steadfast in his commitment to Abba's memory for the full forty days. Sometimes he got orphans to come to our house for Quran Khwani[9], sometimes he just sat in one corner praying for my grandfather and sometimes he joined in the conversation with visitors praising Abba. He continued to come home even after the forty days. He would come at breakfast time and linger on, asking whether he was required. At that point it appeared cruel to tell him that his services were no longer required. So, it was decided that a certain amount of money would be sent to his house every month and he need not bother coming all the way to our house.

But hafizji was a conscientious man. He wouldn't accept money if he was not justifying it by visiting our house at least once a day. So, he continued to come. When my father made his disinterest extremely obvious, plainly telling him to stop coming to our house, he started visiting my uncles (who continued to live in the mohalla) in whom he discovered a renewed interest in Islam and all things Islamic. It was as

[9]Quran Khawani is the recitation of the Quran in one sitting on a specific occasion for somebody else's benefit. It is mostly done by pupils from madrassas (who are given food and some token remuneration), though sometimes family members and friends do it too, invoking the grace of Allah for the person in whose name it is held. It is not specific to mourning rites and can be held even as part of a celebration or the inauguration of a new venture.

though they had only recently discovered Islam and could not get enough of it. My youngest uncle, who lived with his eldest brother in a mixed upmarket locality, turned almost evangelical in his Islamic fervour. In my grandfather's absence, he held his older brothers, especially my father, responsible for keeping him ignorant of Islam. He was determined to correct this inadequacy in his upbringing.

Soon hafizji's benign and flexible opinions were not enough; in fact, he was now regarded as something of an Islamic illiterate. Having tasted some measure of Islamic injunctions, three of my younger uncles started craving more learned and stringent Islamic scholars so that they could become 'proper' Muslims and also teach their kids the proper path of Islam as opposed to apologetic Muslims—a sweeping term that included my immediate family.

A Sky of Possibilities

These changes were so gradual and subtle in the beginning that they were not discernible to my teenaged self. In any case, I was not really paying attention. The world had opened up for me. My father, whose formal education had stopped after Class VIII, and who took private lessons in Urdu, English, and arithmetic as he worked in a shoe factory as a pattern cutter, had become one of the biggest Indian exporters of footwear to what was then the Union of Soviet Socialist Republics (USSR). By the mid-80s, he had also won a handful of awards, including the national award for export volume, quality, and designing. Every year, he travelled a few times to the USSR and other Eastern European countries, including the German Democratic Republic. His worldview had leaped far ahead of his siblings and, in 1987, he presented me with prospectuses and admission forms of several schools in the United Kingdom and the United States. Till then, the idea of studying abroad had not occurred to me.

Of course, he was only kindling my interest. He was not quite ready to send his sixteen-year-old daughter to the West. But the process had started. Being a self-taught man, who learnt largely through his experiences, travels, and exposure to different kinds of people, he was not fixated on formal education or grades. At home, I was encouraged to read all kinds of books, including ones on Islam, which lined one shelf in the study he had built quite ambitiously on the first floor of the house. I was frequently invited to our factory whenever a foreign delegation was visiting. I attended mushairas at home (every few months my father used to invite select Urdu poets for private mehfils)[10] and outside. In addition to sparking my abiding interest in Urdu poetry, poets like Sardar Jafri, Kaifi Azmi, Khumar Barabankvi, and others also exposed me to an irreverent and critical perspective on Islam.

Sure enough, my education was progressing quite unlike that of my cousins. By the time I was writing personal essays as part of the admission process for universities in the US, one of my cousins had successfully memorized the Quran. A small celebration was held for him, the first in our family to have become a hafiz. For younger cousins, he was the role model. Not because everyone wanted to become a hafiz, but because he was someone who had successfully managed the balance between religious and secular education.

I could not go to the US for the undergraduate course. Despite securing admission, and my father's willingness to pay for my education, I was refused the student visa. It was just as well. Had I gone to the US in September 1989 as planned, I would have missed out on the life-altering events that had started to unfold in India.

I joined a bachelor's course in journalism in November 1989 at Delhi University—the first person in my entire extended family to go out of town for an education. In Delhi, the enthusiasm for the coming general elections was at fever pitch in my college. All of us, that is, my classmates, were to be first-time voters.[11] Though I was politically

---

[10]A mushaira is a public event in which several poets, sometimes more than a dozen, are invited to recite their poetry. Whether ticketed or free, these are open to the public, and so take place in auditoriums or public parks. A mehfil is a private gathering in which a single poet or a small number of poets are invited to recite in front of a select audience, comprising the family and friends of the organizer. These are rather like a private party, as the recitation is accompanied and followed by beverages and dinner.

[11]In 1988, Prime Minister Rajiv Gandhi's government had brought down the voting age from twenty-one to eighteen through the Sixty-first Amendment of the Constitution.

conscious, I didn't have strong political views, except that I loved Rajiv Gandhi and was determined to vote for him. To be honest, I would have voted for his party even if I was not in love with him because, as far back as I could remember, my family had always voted Congress, despite my father's momentary straying towards the Communist Party of India (CPI) and my mother's dalliances with the CPI's cultural wing, the Indian People's Theatre Association (IPTA).

In college I discovered that all my classmates were voting for the Bharatiya Janata Party (BJP), still referred to as Jana Sangh in my family. No one at home had a clue about what the party stood for apart from the fact that it was against Muslims. That my newly minted friends were voting for such a party filled me with some amount of unease. I wished that like my school friends they'd ask me questions about Islam and Muslims so that they would realize that Muslims were not the enemy. But nobody asked me anything. In fact, none of them had any curiosity about Muslims. I couldn't figure out if this was good or bad—it appeared they were comfortable in their prejudice and, despite that, had made friends with a Muslim, evidence of their liberal thinking.

Religion surfaced in my parents' decision, too. For the first two years of my stay in Delhi, I was lodged with a Muslim family, business acquaintances of my father. I also made my first Muslim friend in college. He was the only other Muslim in my class, and it was likely because of this that we gravitated towards each other, in some sort of a fellowship of the marginalized. Soon his family claimed me as one of their own and extended a protective shield over me.

Despite my teenaged passion, Rajiv Gandhi lost the elections. V. P. Singh became the prime minister and, within weeks, unleashed the Mandal Commission Report on university campuses. Like all Delhi University colleges, my college was also swept up in the whirlwind. We had heated discussions at Nirula's, the most happening place for students at that time. I had a very strong opinion on the issue, but it was diametrically opposite to that of the rest of my classmates. For the second time in a few months, I found myself alone.

I believed that merit alone was not enough to overcome the centuries of privilege that certain classes had enjoyed and that greater affirmative action on the part of the state was required to ensure that everyone got an equal opportunity to succeed. This made me an oddity in a class where religion was already a divisive factor, even if not overtly. In a few months, this factor became rather more significant once the Babri Masjid–Ram Janmabhoomi agitation picked up steam. The BJP president, Lal Krishna Advani, embarked on a rath yatra in September 1990, symbolically starting from Somnath in Gujarat and aiming to reach Ayodhya on 30 October 1990 in time for the kar seva[12].

By the time this came around, life at college had stopped to matter. As a family—once again a united, large joint family spread across three houses (one still in the mohalla), each home to two brothers—we were beginning to feel insecure. As Advani's rath yatra progressed, fear reverberated in the towns of north India. Ahead of the rath, an improvised Toyota truck, audio cassettes of volatile speeches by Advani, Uma Bharti, Ashok Singhal, Sadhvi Ritambhara, and others were played. My father's closest friend, one of the early converts to the BJP from his circle, volunteered to distribute those cassettes in Agra.

In supposed deference to his long friendship with my father, he delivered the first set of cassettes to our house. Huddled around the cassette player, we heard the speeches on loop. Our emotions ranged from disgust to anger to mirth; some parts were actually comical in their complete disconnect with facts. The contents of the speeches did not arouse fear. What did was the sloganeering that accompanied them: 'Jis Hindu ka khoon na khaule, khoon nahin woh paani hai'—If as a Hindu your blood doesn't boil, it is not blood but water.[13] The vehemence behind each slogan held the promise of retribution, which could only mean violence.

And violence there was.[14] Advani was arrested in October in

---

[12]Kar seva is voluntary religious service. In the context of the Babri Masjid–Ram Janmabhoomi movement, it referred to people collecting at Ayodhya on an appointed day and doing some task at the disputed site which could be considered as service towards the building of the eventual Ram temple on the site of the then existing mosque.

[13]This was an oft-repeated slogan, see Ashutosh Shukla, 'Swords drawn out, they came towards me', *Hindustan Times*, 6 December 2012.

[14]Kabir Agarwal, 'L.K. Advani, the Provocateur in Chief', *The Wire*, 9 November 2019.

Samastipur, Bihar, on the orders of Chief Minister Lalu Prasad Yadav before he could enter Uttar Pradesh. Soon, sporadic violence broke out in various parts of north India. Agra had a history of caste tension, but not communal violence. The acrimony in the air, especially after Advani's arrest, suggested that this was about to change. On 30 October, the planned kar seva was carried out in Ayodhya. As enthusiastic kar sevaks tried to reach the mosque structure, the police opened fire to push them back on the orders of the chief minister of Uttar Pradesh, Mulayam Singh Yadav, later sarcastically referred to as Maulana Mulayam because of his supposed sympathy for the Muslims. The official figure put the dead at sixteen. Retaliation for these killings began soon after, engulfing one town after another in a frenzy of violence, in which, if the state police was not complicit, it was a mute bystander,[15] an indication of how deep the communal virus had penetrated the force.

My family, with no prior experience of communal violence, was in a dilemma. We didn't know where we would be more secure—in an upscale Hindu-majority neighbourhood, where the privilege of the residents would throw a security blanket around us, or in a Muslim majority lower-middle-class mohalla where the numbers would insulate us. Each group kept urging the other to move out. My father told his two brothers who lived in the mohalla to move in with us or with my oldest uncle; and my mohalla uncles kept requesting us to move in with them till the situation improved. All of us stayed where we were. As the communal situation started to worsen all over north India, I was asked to come back home.

Fear Within, Violence Outside

Every day we woke up to the news of violence in some part of the city and hoped that all of us would remain safe. Giving us confidence was the knowledge that, in the last decade, my father and uncle who lived with us had cultivated a vast network of friends from among the bureaucrats who had served in Agra; those district magistrates, senior superintendents,

[15]Asghar Ali Engineer, 'Communal Violence and Role of Police', *Economic and Political Weekly*, Vol. 29, No. 15, 9 April 1994, pp. 835–40.

and commissioners of police had climbed up the bureaucratic ladder in the Uttar Pradesh state administration. Such was my uncle's immediate clout that he had managed to get daily curfew passes for himself and my mother. They used the passes to visit riot-affected areas and hand out relief material.

Then the violence hit home. All through that November morning, our neighbours continued to visit us with solemn advice. 'Shift to your ancestral house for a few days,' they told my father. 'Or at least send bhabhiji (referring to my mother) and the kids away.' Finally, my father booked us a room at the Mughal Sheraton Hotel. My mother drove us to the hotel, leaving my father and uncle at home. However, by late afternoon, anxiety got the better of her. She drove us back home against my father's orders.

As the day drew to a close, we all huddled together in the family room waiting for the attack that my parents were certain would happen that evening. I was handed a diary with the phone numbers of all the police officials we knew, starting from the local police station all the way up to the senior superintendents. I started to make the calls, but none were being answered. 'Doesn't matter, keep trying,' my father said to me.

Then we started to hear the slogans.

At first, they seemed to come from a distance, but slowly they started to come closer. My brother and I ran to the main door, which had a narrow glass panel on the right through which one could see the porch, the gate, and the road beyond. A mob with tridents and flaming torches was marching towards our gate. My brother and I were transfixed at the glass panel—inside, my mother was screaming, asking us to get back. The mob was now at the gate, shouting violently. Right at the front of the crowd was one of our neighbours, a boy whose younger brother was my brother's playmate.

'Sanjay bhaiyya,' my brother whispered and we ran inside to share our discovery.

My father was calm. He told my uncle that Sanjay's presence implied they would not harm us. 'They will shout some slogans and move on,' he said.

Then we heard the sound of windows smashing as the mob started to throw stones. 'Get back to the phone,' my father screamed at me, even as my uncle rushed past him to go to the terrace. He had taken out my father's licensed revolver. 'I will fire a couple of shots in the air to scare them,' he said, taking the steps two at a time.

My father panicked. He screamed at my uncle to stop. My mother chased after him to physically hold him back. 'You fire one shot in the air and they will burn the house down,' my father yelled at my uncle. It was very likely that he was shaking too.

As long as my father was calm, we feared no disaster. But once he voiced his fears, panic descended on us. Fortunately, my uncle saw sense and calmed down somewhat. In those few moments of pure terror, we hadn't realized that the mob had started to disperse. Just as the noise outside receded, my call to the SSP's residence was answered by someone. He made a note of our address and promised to send a patrol car.

Once we were convinced that the silence at the gate was holding, my mother went to the door to confirm that the mob had really left. One of the glass panels had cracked and from the shattered pieces of glass on the porch we figured that several windows had succumbed to the assault as had the car parked in the porch. That evening, no dinner was served. Everyone stayed together in the family room, not daring to step out to assess the damage. Well after ten at night, a few policemen arrived. My father and uncle went out to speak with them; everyone else was instructed to stay inside. The police assured us that they would include our lane in their night patrol and that we should rest in peace.

Somehow, we got through that night. I believed that everything would be fine in the morning. And it was, for a few hours, when our domestic help started to arrive for work. Since ours was not a Muslim area there was no curfew here. Just as we were settling down for breakfast, someone rang the doorbell.

It was my cousin, my middle uncle's older son from the mohalla. Five years younger than me, and still in school, he was dishevelled and quaking with fear. He must have been crying for some time because his voice was hoarse. That morning, the notorious Provincial Armed

Constabulary (PAC)[16] had carried out a cordon and search operation in our old mohalla and had taken away the adult men. My cousin had also been picked up along with his father and younger uncle. However, one of the constables took pity on him and allowed him to jump out of the jeep as it turned onto the main road. From there, he walked the couple of kilometres to our house. During the operation, the police ransacked the house, disconnected the telephone lines, and broke the television sets. My two aunts and younger cousins were at the house but we couldn't reach them because of the curfew orders in that area. And there was no way of knowing where my uncles were. Though I didn't realize it at that time, memories of the Hashimpura massacre[17] must have sent cold shivers down the backs of my parents and uncles.

Leaving the breakfast untouched, my father and my uncle left immediately. My uncle went to the police station next to the mohalla. He was told by the constables there that no such arrest had taken place. But when my uncle insisted he had received the information from reliable sources, he was asked to go to another police station. Convinced that the constables were lying, he stayed put. No officer came to speak with him. My father went to see the police commissioner who had been a guest at our home on several evenings, sharing drinks with my father. At the police station, my father was told that the commissioner was not

---

[16]Prabhu Chawla, 'Provincial Armed Constabulary of Uttar Pradesh becomes focus of controversy', *India Today*, 15 Oct 1980.

[17]During the 1987 communal violence in Meerut, men from the Provincial Armed Constabulary rounded up about forty-five Muslim men in a late-night raid. Instead of taking them to the police station, the PAC took these men to the Upper Ganga Canal in Murad Nagar in Ghaziabad district, where they started to kill them one by one. The bodies were thrown into the canal. Since this was next to the highway, the massacre was interrupted by passing vehicles. After some time, the surviving men were driven to the Hindon River Canal in Ghaziabad where they were eventually killed. Activists filed a case against the PAC; this case dragged on for several years and, in 2015, a district court acquitted all the PAC accused for want of evidence. An Indian Police Service officer, Vibhuti Narain Rai, who was the superintendent of police in Ghaziabad district at that time, was the first person to reach the massacre site and file a first information report (FIR). He later recounted the horror of the incident in his book *Hashimpura 22 May: The Forgotten Story of India's Biggest Custodial Killing*, Gurgaon: Penguin Books, 2016.

available, after which he tried the office of the SSP, another regular at the parties at our home. The SSP briefly met my father, seeming extremely busy, and told him that he was not aware of any such incident.

But he assured my father that if they had been arrested, he would ensure that my uncles would not be harmed. Word was passed down the hierarchy. My uncle was handed a few additional curfew passes. He was also told not to worry and that my missing uncles would return home before the evening. With no other choice, he came back. By that time my father was home too.

I accompanied my mother and uncle to the house of my birth in my uncle's hatchback which, having been parked inside the garage, had escaped the vandalism of the previous evening. The open maidan at the mouth of lane in which our house was located looked like a war zone. Stones were scattered all over the unpaved ground, and there were a few carcasses of two-wheelers. The windows of the houses facing the maidan were broken and most of the doors hung by their hinges. Leaving the car next to the police tents, we walked with great trepidation along the lane towards our house. From the outside, it looked normal. My grandfather had installed a heavy-duty door which had withstood the assault. As always, it was not bolted.

A gentle push opened it. In the central courtyard, the first thing that caught my eye was a Sony television lying face down on the marble floor. Then the pieces of glass, remains of crockery came into the view, and clothes, and toys, and a cricket bat, and the heirloom copper paandaan (an elaborate case in which betel leaves and their accompaniments are kept), and other debris that I could not identify. However, more frightening than this havoc was the eerie silence that permeated the house. When I was growing up there, I always associated this house with noise. There were far too many people in too small a space. But now that there was no sound, my stomach tightened and my legs felt heavy. Where was everyone?

My mother called out to my aunt with what sounded like a shriek. My aunt screamed in response and came tearing out from the room next to the mazar where we used to light incense every Thursday. All at once, the noise returned. My aunts, distraught and dishevelled, rushed out and engulfed my mother in a frightened collective embrace. I tried to hug my cousins but we were all a little embarrassed. We never embraced, even though we used to play together, gossip, and tease one another. So we hung around, looking uncomfortably at the mess strewn around us even as my uncle darted in and out of rooms, taking stock of the damage.

Now my aunts started to recount what had happened, frequently interrupting themselves with loud wails. They told us how my uncles were dragged out in their sleepwear, how a few policemen came back inside to deliberately break things, how they made salacious remarks about my younger aunt, how they scared the kids, and so on. It took me a while to realize that both my mother and I were crying. Perhaps we were crying for my uncles or at the narrow escape that my aunts had had or because of what could have happened to us the previous evening.

But I knew for sure that some of my tears were for the sheer helplessness that I knew my father and my uncle were feeling. Physically they may have travelled a small distance from the Muslim mohalla to an upper-class Hindu colony but emotionally they had travelled the distance of a lifetime. In the family comprising six brothers and four sisters, these two men had most visibly shed their ghettoized Muslim identities. They were at home in the social, cultural, and economic life of Agra, hobnobbing with the who's who of the city. And yet, when it came to communal division, they were nothing but Muslims. Forever suspects, forever scapegoats.

New Realities

My uncles returned home in the late afternoon. A police vehicle dropped them at the mouth of the lane from where they hobbled to the house, whose door had remained unbolted. Their shoulders, backs, and calves were streaked with ugly blue welts. One of them had a wound just below an eyebrow, where he was probably hit by a rifle butt or a baton. My aunt said a few prayers over his head, frequently thanking Allah for sparing his life and, more to the point, his eye. Soon wailing women from the neighbourhood started pouring into our courtyard. Their men were still missing. They pleaded with my mother and my uncle to help get their men back. It was a heartrending scene and I watched from inside the room, hiding behind the door, shaking and frightened. For the first time in my life, I prayed for others. I asked Allah to send their men home just as my uncles had returned.

The other men started coming back to their homes through that night and the next morning. No case was recorded, no charges were filed. It was as if the incident had never happened. Over the next few days, my father and his brothers met frequently and the conversation revolved around safety. Where would we have been safer? My father pointed out that, despite the stone-pelting at our house, we were unharmed. My uncles insisted that the police action in our mohalla was, though not unprecedented, rare. The discussion on where a Muslim might be safe during a communal conflagration remained unresolved.

Slowly, the situation started to calm down. At that time there was no way of knowing how many people died in Agra that week. There was a huge gap between the figures put out by the local Hindi media and what people believed. According to a report compiled by the Institute of Peace and Conflict Studies under Nagarik Mancha by B. Rajeshwari, thirty-one people, most of them Muslims, had died in Agra in November 1990.[18] According to the same study, in the wake of Advani's rath yatra, nearly 1,800 people died in different parts of India between April and December 1990. As happens during communal violence in India, the majority were Muslim.[19]

As I prepared to return to college at the end of November, my mother told me not to mention the two incidents to anyone.

'Why?' I asked her.

'Why!' she retorted. 'Is this something to be proud of?'

I couldn't understand why, as the victims, we should feel shame. She explained that for my father it was not about being a victim, it was about the humiliation. He believed that his successful business, his social

[18]B. Rajeshwari, *Communal Riots in India: A Chronology (1947-2003),* Institute of Peace and Conflict Studies, March 2004, available here: http://nagarikmancha.org/images/1242-Documents-Communal_Riots_in_India.pdf

[19]Asghar Ali Engineer, *Communal Riots After Independence: A Comprehensive Account*, Centre for Study of Society and Secularism in Mumbai, New Delhi: Shipra Publications, 2009.

engagements, such as the mushairas, his national and state awards had placed him in a different league where his name carried respect, and maybe inspired awe. He never went to anyone, everyone came to him. But on those November days he had been helpless and fearful. The hour he spent outside the commissioner's office, which was crowded with people who at a different time would probably have waited outside his own office, devastated him. If he could, he would have erased those two days from his life.

So we collectively worked towards erasing the memory of those days from our lives. Perhaps, to some extent, we succeeded. Since nobody spoke about that time, the memories started to fade, despite the trail of blood that the 1991 elections left across India.[20] The following year, the Babri Masjid–Ram Janmabhoomi drums started beating again. In a special April Fools' Day edition, one of the local Hindi newspapers of Agra carried an article about a secret meeting between Prime Minister Narasimha Rao and the BJP's Advani in which the two agreed to build the temple at the site of the mosque. This joke hit so close to truth.

As the drums became louder, old fears returned. This time the chief minister of UP was the BJP's Kalyan Singh, whose government contributed to hate-mongering.[21] I returned to Agra a few days before the scheduled shilanyas[22] at Ayodhya on 6 December 1992. It was a weekend, when I would often go home. But, more importantly, my parents wanted all of us together in case violence broke out again.

Though 6 December was a Sunday, we all woke up early and planted ourselves in front of the television set in our family room. Selecting the BBC news channel, my uncle announced that the mosque would be blown up before the end of the day. His theory was that dynamite sticks had already been planted all around the structure. My father maintained that nothing of the sort would happen.

'It's all political gimmickry,' he declared.

---

[20]This has been chronicled in detail in Chapter 5.

[21]Nilanjan Mukhopadhyay, 'Past Continuous: How the Kalyan Singh Government Aided the Ram Mandir Movement', *The Wire*, 11 November 2018.

[22]Laying of the foundation stone of the proposed Ram temple.

As a journalist in the making, I did not indulge in speculation. 'We will know very soon,' was all I said. Over the last two years, I had grown up very fast. My family often sought my opinion and I was frequently allowed to participate in 'grown-up' conversations.

As the morning progressed, I started to feel increasingly confident about my father's assessment. Finally, bored, I left the room and went upstairs to the study to rifle through old books. In less than half an hour, I heard loud voices from downstairs. At first, I ignored them, but when my mother called my name, I went down and saw a cloud of dust on the TV screen.

My father and uncle were staring at the screen, speechless. For all his claims, even my uncle hadn't believed that the mosque would be demolished, let alone clawed down by a frenzied mob. Maybe dynamite blasts would have been less brutal. But to see people atop the dome, manually pulling down a structure conveyed a sense of extreme hatred and brutality. And then to see a joyous Uma Bharti with her arms around a seated Murli Manohar Joshi was surreal.

I was speechless too. Could this be another April Fools' joke in December? The ferocity on the screen filled me with terror. Memories of two years ago and what we escaped came back to me. I was silently repeating to myself, 'They couldn't have torn down the mosque', perhaps in an attempt to negate what I was seeing on screen. Then I heard my uncle tell someone on the phone, 'Masjid gir gayee' (the mosque has fallen). The cloud of dust on the screen settled. In place of the dome was debris. The illusion had shattered. Reality had hit hard.

The Indian Muslim

I expected my family to react a bit more forcefully to this earth-shattering moment. But there was equanimity in their attitude. I also expected them to panic about a possible outbreak of violence. Even on that count they surprised me. There was resignation and a strange sort of hope, rooted not in the realities as they were emerging but in wistfulness. Perhaps nothing we fear will happen, my father told my uncle, who had also lost the impulsiveness of two years ago. This defeatist attitude unnerved me more than the fear I had felt in them in 1990.

Over the next few years, I realized that 6 December 1992 had been a turning point not just for my family, but for most Indian Muslims. We may ignore politics and turn our backs on it, but politics doesn't ignore anyone. And so, we too were caught up in the whirlwind that became the Indian political milieu after 1992. Civility was the first casualty. It was replaced by communal prejudice, which was no longer considered an individual predilection, but an assertion of facts. While earlier, one wouldn't voice anti-Muslim views for fear of being judged as intolerant, now the public expression of such opinions was seen as the mark of an assertive Hindu.

Suddenly, demonstrative religion was all around us. As the benign 'Ram-Ram' was replaced by the militant 'Jai Shri Ram', people started huddling with their own kind. A lot of business-class Muslims who had stepped out of the mohallas and built swanky houses in mixed localities returned to the smothering comfort of narrow lanes and closed minds. My uncle, who, perhaps under my father's influence, had begun charting a modern course for himself, abandoned it. He moved out of our house into his own. The area he chose to raise his family was indicative of his state of mind. It was a mixed neighbourhood but with a preponderance of Muslims. For good measure, there was a mosque across the street, though not as formidable as the one in our old mohalla. And he renewed contact with hafizji, who, now retired from his masjid duties, started visiting my uncle every morning and, later, accompanied him to his shoe factory.

Hafizji was no Islamic scholar. His information and advice were based on popular beliefs or what he picked up by listening to others. And because he depended completely on his benefactors, he was always careful not to annoy or anger them. By seeking hafizji's benediction on a daily basis, my uncle thought that he remained a moderate Muslim as he was not reaching out to the hard-line ulema. Perhaps he did not realize that by exposing himself to a semi-literate mullah he was increasingly crippling his own mental faculties. I often heard him ask hafizji pointless questions like 'If I contribute to the reconstruction of the mosque, would the benefit that will accrue to me be equal to that of annual zakat?' Or

'If I'm having dinner with someone who is drinking alcohol, would it be sinful for me to share food with him, even though I am not drinking?'

These were silly, almost pointless, questions, and I sometimes felt that my uncle was asking them only in jest to tease hafizji or to test his knowledge, because some questions would stump hafizji and he would be forced to invent answers as he went along, frequently contradicting himself. But, over time, hafizji gained confidence and became more assertive in his responses, even becoming offended if he were not taken seriously. And, over time, my uncle, who had not read the Quran himself, started to take him seriously.

I had stayed on in Delhi after my graduation on one pretext or the other, returning to Agra only on the weekends. My siblings had followed me to Delhi and we now rented an apartment together. Finally, after much acrimony at home, I successfully convinced my father that the next step after completing an education was finding a job, not getting married. After I started working, my visits to Agra became less frequent, sometimes I would go only once a month. My visits to my uncles and cousins became even rarer, often months would go by before I met them.

Around this time the family business was also unravelling following the disintegration of the Soviet Union in December 1991. Perhaps professional stress added to the overall sense of insecurity. Most of my cousins were now regular practitioners of namaz and roza. Though they had gone to the same school as my siblings and I, they forged new friendships with Muslims, many of whom sported small token beards and wore skullcaps with pride in public, perhaps in an assertion of their identity. While my immediate family moved away from religious conservatism and ritualism, finding them constricting, the rest drew comfort from them, happy with the assurance it provided.

I saw how far this had taken them at my niece's first birthday party about a decade ago. As has been traditional in our extended family, after the party, all family members lingered on the lawn, reminiscing about the old days and exchanging gossip. The conversation drifted to marriage and someone brought up a Sunni man we knew who had married a Shia woman and the confusion the marriage had led to for the kids. When I pointed out that this should not have been grounds for confusion because, forget Sunni–Shia, Islam allows marriages between the adherents of the book (which includes Jews and Christians), my uncle, with whom we had lived through the horror of communal hatred in the 1990s, snapped at me.

'Shias are kafir[23],' he declared.

Nobody spoke after that. Having grown up hearing that there was no such thing as kafir, and that everyone was equal in the eyes of Allah, my uncle had said the unspeakable. I had grown up believing we were Muslims not because of our devoutness, but simply because we believed we were Muslims. Intolerance had crept into our family of liberal religious values and there was now a clear divide. Only my immediate family stood with me. The party broke up.

While several family members, especially the younger ones, of my extended family had crossed the threshold by flaunting their faith in public, my uncle lingered in the middle, hoping he would never be asked to choose sides. That evening, he made up his mind and stepped across. In the new emerging India, there was no place for old family philosophies.

More recently, at another family occasion, I discovered that my youngest cousin, all of sixteen, had started to wear a headscarf. No one in my paternal family, including in my parents' generation, had ever worn a hijab or a burkha. I overheard her telling another cousin that she found living in India restrictive to her practice of Islam. Her Islam had shrunk from a faith to practice. Her problem was threefold, she explained to me.

One, she was studying at a missionary school like I had, which though not overtly religious, had Christian characteristics, and started the day with the Lord's Prayer every morning. In Agra, the other option for modern education would be a public school, which would be largely Hindu in ethos. The Lord's Prayer would be replaced by the Gayatri Mantra! Ideally, she would have preferred a modern school with an

[23]The word kafir comes from the Surah Al-Kafirun of the Quran. It refers to those who disbelieve the message of Allah. Over time, fanatic Muslims started to refer to all non-Muslims as kafir.

Islamic ethos, including classes on the Quran and Hadith[24] and if not that, then an agnostic school. When I was growing up, there were hardly any good public schools in Agra, but in cities like Delhi mainstream public schools were neutral as far as religion was concerned.

Two, wearing a hijab had had the opposite of the intended effect. Instead of taking attention away from her, it drew attention to her. Since hardly anybody else wore a headscarf in her school, it came in the way of her social life and ability to make friends. She was a double minority.

Three, there was too much 'Hinduization' of public places. While schools and other public organizations make allowances for Hindu sentiments, festivals, and food preferences, no such accommodation is extended to Muslims. Sometimes school examinations are scheduled without regard to important Muslim festivals like Eid ul Zuha.

Needless to say, she was more comfortable with Muslims as friends. 'We don't have to pretend with one another,' she said, because, according to her, all she was to her Hindu friends was a validation of their liberal outlook.

Was this not true of her too? Did she not pretend to be a liberal when she was not?

'Yes,' she shot back at me. 'That is why I feel that living in India restricts my practice of Islam. I don't like to pretend.'

The conversation continued to disturb me for a long time. I had never perceived two distinct identities in myself—Muslim and Indian. When had this split taken place in others like me? Had it begun to take place in me? Had Muslims become more Muslim and less Indian? Was it even a question of 'either-or'? Or had I become a closet xenophobe by even raising this question? Was I suppressing the former so that I would be trusted as the latter?

The issue was rather more complex. So, what did it mean to be a Muslim in India? More to the point, what did Islam mean to Indians, Muslim and non-Muslim? Was it a religion of peace, tolerance, and coexistence or was it a faith that insisted on exclusivism, rigidity, and unquestioning adherence to inflexible ideas? Was it a living religion for

[24]Compilation of Prophet Muhammad's teachings, sayings, and actions.

all time to come or it was an archaic, tribal belief system that managed to spread its creed by the power of the sword?

What about most Muslims in India? Were they like my grandfather and my immediate family who believed that Islam should be a personal guiding light that provided solace and not a governing force that determined the choices they made?

Or were they like my cousin and her family who believed that their life's choices must be based upon Islam? For them it was not enough that they were Muslim; they asserted this fact in private and public.

Could this then be a question of identity itself? An Islamic identity superimposing itself on the Indian Muslim identity, which was an all-encompassing intricately woven coat of faith, superstition, culture, literature, music, and poetry? A geographically-rooted concept distinguishing, let's say, the Muslims of Uttar Pradesh from those of Kerala and Gujarat?

More to the point, could Muslim issues be broadly categorized into these neat boxes? Or were there bigger issues here which had shaped the worldview of Indian Muslims and how they regarded themselves vis-à-vis other religious groups? Issues like insecurity, discrimination, injustice, and criminalization?

While Muslims in India have never been a monolithic group even in terms of religious belief, today, three factors (in varying degrees) unite them—a craving for a uniform pan-Islamic identity created by Saudi Arabia; relative socio-economic backwardness; and the discrimination by state authorities because of religious prejudice and, to some extent, violent persecution.

The idea of this book developed from these disparate questions. More than describing the Muslims of India, I wanted to represent the case of Muslims to those who wonder about them. But as I began to work on my representation, I realized that, perhaps, there was a need to represent Islam itself in a contemporary mould to Muslims. After all, they are the ambassadors of the faith they espouse. If they do not understand the context of the Quranic verses as they were revealed then they were guilty of misrepresenting their religion. For most Indian Muslims, the source of their understanding does not come from an educated study of Islam, but from the practices handed down in their families and reinforced periodically by semi-literate mullahs who are products of largely ill-equipped, single-room madrassas dotting the Indian landscape. When they attempt to find solutions to twenty-first-century problems using a seventh-century template, it's no surprise that these often miss the mark. And when the answers do not wholly address the questions, they serve to distort the narrative.

Ideas that don't evolve or keep pace with the changing world atrophy or, worse, become distorted. The idea of Islam has suffered from both atrophy as well as distortion. This is the reason that all the so-called Islamic 'reformers' or preachers have tried to take Muslims back in time to the seventh century when Prophet Muhammad established the first Islamic state in Medina. As a consequence, the more Muslims strive to be true to the Islam of Prophet Muhammad, the more out of time and backward they appear. Is it not possible to be Muslim *and* forward-looking?

As questions continued to sprout, this book started to grow. The central discussion, however, remains Muslims in India—their faith, their strengths, their insecurities, their aspirations, their limitations, their petty compromises, and their dogmatism. Today, twin prongs of external and internal forces hold Muslims in a pincer grip. The external prong is the sociopolitical discrimination that they face at the hands of both lawmaking and law-enforcing authorities, which often manifests as mental and physical violence. It denies not only equal opportunity to the Muslims, but also justice, when required. This situation has worsened with the rise of Hindu right-wing political forces that demonize Islam and Muslims, holding them responsible for countless supposed wrongs throughout history. This forces Muslims to seek security in their own numbers, and they withdraw into ghettos on the periphery of the mainstream, thereby limiting their choices in terms of accommodation, education, and profession. The primary internal factor is the vicious cycle perpetuated by illiteracy, poverty, and the disproportionate influence of the mullahs on the community. This influence of the mullahs, which commenced after the collapse of the Mughal Empire in 1857, has, on the one hand, kept a large number undereducated and therefore unemployable; on the other hand, it has prevented the emergence of progressive, secular Muslim leadership. Since the ulema represent the community, they have engaged with political institutions on behalf of the people. Successive political regimes also started to turn to them as the leaders of the Indian Muslims and a cycle was started. Consequently, even when a progressive, or non-conservative Muslim politician emerges, she has to kowtow to the conservative few for credibility and acceptability.

A large number of Muslims, especially in India, remain uncertain about the correctness of their religious practices. They need frequent validation from those whom they perceive as experts in Islam. These so-called experts are largely semi-literate people who derive their authority from having learnt the religious texts by rote. With no exposure to any other learning, they remain intellectual pygmies. Hence, their default setting is always conservative and unyielding towards ideas that challenge them. Yet, they preside over nearly 200 million Indian Muslims, holding the fear of hell over them. And just as the external prong does, these self-imposed religious conditions also limit the Muslims' access to secular/modern education, employment in the organized sector, and critical thinking.

Today, not just the Muslims, but Islam itself is in a strange place. While it continues to be a great source of spiritual and emotional succour for a large number of people (peaceful conversion to Islam is a worldwide phenomenon), it is also a source of suspicion and fear for an equal number, who vilify it, either deliberately or because they do not understand it. For example, scholars, respected writers, and journalists often write about how the problem is not with the Muslims, but with the religion itself. In their view, it is Islam that promotes separatism and intolerance towards non-Muslims and ranks women as inferior to men. These scholars selectively quote Quranic verses to make their point not only to put Muslims on the defensive but also justify the discrimination against them.[25] Ironically, radical Muslims

---

[25]See Ayaan Hirsi Ali, 'Islam Is a Religion of Violence', *Foreign Policy*, 9 Nov 2015 and Rafiq Zakaria, 'Book review: Arun Shourie's "The World of Fatwas"', *India Today*, 30 Nov 1995.

use these same verses to brainwash the gullible into believing that the Other is always the enemy.

This book tried to get at the truth about Islam and Muslims in India by looking at the broad sweep of issues that bedevil the Muslim community—from the origin of Islam in India and multiplicity of Islamic sects to fatwa, jihad, and triple talaq.

The book addresses both Muslims and non-Muslims. It aims to show Muslims what the spirit of Islam stood for and how they have allowed it to putrefy over the centuries; and it tells those who are suspicious of Islam that not all that they read and think is correct. I believe that this book needed to be written because the exclusivism that today's Muslims want to claim for themselves is the first step towards intolerance and intolerance only breeds more intolerance.

The violent, overt manifestation of intolerance is rare, therefore less worrisome. It's the mental intolerance that creates divided societies and reinforces ghettos, both psychological and physical. In addition, it creates a class of vulnerable people who constantly need validation from religion, access to which is controlled by the clergy, something not traditionally required in Islam.

In this book, I will examine the changes that Islam sought to bring about in Arab society and, subsequently, in other parts of the world. I will also delve into why tribalism and political power play triumphed over the original vision of Islam, reducing it to a sectarian faith. I want to suggest ways to reclaim a faith that came into being by trying to build an inclusive, egalitarian society based on the principles of justice, equality, and humanity.

I am not an Islamic scholar. However, I have been both a student and observer of Islam. But more importantly, I think a lot about my religion. I like my Muslim identity. It hurts me to see a large number of Muslims reducing themselves to caricatures; and it troubles me to see how this caricature has become an object of ridicule for the majority, and deserving of neither respect nor civility. This book tries to address both the misconceptions and misgivings about Islam and Muslims in India.

◆

On the afternoon of 25 February 2020, my father's youngest sister who lives in northeast Delhi with her husband called me in a panic. A couple of days earlier, communal violence had broken out in parts of northeast Delhi triggered by virulent sloganeering and provocation by members of the BJP. The most prominent of these was: 'Desh ke gaddaron ko, goli maaro saalon ko' (Shoot the traitors of the country).[26]

It was not difficult to understand who the 'traitors' were meant to be. The slogans were shouted by those who were part of the processions being taken out through the Muslim areas of northeast Delhi by BJP leaders. In the just concluded Delhi state elections, the BJP had lost badly to the local Aam Aadmi Party. It was believed that the Muslims had voted en masse for the latter,[27] shaping its huge victory. Hence, the anger against the Muslims.

Muslims had also been holding peaceful demonstrations in various parts of Delhi since December 2019, protesting against the Citizenship (Amendment) Act which allows for the fast-track citizenship of all migrants from Pakistan, Afghanistan, and Bangladesh, except Muslims. The middle-level BJP leadership tried to harness the Hindu rage against Muslims for these protests, labelling the latter as anti-national.

Finally, heeding these calls to arms in the name of nationalism, mobs started attacking Muslims on the night of 23 February 2020. Remembering what had happened in 1990, I started calling my aunt every few hours, urging her to move in with me for a few days. She continued to resist. It was not only about her immediate family, but her husband's extended family, all of whom lived there; some even ran businesses in the locality. They had properties and investments in the neighbourhood.

'You expect me to abandon my whole life and run away,' my uncle bellowed on the phone. He hoped that the mob would not reach their

---

[26]Revathi Krishnan, 'Days before Budget, minister Anurag Thakur chants "desh ke gaddaron ko, goli maaro saalon ko"', *The Print*, 27 January 2020.

[27]IANS, 'Muslims overwhelmingly voted for AAP in Delhi polls', *Outlook*, 8 February 2020.

area. That hope was not based on anything concrete. But what else could one do but hope?

On 25 February, a mob reached the area where my aunt lives. Around 3 p.m., she called me. Armed assailants were at the head of her lane. The men of the neighbourhood, including my sixty-five-year-old uncle, were standing at the entrance to the lane, armed with wooden staffs and bricks, in the hope of fighting off attackers armed with swords and country revolvers.

'Can't you do anything?' she asked me.

Do something? My mind raced. What could I do, sitting 25 kilometres away and in a different state?

The fear, the helplessness, the anger of 1990 returned.

Although my family members were not harmed by the violence, when order was finally restored, the government put the total dead at fifty-three, of which thirty-six were Muslims.[28] The most devastating aspect of this round of communal violence was the open and blatant prejudice showed by the Delhi police. Several videos, shot by citizens, have surfaced that show how the police, in many parts of Delhi, egged the mob on to attack Muslims. In some areas, the police left the scene of rioting so that violence could go on uninterrupted. In one particularly gory video, police personnel are seen repeatedly hitting injured men lying on the ground, forcing them to say 'Bharat Mata ki Jai'. One of those men died of his injuries later.

When I started to write this book, what I wanted to do was address fellow Muslims and tell them that they needed to look beyond the mullahs and embrace modernity because nothing in Islam tells them to stick to dogmas which are past their sell-by date. However, I increasingly became conscious of just how vulnerable Muslims in India are, and how this made them extremely fearful, to the exclusion of pretty much everything else. How does one tell people just struggling to stay alive that they need to change their thinking, their manner of living, their approach to religion?

[28]'Delhi Riots Death Toll at 53, Here are the Names of the Victims', *The Wire*, 15 July 2020.

I have tried to weave those fears into my narrative. I have equally tried to inform non-Muslim Indians how their perception of Muslims is based on prejudice and hearsay, not facts. I hope with this book we are able to build a bridge of conversation.

1

MUSLIMS IN INDEPENDENT INDIA

In 2016, I bought an apartment in a newly developed gated residential complex in the National Capital Region. Before I moved in, the estate manager introduced me to a handyman, a young boy really, Jiarun, who would help me settle down—by helping with the hiring of electricians, plumbers, masons, carpenters, etc.

Jiarun, I rolled the name around on my tongue a few times. What kind of a name is that? Jiarun grinned affably without offering an explanation. The estate manager told me sheepishly, 'Actually, his name is Ziarun, but since others had difficulty pronouncing Zia, it became Jia.'

'But you can pronounce Zia,' I pointed out unnecessarily.

He looked embarrassed. 'Everybody calls him Jiarun, so I also got in the habit of calling him that,' he said, hastily adding, 'He doesn't mind it.'

Then, regaining his confidence, he asked Ziarun cheerily, 'Do you mind it, Jiarun?'

Ziarun's grin stretched to his ears. 'Kya baat karte hain, sir' (What are you saying, sir), he said, shaking his head.

As Ziarun walked me to my flat, I repeated the name a few times, trying to figure out its origin. 'It's an unusual name,' I told him. 'I have not heard it before.' I didn't tell him that, of course, but my question partly rose from class prejudice. People from his socio-economic background usually had simpler names—Mahesh, Suresh, Ramesh, Raju....

'Where are you from?' I asked him.

'Assam,' he replied.

'What's your full name?'

He paused for a moment. Then, looking straight at me, he replied, 'Mohammed Ziarul Haq.'

The journey from Mohammed Ziarul Haq to Jiarun was a short one. His middle-aged supervisor, the aforementioned estate manager, a kind-hearted soul, had told him that his name was very complicated. A lot of flat buyers would not be comfortable with it. So, while Mohammed and Haq were dropped, Ziarul was modified to Jiarun, which was pronounced as Ji-Arun. Some dispensed with Ji also.

'Naam se kya farq padhta hai (What difference does the name make),' reasoned Ziarul, narrating his story.

I agreed with him. Only, in his case, the change of name had caused a change of identity, too. Since his company-issued identification card bears the name Jiarun, when the employees all went together to register for their Unique Identification Number at the nearby Aadhaar camp, Ziarul was enrolled as Jiarun. For all practical purposes he is Jiarun now. His faith no longer poses a threat to him—neither in the urban village where he lives next to the gated society, nor on the trains which he takes once a year to visit his parents in Assam.

Over the next few weeks, I was introduced to a contractor called Sonu and his cousin Babloo, the ironsmith. They both greeted me respectfully with a 'Namaste'. Sonu and Babloo came recommended by the estate manager, as well as their previous clients. As they started work, I saw more and more of them. One day, for some reason, Sonu decided to greet me with 'As Salaam Aleikum', instead of 'Namaste'. Though surprised, I replied spontaneously: 'Walekum As Salaam'. I thought he was just trying to please me, and didn't question this change of greeting.

But Sonu couldn't hold himself back for long. One Sunday afternoon, as I was going over the printouts of designs I had chosen for the wardrobes he was to build, Sonu mumbled, 'Hum bhi Musalmaan hain (We too are Muslims).'

I looked up at him with a start.

'My real name is Imamuddin.'

'In that case, I will call you Imamuddin,' I told him, without asking any questions. He seemed pleased at having found a co-religionist among his customers. Soon he started telling me more about himself.

'My wife and children live in my ancestral village. Near Amroha,' he said once.

On another occasion, 'My son goes to school. He is in Class II. I will let him study till Class V in Amroha, only then I will bring him here and put him in a good school.... Next year, I will put my daughter also in school.'

'I have told my wife that education is very important, but religious education comes first. Both my children must finish the recitation of Quran Pak (holy),' he said, adding that he doesn't want his children to be like him. 'I couldn't study much,' he said.

'How much have you studied?'

'I only managed to finish the Qaeda,' he said, referring to the primer that one reads before moving on to the Quran. He assumed that I was not asking about his school education. When I clarified, he shrugged.

'Zyada padh ke kya kar lete (What more could I have achieved by studying more),' he said. 'By Allah's grace, I am earning all right. In fact, I single-handedly got my sister married and helped my younger brother settle down,' he said with a touch of pride.

Most of the time, I let him talk. In his garrulity, I detected a touch of isolation. With a nebulous religious identity, he clearly couldn't talk like a Muslim with his friends or neighbours here. This bothered him. Maybe it filled him with religious guilt too, having hidden his Islamic identity in the pursuit of worldly objectives, instead of proudly proclaiming it.

As his trust in me grew, his soliloquies started to go beyond his family and his dreams for his children. He started talking about the religious prejudice that Muslims face—how even in the village, festivals are now celebrated in a low-key manner.

'Pata nahi kab danga ho jaye. Koi wajah toh hoti nahin hai, bas bahana hota hai (Who knows when a riot may break out; these things don't need a provocation, they only need an excuse). One has to be careful these days, especially the poor. We are the ones who suffer the most.'

Then, a few weeks later, he went back to namaste. 'Please call me Sonu only,' he requested. There had been some gossip about his faith. 'If word gets around that I am a Muslim my prospects might suffer.'

I didn't argue.

It was only later that the irony of the reality of Ziarul and Imamuddin's hit me. Ziarul's supervisor, only slightly better placed than him in terms of education and employment, had no problems with his religion. But he sensed that the residents at the luxury gated housing complex—people with better education, exposure, and income—might have a problem with a Muslim handyman. This was not something he would have just made up. Either his supervisors had mentioned it to him or this was his experience while being an estate manager for various housing complexes. Similarly, Imamuddin was hiding his religion from his potential customers, people who could potentially spend lakhs of rupees on doing up their flats!

The even bigger irony is that for generations, a disproportionate number of tradesmen, from carpenters to house painters, mechanics, ironsmiths, potters, etc. have been Muslims. They are school dropouts who pick up their fathers' trade and start working young. This is the reason a fairly large number of them have a reputation of excellence in their particular field and customers often seek Muslim tradesmen because of the deftness of their hands.

Yet, today, these same tradesmen fear that they will not get work if customers find out that they are Muslims. Where has this fear come from?

On the other side, customers most likely know that the people they are employing are Muslims who are pretending that they are not. Do they feel smug that a disadvantaged Muslim can't dare to show his faith?

'The Muslim identity has never been under such overt attack in the past as it is today,' says former vice president of India, Hamid Ansari. He explains: 'The Partition of India impacted the north Indian Muslims the most. To some extent, one can include Hyderabad in this, but not beyond that. States like Maharashtra, Kerala, Karnataka, and Tamil Nadu were not affected. Because of the bloody nature of the Partition and the trail of violence, security has always been a major concern with the north Indian Muslims. The series of communal riots [following Partition] only reinforced this insecurity. Through the 1960s, 70s and 80s, people knew that in instances of riots, the government was often guilty of acts of omission, and sometimes commission too, but it did not affect the question of identity.'[1]

That happened with the rise of the BJP in the 1980s.

[1]In conversation with the author, New Delhi, 25 February 2019.

'The Muslims' fear of loss of identity was added to the fear of security,' says Ansari.

This had two consequences. As individuals, poor Muslims started to underplay their identities and, as if to compensate for that, when in strength, they started to assert it more and more.

Hence, today one sees two kinds of Muslims in public places in India. The first kind comprises those who work in mixed environments. They try and merge with their surroundings, becoming as invisible as possible. It's not very difficult to do this, aided as they are by their non-Muslim colleagues, neighbours, and acquaintances, who would ideally prefer a Muslim to not show her Muslimness.

'Yet, when they unexpectedly come across a Muslim in a non-Muslim situation, they immediately try to build a brotherhood of Muslimness,' chuckles Saif Habibullah, who works with non-government organizations such as Asian Heritage Foundation and others. 'They try and talk in hushed tones, making Muslim connections and generally telling the other "I have your back" even when they don't mean it.'

'Don't mean it?'

'Never doubt that,' he says. 'A Muslim is least likely to stand up for another in a public place. His insecurity is too deep-rooted for him to take a stand.'[2]

Dr Shah Alam Khan, an orthopaedic surgeon and orthopaedic oncologist at the All India Institute of Medical Sciences (AIIMS), agrees. 'A Muslim carries a greater burden of proving that he is a secular person. He always holds back on the side of caution to establish non-parochial credentials, particularly when in the company of non-Muslim people.'

But this goes the other way too, says Dr Khan, who has authored two books on the rise of Hindu right-wing politics in India. He has started calling himself a Muslim despite being a 'practising atheist'. He gives an example from the hospital he works at. 'Usually, I am not asked to serve on any internal disciplinary committee. However, a couple of years ago, I was asked to be a part of one internal enquiry committee. I soon figured out why this happened. The young doctor under investigation

[2]In conversation with the author, New Delhi, 23 October 2018.

was a Muslim. Even as my presence obviated the risks of allegations of prejudice against him, it was expected that I would not stick my neck out to protect him.'

'Did you stick your neck out?'

'Thankfully, I was not put to the test,' he chuckles. 'It was a clear case of indiscipline.'[3]

The second kind of Muslims are those who live and work among co-religionists. They proudly exhibit their religion on their person, gleefully living up the stereotype. However, for all their brashness, these people are the most desperate and worried. Desperate to not let go of any opportunity that comes their way, given how rationed these are. And worried of the cost it may extract of their faith and, perhaps, even their lives. Within these two extremes lies the full range of contradictory emotions the community experiences—from fear to defiance, from sadness to anger, and from parochialism to self-preservation.

Yet, the popular narrative does not see this. What it sees is a retrograde, intolerant, unclean, dogmatic community dressed in a manner that is an eyesore in any progressive and modern society. Despite having partitioned the country and having got their own Islamic state in the form of Pakistan, they continue to live here. They get concessions from the government, like being allowed to practise their personal law. Worse, they still demand benefits from the government by way of reservations and subsidies!

Aware that this popular narrative is far from the truth, in March 2006, the Manmohan Singh government appointed a committee under Justice Rajinder Sachar to study and prepare a report on the social, economic, and educational status of the Muslim community of India. The study, popularly known as the Sachar Committee Report, was submitted to the Prime Minister's Office in November 2006, and put on record facts that were pretty well known to those who wanted to see it.

'...the Community,' the report said in reference to Muslims, 'exhibits deficits and deprivations in practically all dimensions of development. In fact, by and large, Muslims rank somewhat above SCs/STs but below

[3]In conversation with the author, Noida, 6 October 2019.

Hindu-OBCs, other minorities and Hindu General (mostly upper castes) in almost all indicators considered. Among the states that have large Muslim populations, the situation is particularly grave in the states of West Bengal, Bihar, Uttar Pradesh and Assam.'[4]

In the report, which curated an exhaustive list of recommendations for the amelioration of the Muslim community in India, Justice Sachar was candid and accurate in describing their predicament. He observed in his introductory note, '[Muslims] carry a double burden of being labelled as "anti-national" and as being "appeased" at the same time.'

These, then are the Muslims in India today—fearful, marginalized and yet accused of being the king's favourite wife who gets precedence over others. For that reason, they are diffident and apologetic—invisible for the most part and visible only as exhibits to validate the stereotype.

Laila Tyabji, one of the founding members of Dastkar,[5] who comes from a family of bureaucrats (her father was an Indian civil service officer who shares the credit for designing the Indian national flag; her mother tailored the first version of the tricolour that fluttered on Prime Minister Nehru's vehicle as he drove to the Red Fort for his famous 'tryst with destiny' speech) recounts an interesting conversation to convey how the Indian mainstream chooses to 'not see' the Muslim beyond the stereotype.

'I once had a conversation with a retired bureaucrat who was making sweeping statements about Muslims being radical and intolerant. I interrupted him. "I am a Muslim, too," I told him. He was taken aback. Then saying that I was an exception, he continued his rant. I interrupted him again and asked him if he had not come across any other Muslim in his entire career or while he was growing up in north India. I insisted that he think about it before answering. Gradually, he recalled a tailor who used to come to his house, then a carpenter and then a few fellow bureaucrats that he met during the course of his career. In all, he managed to count about fourteen Muslims he had interacted

[4]'Social, Economic, and Educational Status of the Muslim Community: A Report', Prime Minister's High Level Committee, Cabinet Secretariat, Government of India, November 2006, available here: http://www.minorityaffairs.gov.in/sites/default/files/sachar_comm.pdf

[5]An organization that promotes traditional Indian craft and craftspeople.

with in his sixty-five years. And he called all of them exceptions!'

Seizing the advantage, Laila then asked him to list one Muslim he had met who fit the description of radical and intolerant. He hadn't met any. The stereotype was in his mind, born partly of prejudice and partly out of propaganda. Yet it was so deeply ingrained in him that he continued to ignore his own experiences to the contrary, labelling all the Muslims he had met as exceptions to the rule.

'That is the problem,' she says. 'As the moderate Muslim doesn't fit the stereotype, she is brushed aside as an exception, whereas the truth is: she is the rule. The retrograde is the exception.'[6] This is the reason that nearly all Muslims who do not fit the stereotype are told 'but you don't look like a Muslim', at some point in their lives, because this allows them to be rendered both invisible and inconsequential.

Yet, despite the best of efforts across the religious divide, Indian Muslims can neither hide nor be hidden. The 2011 Census puts the Muslim population at 17.22 crore, 14.23 per cent of the total population of the country.[7] Muslims are spread out all over India, except for the union territory of Lakshadweep and the former state of Jammu and Kashmir (J&K), where Muslims are in the majority.

While 96.58 per cent of Lakshadweep's population is Muslim, in actual numbers this constitutes only 62,268 people. In the erstwhile state of J&K, 68.31 per cent are Muslims. In sheer numbers, it is 8,567,485.[8]

On 5 August 2019, the Government of India announced its decision to withdraw the status of 'state' from J&K and replace it with two UTs—Jammu & Kashmir being one and Ladakh the other. Unless there is a movement of people from the rest of India into the two UTs, Muslims are likely to remain the majority, even in Ladakh, which also has a large Buddhist population.

In the rest of India, the Muslim community is spread all across with substantial populations in states such as Assam (34.22 per cent), West

[6]In conversation with the author, New Delhi, 22 March 2019.

[7]Religion Census 2011, Census 2011, available here: https://www.census2011.co.in/religion.php.

[8]Ibid.

Bengal (27.01 per cent), Kerala (26.56 per cent), Uttar Pradesh (19.26 per cent), and Bihar (16.87 per cent). In the states of Jharkhand, Uttarakhand, Karnataka, Delhi, and Maharashtra, the Muslim population goes from 15 to 10 per cent. In the remaining states, it is under 10 per cent. Mizoram has the smallest population ratio of 1.35 per cent, though in actual numbers, Sikkim has a mere 9,867 Muslims out of a population of 610,577.[9]

Contrary to the propaganda narrative of 'Hum Panch Hamare Pacchees',[10] the Muslim fertility rate has been consistently falling since Independence. According to the National Family Health Survey-4 of 2015–16, for the first time the Hindu and the Muslim rates of procreation were roughly the same. While the Hindu woman's fertility rate is 2.1, the Muslim's is 2.6.[11] This is reflective of increasing levels of education and decreasing resistance to family welfare initiatives.

There is another interesting statistic about Muslims in India. Like all impoverished communities, such as Scheduled Castes and Scheduled Tribes (SC/ST), a large number of Muslims live in villages. However, as a percentage of their overall population, more Muslims live in urban areas than any other community with the exception of upper-caste Hindus.[12]

'In 2001, 35.7 per cent of the Muslim population was urban compared to 27.8 per cent of the overall population.... As per the NSS (National Sample Survey), 35.1 per cent of the Muslims lived in urban areas against 28.6 per cent of the general population in 2011–12,'[13] noted the Amitabh

---

[9]Ibid.

[10]'Hum Panch Hamare Pacchees' is a propaganda slogan of the Hindu right wing. It alludes to a Muslim man's privilege of being allowed to have four wives, therefore allowing him to have a large number of children. During his Gujarat Gaurav Yatra in September 2002, Narendra Modi, then chief minister of Gujarat, not only used this phrase but also referred to refugee camps housing Muslim victims of the communal carnage of March 2002 as 'child producing centres'. See 'Should We Run Relief Camps? Open Child Producing Centres?', *Outlook*, 30 Sep 2002.

[11]'Drop in fertility rate among Indian Muslims and the impact of girls' education', *The Telegraph*, 23 Nov 2020.

[12]Prof Amitabh Kundu, Report of the Post Sachar Evaluation Committee, Ministry of Minority Affairs, Government of India, 2014, available here: https://sabrangindia.in/sites/default/files/audio_listing_images/kundu_commission_report_0.pdf?698

[13]Ibid.

Kundu Committee, which was appointed by the Government of India in 2013 to evaluate the status of the Muslim community in India since the implementation of recommendations made by the Justice Sachar Committee.

Since their arrival in India, Muslims have largely been urban people, employed as they were in government positions. The rural population grew out of this class of powerful city-dwellers, through the award of land or territory by rulers. Eventually, two classes of rich and powerful Muslims grew in India, those in royal employment and those who were allocated cultivable land in exchange for their service, largely in the army. From this emerged the class of Muslim talukdars/zamindars or landholders. To service these elite classes, a third category emerged—artisans, craftspeople, and tradesmen, most of whom were locals who embraced Islam. Given the nature of their work, these people also lived in urban areas, working for the rich and the powerful.[14]

The Partition of India changed this demographic distribution. A lot of the Muslim landed gentry moved to Pakistan along with the urban educated employed with the government. Left in the cities were semi-literate craftspeople and tradesmen. In the villages were tillers, landless labourers who worked seasonally and, in the absence of work in the villages, moved to towns to work as daily wagers—roadside mechanics, construction workers, ironsmiths, and so on. Poor education levels ensured that they did not become part of the organized employment sector.

Professor Kundu notes:

> One of the major inequities observed among the Muslim community, highlighted by various researchers as also the JSCR (Justice Sachar Committee Report) is in the field of education.... The livelihood of Muslims is mostly dependent on self-employment in the informal sector which is also evident from their lower share of households living on earnings from regular wage employment (28 per cent

[14]'Report of the Expert Group on Diversity Index', Ministry of Minority Affairs, Government of India, 2008; also see Laurent Gayer and Christophe Jaffrelot (ed.), *Muslims in Indian Cities: Trajectories of Marginalisation*, London: Hurst Publishers, 2012.

> households for Muslims versus 43 per cent households for Hindus and 42 per cent for urban households overall). Over the recent years, it appears that more of urban Muslim households have shifted to self-employment as a major source of household income.[15]

The Government of India had unhesitatingly accepted the Sachar Committee recommendations. As a first step towards providing Muslims greater access to education, microfinance, as well as equal opportunities, it carved out the Ministry of Minority Affairs (MoMA) from within the Ministry of Social Justice and Empowerment in 2006 with Abdul Rahman Antulay as the first minister. Though the ministry's mandate covered all listed minorities—Muslims, Sikhs, Christians, Buddhists, Zoroastrians, and Jains, the fact that all ministers so far have been Muslim suggests that the government intended to focus to a greater degree on the Muslim community which, as Justice Sachar had observed, was the most backward and impoverished among all minorities.

In August 2013, MoMA appointed a Post Sachar Evaluation Committee (PSEC), under the chairmanship of Professor Amitabh Kundu to 'evaluate the process of implementation of Sachar Committee and the outcome of the programmes being implemented by the MoMA and other ministries and to recommend corrective measures'.[16]

In the PSEC report submitted to the minister of MoMA, Dr Najma Heptulla, in September 2014, the Kundu Committee observed that 'available financial resources and physical targets have been meagre in relation to the deprivation of the minorities, especially Muslims, and for some of the schemes this meagre amount has not been fully utilised and this requires that allocation of resources to the Ministry of Minority Affairs be increased'.[17]

Worse, 'MoMA reports that the share of priority sector lending (PSL) to minorities has increased to 16.09 per cent in 2013–14 of total

[15]Kundu, Report of the Post Sachar Evaluation Committee.

[16]Ibid.

[17]'Action Taken on The Report of Amitabh Kundu Committee', Press Information Bureau, Government of India, Ministry of Minority Affairs, 3 March 2015, available here: https://pib.gov.in/newsite/PrintRelease.aspx?relid=116357

PSL by banks in the country. However, Muslims could get only 44.31 per cent, while Sikh[s] had 24.58 per cent, Christian[s] 21.87 per cent, Buddhists 2.06 per cent, Parsis 2.23 per cent and Jains 4.96 per cent in total PSL to minorities in the same year. This shows that except Muslims and Buddhists, the two most deprived minorities, other minorities are able to corner larger share in PSL. This distortion needs to be corrected at the earliest.'[18]

Simply put, a Muslim's capacity to take advantage of the government's affirmative action programmes in comparison to others remains poor. Not only are Muslims unable to help themselves, they are unable to get help as well.

Five possible factors might explain this phenomenon and we will examine each of these below.

The first factor is the Partition of India. As we have seen, nearly 8 million Muslims crossed over to Pakistan during and immediately after Partition;[19] a sizeable proportion of these migrants comprised the elite or the educated class of Indian Muslim society. In a paper for Yale University, scholars Prashant Bharadwaj, Asim Khwaja, and Atif Mian have offered a very interesting statistic. Exploring the changing demographic profile of India and Pakistan, they write that the outflow of Hindus and Sikhs from Pakistan and the inflow of Muslims from India only marginally affected the literacy ratio of Pakistan because even though the migrating Hindus and Sikhs were far more literate than the resident Muslims of Pakistan, this deficiency was offset by

[18]Kundu, Report of the Post Sachar Evaluation Committee Report. When the population of all minorities in India is put together, Muslims form 71 per cent, Christians 12 per cent, Sikhs 9 per cent, Buddhists 3 per cent, Jains 2 per cent and Others 3 per cent. Despite this, Muslims are able to avail only 44.31 per cent of priority sector lending schemes, whereas, Jains who comprise 2 percent manage to get 4.96 per cent of PSL. Parsis are not even categorized separately in the Census. They are clubbed together with other smaller minority groups and listed as Others, which forms 3 per cent of all minorities. Yet, they are able to get 2.23 per cent of PSL.

[19]Sarah Ansari, 'The Movement of Indian Muslims to West Pakistan after 1947: Partition-Related Migration and its Consequences for the Pakistani Province of Sind', *Migration: The Asian Experience*, London: Palgrave Macmillan, 1994, pp. 149–68.

the emigrating Muslims from India who were also highly literate.

Using Karachi as an example, they write:

> The district of Karachi received a large influx of migrants—in 1951, nearly 28 per cent of the population was migrant.... Hindus and Sikhs in Karachi in 1931 were also much more literate than the resident Muslims—21 per cent as opposed to just 3.7 per cent. After partition, nearly all Hindus and Sikhs left Karachi (only 1.5 per cent of the population in 1951 was composed of minorities). Yet, the aggregate effect on Karachi's literacy is very small—this was due to the highly literate migrants who moved into Karachi. In the city of Karachi, 91 per cent of the literate population were migrants! What is important here is while overall literacy rates remained largely unchanged, who the literate population was composed of certainly changed. Partition thus replaced existing minority-majority literacy differences with within majority literacy differences.[20]

This wasn't simply a case of brain drain from India. This created an intellectual deficit which continues to have a cascading effect on the community. After all, education is not about literacy alone. It's about exposure to diverse ideas, being challenged by new concepts, and learning to go beyond inherited wisdom. Above all, education adds to confidence and encourages people to overcome insecurities.

'The Partition of India had a devastating impact on the Indian Muslims,' rues Maulana Mahmood Madani, general secretary, Jamiat Ulama-i-Hind, which was closely aligned with the Congress and opposed Partition. 'When some Muslims decided to move to Pakistan after Independence, they left behind a legacy of hatred. Those who stayed behind had to start their journey from the position of less than zero. Given where we started from, I have to say that I am proud of the progress Indian Muslims have made.' Then, for good measure, he adds, 'The credit for this has to be jointly shared by both the Muslims

---

[20]Prashant Bharadwaj, Asim Khwaja, and Atif Mian, 'The Partition of India: Demographic Consequences', Harvard KSG and Chicago Booth School of Business, 2009.

as well as the [rest of] Indian society which created this enabling environment.'[21]

The second factor is a result of the first. The bloodletting during Partition—roughly 16.7 million people moved between India and Pakistan over a period of four years from 1947; however, only 14.5 million have been accounted for, which suggests 2.2 million missing (probably dead)[22]—created deep-rooted distrust of the Other. In India, not only did ordinary citizens dislike and distrust Muslims, it percolated to the government too.

In his eponymously titled biography of Jawaharlal Nehru, S. Gopal writes:

> The old stalwarts of the Congress, however, such as Patel and Rajendra Prasad, with the backing of the leader of the Hindu Mahasabha, Syama Prasad Mookerjee, believed not so much in a theocratic state as in a state which symbolised the interests of the Hindu majority. Patel assumed that Muslim officials, even if they had opted for India, were bound to be disloyal and should be dismissed; and to him the Muslims in India were hostages to be held as security for the fair treatment of Hindus in Pakistan.[23]

Nehru, says A. G. Noorani, quoting from Durga Das's *Sardar Patel's Correspondence 1945-50*, dismissed the suggestion.[24]

However, the matter did not rest there. As the division of the nation's armed forces was underway, Wajahat Habibullah, former secretary of the union Ministry of Panchayati Raj, and former Chief Information Commissioner of India recalls, a directive was issued by the union Home Ministry that while Muslim officers of the Indian Army were free to stay in India, they would have to resign their commission. Of course, if they opted to join Pakistan, they would be allowed to continue in service.

[21]In conversation with the author, New Delhi, 15 November 2018.

[22]Bharadwaj, Khwaja, and Mian, 'The Partition of India'.

[23]S. Gopal, *Jawaharlal Nehru*, Vol. II, New Delhi: OUP, 2014, pp. 15–16.

[24]Quoted in A. G. Noorani (ed.), 'The Muslims of India: A Documentary Record' (Oxford India Collection) from Durga Das (ed.), *Sardar Patel's Correspondence 1945-50*, Vol. VII, Ahmedabad: Navajivan Publishing House, 2004, p. 670.

'Perhaps they were suspicious of Muslim officers wanting to serve in the Indian Army, as opposed to the all-Muslim army of Pakistan,' Habibullah says.[25] He was only two at that time, but this is the story he had heard over the years.

His father, Colonel Enaith Habibullah, and his colleague, Colonel Mohammed Usman (they both became brigadiers soon after this),[26] protested this directive. They sought a meeting with Prime Minister Jawaharlal Nehru and presented their case. Eventually the order was rescinded. Brigadier Habibullah was subsequently promoted to major general and, in 1953, he went on to establish the National Defence Academy (NDA) in Pune, India's only tri-service entry-level military academy. He remained at NDA until 1960, becoming its longest-serving commandant. Habibullah claims that his father refused both promotion and command of the army because of his deep commitment to the academy he had set up. However, this did not stop tongues from wagging in the political set-up.

'In 1978, when Air Marshal Idris Hasan Latif was appointed Air Chief Marshal (ACM) by the Janata government, then industry minister George Fernandes took credit for ACM Latif's elevation and said that Major General Habibullah could not become the army chief because the Congress government didn't have the courage to appoint a Muslim as army chief, but the Janata government made a Muslim the air force chief,' Habibullah recalls.

'By stripping all their capabilities down to their religious identity, this was an insulting statement for both my father and ACM Latif,' says Habibullah, adding, 'the truth is, as major general, my father couldn't have become the army chief. And he had himself refused postings out of NDA.'

The Habibullahs have been a privileged family, a badge they wear

[25]Interview with the author, New Delhi, 21 October 2018. Also see Wajahat Habibullah, *My Years with Rajiv: Triumph and Tragedy*, Chennai: Westland Publications, 2020, p. 7.
[26]Also called Naushera ka sher (the lion of Naushera) for his leadership in that sector of Jammu and Kashmir during the 1947–48 India–Pakistan war. Brig. Usman died during the war and was posthumously awarded the Maha Vir Chakra, the second-highest gallantry award of the Indian Army.

lightly, but consciously. 'I have realized over the years that my experiences are not reflective of what an average Muslim goes through in India,' he says. 'I am conscious of the fact that a vast majority has faced exclusion and they continue to face exclusion, including in the bureaucracy.'

In November 2011, a retired home secretary also alluded to this systemic exclusion of Muslims from the bureaucracy in an off-the-record conversation with me. We were talking about challenges to internal security. He said that since the Partition, partially out of communal prejudice, and partially out of genuine fear of national security, Muslims were filtered out of the intelligence agencies. Over a period of time, to overcome this shortfall, intelligence agencies infiltrated non-Muslim agents (pretending to be Muslims) into conservative mosques to keep a tab on what was happening. This has been a hit and run approach, which worked sometimes, but mostly did not.[27]

Najeeb Jung, former Lieutenant Governor of Delhi (and the course mate of the secretary mentioned above) endorsed this opinion. According to him, Muslims were at times also filtered out of the Intelligence services because of concerns of leaks across the border rather than mere prejudice. 'Most north Indian Muslims have families across the border. In the early post-Independence decades, there used to be a lot of movement among families, including marriages, across the border. It was because of this that there was a concern that sensitive matters may inadvertently get leaked through the intermingling of families,' he reasons.[28]

However, he admits that some Muslims could have been eliminated during the selection process for government employment due to prejudice. 'And this may have happened even if there was a Muslim on the selection panel,' he says, linking this to the legacy of the Partition. 'Muslims on a selection panel may be hesitant to push for a Muslim candidate for fear of appearing parochial or communal. This could well be because some may still carry a complex over Partition. Muslims

---

[27]Pravin Sawhney and Ghazala Wahab, *Dragon On Our Doorstep: Managing China Through Military Power*, New Delhi: Aleph Book Company, 2017, p. 218.

[28]In conversation with the author, New Delhi, 13 February 2019.

demanded and got Pakistan. Those who chose to stay back were forced to feel apologetic.'

If the government with all its checks and balances can't keep prejudice out of policy execution then what chance do private citizens have? In the early decades after the Partition, many private sector companies, especially legacy corporations of the departed British, were chary of hiring too many Muslims. Their reluctance didn't stem from national security concerns, but a general resentment towards Muslims for not leaving India despite having got their 'own Pakistan'.

Irshad Khan[29] retired as the chairman of a leading Indian company, part of one of the country's biggest business houses a few years ago, after having worked there for over four decades. He came to the Indian corporate world with impeccable credentials—Doon School (Dehradun), St. Stephen's College (Delhi), and the London School of Economics.

However, before he landed the job at the company he describes as one of India's most secular, he had an inexplicable experience while applying for a job in another company when he first returned to India after having worked in London for a few years.

'I was asked to undergo a complete medical test, in which I was diagnosed with a mild cardiac condition. I was in my late 20s and it was not a big deal, but an aberration, caused by overindulgence in London, which was soon corrected. Yet, the management kept my application pending asking me to undergo more tests repeatedly, seeking multiple medical opinions and so on,' he recalls. 'I couldn't understand what the issue was until somebody from within the company told me informally that I was wasting my time. I would not be hired because I am a Muslim. That was the first time I felt that prejudice was a reality. It may not be widespread, but it was there.'[30] However, that did not stop him from encouraging other Muslims to keep trying for employment in the mainstream corporate world.

And this leads to the third factor—Muslims' reluctance to even try. Convinced that they will not get a fair deal, a large number of Muslims

[29]Name changed.

[30]Telephonic conversation with the author, 12 September 2019.

do not even want to make an effort. Habibullah explains this as the perception of exclusion.

He says, 'There are two issues here—actual exclusion of the Muslims and the feeling of exclusion from the national mainstream. Both evoke different sentiments and reactions.'[31]

Khan says, 'I recall that when I was posted in Calcutta in the early 1980s, one morning a young man rang my doorbell. He was a graduate and wanted to apply for a job in one of my Group companies which had advertised some vacancies. He told me that he had come to tell me that though he is qualified he will not get the job because he is a Muslim. And that is the reason he has decided that he will not even apply. I was taken aback.'

After going through that person's documents, Khan persuaded him to apply. Finally, to convince him further, he told him that, 'If you do not get the job, I will personally call up the person in charge of recruitment and push your case.' It was not required. The applicant got the job.

'If you don't make the effort, you will not get anything,' Hamid Ansari emphasizes. This was something he often said to the students at Aligarh Muslim University (AMU) during his tenure as the vice chancellor. Though he often held himself up as an example, the majority remained unconvinced.

'Of course, there is prejudice, but despite that the Indian system has room for people to find their own space, provided you go out and claim it. If you start with the conviction that you will not get a fair deal, you will not get it,' he says.[32]

Notwithstanding the prejudice, many Muslims use it as an excuse to not make an effort although the real reason for their lack of success might lie elsewhere. Former vice chancellor of AMU as well as former Deputy Chief of Army Staff, Lieutenant General Zameeruddin Shah minces no words when he says, 'Muslim children are ill-equipped to get admission in any good university.' Subsequently, they remain ill-equipped to compete for jobs.

[31]Interview with the author, New Delhi, 21 October 2018.

[32]In conversation with the author, New Delhi, 25 February 2019.

This was true when I was in school and this remains true, perhaps to a lesser extent, even today. I remember my father trying to persuade his cousin to admit his daughter to the same convent school as me. However, my uncle stood his ground, arguing that he would not send his daughter there because he didn't want her to be exposed to discrimination. His daughter studied in an Urdu-medium school. Several years later, he enrolled his younger daughter in the same school as me. As she repeatedly fared poorly, the headmistress advised the family to let her repeat Class VII. Citing discrimination, the family pulled her out of that school and sent her to the same Urdu-medium school her older sister had gone to.

A historical disdain of secular education is the fourth factor why many Muslims, especially those from the socially and economically weaker strata, do not make too much effort to access modern schools even when they are subsidized. In this, the ulema also play a role by telling the intellectually weak that for true Muslims, knowledge of the Quran and Hadith is sufficient to secure one's afterlife—and that is the purpose of this life.

The origin of this sort of thinking can be traced back to the beginning of Islam. At the time of Islam's revelation, the majority of the Arabs, including the Prophet, were not lettered. The ulema have argued over the centuries that despite their lack of education, the fact that Allah chose the Arabs for his last message meant that worldly education was not necessary for the attainment of paradise. This, despite the fact that Islam laid enormous emphasis on learning. The Prophet is reported to have said, 'Seeking knowledge is an obligation upon every Muslim'.[33] However, certain ulema interpret this narrowly as pertaining only to seeking knowledge about Islam and the afterlife.

This thought became nearly institutionalized in the eleventh century when military rulers from Central Asian khanates started arriving in Persia to establish the Seljuq dynasty. Though the Seljuqs paid obeisance

[33]'Hadith on Knowledge: Seeking knowledge an obligation on every Muslim', Daily Hadith Online, available here: https://abuaminaelias.com/dailyhadithonline/2012/08/30/talab-ilm-wajib-faridah/

to the Abbasid caliphs who are credited with ushering in the golden age of Islam[34] in terms of scientific learning, independent enquiry, and engagement with the West[35], the neo-convert Seljuqs shifted focus to religious learning at the cost of scientific education.

Writing for *Deutsche Welle*'s German-Arabic project *Qantara*, Hasan Hasan says, 'Abu Ali al-Hassan al-Tusi (1018–1092), better known as Nizam al-Mulk, the grand vizier of the Seljuq dynasty...created a system of education known as "Nizamiyah" that focussed on religious studies at the expense of independent inquiry. For the first time in Islamic history, religious studies became institutionalized and religious studies were seen as a more lucrative career path. Previously, sciences and Islamic law were intertwined.'[36]

Over the centuries, this thinking became so pervasive that when Syed Ahmed Khan, subsequently knighted by the British, started a madrassa of modern education called the Mohammedan Anglo-Oriental (MAO) College in 1877 in Aligarh, he faced enormous resistance not merely from the ulema but from ordinary citizens too. Modelled after the great British universities of Cambridge and Oxford, which he had visited for inspiration, the college grew into the Aligarh Muslim University by 1920.

For all the exertions of Sir Syed, a large number of Muslims refused to send their children to MAO College lest they became irreligious or 'westernized'. Hence, Sir Syed had to repeatedly fight on two fronts. On the one hand, he had to convince the British to start trusting the Muslims again and not to apportion the entire blame for 1857 to them. On the other hand, he had to convince the ulema that he was not anti-Islam and that the modern education he was offering to Muslims was not against the tenets of the faith.[37] This was no easy task. Numerous

---

[34]Christopher de Bellaigue, *The Islamic Enlightenment: The Modern Struggle Between Faith and Reason*, London: The Bodley Head, 2018.

[35]The best known Muslim scholars, mathematicians, authors such as Ibn-e-Sina (popularly known as Avicenna), Ibn Rushd (popularly known as Averroes), Muhammad ibn Musa al-Khwarizmi, Omar Khayyam etc. thrived during the Abbasid Caliphate between 750 CE and 1258 CE.

[36]Hasan Hasan, 'Don't blame it on al-Ghazali', *Qantara.de*, 9 Jan 2013.

[37]Nadeem F. Paracha, 'The forgotten past: Sir Syed and the birth of Muslim nationalism

fatawa (plural of fatwa), the considered opinion of the ulema, were issued against him, some even calling for his death.

More than twenty years after Sir Syed's death, Maulana Muhammad Ilyas Kandhalwi founded the Tablighi Jamaat, a proselytizing Islamic movement, in response to the Aligarh movement started by Sir Syed. In one of his early discourses, Maulana Kandhalwi said, 'The evil and harm that goes with "Molvi Fadil" examinations (MA, PhD degrees etc.) offered by the government is not fully realized by us. These examinations are given so that the candidates may get certificates in order to find employment in English schools... There can be no greater injustice to religious education than the fact that those who are equipped with it, ultimately become instruments in serving the interest of the enemies of Islam.'[38]

The public intellectual Professor S. Irfan Habib, a historian of nineteenth- and twentieth-century South Asia, says that religious restrictions apart, the resistance to modern education also stemmed from the deep-rooted hatred and disdain towards the British after the revolt of 1857. 'This aversion to secular learning suited the ulema as it ensured that people remained in their clutches so they continued to fan the notion that Islam disapproves of modern education as it takes the faithful away from the path of Allah.'[39]

Throughout his career, Sir Syed had to accommodate the demands of the ulema and conservative parents. In its early years, the MAO College not only retained an Islamic core but also an upper-class (and caste) bias in its student profile. As Sir Syed himself came from a rich, landed Delhi Muslim family that claimed descent from the Prophet's family, he suffered from the same prejudice that most people at that time had towards the 'low caste/class'. In several articles and speeches, he emphasized the importance of modern education for 'Sharif' Muslims—that is, Ashrafs or upper-caste/class Muslims as opposed to Ajlafs or the working class.[40]

---

in South Asia', *Scroll.in,* 21 Aug 2016.

[38]Ghazala Wahab, 'In the Name of God', *FORCE*, July 2007.

[39]In conversation with the author, New Delhi, 27 August 2019.

[40]Arshad Alam, 'Syed Ahmed Khan and His Educational Ideas', Contemporary Education Dialogue, SAGE Journals, 2018.

Sir Syed's narrow view was not his alone. 'Knowledge was a means to social and economic success and was jealously guarded by those in possession of it,' Bellaigue wrote.[41] This was true of all caste Indians who wanted to retain not just their social and economic superiority but also, by some convoluted reasoning, societal balance. Sir Syed furthered the argument of maintaining the balance to deny Muslim women the access to modern education he was offering upper-class Muslim men. He argued that women could not be better educated than men as it would disrupt domestic harmony and 'raise their expectations'[42]. According to him, as well as those he was reaching out to modernize, a woman was only required to learn religious texts and home-making skills. AMU established its first women's college in 1922, twenty-four years after the death of its founder.

The result of this controlled outreach was that despite the revolutionary nature of the 'Aligarh Movement' as Sir Syed's endeavour was called, its reach was extremely limited; not only socially but geographically too. It remained largely a north Indian, upper-class Muslim movement. The working classes remained beyond the pale of AMU for several decades and only started to see any advantage from it well after Independence.

But the lack of interest in modern education lingered on, now prompted by post-Partition prejudice that led to limited employment options for Muslims. If education did not result in immediate employment, what good was it? Had one learnt some skill instead of wasting time and money on schools, one would have at least been able to make a living, was a common refrain in many sections of the Indian Muslim community.

Dr Shabista Gaffar, who has served as chairperson of the committee on girl's education instituted by the National Minorities Commission during the United Progressive Alliance government, points out: 'During my travels across India researching reasons why Muslims do not take

[41]Bellaigue, *The Islamic Enlightenment*, p. 76.

[42]Nasreen Ahmed, 'Sir Syed Ahmed Khan and Muslim Female Education: A Study in Contradictions', Proceedings of the Indian History Congress, Vol. 68, Part One, 2007.

modern education seriously, one of the recurring reasons across the gender divide was lack of employment avenues. The other inter-related factor was lack of awareness about career options. Most Muslims even today only look at traditional careers.'[43]

The employment situation started to change in India in some measure with the oil boom in the Middle East which opened up unprecedented opportunities for Indian Muslims. Politician Asaduddin Owaisi, president of the All India Majlis-e-Ittehadul Muslimeen, says, 'When employment opportunities opened up in the Gulf, the clamour for education also increased among Muslims. They started doing what they never did before—demand modern, job-oriented education and even borrow money to pay for it.'

Eventually, as earnings increased, so too did the demand for more schools catering to Muslim students. 'Today, all Muslims want schools in their areas, but there are hardly any good schools because both the government and the private sector have not prioritized this demand of the Muslims,' he says, adding, 'eventually, Muslims have to rely on Muslim-run schools of whatever quality.'[44]

As this 'demand' for education was directly linked to the 'supply' of jobs in the Gulf, for instance, that of technicians, foremen, office assistants, etc., it did not add any intellectual value to the community back in India. Rather, it had a few drawbacks. One, the extended stay in the Gulf exposed workers to Wahhabi Islam. The prosperity Indian Muslim expatriates encountered in the Gulf countries after the oil boom stood in sharp contrast to the abjectness of their existence in India. Over time, their exposure in the Gulf began to condition their thinking and they became conduits of the Wahhabi form of exclusionary Islam into India, which started replacing the syncretic Indian Islam.

Two, says Irshad Khan, 'The remittances that the Muslims working in United Arab Emirates and Saudi Arabia sent home transformed their lives here. The families became prosperous and in the villages of Bihar and eastern Uttar Pradesh, this prosperity became a source of envy

[43]In conversation with the author, New Delhi, 23 August 2019.

[44]In conversation with the author, New Delhi, 17 August 2019.

and to some extent communal tension.... This disturbed the delicate social balance.'[45]

The third consequence of this has been that as more Muslim youth aspired to go to the Gulf countries, their connection with India became increasingly tenuous. 'They have stopped trying in India because they feel that they can improve the quality of their lives in the Gulf,' says Khan.[46] Hence, at some level, even the government remained complacent about working towards the uplift of Muslims. When they don't even take advantage of the existing ameliorative schemes, as noted by the Kundu Committee, why would the government bother with more?

The fifth factor is insecurity, which has been brought about by repeated instances of violence against Muslims. This leads a large number of Muslims to prefer to keep their heads down, not wanting to attract unnecessary attention to themselves. They want to live with other Muslims, not venturing too far from their chosen ghettos for education or employment. Justice Sachar wrote in his report:

> Schools beyond the primary level are few in Muslim localities. Exclusive girls' schools are fewer, and are usually at a distance from Muslim localities. This has its repercussions because after any incident of communal violence, parents pull out their girls from school fearing [for] their security.[47]

In the same report he notes that the sense of insecurity comes in the way of Muslims accessing various government schemes from employment to healthcare as it will require that they step out of their ghettos.

He writes:

> Fearing for their security, Muslims are increasingly resorting to living in ghettos across the country.... However, while living in ghettos seems to be giving them a sense of security because of their numerical strength, it has not been to the advantage of the

[45]Telephonic conversation with the author, 12 September 2019.

[46]Ibid.

[47]Kundu, Post Sachar Evaluation Committee Report.

> Community. It was suggested that Muslims living together in concentrated pockets (both because of historical reasons and a deepening sense of insecurity) has made them easy targets for neglect by municipal and government authorities. Water, sanitation, electricity, schools, public health facilities, banking facilities, anganwadis, ration shops, roads, and transport facilities—are all in short supply in these areas.

An urban Muslim ghetto has to be seen to be believed. No matter how many times you go there, the reaction upon crossing the invisible border between the megalopolis of Delhi and the tenements of Jamia Nagar/ Zakir Nagar in the area of Okhla is always the same—shock and dismay.

In November 2018, for one of my visits to the area in the course of writing this book, I requested a junior colleague from my office to accompany me as I was unsure about finding space to park my car there. In the last days of autumn, just before winter sets in, a haze of smoke and air pollutants descends on the whole of Delhi. But it is not the pollution or dirt alone that dismays the visitors to this 'Muslim area'. It is something else—a combination of poverty, backwardness, fear, and an awareness of something different.

We drove past the Yamuna barrage onto a narrow road flanked by Lego-style boxes one atop the other passing off as houses on one side, and a strip of the Yamuna, a travesty of a river, on the other.

Not only did the landscape change in a matter of minutes, from posh South Delhi to the decrepit habitations south of the river, the type of people changed too. Most men had beards, some wore skullcaps. Their trousers or pyjamas were hitched up to reveal the ankles. Women were attired in shape-concealing salwar-kurtas. While some wore pinned headscarves, some had covered their heads with their dupattas. Thankfully, only few wore full burkhas.

'I have never been here before,' my colleague confessed sheepishly; that was the reason he had been enthusiastic about accompanying me. 'I was always scared of coming to this side.'

'Not even for Mughlai food?' I asked, joking.

'No,' he shook his head. 'I have heard so many stories about places like these. I never thought it was worth the trouble.'

'Places like these?'

'You know, Muslim areas,' he blurted, before adding, 'Of course, those are all exaggerations. I never had an opportunity to come here....'

His words were crashing into one another. To comfort him, I told him that even I didn't come here very often. 'It's very congested. It's very dirty too.' He relaxed. I was not offended. He was not prejudiced—he was just a victim of the popular narrative.

The conversation brought to mind the Batla House encounter of 2008.[48] This incident features prominently in the long list of grievances that Muslims hold against the Indian state. In this case, they have reason to.

On 19 September 2008, a team belonging to Delhi police's special cell, led by Inspector Mohan Chand Sharma, carried out what it claimed was an anti-terror operation at a rented accommodation in Batla House—a congested locality in Jamia Nagar. Two boys, whom the police claimed were notorious terrorists from Indian Mujahideen, were killed. The locals of the area believed that the boys were innocent. During the course of this operation, Inspector Sharma was also killed. Sharma, a veteran encounter-specialist, had not been wearing a bullet-proof jacket, while the rest of his team was kitted out in bullet-proof gear. This raised questions about the encounter.

The other question raised was about the timing of the operation itself—six days after the serial bomb attack in Delhi on 13 September 2008 in which thirty people died.[49] Delhi police personnel had started scouting the area on the evening of the 13th, picking up people for questioning. Several men and boys were picked up from the Jamia and Zakir Nagar areas and were charged with multiple cases of terrorist violence, including those that had occurred in other cities. It was as though these localities had produced made-to-order terrorists ready to

---

[48]'9 years of the Batla House "Encounter": details of the case so far that we must know', *India Resists*, 17 Sep 2019.

[49]Jamia Teachers' Solidarity Group, '"Encounter" at Batla House: Unanswered Questions', available here: https://revolutionarydemocracy.org/batla/batla.htm

be nabbed at short notice whenever necessary.

The locals vehemently protested the police action. Sit-downs and marches were carried out against the Delhi police and the administration. These protests continued for the next few years.[50] An impartial enquiry into the encounter was demanded, but dismissed as being demoralizing to the police.[51] Police morale was important, never mind that people who lived in these localities were on edge.

Even a decade after the incident, the ghost of Batla House lives on in the area where police checkpoints outnumber schools, where food delivery services refuse to cater, where banks refuse credit cards to those living in that area. Intelligence Bureau agents in plain clothes keep tabs on the residents, especially the students.

Ghettos are most often found in cities with a history of communal violence. For instance, in a city like Bengaluru, there are areas with a majority Muslim population, like Vasanth Nagar or Shivaji Nagar. Situated right in the middle of the city, at walking distance from the famous Benguluru landmark, Cubbon Park, these localities are not ghettos, but just another part of the city unlike Okhla. The Muslim-dominated areas in Okhla have not grown organically during the course of the development of cities, like the Jama Masjid/ Nizamuddin West area of Delhi or the Mohammed Ali Road neighbourhood of Mumbai. Places like Ohkla, Mumbra on the outskirts of Mumbai, or Juhupura in Ahmedabad are urban islands created as a result of the action of the state and the attitudes of sections of non-Muslim inhabitants of the city. They are an indictment of the cities in which they exist.

Take Mumbra, for instance, a township developed entirely by Muslims who built one facility after another, following the 1992–93 riots in Mumbai. Muslims started to move there as the city of dreams turned into a nightmare. Today, it enjoys the dubious distinction of being the largest Muslim ghetto in India, housing more than 900,000 people

---

[50]'Students hold protest march on 5th anniversary of the Batla House encounter', *News 18*, 19 Sep 2013.

[51]Praveen Kumar, 'Batla House encounter: Cops' no to judicial probe', *India Today*, 9 Apr 2009.

according to the 2011 Census.[52] Even today, Mumbra is an oversized urban village tied to Mumbai through an umbilical cord of memories. Like the Okhla area of Delhi, a Mumbra address also limits options of education and employment in the mainstream for its residents.

Basharat Peer, in a column in *The Hindu*, says: 'A Mumbra address often carries a degree of prejudice and suspicion. A lawyer spoke of trying to buy an Idea Internet dongle at a Thane shop and being turned away; an Urdu publisher spoke of waiting months to get a landline and broadband connection from BSNL. A few weeks ago, a private school in Panvel, a suburb 24 kilometres from Mumbra, decided to ban admissions of students from the ghetto, claiming that they behave badly....'[53]

As previously stated, the ghettos provide a convenient array of suspects for the police whenever they are pushed by their superiors to 'close cases' especially after a terrorist attack. While a Batla House or an Ishrat Jahan[54] are uncommon incidents, its common knowledge that young Muslim men are frequently picked up and held without charges indefinitely under some anti-terrorist law or another. Several reports list the disproportionate number of Muslim undertrials throughout India.[55] One such man, Mohammad Aamir Khan, recently published a book on the fourteen years he spent in the jail as an undertrial on trumped-up charges of terrorism.[56] Eventually, he was honourably acquitted, like so many others, because in most instances, the police cases fall apart in the courtrooms. Unfortunately, they often take decades to get there.

---

[52]Basharat Peer, 'In India's largest Muslim ghetto', *The Hindu*, 19 Jun 2015.

[53]Ibid.

[54]Ishrat Jahan was a nineteen-year-old woman from the Mumbra area who was killed (along with two men) by the Gujarat police in an encounter on the outskirts of Ahmedabad in June 2004. The police had alleged that the three were Lashkar-e-Taiba operatives and were on a mission to assassinate the Gujarat chief minister, Narendra Modi. The encounter raised several questions, forcing the Gujarat High Court to constitute a special investigation team which declared the encounter as staged. See Sreya Roychowdhury, 'Ishrat Jahan Encounter Case: A Timeline of Events', *The Wire*, 2 May 2019.

[55]Status of Policing in India Report 2018: A Study of Performance and Perceptions, Common Cause India, 2018, available here: http://commoncause.in/pdf/SPIR2018.pdf

[56]Mohammed Aamir Khan (with Nandita Haksar), *Framed As a Terrorist: My 14-Year Struggle to Prove My Innocence*, New Delhi: Speaking Tiger, 2016.

State indifference and persecution are not the only reasons Muslims are pushed into ghettos. Property owners refuse to rent accommodation to Muslims—this again is related to a history of communal violence. More Muslims find it difficult to find an apartment in Mumbai or Ahmedabad than in Delhi or Kolkata. Similarly, between Delhi and Bengaluru, it is easier for Muslims to find accommodation in the latter.

When I first started to look for rented accommodation in Delhi in 1992, I had no problem. I lived in rented apartments for over a decade in south and east Delhi. Not once did my religion come in the way. However, when my cousins shifted to Delhi in 2007, they had to struggle, and property dealers frequently advised them to opt for Okhla.

Professor Habib says that this has more to do with the make-up of Indian society than religion. 'Indians are a parochial and identity-conscious people. They prefer living with their own kind, which is why in Delhi you have Bengali-dominated or Punjabi-dominated areas. Religion just adds another layer to this behaviour. Of course, upwardly mobile Muslims have a problem because the Muslim areas are mostly backward.'[57]

Apart from providing fodder to the police, the ghetto perpetuates two other conditions—poverty and stereotyping. Since their address restricts their options in the mainstream, a large number of Muslims live and work within the supposedly 'safe' confines of their areas, as noted by both Justice Sachar and Professor Kundu in their respective reports. This creates a cycle of poverty and poverty-induced despair. As we have seen, most Muslims resort to self-employment as small businesses catering largely to Muslims or services like carpentry, auto repair etc., because of poor education levels. This is also evident by another statistic that Professor Kundu recorded. According to him, a higher number of Muslims from the 'lower educational category' who are employed in jobs like these are fifteen years of age or thereabouts. This, he concludes, suggests poor economic conditions. In rural areas, it is also common to find a higher percentage of Muslims employed as casual labourers rather like the SC/ST and other OBC communities.

---

[57]In conversation with the author, New Delhi, 27 August 2019.

One of the positive signs on the employment front is that a certain percentage of Muslims are employed in professional categories such as 'teachers, government officials, managers, service shop owners and sale persons'. In this respect, though much poorer than the upper-caste Hindus, they fare better than the SC communities.

Interestingly, one statistic that does not find mention in either the Sachar Committee or Kundu Committee reports is the high representation of Muslims in the media and performing arts, like films, theatre, etc. This is ironical because a large number of conservative Muslims believe that Islam forbids imagery, and hence films and entertainment are considered un-Islamic careers.

At least two ulema, including Maulana Mahmood Madani, told me that the purpose of a Muslim's life is prayer and devotion to Allah. 'There is no room for entertainment in this world because it is a temporary realm. A true Muslim will partake of real entertainment in the afterlife.'[58] And yet, the Indian film industry, since it came into being, has always had a preponderance of Muslim artists, both on-screen and off-screen. More recently, one finds a disproportionate number of Muslims in journalism, both print and broadcast. Lack of education or prejudice does not seem to come in their way in these streams.

One reason for this could be aptitude. Perhaps Muslims are better at creative pursuits than analytical ones. At least, that is what the Muslim Personal Law Board thought when it wrote to the Human Resource Development minister a few years ago. Feminist activist and writer Sheeba Aslam Fehmi explains that the Muslim Personal Law Board wrote to the government 'urging it to exempt Muslim children from mathematics Class 10 Board examinations saying that they do not have the aptitude for that. Can there be a more demeaning internalization of weakness and inferiority?'[59] That's certainly one way of looking at it. However, that is not how the Central Board of Secondary Education (CBSE) views it. In early 2019, it announced that it would bifurcate the

---

[58]Maulana Madani in conversation with the author, New Delhi, 15 November 2018.
[59]In conversation with the author, New Delhi, 23 August 2019.

mathematics examination into two categories[60]—standard and basic—from 2020, to enable children who did not want to study the subject beyond Class X to clear the board examination without anxiety about failure or poor overall percentage. Perhaps the Muslim demand did play a role in this, although it wasn't exactly a welcome development.

But to get back to the high representation of Muslims in the arts, especially popular culture and journalism. 'There are three possible explanations for this phenomenon,' says journalist Arfa Khanum Sherwani. 'One is the legacy factor. The Mughals nurtured fine arts across domains. Pursuing vocations such as music, poetry, public performances ensured both recognition by the court and social mobility. Hence, a large number of Muslims trained and worked in these areas which, over time, became family vocations.'

The second factor, according to her, has to do with Muslims being a minority in India facing a certain degree of prejudice and sometimes persecution. Given this, expressing one's angst through poetry or literature has been a form of resistance. 'You will find several Muslims employed in non-creative fields, but still writing as a hobby.'

The third factor reflects more on Indian society than Muslims per se. 'An average Muslim from one of the higher castes, those who are called Ashrafs or Shurafas, tend to speak a more sophisticated language, their diction is better and, like it or not, they are usually fair-skinned and good-looking. All of this opens doors for them, both in television media and, to some extent, films. This social capital at times helps them beat the prevalent discrimination against the Muslims but ends up [with these industries] having a disproportionate representation of upper-caste Muslims.'[61]

'It is not just the women and it is not just the media,' says Dr Shah Alam Khan. 'Like the upper-caste Hindus, the upper-caste Muslims—fair-skinned and well-built—have it easier than the low-caste Muslims.'[62]

---

[60]CBSE class 10 Maths Basic and Standard in 2020, available here: https://mycbseguide.com/blog/cbse-class-10-maths-basic-and-standard-in-2020/

[61]In conversation with the author, New Delhi, 24 October 2019.

[62]In conversation with the author, Noida, 6 October 2019.

The caste system among the Muslims of the Indian subcontinent is the worst-kept secret of the community. The egalitarian faith of the desert that established the equality of all humans by freeing the slaves and insisting that when men offer namaz they should stand so close to one another that their ankles touch could not overcome the deep-rooted prejudice of birth in India.

Indian Sunni Muslims have divided themselves into neat boxes of differences based on birth and circumstance of their conversion to Islam. Hence, as previously noted, there are three categories of Muslims. At the top of the pyramid are Ashrafs—these include the Syeds, Sheikhs, and Pathans. All consider themselves of Arab-Persian-Turkish-Central Asian descent. These are the people who are descended from migrants to India over several centuries, right from the time of the revelation of Islam. A lot of them were traders who came for business and settled down here, marrying women from upper caste or powerful families. Also included in this category are upper-caste Hindus who converted to Islam and automatically assumed Ashraf status because of their erstwhile caste.[63]

Among Ashrafs, Syeds are at the top as they claim descent from the Prophet's family through his daughter Fatima. Some Syeds are Shia and claim the same lineage. For years, Syeds in India tried to maintain their racial purity by marrying only among themselves. Eventually, they deigned to marry from among Sheikhs, the second in the pecking order. Sheikhs also marry from Pathan families. The second category is of working-caste Hindus who converted to Islam in one of three ways—of their free will, to further their commercial interests, or under duress. However they came to Islam, they formed the working castes among Muslims, referred to as Ajlafs and include tillers, barbers, butchers, cobblers, weavers, etc. These are the people who now refer to themselves as other backward communities (OBC). The Kundu Committee, based on the 68th NSS data (2011–12) reported that nearly half the urban Muslim population listed itself as OBC.

---

[63]See Sadia Dehlvi, *Sufism: The Heart Of Islam*, New Delhi: HarperCollins, 2009 and Khalid Anis Ansari, 'India's Muslim community under a churn: 85% backward Pasmandas up against 15% Ashrafs', *The Print*, 13 May 2019.

Interestingly, when it comes to marriage, each community prefers their own, shunning even the caste supposedly higher than theirs. My own barber takes great pride in his caste—'Salmani'. He says that denouncing one's caste is akin to denouncing one's parentage.

'The only reason I will agree to my daughter marrying outside our caste is if we are unable to find a man as educated as her in our community,' he told me, adding a caveat. 'But if I have to go out of my caste, it will be to a caste higher than mine. Even if the man is well-educated, I will not give up my caste for another lower caste.'

For marrying within one's own caste/ community, Muslims take recourse in the Islamic tradition of 'Kuf' which recommends marriage within economic and intellectual compatibility so as to minimize the chances of an unhappy marriage that could lead to divorce. Explains Professor Faizan Mustafa, vice chancellor, National Academy of Legal Studies and Research (NALSAR) University, 'The Hanafi jurisprudence[64] recommends that one should marry so that one is compatible in terms of wealth, education, and thinking. This recommendation is referred to as Kuf. It has nothing to do with caste or social standing. That in India caste determines wealth and education to a large extent is incidental.'[65]

The third category includes those who call themselves Scheduled Caste Muslims. These are essentially Scheduled Caste Hindus who converted to Islam but couldn't shake off the yoke of their caste. Given that a miniscule percentage, according to the Sachar Committee Report, lists itself as Scheduled Caste (1.5 per cent of total Muslim households), clearly the majority of them have managed to move up the ladder by assuming 'Ashraf' family names like 'Khan' and finding jobs outside the family trade.

Professor Khalid Anis Ansari, senior assistant professor of sociology, Glocal University, and a social activist, has an explanation for the small percentage of Scheduled Caste Muslims: 'The NSSO data is based on self-reporting. As we know, Clause 3 of the Presidential Order, 1950, and subsequent amendments have resulted in the official non-recognition of

[64]Schools of Islamic jurisprudence have been dealt with in another chapter.

[65]In conversation with the author, New Delhi, 13 September 2019.

Dalit Muslims and Dalit Christians as SCs. In most states the Muslims of SC origin are recognized as OBCs and so most Dalit Muslims return themselves as OBCs in official surveys. However, broadly, most Dalit Muslims do not identify as Dalits because they do not have the tools—education and awareness—to distinguish themselves. They believe what they are told by religious leaders—that Islam is an egalitarian religion with no social hierarchies.'[66]

Since caste has no religious sanction in Islam and is a result of social conditioning, it is commonplace to deny its existence. Curiously, it is not only the upper-caste Muslims who deny it, even the so-called lower castes deny it. I spoke to a number of tradesmen about the problems they face at the hands of the Ashraf communities. Not one accepted that there was a thing called caste in Islam. The only people who speak for them are the community leaders or activists.

Perhaps because they find themselves on the periphery, it is this class of Muslims, described as Pasmanda, Persian for those left behind, who lead the charge of the conservatives. They also contribute the maximum numbers to the low-level ulema class comprising hafiz and local muftis[67]. As always happens in such cases, they are the most righteous and devout segment of the community. Given their large numbers they are the group that reinforces stereotypes.

The Moderates' Dilemma

Striking a balance between prejudice and stereotypes, faith and modernity, moderate or progressive Muslims are increasingly being pushed to the margins.

Since there is no data on the number of Muslims who call themselves moderate, it is not possible to quantify their number. But going by the assertiveness of the conservatives and their penchant to assign labels to those who do not agree with them, moderates do seem to be at a disadvantage. And not just in India.

Dr Qamar Rahman, a scientist who retired from the Council of

[66]In conversation with the author, New Delhi, 21 November 2019.

[67]Scholar with expertise in Islamic law and is qualified to issue fatawa.

Scientific and Industrial Research (CSIR) a few years ago, and is currently dean of research science and technology, Amity University, Lucknow, narrates an incident from the time she used to work at Rostock University in Germany.

'Religion is very important to me. I have always been diligent in saying my namaz and keeping my rozas,' she says. 'When I moved to Rostock many years ago, I went to a local mosque to get the schedule of namaz timings. This has been my practice throughout my life. Wherever I travel abroad I always visit the local mosque. Getting the prayer timing is just one of the reasons. Another is to see the mosque. The architecture and its state give insight into who built the mosque and the status of the local Muslim community. While I was looking at the mosque, I spotted a man dressed like an important religious person. He gestured to the person I was talking with. My guide returned to tell me that I should not come to the mosque with my face exposed. I was shocked and hurt by his stricture. I told my guide to tell him that while I will do my best to adhere to the spirit of Islam, even he should do that. He should not look me in the face because the Prophet advised men to lower their eyes when they came across a woman.'[68]

According to Rahman, since she never let her work and faith interfere with one another, conservative Muslims always find reasons to point fingers at her, questioning her practice of Islam. Rahman's professional achievements have insulated her to a large extent, as has her outspokenness. Not everyone has these advantages, which is why a large number make excuses for their beliefs. Often, they fear that the larger community, which is disdainful towards them, will ostracize them. This is particularly worrying because given the sociopolitical environment of India today, their moderate beliefs are of no help when they are viewed and condemned as Muslims by Hindu fanatics. On the one hand, conservative or devout Muslims disparage them; on the other hand, Hindus suspect them.

'A moderate Muslim really has no voice or traction within the larger Muslim society today,' says Professor Mustafa. 'When I speak,

[68]Interview with the author, New Delhi, 18 August 2019.

non-Muslims listen to me more intently than Muslims who doubt my knowledge because I do not fit the bill of a "learned" Muslim.'[69] To be taken seriously by the Muslim community he would need to grow a beard and dress in a certain manner.

Professor Habib says, 'Progressive Muslims have been totally marginalized. They are considered apologists.' In 2016, he was invited to speak at a conference, 'Rethinking Islam' at the AMU. While Habib spoke of opening Muslim minds to new ideas, the audience was more worried about the dangers to Islam from the West. 'This self-righteousness is the main problem,' he says. 'Instead of changing themselves, they talk about changing the world.'[70]

This marginalization impacts all aspects of the life of a 'less devout' Muslim. Take, for instance, something as ordinary as finding a 'like-minded' Muslim spouse, especially in an arranged marriage set-up.

Says Uzmi Athar, a young journalist, 'Since I am not in a relationship, my parents offered to find me a match. But despite their best efforts, they have been unsuccessful.'[71] Even when they find Muslim men with similar liberal values, the men and their families are reluctant to accept a progressive Muslim woman, and a journalist to boot! A moderate woman is doubly disadvantaged, as her ability to guide her eventual progeny on the Islamic path is suspect. So, while men can display their moderation as a mark of progress, women are required to have an Islamic core. This dichotomy adds to their disadvantage vis a vis those who are unambiguous about their religious beliefs.

'I do not see myself as a moderate Muslim,' says deputy general manager, Broadcast Engineering Consultants India Ltd, Mazhar Umer. 'I am a religious Muslim, and this is nothing to be embarrassed about. Nobody has a problem with a religious person. I have no problems with a religious Hindu or a religious Christian, and they don't have a problem with me because we are not stepping on each other's toes.'

The difference between the moderate and the religious, according

---

[69]In conversation with the author, New Delhi, 13 September 2019.

[70]In conversation with the author, New Delhi, 27 August 2019.

[71]Interview with the author, Noida, 19 March 2019.

to him, lies in the sentiment towards religion. 'I try to pray five times a day. I have kept a prayer mat in my office,' he says. 'Sometimes when I am unable to pray because of my work, I feel bad about it and read the qaza (penance prayer) the moment I am able to.'[72] Umer is equally diligent about fasting in the month of Ramzan as well as meeting his zakat obligations.

Many Muslims such as Umer do not view moderates favourably. They dismiss the fact that moderate Muslims have arrived at their way of being through an intellectual assessment of Islam and feel that the moderation rises out of a lifestyle borne of sloth, desperation to merge with the majority, and lack of courage to stand up for one's faith. People like Umer believe that his choice of openly professing and practising his religion reflects his rectitude and intellectual courage.

It is pointless to blame people like Umer for their assessment of the moderates. The fact is that most moderate Muslims lack confidence about their faith. Indeed, their beliefs or liberal views are not always an intellectual choice, but the lifestyle that they drifted into, inherited from their parents, or imbibed from peers. Quite like the Hindu stages of life, where renunciation is undertaken post-retirement, moderate Muslims tell themselves that they will give up pleasures for piety in old age. As the Urdu poet Brij Narayan Chakbast wrote a century ago:

> Jab tak tha jawani ka aalam, kya aish ki masti rehti thi
> Jab piiri maut ki layee khabar, phir zuhd bhi hai aur taa-at bhi
> (In the headiness of youth, one indulged in all kinds of pleasurable activities
> When old age brought the news of death, only then did one turn to abstinence and devotion)[73]

Perhaps that also explains why a large number of Indians perform the hajj pilgrimage only towards the end of their lives, because they hope to give up sinful habits after that.

---

[72]Interview with the author, Noida, 1 April 2019.

[73]Maulvi Mohammed Ibrahim and Fida Hussain Khan Sahab (ed.), *Shahkaar-e-Nazm*, Allahabad: Rai Sahab Ram Dayal Agarwal, 1988, p. 27. (Translation by the author.)

Islam didn't hold much interest for Najeeb Jung as a child despite his mother's attempts to teach him the religion. He remained ambivalent about it throughout his youth. Most moderate Muslims blame their lack of piety on everything from pressure of work to lack of facilities (to pray) rather than confess that it is a lack of will. This is primarily because of the immense pressure from conservative Muslims who mock them as apologists or sell-outs to the cause of Islam. Not surprisingly, they can seldom explain the moderation of their beliefs. In sharp contrast is the devout Muslim who is articulate and speaks with the authority of the scriptures, spouting verses and Hadith at the whiff of an argument.

When I was growing up, my faith was frequently challenged by my more religious cousins. They not only knew quite a few Quranic verses, they were also familiar with a range of Islamic texts written by various scholars over the centuries. It was immaterial whether they had actually read the text or simply heard an Islamic demagogue on an audio or a video tape. The fact was that people like me had no interest in the disciplined practice of religion and hence never bothered to access such religious material. Besides, as a teenager, I had not dwelled upon my choices, which to a large extent were inherited.

But inheritance is no argument. I could not explain why I didn't feel inclined to offer namaz five times a day, so to escape the harangue I used to face whenever I visited the maternal side of my family during vacations, I would quietly join them in prayer. This further weakened my position, as it now appeared that I was lazy or worse, a hypocrite, hence morally weak and corruptible—someone who needed to be constantly pushed towards doing the right thing. What made my situation worse was my inability to express what I felt towards God. Did I believe in Allah? If I did, why didn't I obey his commandments? And if I didn't believe in Allah, then on what basis did I call myself a Muslim!

When I was young, I wasn't aware of the Quranic verse which says there should be no compulsion in religion.[74] I also didn't understand that non-conformists or independent thinkers threaten the carefully

[74]Surah Al-Baqarah, Verse 2:256, Translation by Dr Mustafa Khattab (https://quran.com/2/256-266).

built structures that conformists nurture—today they refuse to obey, tomorrow, what if they start to question? This is the reason apostasy or irtidad worried the early Islamists—all it takes is for one challenger to stand up for the floodgates to open. Despite the fact that the Quran does not mention apostasy, or prescribe any punishment for it (just as it does not prescribe any punishment for blasphemy), conservative ulema use it as a threat to keep in check those who they view as wayward.

Apostasy, or the renunciation of one's faith, became a sin after it was conflated with treason during the caliphate of Abu Bakr. As the first caliph was engaged in consolidating the Muslim community and its territory, which entailed subduing rebellion in various parts of the Islamic world, 'religious affiliation and citizenship were nearly identical terms in 7th century Arabia, so therefore were apostasy and treason considered one and the same.'[75]

When Islamic laws were being written, apostasy was described as treason. Death was the prescribed punishment for the crime. Even after the emergence of modern nation-states, where citizenship had nothing to do with religion, the ulema continued to treat apostasy as a grave sin against Allah, a position the conservatives take against moderates or those they deem as 'not adequately Muslim'. Such people, they believe, must be preached to until they return to the fold or leave for good—there are no half measures.

Since I was ignorant of all this, I continued to be on the defensive whenever challenged by any argument in the name of Islam. There are others like me. Rizwan Ahmed, a businessman and an aspiring writer, struggled with several labels, calling himself agnostic and atheist before settling for non-practising Muslim. 'When I was younger and more rebellious, I preferred calling myself an atheist. Perhaps it was fashionable those days. But I was never an atheist. Despite my nebulous belief in God, I did find the idea of an Almighty comforting. Besides, I never left my Muslim identity, in terms of culture, language, festivals, and habits, and now more than anything else, empathy for fellow Muslims.'

[75]Reza Aslan, *No God But God: The Origins, Evolution and Future of Islam*, London: Random House, 2011, p. 121.

Moreover, he also reads namaz occasionally, during Ramzan or on Eid.

Today, when a family member urges him to pray more regularly, he has a standard reply. 'I tell them: "You have asked me to come to the mosque to pray. You have earned your credit and place in paradise by showing the right path to a sinner. I have said no. The sin is upon me now. Let me rot in hell." This shuts them up all right,' he chuckles.[76]

Ahmed is fortunate in that his self-appointed minders back off when told to. Not all are this fortunate. Some face such strictures on a daily basis, if not from relatives, then from Muslim neighbours or the visiting jamaatis (members) of the Tabligh,[77] the proselytizing sect founded in the late 1920s by Maulana Mohammed Ilyas Kandhalwi with two objectives: self-improvement and the improvement of others. Hence, not only do they strive to turn themselves into an increasingly medieval version of Muslims, they also reach out to others, through a process called da'wah (invitation). Umer encountered the Tablighi Jamaat in the mosque he used to frequent in his university years in Benares. 'The Tabligh has been a big influence on my life,' he says. 'I have participated in several short-term Jamaat activities. It is my desire to go on a forty-day chilla (proselytizing trip) with them.'

While Tablighi Jamaat is a Sunni organization, proselytizing is not confined to this group of Muslims. In fact, it is even more pervasive in smaller and closed communities like the Bohra Muslims, where community minders keep track of everyone through Aadhaar-like Bohra ID cards.

Says journalist-activist Aarefa Johari, 'The Bohras are an extremely close-knit community, particularly if you live in a Bohra-dominated locality in your town or city. For many Bohras, even if they are not intensely religious, social, community, and economic life are all intertwined. Many family businesses operate in Bohra localities with Bohra clients. Their social circles are all people they keep meeting in the mosque. Hence, there is always a need to maintain good relations with other community members and the community authorities. Of

[76]Interview with the author, New Delhi, 24 August 2019.

[77]The Tablighi Jamaat has been described in detail in Chapter 4.

course, all of this affects individual freedom and choices.'[78]

Given this, the community authorities know who comes regularly for prayers to the mosque and who doesn't. 'Every year before Ramzan, some mosque representative will show up to ask my mother why her daughters never go to the masjid. And they try to convince her to convince us, or sometimes try to convince me directly,' says Johari, who now identifies as a non-practising Muslim.

According to her, ostracization from the community is a 'real threat' that forces many to fall in line. It comes down to three primary concerns: 'If we are ostracized, who will officiate at my child's nikah (marriage)? Who will conduct my funeral? And how will I get a place in the kabarastan (graveyard)? The latter, especially, is very understandable, because ostracized Bohras have been barred from attending their loved ones' funerals,' says Johari.

As if this were not enough control, the community elders also encourage members to publicly name and shame dissenters. Says Johari, 'Bohras are taught to pray laanat (curse) on dissenters. Every Moharram, when the story of the Karbala war is narrated, the congregation collectively names the enemy soldiers who killed members of the Prophet's family, and then prays laanat on them. They literally say, "kaho (enemy) ke upar laanatullah" (say Allah's curse on so and so). The Syedna[79] has, over the years, asked the community members to pray laanat on different reformists and rebels who are officially ostracized. And it's a really big deal. Because it's seen as the worst kind of curse someone can throw at you.'

While Johari is among the exceptional people who were driven to rebel because of this all-pervasive style of herding the flock, most people do not react the same way. Perhaps because of their insecurities and inability to take their own decisions, they prefer to belong rather than stand out. It is people like this who also form the foot soldiers

[78]Email interview with the author, 9 January 2019.

[79]Syedna Abu Jafar us Sadiq Aaliqadr Mufaddal Saifuddin is the fifty-third and current Da'i al-Mutlaq of the Dawoodi Bohras. As Da'i al-Mutlaq, he is both royalty and spiritual leader rolled into one, and demands unquestioning subservience. Syedna is an exalted title which refers to his descent from Prophet Muhammad's family.

of the Tablighi Jamaat, leading to an unusual phenomenon where an increasing number of children today are more religious and conscious of their Islamic identity than their parents were, despite globalization and unprecedented exposure to liberal values both through multimedia and individual travels.

According to a research published by the Pew Research Center in June 2018, the younger generation in developed countries is becoming less religious than their parents. However, in the developing world, with fast-growing populations, the young tend to be as religious, if not more so, than their parents.[80]

For instance, Umer claims that he is more religious than his parents were. He has formally initiated his children into Islam and has a mufti coming home regularly to teach them about Islam, something his parents never did. In fact, he didn't even learn to read the Quran in Arabic till a few years back. His turn towards conservative Islam has been a personal journey.

According to Hamid Ansari, one doesn't really need a survey to realize that Muslims are increasingly turning towards demonstrative Islam. Both an alumnus and later the vice chancellor of AMU, Ansari uses his experience at the university to make his point. 'During my student days, AMU was a pan-India institution and because of that, the culture was liberal, inclusive, and open. However, by the time I returned as vice chancellor (2000–02), it was fast turning into a north Indian, specifically, an Uttar Pradesh–Bihar institution. The changed students' profile affected the cultural ethos of the university too.'[81] This profile is also reflective of the upward mobility of the 'left behind communities' or the Pasmandas, who consider religious conservatism as stepping stones to the hallowed portals of Islam.

Going by the incidents of the last few years at the AMU campus, perhaps the situation is worse today. Says Rana Safvi, author-historian and a proud Aligarian, 'It breaks my heart to see how religious politics

---

[80]Stephanie Kramer and Dalia Fahmy, 'Younger people are less religious than older ones in many countries, especially in the U.S. and Europe', Pew Research Center, 13 June 2018.
[81]In conversation with the author, New Delhi, 25 February 2019.

has been ruining the great institution that AMU used to be. In my times, it was an extremely liberal campus. Of course, there was a section of ultra conservatives, but it was a very small section. Hardly any woman wore hijab. But today, you would really have to look hard to spot one who does not wear it.'[82]

Safvi believes that this has as much to do with faith as with the need to conform. 'As a student you don't want to draw unnecessary attention to yourself,' she says, 'especially in the current sociopolitical atmosphere.' In the last few years, AMU has been relentlessly targeted by the Hindu right wing,[83] which has made the students reactive. But at the same time, the growing influence of the Muslim right wing on the campus is also a reality.

Ansari gives another example, this time from his days in Delhi as vice president of India between 2007 and 2017. 'In the early years of my term, I used to go to the Parliament Street mosque in central Delhi for the Friday afternoon prayers. Those days, the mosque used to be nearly empty,' he recounts. 'But in the last couple of years of my term, I started noticing larger numbers. I am told that this is the situation in most mosques.'[84]

Religiosity apart, mosques have also become places to hang out and befriend fellow Muslims, which is otherwise difficult given their sparse distribution in mainstream educational institutions and professional workplaces. And in times of adversity, perceived or real, people tend to look for those they can unite with. In fact, adversity, personal or public, is one of the driving factors which pushes the ambivalent towards religion. In such cases, the degree of religiosity depends upon the insecurity that the adversity instils.

While the growing conservatism of the young can be attributed to the widespread network of the Tablighi Jamaat and Jamaat-e-Islami

---

[82]Interview with the author, Greater Noida, 22 April 2019.

[83]Mohammad Sajjad, 'Aligarh Muslim University is being accused of fostering "anti-nationalism" for cheap electoral gains', *Economic Times*, 4 May 2018 and Shreya Roy Chowdhury, 'Anatomy of AMU attack: Why Aligarh's Hindutva groups are rankled by the university', *Scroll.in*, 13 May 2018.

[84]In conversation with the author, New Delhi, 25 February 2019.

as well as a reaction to the emergence of the Hindu right wing, what explains the relative liberalism of previous generations?

'Those were simpler times,' reminisces eighty-year-old Jamaluddin Sheikh, a retired businessman, who dabbled in everything from social activism to Communism and IPTA in his youth, as well as his family business.

'Life is too short to spend it worrying about afterlife,' he chuckles, before reciting an Urdu couplet:

Kya talkh Shaikh ki zindagani guzri
Ek shab na bichare ki suhani guzri
dozakh ke takhaiyyul mai budhapa guzra
jannat ke tassawur mai jawani guzri

(What bitter life the devout led
Not one evening was joyous
Old age was spent fearing hell
Youth was wasted dreaming of paradise)[85]

'In my time, a Muslim was a person who called himself one,' he says. 'It didn't matter how many times one prayed or how many days one fasted in Ramzan. I was born a Muslim and I will die a Muslim. Beyond that I did whatever I desired. My only guiding principle was that if I could, I must help and not harm anyone. My conscience is clear.'

Echoing similar thoughts, lawyer-politician-author Salman Khurshid says, 'I grew up holding religion more as a cultural experience. There were no clear-cut categories dividing religion, decency, social behaviour etc. Mazhab (faith) was seamlessly interwoven with tehzeeb[86].' As a child, Khurshid was taught how to read the Quran and namaz, but it was more in the spirit of the family heritage rather than a strict way of life.[87]

Wajahat Habibullah's initiation into religion was even more informal. His father, an Indian Army officer who retired with the rank of major

[85]Interview with the author, Agra, 26 May 2019.

[86]There is no corresponding word for tehzeeb in English. Tehzeeb includes everything from decency and etiquette to cultural heritage.

[87]In conversation with the author, New Delhi, 22 October 2018.

general, was anglicized and identified as agnostic. While his mother was a modern army wife, 'she retained a strong religious core, which was more internal than demonstrative', recalls Habibullah. 'I am proud of my Muslim identity,' he says, 'but it is more spiritualistic than ritualistic.'[88]

In those days, this easy-going relationship with Islam was not limited to upper class, educated Muslim families alone, rather it was even more rampant amongst the working classes, simply because their access to religion was through local pirs (holy men) and Sufis, both of whom preached brotherhood over dogmatism, and hence were deplored by the revisionist Islamist movements which have been trying to rid Muslims of these very evils.

In that sense, the moderation of Indian Muslims owed its preponderance to the influence of the Sufis who had crafted a very Indian style of Islam which was inclusive, tolerant, forgiving, and benign. Even two decades ago, not only were most Indian Muslims aligned with one Sufi order or the other, several of them devoted part of their time and money to the maintenance of a particular dargah. For instance, the Habibullah family is among the caretakers of the Haji Waris Ali Shah dargah near Lucknow, better known as Deva Sharif, with Wajahat Habibullah being the head of the trust that oversees the affairs of the shrine.

Another reason why Muslims of a certain generation were more progressive in their religious beliefs was because of the influence of the Communist movement. While the pre-Independence Progressive Writers' Movement had a disproportionate representation from among the Muslim intellectuals, even after Independence, Muslims were drawn to Communist ideology. In that ideology they found echoes of the Islamic ideals of justice, equality, and so on. So, though they did not renounce Allah, they reasoned that as long as they adhered to the spirit of the Quran, they were fulfilling their obligations, both as Muslims, as well as responsible citizens.

Says Laila Tyabji, 'Islam is a very beautiful and practical religion. It has to be taken in its spirit, more as a metaphor rather than literally.'

---

[88]Interview with the author, New Delhi, 21 October 2018.

Or as Qamar Rahman says, 'A Muslim who follows Islam in its truest form will always be moderate and progressive; while a conservative will always distort it to fit his dogmas and prejudices.'[89]

In today's India, the moderates are a social, if not a numerical, minority, despite Khurshid's assertion that, 'The majority, irrespective of faith, is always moderate.'[90] The unfortunate part is not their numerical status, but their silence. Why do they prefer to remain silent instead of reclaiming the inclusiveness and syncretism of their faith from obscurantist evangelicals?

Tyabji hazards an explanation, 'Whenever I write a post critical of some aspect of Islam on Facebook, I get three kinds of responses. The smallest kind is of pure appreciation. The second is from the Hindu right wing which latches on to my criticism to make sweeping statements against Muslims in general. The third kind of response, which is seldom posted on the public forum but is conveyed through personal conversations, is that in times like today, why must Muslims give fuel to the right wing for further Muslim bashing. I see their point. I wish the situation in India hadn't come to this.'

Tyabji believes that India's Sufi-syncretic culture, nurtured and promoted by the Mughals, was its biggest strength. 'Had Partition not happened, the Indian subcontinent could have been a very strong counterbalance to the Saudi-exported Wahhabism,' she laments.[91] The world would have been different.

Caught between the Hindu right wing (which disregards them as exceptions not representative of their community) and the Muslim right wing (that disparages them as apologists and disgrace to the faith), the moderates prefer to keep their heads down and hope that they won't be called upon to take a stand.

These, then, broadly speaking, are the various kinds of Muslims in independent India. Diverse as far as their religious beliefs and practices are concerned, but united in their insecurities and anxieties.

[89]Interview with the author, New Delhi, 18 August 2019.

[90]In conversation with the author, New Delhi, 22 October 2018.

[91]In conversation with the author, New Delhi, 22 March 2019.

For over seventy years, they have been charged with being recipients of state appeasement, and yet continue to fall behind on all parameters of progress. Clearly, it is a community that needs the right sort of institutional help in order to reach its full potential—this is as important as its imperative to help itself.

2

THE STORY OF INDIAN ISLAM

On the south-west bank of the Brahmaputra, Raja Ram Singh, a general in Aurangzeb's[1] army, had a massive problem. His soldiers were dropping dead for no apparent reason. Sent by Aurangzeb to quell the rebellion of the Ahom king Chakradhwaj Singha, Ram Singh had been stuck at Dhubri, unable to make further headway into Assam. The fact that soldiers were dying of a mysterious cause was demoralizing the troops who were reluctant to advance. Could it be sorcery that the Ahom were using against them or simply the mosquitoes breeding in the hot and humid climes of the Brahmaputra region that were preying on the soldiers?

For Ram Singh, this was a matter of his Rajput reputation and his standing with the Mughal emperor. Finally, he sought divine intervention. He requested the ninth Sikh Guru, Tegh Bahadur, to visit Dhubri and bless his troops. For good measure, he also requested five pirs who had just returned to the Mughal capital after a pilgrimage to the Ajmer dargah to come to Dhubri.

The gods, however, were not on Ram Singh's side. At Dhubri, Guru Tegh Bahadur and the five pirs saw the formidable army of an ambitious emperor arrayed against poorly armed and frightened locals. Instead of blessing the army, the saints blessed the locals that they would be unharmed and undefeated. Eventually, Ram Singh had to sue for peace and agree that the Mughal Empire would end at the western bank of the Brahmaputra, before returning to the capital.

While Guru Tegh Bahadur returned from Assam after a year and faced the wrath of Aurangzeb for his supposed betrayal, the five pirs

[1]Aurangzeb (1618–1707) was the last of the great Mughals. The empire started to decline after his death.

stayed on in Dhubri, attracting devotees from all over the Brahmaputra region, many of whom embraced Islam. After the death of the pirs, the locals converted their resting place into a dargah known as Dargah Panch Pir, which even today is an important place of pilgrimage for the people of that region.

Filmmaker Shahnaab Alam narrated this story to me—part history, part folklore—with dramatic flourishes. His most recent production was the acclaimed Assamese language film *Bhoga Khirikee* (2018) directed by Jahnu Barua.

'Since the introduction to Islam [of the Assamese] was through the Sufis, the neo-converts adapted the religion to their local culture. The Assamese Muslims were not expected to give up their traditional customs and historical practices, including in matters of marriage and death, two major social events,' he says.[2]

The five pirs went to Assam in 1670, but Assam's first brush with Islam occurred nearly four centuries earlier. Muhammad bin Bakhtiyar Khalji, a military commander of Mohammed Muizuddin of Ghor (popularly known as Muhammad Ghori), on an expedition to the east, entered Assam's Kamarupa district from northeastern Bengal (now Bangladesh). He invited the local tribes to embrace Islam and become part of his expedition. Some joined. Apart from those who converted, many soldiers, including those of Turkish, Persian, and Afghani origin that were part of the expedition, stayed back in various parts of Assam, marrying local women and starting families there.[3]

Over the next few centuries, the Muslim population grew organically in several pockets of Assam. As the population grew, various Sufis also started visiting the state. Some stayed on and some moved further east into Manipur, Tripura, Meghalaya, and Nagaland. According to the Government of India Census of 2011[4], Muslims comprise 8 per cent of the Northeast's population, the bulk of whom live in Assam and make

[2]Telephonic interview with the author, 10 March 2019.

[3]Irfan Habib (ed.) *Medieval India I: Researches in the History of India 1200-1750*, New Delhi: OUP, 1995, p. 7.

[4]Religion Census 2011, available: https://www.census2011.co.in/religion.php

up 34.22 per cent of the total population.

'These are Assamese Muslims who are linguistically and culturally different from other Muslims, including the Bengalis,' Alam points out.

This distinctness is not unique to Assam. Despite the collectiveness the term 'Indian Muslims' connotes, Muslims in India have been a diverse group, not just linguistically and culturally, but also in the manner in which they relate to Islam. This relationship with the faith depends on two factors: one, how Islam came to a particular region; and two, where it came from. In Assam, as in most of north India, Islam came in three parallel waves via the invaders, the mystics, and the settlers who came looking to make their fortune.

The religion all these groups brought with them combined piousness with pragmatism and spirituality with temporal matters—these components of the religion differed only in degree depending on the sort of person who espoused it. The Prophet of Islam, Muhammad, epitomized this sort of composite faith in the way he lived—living an ascetic life, preaching moral uprightness and fairness, but also leading his people into 'just wars' for survival.

The Life of the Prophet

Prophet Muhammad's early life was spent in hardship and struggle for mere survival. His father, Abdullah, died before his birth in 570 CE. His young mother, Amina, unable to raise him herself, sought the help of his paternal grandfather, Abdul Muttalib. Amina died of an illness when Muhammad was only six. His grandfather died soon after. Muhammad then came into the care of his uncle Abu Talib, who ensured that he didn't starve. But beyond that, there wasn't much that he could do for his nephew as his own fortunes as the chief of the Banu Hashim tribe were waning.[5]

Muhammad had barely reached adolescence when he started accompanying trading caravans to make a living. However, even as he

[5]A. Guillaume, *The Life of Muhammad: A Translation of Ibn Ishaq's Sirat Rasul Allah*, New Delhi: OUP, 2002, p. 70.

was trying to just stay alive, popular legends, compiled by his chroniclers[6] over a century after his death in 632 CE, tell us that he was equally sensitive to the yearnings of his soul. As an adolescent he would engage with the wandering minstrels that he encountered during his travels, asking them questions about God, life, the afterlife, and the world. Some of these minstrels lamented the corruption of the Abrahamic faith by the Arabs.[7] Muhammad came to see that the faith he had inherited from his family had begun to increasingly veer towards paganism.[8]

In his adulthood, he found employment with a successful businesswoman Khadija, who had some of the biggest caravans traversing Mecca. Khadija, a widow, hired Muhammad based on his reputation for honesty, piety, and business acumen. Eventually, she proposed marriage to him, which he accepted. According to his chroniclers, he continued to work for his wife for a salary, not partaking in her wealth. Revelling in his poverty, he often said, 'Al fakhru fakhri' (Poverty is my pride).[9]

He was also given to withdrawing into seclusion for meditation and reflection. It was during one of these moments of seclusion at Mount Hira in his fortieth year in 610 CE that he heard a voice telling him to read. Being unlettered, he was perplexed at this command that he could not heed. At that moment, he felt such a strong constriction in his chest that he was unable to breathe. By some accounts, this was because Archangel Gabriel, Jibreel in Arabic, who was the (invisible) bearer of Allah's message, was holding him in a tight embrace.[10] Once again, he heard the same command and, once again, he felt the same constriction. When the command was repeated a third time, the embrace was tighter than before. He almost collapsed. However, once the grip

---

[6]The first chronicle of Prophet Muhammad's life, written rather like a hagiography, was by Ibn Ishaq in 767 CE. This has been the primary source of all the subsequent books on the life and times of the Prophet.

[7]Guillaume, *The Life of Muhammad*, p. 70.

[8]Ibid.

[9]Dehlvi, *Sufism:* p. 408.

[10]Maulana Mufti Mohammed Shafi Usmani Sahab, *Ma'ariful Qur'an: A comprehensive commentary on Quran*, Deoband, Uttar Pradesh: Maktaba-e-Darul Uloom, 2017.

on his chest eased, he became conscious of the following verse, as if it were planted on his heart:

> Read, 'O Prophet,' in the Name of your Lord Who created—
> created humans from a clinging clot.
> Read! And your Lord is the Most Generous,
> Who taught by the pen—
> taught humanity what they knew not.[11]

He returned home trembling. The experience in the cave of Mount Hira unnerved and frightened him. If it wasn't for the faith that his wife Khadija had in his vision, he would have dismissed the experience as a hallucination or sign of madness.

'Khadija believed in him and accepted as true what he brought from God, and helped him in his work. She was the first to believe in God and His apostle, and in the truth of his message.'[12]

This relief, however, was short-lived.

'The revelations stopped for a time so that the apostle of God was distressed and grieved. Then Gabriel brought him the Sura of the Morning, in which his Lord, who had so honoured him, swore that He had not forsaken him, and did not hate him.'[13]

And so, Muhammad started to believe that Allah had chosen him as His messenger from among the line of prophets from Adam onwards. His tribe claimed lineage from Abraham, so it was not difficult for them to accept the notion of prophethood. The first person to bear witness to his claims or shahadah[14], other than his wife, was Ali, his cousin and later

---

[11]Surah Al-Alaq, 96:1-5, translation by Dr Mustafa Khattab (https://quran.com/96)

[12]Guillaume, *The Life of Muhammad*, p. 111.

[13]Ibid.

[14]Shahadah means to bear witness. It is a root word, which is also the name of the second Islamic Kalima—Ash-hadu Al-laaa Ilaaha Illa-llaahu Wahdahoo Laa Shareeka Lahoo Wa-Ash-hadu Anna Muhammadan 'Abduhoo Wa Rasooluhu. It means: 'I bear witness that there is none worthy of worship except Allah, the One alone, without partner, and I bear witness that Muhammad is His servant and Messenger'. All Muslims are supposed to recite this. Often, conversion to Islam is possible simply by reciting this kalimah or taking the shahadah. A person who takes it is called a shaheed. Similarly,

son-in-law. To convey to the Meccans that a 'true' faith, a renewal of the Abrahamic religion, had been revealed by Allah, Prophet Muhammad led Khadija and Ali in prayer, facing the Kaaba, a prehistoric symbol of faith in Arabia, inside which people of all religious persuasions kept their chosen deities. Several people were moved by this act to stop and make enquiries. Some embraced the message at once and some others took time to accept the Prophet.[15]

However, the powerful Quraysh tribe of Mecca didn't take kindly to this. The leaders of the tribe viewed Prophet Muhammad as a pretender and disruptor of the well-established pattern of Meccan life. As long as Khadija was alive, her wealth and stature provided protection to Prophet Muhammad's evangelical activities. However, after her death, the hostilities increased to such an extent that he had to escape to Yathrib (later called Medina) in 622 CE with his followers. This escape, called Hijrah, marks the beginning of the Islamic calendar, because it led to the establishment of the first model Islamic state.

In Medina, Prophet Muhammad entered into a treaty of coexistence with several powerful Jewish tribes. The Jewish merchants of Medina regarded him as non-partisan and sought him as a hakam or judge for the resolution of disputes. This was also the time that the revelation of Quranic verses became more event-specific, rather than philosophical and historic (as had been the case in Mecca). Now, they addressed the immediate challenges faced by the fledgling Muslim community and provided answers to questions that emerged as more people embraced Islam.

The rapidness with which Islam grew in subsequent decades belies the violent challenges it faced in the early years. From 622 CE till the Prophet's death in 632 CE, the Muslim community of Medina had to fight several battles for survival, starting with the famous Battle of Badr in 624 CE to the final victory over its entrenched adversary, the Quraysh, in 630 CE.

In this decade of struggle for survival, the Muslims faced open hostility, treachery, doublespeak, and recantation by those who

---

Islamic warriors who waged jihad or died for the 'cause of Islam' were shaheeds.

[15]Guillaume, *The Life of Muhammad*, p. 113.

pretended to swear allegiance to the Prophet. The categories of mushrikeen, munafiqeen, and kafiruns came about at this time. Mushrikeen referred to those who believed that Allah could have a wife or a son. This was a direct reference to the Christian belief that Jesus was the son of God. It meant not accepting the soleness and oneness of Allah, hence committing the greatest sin of all—shirq—sharing Allah's godliness with others. Munafiqeens were those who pretended to be Muslims but were not. These were hypocrites that needed to be carefully watched because they could cause grievous harm to the Muslims. Kafiruns were non-believers or those who did not believe in the message of Allah. The term was used for pagans or people who did not believe in any of the Semitic books, such as Torah (revealed to Moses or Musa), Zabur (revealed to David or Daoud) and Injeel (revealed to Jesus or Isa).

It was in this period that the Quranic verses on the code of conduct, principles of war, treatment of prisoners of war, punishment for treachery or hypocrisy, and the obligation of fighting a just war (jihad) were revealed. The 'sword verses', some of which prescribe death for infidels and hypocrites, including those who 'repent', were the products of this period. Jihad, once declared, was obligatory on all Muslims. It was similar to the concept of conscription in the modern era. Given the small size of the Muslim ummah (community), and the hostility the Muslims faced, if fighting were not made compulsory, many would have refused to fight for fear of death, putting an unfair burden on a few to defend the whole community. This was the reason that even women, including the Prophet's wives, joined battle. However, the rules for declaring jihad were very stringent. One, it was defensive in nature; and two, it could only be declared by a just leader of the ummah, which referred to the Prophet himself and, thereafter, the caliphs.

In practice, however, the Islamic state under Prophet Muhammad was based on the 'principles of tolerance and respect of creeds and conscience, especially towards Jews and Christians, i.e., the followers of Revealed Books acknowledged by Islam'.[16] But non-Muslims were

[16]Muhammad Abdullah Enan, *Decisive Moments in the History of Islam*, New Delhi: Goodword Books, 2007, p. 15.

required to pay an additional tax, called jiziya, to ensure their freedom to practise their faith and conduct their business. Over the years, as Muslims came in contact with other religious groups, this model of coexistence and revenue collection was applied to them as well, including in India.

The last decade of the Prophet's life was spent teaching Muslims the importance of survival; of choosing life over death and living to fight another day. This vital lesson was taught by the Prophet himself at the Battle of Uhud in 625 CE, a year after a small, ragtag Muslim force led by the Prophet had defeated the huge army of Quraysh (from Mecca) at Badr. At Uhud, the Quraysh attacked in greater numbers. Realizing that they were greatly outnumbered, the Prophet Muhammad hesitated to join battle. But his followers were confident that under his leadership they would be able to vanquish the Meccans once again.

Prophet Muhammad allowed himself to be persuaded. But, as he had feared, the Battle of Uhud turned into a massacre of the Muslims. The few who survived, including the Prophet, fled the battlefield to regroup and recover.

Two years later, when the Quraysh mounted yet another attack on the Medinan Muslims, putting together a confederacy of several tribes, including the Jews who had earlier agreed on peace and coexistence with the Muslims, the Muslims were not only able to withstand the siege for several days but also repulse it. This came to be known as the Battle of Trench (627 CE) and it degraded the power, reputation, and influence of the Quraysh even as it established the reputation of Prophet Muhammad as a formidable leader of the people.

In popular discourse, the Battle of Trench is better known for the massacre of the Jewish tribe Banu Qurayza with whom Prophet Muhammad had made an agreement for coexistence. The Banu Qurayzas reneged on the agreement—perhaps they believed that the Meccans would manage to vanquish the Muslims, given their victory at Uhud—and started surreptitiously supplying material, including weapons, to the Quraysh army.

Writing in *Muhammad: His Life Based on the Earliest Sources*, Martin Lings speculates that the Banu Qurayza believed that the worst that would happen if Prophet Muhammad's army won was they would be banished from Medina, as had happened to the Jewish tribes of Banu Nadir and Banu Qaynuqa after the Battle of Badr.[17] Both these tribes had reneged on their agreements on the eve of battle, leaving the Muslim forces vulnerable. Despite the precedents of Arab tribal justice, in which the punishment for treachery was death, Prophet Muhammad had decided to spare their lives. They were ordered to leave Medina. However, at the Battle of Trench, the Banu Nadir had joined hands with the Quraysh. Having learnt his lesson, after the Battle of Trench, Prophet Muhammad reverted to tribal justice.

Consequently, a neutral judge—hakam—was appointed. He sought guidance from the Jewish book of law, Deuteronomy, and pronounced that all men of fighting age, nearly 600 of them, should be put to death and women and children should be enslaved as the spoils of war.[18] This massacre of the Banu Qurayza has, perhaps, been the most violent and controversial event in early Islamic history, and has helped spawn the Islamic stereotype of bloodthirsty marauders.

However, from the Muslims' perspective, this was a defining event. For all its abhorrent nature, the massacre was a strong deterrent to future challengers. It led to peace between the Medinans and the Meccans (through the Treaty of Hudaybiyyah in 628 CE), which allowed the Prophet to lay the foundations of an Islamic society that invited both awe and inspiration. Quranic verses pertaining to civil laws such as business, marriage, divorce, inheritance, responsibility towards orphans, the role of women, and so on, were revealed, which created the body of Shariah or the Islamic rule book. The reputation of Islam as a just and egalitarian religion spread, leading to mass conversions, especially among the Meccans and Quraysh.

Most importantly, the Meccans welcomed Prophet Muhammad and his entourage when he marched into the city in 630 CE as the leader not just of Medina, but Mecca too. None objected when he proceeded to destroy the idols inside the Kaaba and claim the prehistoric nondescript

---

[17]Martin Lings, *Muhammad: His Life Based on the Earliest Sources*, Cambridge, UK: Islamic Texts Society, 1983, p. 221.

[18]Guillaume, *The Life of Muhammad*, pp. 461–64.

structure which was rebuilt by Abraham and his son Isaac (Ibrahim and Ishaaq) at the command of Allah.

Since antiquity, the Kaaba had been regarded as the earthly abode of Allah by the Arabs. It had been the nucleus of Arabian life.[19] Arabs, irrespective of their faith, held the Kaaba as sacred, and placed the idols of their beloved deities inside the quadrangle structure. Now, with the Kaaba rid of idols and claimed as Islamic, the religion of Islam had truly arrived in Arabia—twenty years after Prophet Muhammad had the first revelation on Mount Hira. All Muslims now turned to Kaaba while offering their prayers instead of facing Jerusalem.

The March of the Muslims

The neo-Muslims were not only devout but also hugely enthusiastic about their faith. They carried the message of Prophet Muhammad everywhere they went. In his book *A History of the Arab Peoples*, Albert Hourani chronicles this outward surge of the Arabs charged with the fervour of their new faith.

> They established their first important base at Qayrawan in the former Roman province of Africa (Ifriqiya, present-day Tunisia); from there they moved westwards, reached the Atlantic coast of Morocco by the end of the seventh century and crossed into Spain soon afterwards; at the other extreme, the land beyond Khurasan reaching as far as the Oxus valley was conquered and the first Muslim advances were made into north-western India.[20]

Consequently, the first Muslims that came to India were Arabs. They came as early as 636 CE during the term of the second caliph, Umar—just four years after the death of the Prophet. Following the trail of pre-Islamic Arab traders, the Muslim fleet landed on the coast of Malabar—this time, not only to trade but also to preach the newly-revealed religion.

Around the same time, other Muslim Arab traders landed on the coast of Gujarat and were warmly received by the locals. They were

[19]Desmond Stewart, *Mecca*, New York: W. W. Norton & Company, 1980, p. 168.

[20]Albert Hourani, *A History of the Arab Peoples*, London: Faber and Faber, 2013, p. 26.

provided land where they settled and plied their business. Over the next hundred years, several Muslim settlements developed all along the western coast of India and in the hinterland as well.

Even as the sea trade between Arabia and India was yielding unexpected consequences, efforts were on to discover the land route to India. This was the route that Muhammad bin Qasim, a commander of the Umayyad Caliphate[21], took when he conquered Sindh to avenge the hijacking of a vessel by Kutch-based pirates. After defeating the king of Sindh, bin Qasim established Umayyad control over the province by appointing a local governor before returning to Arabia. Now Arabs were coming to India over land and sea although they remained contained in and around Sindh and Kutch for at least another century. In this period, the foreign community got truly indigenized by marrying local women.

Writes Tara Chand in his seminal book *Influence of Islam on Indian Culture*, which was published in the 1920s, and still remains a source of reference for scholars:

> Henceforth Muslim influence grew rapidly.... They were welcomed as traders, and, apparently, facilities were given to them to settle and acquire lands and openly practice their religion. They must have entered upon missionary efforts soon after settling down, for Islam is essentially a missionary religion and every *Mussalman* is a missionary of his faith. Many were undoubtedly held in respectful esteem.... Before the ninth century was far advanced they had spread over the whole of the western coast of India and had created a stir among the Hindu populace, as much by their peculiar beliefs and worship as by the zeal with which they professed and advocated them.[22]

Their pace of growth was more rapid in the south as compared to the west and central regions, primarily because there was great religious, social, and political turmoil in southern India during the eighth and ninth centuries. There was a tussle for supremacy between Hinduism,

---

[21]The first Islamic empire, 661–744 CE, based in Damascus.

[22]Tara Chand, *Influence of Islam on Indian Culture*, New Delhi: Manakin Press, 2018, p. 33.

Buddhism, and Jainism. In addition, the old kingdoms were in disarray in the face of new claimants to power. Into this situation, 'Islam appeared upon the scene with a simple formula of faith, well-defined dogmas and rites, and democratic theories of social reorganization. It produced a tremendous effect, and before the first quarter of the ninth century was over, the last of the Cheraman Perumal kings of Malabar who reigned at Kodungallur had become a convert to the new religion.'[23]

This was not very different from the way Islam was being accepted by people in other parts of the world where the Arabs ventured with the message of Allah. As Hourani says: 'Some Christians, however, touched by controversies about the nature of God and revelation might be attracted by the simplicity of the early Muslim response to such questions, within what was broadly the same universe of thought. The absence of a Muslim Church or an elaborate ritual of conversion, the need only to use a few simple words, made acceptance an easy process.'[24]

By the late tenth century, Arabs had started to move well into the southern plateau—east into Tamil Nadu and north into Karnataka and Maharashtra. In these parts, the traders, mainly suppliers of West Asian horses, were accompanied by Sufi saints. Though the primary purpose of the accompanying saints was most likely to provide religious guidance and succour to the traders, the locals also started visiting them to seek help and benediction. As a result of these exchanges, many locals embraced Islam. Gradually, these saints acquired their own stature and position independent of the people who brought them to this land. Consequently, by the twelfth century the south Indian landscape was dotted with mosques and tombs of these saints. They turned into places of mini pilgrimage and were visited by both Muslims and Hindus.

By the thirteenth century the value of the equine trade had increased greatly and the Arabs were gradually co-opted into the ruling elite in states like Karnataka and Tamil Nadu, with some being appointed as advisers and even commanders. In his book *The Madura Country: A Manual*, British civil servant James Henry Nelson quotes Marco Polo's

---

[23]Ibid., p. 34.

[24]Hourani, *A History of the Arab Peoples*, p. 29.

account, where he records one 'Taqi Uddin as the deputy minister and adviser of king Sundar Pandya'. He also notes that the Pandya king sent 'Fakhr Uddin Ahmad, son of Jamal Uddin as his envoy to the Mongolian emperor Kublai Khan in 1286 or 1287'. Later, after the death of the Pandya king in 1293 CE, an Arab envoy, Jamal Uddin, became the king.[25]

Even as the trader-led Arab-origin Muslim population was growing organically in south, the trajectory in the north was rather different. Here, the motive was not trade alone but empire-building as well. The invasions into north India commenced with the ascendancy of Mahmud of Ghazni (in present-day Afghanistan) in 997 CE. The attacks on neighbouring kingdoms, Kandahar to the southwest and Peshawar to the east, were a means of consolidating Mahmud's rule. Buoyed by his victory in Peshawar, by the early eleventh century, Mahmud had started to move further into the fertile plains of Punjab, defeating one ruler after another. With each victory, his army inched further south, reaching Somnath in Gujarat by 1023 CE.

A pragmatic ruler, Mahmud was aware of his limitations. Instead of trying to annex the defeated land to his empire, he simply collected the booty, appointed local vassals who would help him in his next campaign, and returned to Ghazni.

However, his plundering of the Somnath temple has repercussions even today. This event became the rallying point for right-wing Hindu ideologues of the twentieth century to buttress the narrative of hundreds of years of oppression at the hands of Muslim invaders. There is no reliable account that Mahmud attacked Somnath for reasons other than its wealth. Theories suggesting that he attacked the temple complex to destroy the idol of the pre-Islamic goddess, Manat, which some believed had been taken away from Kaaba[26] and sent to Kathiawar in India to

---

[25]J. H. Nelson, *The Madura Country: A Manual,* New Delhi: Asian Educational Services, 1989 (1st edn. 1866), available here: https://archive.org/stream/in.ernet.dli.2015.172487/2015.172487.The-Madura-Country-A--Manual-I-To-V_djvu.txt

[26]As noted, the Kaaba is the holiest Islamic shrine and the site of the annual hajj pilgrimage. In Islamic history, Kaaba was built by Abraham and his son Ishmael. With the rise of the age of ignorance (Jahiliya) in Arabia, the pagan tribes started to place idols of their gods inside the Kaaba. When Islam was revealed to Prophet Muhammad, he

escape destruction at the hands of Prophet Muhammad, are mere conjecture. According to historian Romila Thapar, Mahmud understood the importance of the plunder of Somnath to his reputation. Hence, his courtiers and chroniclers deliberately exaggerated its destruction as well as its worth so as to project their king as a mujahid or holy warrior to the Abbasid Caliphate in Mecca.[27] The ploy worked. Mahmud received a commendation from the caliph and this enhanced his standing amongst the Muslim royalty.

Mahmud's campaigns into India opened a new passage into the north of the country, which was then used by invaders, adventurers, and saints alike. Another distinguishing aspect about Mahmud's invasions into India was that, despite his Afghan ancestry, he was Persianized in his upbringing because his mother was a Persian princess. Moreover, he commanded a mixed army of Afghan, Persian, Turkish, and Central Asian soldiers. Consequently, after he returned to Ghazni, he left behind multiple cultural influences on north India, in addition to paving the way for the incubation of Indo-Persian culture.

A few decades later, another ambitious Afghan, Muhammad Muizuddin, of the Ghor province, turned his eyes to India. Better known as Muhammad Ghori, he captured the erstwhile territory of Mahmud Ghazni in Afghanistan, then followed his footsteps southeast and reached Gujarat in 1178. However, he was defeated and retreated to Ghazni. En route, he was able to subdue Multan and Lahore, which he left to the charge of his governors.

Back in Ghor, he explored the possibility of breaching the Khyber Pass and in his next campaign, entered northwest India, getting all the way to Tarain on the outskirts of Panipat in modern-day Haryana. He faced yet another defeat in his first major battle with the Rajput king Prithviraj Chauhan in 1191 CE. He returned the following year with a larger army and met Chauhan on the field again. This time he prevailed. The victory

---

sought to purify the Kaaba by destroying the idols. The chronicler of Mahmud Ghazni, Farrukhi Sistani, claimed, after the sacking of Somnath, that Mahmud had done so to destroy the idol of Manat which escaped destruction in Mecca.

[27]See Romila Thapar, *Somanatha: The Many Voices of a History*, New Delhi: Penguin Books, 2008.

against Chauhan was followed by conquests throughout the Indo-Gangetic plain, Rajasthan, and parts of Bengal. By 1200 CE, most of north India had been conquered by Muhammad Ghori's troops, with his commanders Qutubuddin Aibak subduing the north Indian plains and Muhammad bin Bakhtiyar Khalji capturing the territories of Bihar and Bengal.

Like Mahmud, Ghori returned to Ghazni after his campaign against Chauhan, leaving his Turkish slaves Aibak and Khalji to administer the captured territories as his viceroys. Ghori was assassinated in 1206 CE. As he did not have any heirs, his territory was divided among his slaves, with Aibak and Khalji holding on to the Indian territories under their control. This was the beginning of Muslim rule in India with Aibak founding the Delhi Sultanate and Khalji establishing the Bengal Sultanate.[28]

Even as the foundations of these sultanates were being laid, 'numerous Muslim men of learning and religion poured into India'.[29] While most came from the western provinces of Afghanistan, some came from as far away as Persia and Iraq. Many were wandering mystics who left behind a trail of converts and devotees as they moved on to other places in search of enlightenment. Some made India their home.

Alongside came adventurers, historians, and men seeking opportunities in a new land. These Muslims were mainly of Turkish and Central Asian origin but culturally influenced by the Persians more than the Arabs. Hence, the Islamic values that they brought with them were Turco-Persian. This influx not only influenced the cultural landscape of north India in terms of customs, cuisine, clothes, and music, it also led to the evolution of Urdu, inspired by Farsi with smatterings of Arabic and Turkish married to the Hindi dialects.

Since by this time the Arab empire or caliphate[30] was waning with

---

[28]Habib, *Medieval India Vol. 1,* p. 9.

[29]Chand, *Influence of Islam on Indian Culture*, p. 46.

[30]The Abbasid Caliphate succeeded the Umayyads in 750 CE. Its reign till 1258 CE is called the Golden Age of Islam, which was brought to an end by the Mongol invasion of the Middle East. Starting with the most famous of caliphs, Harun al Rashid, the Abbasids shunned traditional Arab tribalism and parochialism in favour of close engagement with Persia, Turkey, Europe, and India. Putting into practice Prophet Muhammad's injunction to the believers that attainment of knowledge was of utmost importance,

spiritual and temporal power in the region shifting to the Ottomans (in Turkey), the exposure of the inhabitants of north and northeast India to the Arabized religion was limited, unlike southern India where Muslims were either of Arab origin or Arab influence. In the south, those who converted to Islam were conversant with Arab culture rather than Persian or Turkish culture which was the norm in north India.

However, by the end of the thirteenth century, these clear distinctions between the north and south, Arab and Persian influences began to blur. In 1296, Alauddin Khalji, the twelfth of the Delhi sultans, defeated the Yadavas of Devagiri in modern-day Karnataka. By 1308, his commander Malik Kafur had established the rule of the Khaljis on the Deccan plateau.[31] By the time Babur upended the Delhi Sultanate in 1526 by defeating its last ruler, Ibrahim Lodhi, almost all of the Deccan, except Kerala, parts of coastal Tamil Nadu, north Andhra and Orissa, were under the control of the Delhi/Agra sultans.

The early Muslim rulers were of Afghan–Turkish–Persian origin. Their reign of over 200 years infused the plateau with Persian, Turkish, and Central Asian influences in food, culture, music, language, literature, and lifestyle. The arrival of the Mughals, whose powers remained north of the Vindhyas until Aurangzeb's ascent, gave greater autonomy to these sultans, each of whom founded his own dynasty, many of which barely survived two generations.

Nevertheless, they wrought substantive changes to society. Persian influence now swept across India, from north to south, barring a few regions. Its dominance was even more impactful as the ruling classes patronized it too, considering the culture a measure of courtliness and sophistication. The prevailing view was: when even Arab Abbasids and the Ottomans accepted the superiority of Persian culture, architecture, and polity, who were the Indian Muslims to protest?

In India, however, the mingling of Islam and Hinduism led to a

---

scholars were revered during the Abbasids' term. All Arab literature, poetry, the sciences, and philosophies were from this period.

[31]Manu S. Pillai, *Rebel Sultans: The Deccan from Khilji to Shivaji*, New Delhi: Juggernaut, 2018, p. 299.

distinctively regional syncretism as Tara Chand explains:

> Muslim authority...had also to impose upon itself other restraints. The employment of the Hindus was a necessity of their rule. Mahmud of Ghazna had a numerous body of Hindu troops who fought for him in Central Asia, and his Hindu commander Tilak suppressed the rebellion of his Muslim general Niyaltigin. When Qutb-uddin Aibak decided to stay in Hindustan, he had no other choice but to retain the Hindu staff which was familiar with the civil administration, for without it all government including the collection of revenue would have fallen into utter chaos....
>
> The Muslims who came into India made it their home. They lived surrounded by the Hindu people and a state of perennial hostility with them was impossible. Mutual intercourse led to mutual understanding. Many who had changed their faith differed little from those whom they had left.... The effort to seek a new life led to the development of a new culture which was neither exclusively Hindu nor purely Muslim. It was indeed a Muslim–Hindu culture.[32]

In this, the biggest contribution was made by the Sufis, who were not only a bridge to the Almighty for the common people but also spiritual, and, in some cases, political, advisers to the rulers. Hence, while the Muslim sultans handled the administration of the empire, the Sufis took care of the people. This led to the evolution of a non-competitive and non-threatening Islam, which embraced diversity without making a virtue of its exclusivity—'...Muslim Sufi orders and Muslim writers and poets show a strong tendency to assimilate Hindu practices and doctrines, in some cases going so far as to adopt even the adoration of Hindu gods.'[33]

Selfless Sufis

Regarded either as an offshoot of Islam or a separate sect, Sufism was the earliest disruptive movement that sprang from within the religion.

---

[32]Chand, *Influence of Islam on Indian Culture,* pp. 136–37.
[33]Ibid., p. 138.

The Sufis were variously called the people of the bench (referring to their seat outside the Prophet's mosque), or 'ahle suffa' because of the patched woollen garment, 'suf', that they wore. It was a movement that was concurrent with the revelation of Islam itself, and some people regarded it as the real spirit of Islam, calling Prophet Muhammad the first Sufi or Auliya—one whom Allah regarded as a friend or beloved.

During the lifetime of Prophet Muhammad, the Sufis were driven by unconditional love for Allah and his Prophet. They considered Prophet Muhammad as the greatest of all—the one who was created even before Adam, and sent to earth as the last and final Prophet. He perfected the religion of Allah for all of humanity. And they were convinced that Prophet Muhammad was showing everyone the righteous path to reach the divine. On the other hand, the ulema, who emerged subsequently, swore by rules and dogmas, and resented the simplicity and flexibility of Sufism.

There is a famous legend associated with the greatest woman Sufi ever, Hazrat Rabia of Basra, who died in 801 CE. Once she was found running in the desert with a torch in one hand and a pitcher of water in another. When somebody stopped her to ask what she was doing, she replied that she intended to burn paradise with her torch and douse the flames of hell with water so that 'people [would] love God for the sake of God and not for want of paradise or fear of hell'.[34]

Rabia was preceded and succeeded by a long line of Sufis who regarded Islam not as a religion of set principles, of do's and don'ts etched in stone, but as a pure yearning for God. These mendicants were selflessly devoted to the Prophet, not because they believed that he would lead them to paradise and all the pleasures promised therein, but because they loved Allah unconditionally. All they desired was to subsume their being into God or achieve the state of fana. Lost in love, they trampled on their egos, reduced themselves to beggary, because ego, they believed, led to arrogance and intolerance. The Sufis remained seekers of knowledge, whether through structured, institutional learning or through reflection and meditation. But even in cases of institutional

---

[34]Dehlvi, *Sufism*, p. 408.

learning and government patronage, once the heart beckoned, they retreated into seclusion.

Describing this indescribable mystical phenomenon, a tenth-century Sufi of Baghdad, Junayd, wrote: 'Sufism is not achieved by prayer and fasting but it is the security of the heart and the generosity of the soul.'[35] Another Sufi Uwaymar bin Zaid, said, 'One hour of reflection is better than 40 nights of prayer, and that one act of righteousness with godliness and faith is preferable to unlimited ritual observance.'[36]

During Prophet Muhammad's lifetime, the Sufis used to be fed from his household, as the Prophet believed that they were Auliya.[37] He advised his followers to show respect and even reverence towards these people who undertook incessant fasting and spent all their time praying, unmindful of worldly pleasures. In one of the earliest Persian books on Sufism, translated by Reynold A. Nicholson, *The Kashf Al Mahjub*, Prophet Muhammad is quoted as having said: 'He who hears the voice of the *ahl-e-tassawwuf*, people of spirituality, and does not say *Ameen* to their prayers is inscribed before God among those with *ghafla*, heedlessness.'[38]

The Sufis believed that God had blessed Prophet Muhammad with both knowledge of the world (Ilm-e-Safina) and the mystical knowledge of the heart (Ilm-e-Ladduni). The Prophet shared this knowledge of the heart with his cousin and son-in-law, Ali, according him the title of Imam of the Walis or Leader of the Auliyas. The Sufis trace their spiritual lineage to Ali. It is his name—Hazrat Ali—that is invoked in Sufi music and at the dargahs. Moreover, identifying with Prophet Muhammad's proclamation that 'poverty is my pride', these wandering minstrels who conveyed the most complex of thoughts through verses, craved neither wealth nor power. Committed to solitude, their only social outreach was helping the poor.

Despite the Prophet of Islam's enthusiastic support for the Sufis,

---

[35]Ibid.

[36]Ibid.

[37]Ibid.

[38]Ali B Uthman Al-Jullabi Al-Hujwiri, R.A. Nicholson (trans.), *The Kashf Al Mahjub: The Oldest Persian Treatise on Sufism*, New Delhi: Cosmo Publications, 2010, p. 467.

mere decades after his death these mendicants were pushed outside the mainstream of Islam, which at that time was fully engaged in and committed to both territorial and theological expansion. The Sufis had no role or interest in this. Since theirs was a personal quest, they were happy to withdraw, physically and spiritually, from the ever-expanding Arab empire.

Sufi and non-Sufi Muslims coexisted without strife during the reign of the four Rashidun caliphs (or the rightly-guided ones)[39]—Hazrat Abu Bakr Siddiq, Hazrat Umar, Hazrat Uthman, and Hazrat Ali (632 CE–661 CE)—as both groups derived their knowledge from the Quran and the example that the Prophet had set. To a large extent, the ulema and the Sufis were interdependent and sought each other out for advice on law or for emotional succour and spiritual guidance.

This state of harmony was disrupted when Islamic intellectuals started to emerge in the ninth century. These learned men, with expertise in the theory of the Quran and the life of the Prophet through the Hadith started to interpret the Shariah so as to convert it into a codified law of the land.

Hourani explains that '[m]ore systematically than the Umayyads, the Abbasids tried to justify their rule in Islamic terms' in an effort to solidify their power.[40]

After the passing of the Rashidun caliphs, the caliphate deteriorated into a hereditary dynasty. These rulers were aware of their religious illegitimacy, because instead of being elected by consensus because of their piety, they assumed power through family loyalties and strife (more on the election of caliphs in a later chapter). To retain control over the population, they created and supported a class of ulema—muftis and imams—who would be in charge of the religious domain while the caliphs focussed on the running of the state and expansion of the empire. With royal patronage up for grabs, opportunist ulema started to make pronouncements on religious matters to suit the requirements of

---

[39]They were called so because they were all among the first ones to convert and were the companions of the Prophet. After them, the caliphate became hereditary.

[40]Hourani, *A History of the Arab Peoples,* p. 36.

the rulers. This led to contradictory fatawa, deliberate misinterpretation of Quranic verses, and intolerance towards critics or non-conformists.

The counter to this corruption was provided by the peerless imams who did not fear the caliph. Even on pain of death, they refused to recant their interpretation of Shariah, and, therefore, left behind a well-regarded legacy of fortitude and uprightness. These imams interpreted and codified the Shariah into implementable laws, or what is called Islamic jurisprudence. From this painstaking labour emerged four schools of Sunni and three of Shia jurisprudence (these are dealt with in detail in the next chapter).

In the face of this towering intellectualism, the Sufis increasingly started to appear like simpletons and often became objects of ridicule because of their appearance, poverty, pithy proverbs, and insistence on relating to faith through the heart and not the mind. They continued to withdraw from the mainstream, preferring isolation. Yet, ironically, and much to the frustration of the ulema who were striving to build a structured edifice for Islam, people continued to flock to the Sufis, both for guidance and benediction. This created a rival power centre. Even the caliphs sought out the Sufis, and they became an existential threat to the institution of the ulema. The Sufis were accused of heresy, denounced as un-Islamic, punished, banished, and sometimes killed.[41]

None of this could curb the call of the heart. And the tribe of the mystics continued to grow. But they moved out of the Arabian peninsula. The first scholar to lend intellectual heft to Sufi mysticism was Abu Hamid al-Ghazali (1058 CE–1111 CE), one of the most respected thinkers and writers on Islamic philosophy, reasoning, and mysticism, who actively engaged in academic debates with Grecian philosophers. Of Persian origin, al-Ghazali studied Islamic theology and law under some of the leading exponents of the time and was employed in Sunni Islam's biggest theological institution, the Nizamiya Madrassa in Baghdad.

---

[41]Megan Specia, 'Who Are Sufi Muslims and Why Do Some Extremists Hate Them?', *New York Times*, 24 Nov 2017 and Brian Rohan and Samy Magdy, 'Militants attack Egyptian mosque, kill at least 235 people', AP News, 27 Nov 2017.

The chain of Nizamiya madrassas was established towards the waning centuries of the Abbasid Caliphate to draw Muslims away from scientific, argumentative, and independent learning and towards purely Sunni Islamic education. With these madrassas, the rising dynasty of that time, the Seljuq, which began as a vassal of the Abbasids but gradually came into its own, used religion to keep the people obedient (out of fear of Allah) and under its thumb. This was perhaps the first instance in Islamic history where a political power used religion to subjugate the people.[42]

Despite the prestige of his job, al-Ghazali suffered a crisis of heart and mind sometime in his late thirties. He quit his government job and went to perform hajj in 1095 CE. On the way back, he visited different places of Islamic significance, including Jerusalem, and returned to Persia to resolve his spiritual dilemma.

Gradually, his soul-searching brought him closer to the Sufi way of Islam. He refused to resume his position at the Nizamiya Madrassa. He argued that 'benefiting from the riches of the military and political elite implies complicity in their corrupt and oppressive rule and will jeopardize one's prospect of redemption in the afterlife' because 'the high ethical standards of a virtuous religious life are not compatible with being in the service of sultans, viziers, and caliphs.'[43]

Eventually, al-Ghazali founded a khanqah (Sufi seminary) in Tus, on the Iran–Afghan border, where he resumed his teaching. This time, his disciples were not orthodox Muslims but people drawn to an informal and personalized way of reaching the Almighty. Such was al-Ghazali's influence on Islamic thinking that he was referred to as Hujjat-ul-Islam or Proof of Islam in his lifetime.[44] Though al-Ghazali wrote more than seventy books in Persian and Arabic on subjects as varied as science, philosophy, and Islamic reasoning, his biggest contribution was in evolving a theology of Sufism, marrying it with the Shariah.

---

[42]Hassan Hassan, 'Don't blame it on al-Ghazali', Qantara.de, available here: https://en.qantara.de/content/the-decline-of-islamic-scientific-thought-dont-blame-it-on-al-ghazali

[43]Al-Ghazali, Stanford Encyclopedia of Philosophy, available here: https://plato.stanford.edu/entries/al-ghazali/

[44]Frank Griffel, *Al-Ghazālī's Philosophical Theology*, New Delhi: OUP, 2009, p. 34.

Through this, he helped develop a 'systematic view of Sufism and its integration and acceptance in mainstream Islam'[45]. The Sufi philosophy that he conceived had three sequential components: the Shariah, Islamic principles, through which the Sufi chisels his devotion to Allah; the tariqah, the path the Sufi must follow to reach the divine; and, finally, the haqiqah, the divine truth, the object of the Sufi's labour.

Al-Ghazali argued that as long as one believed in Allah and Prophet Muhammad one could practise Islam several different ways, and that 'any of the many traditions practised in good faith by believers should not be viewed as heretical by other Muslims'[46]. With this al-Ghazali sought to respond to the Islamic orthodoxy that viewed everyone who disagreed with them as heretical. Professor of Religious Studies Frank Griffel explains:

> While Ghazali does state that any Muslim practicing Islam in good faith is not guilty of apostasy, he does outline in The Criterion that there is one standard of Islam that is more correct than the others, and that those practicing the faith incorrectly should be moved to change. In Ghazali's view, only the Prophet himself could deem a faithfully practicing Muslim an infidel, and his work was a pushback against the religious persecution and strife that occurred often during this time period between various Islamic sects.[47]

Al-Ghazali opened the floodgates for the development of Sufi philosophy, which spread out of Persia, Turkey, and Afghanistan to other parts of the world, including Europe, finally reaching its pinnacle in South Asia. Over the next hundred years, a number of Sufi philosophers emerged, the most towering of whom was Ibn al-Arabi.

Born in the Valencia region of Spain in 1165, Ibn al-Arabi 'gave the esoteric, mystical dimension of Islamic thought its first full-fledged philosophic expression'[48]. He wrote a number of books propounding

---

[45]Ibid.

[46]Ibid., p. 120.

[47]Ibid., p. 104.

[48]Ibn al-Arabi, *Encyclopedia Britannica,* available here: https://www.britannica.com/biography/Ibn-al-Arabi

his idea of unity of the soul with Allah.

By the time Al-Arabi died in Damascus in 1240, after travelling all through the Arab empire, from southwest Europe to North Africa and the Middle East, including pilgrimages to Mecca and Jerusalem, his fame as a Sufi saint was widespread. People from all over the region came to visit him in Damascus, for learning, guidance, or simply to pay obeisance. The Arab ulema were livid. People were prohibited from reading his books, but that did not stop his growing following, especially in the rest of the world where Sufis were charting their own course.[49]

The East—Persia, Turkey, Central Asia, and South Asia—became fertile ground for the incubation of Sufi philosophies and orders. Almost all Sufi orders or silsilas, from the quietest and most conservative like the Naqshbandis to political influencers like the Suhrawardis to those that aligned Indian Vedic thinking with Islamic mysticism like the Rishis (of Kashmir), made their home in the Indian subcontinent despite having originated in Persia, Afghanistan, Turkey, or Central Asia. Abul Fazl, Emperor Akbar's chronicler, recorded fourteen Sufi silsilas in the *Ain-e-Akbari*.

However, the most famous, revered, and far-reaching Sufi order in India has been the Chishtiya silsila. It was founded by Moinuddin Chishti, who came to India from the Sistan province of Persia and settled down in Ajmer in 1197. Chishti, who earned the honorific 'khwaja' for his benedictory powers, based his outreach on the principles of 'redressing the misery of those in distress, fulfilling the needs of the helpless and feeding the hungry'.[50] This is the reason he is reverentially called Khwaja Gharib Nawaz or the one who takes care of the poor. All Chishtiya Sufis who inherited the mantle from him adhered to these values. They shunned personal wealth and royal patronage, focussing instead on creating community kitchens and hospices for the poor within their khanqahs, which evolved into more than mere seminaries, as the saints lived there as well.

---

[49]Ibid.

[50]Dehlvi, *Sufism*, p. 408.

Another well-known and well-regarded Sufi of the Chishtiya order was Hazrat Nizamuddin Auliya who built his khanqah in Delhi. Lovingly called Mehboob-e-Ellahi (Beloved of the Almighty), Nizamuddin despaired of any association with the nobility. A fable associated with him mentions that he had a special door in the rear of his cottage. Whenever the sultan (perhaps a reference to Alauddin Khalji of the Delhi Sultanate) entered the front door, he left through the rear.

While nearly all of the Sufis composed devotional poetry in praise of Allah and his prophets, they encouraged the musical rendition of these in their khanqahs to create an atmosphere of sublimity or sama mehfils, thereby contributing to the evolution of a new genre of music called Sufi music. While the Sufis were deeply religious in their practice of Islam, their khanqahs (during their lifetime) and (after their deaths) their dargahs, were open to people of all faiths. The Sufis did not distinguish between people on the basis of religion or creed.

It was Sufis such as these who brought about the confluence between the Arabian religion and the native beliefs of India, causing greater conversion to Islam. This intermingling could not have occurred if conversions had taken place on pain of death.

It must be said here that the Sufi interpretation of the faith aside, the Quran itself discourages forcing one's faith on another. For instance, the verse Al-Kafirun says:

> I do not worship what you worship,
> nor do you worship what I worship.
> I will never worship what you worship,
> nor will you ever worship what I worship.
> You have your way, and I have my Way.[51]

From the rulers' point of view as well, forcing conversions made little sense since non-Muslim communities were required to pay additional tax. Writing about the rise of Islam in Europe, American Sufi writer Stephen Schwartz says in his book *The Two Faces of Islam*: 'But numerous

[51]Surah Al-kafirun, Verse 109:1-6, translation by Dr Mustafa Khattab (https://quran.com/109).

Islamic rulers, however intense their devotion to the faith, found it convenient to encourage Jews and Christians to remain outside Islam, as a financial resource. This historical fact contradicts common Christian legendry claiming that multitudes were forcibly converted to the faith of Mohammed.'[52]

In India, this approach went further. According to Khalid Anis Ansari, 'The Muslim ulema were reluctant to convert low-caste Hindus because who would have done the dirty work then?'[53]

However it happened, the advent of Islam into the subcontinent, and the resultant conversions to the faith, led to all manner of changes in Indian society. Quoting Dinesh Chandra Sen's history of the Bengali language, Tara Chand writes: 'This elevation of Bengali to a literary status was brought about by several influences, of which the Mohammedan conquest was undoubtedly one of the foremost. If the Hindu kings had continued to enjoy independence Bengali would scarcely have got an opportunity to find its way to the courts of Kings.'[54]

In the same chapter he writes that the rise of Brahminism had pushed native beliefs to the margins, fostering both class and caste divisions, which was resented by a large section of the people. 'The representatives of the older faiths were highly gratified with the suppression of Brahminism and even with Muslim vandalism. The followers of the Dharma cult, a modified form of Mahayanism could hardly contain themselves with glee at the chastisement which their erstwhile oppressors suffered.'[55]

Then quoting a Dehara Bhanga (breaking of a temple) song titled 'Dharma Puja Paddhati' (the method of worshipping Dharma), he writes:

Some worship Alla, some Ali, and others Mamud Sai (Lord)
The mian kills no living things nor eats dead ones

---

[52]Stephen Schwartz, *The Two Faces of Islam: The House of Sa'ud From Tradition to Terror*, New York: Doubleday, 2002, p. 32.

[53]In conversation with the author, New Delhi, 25 February 2019.

[54]Chand, *Influence of Islam on Indian Culture*, pp. 213–14.

[55]Ibid., p. 215.

> He is cooking his food over slow fire
> The caste distinction will slowly be broken—for, behold, there's a Mohammedan in a Hindu family[56]

According to Tara Chand, this close interaction between Hindus and Muslims led to the emergence of several practices common to both communities. For instance, Hindus would not only offer sweets at Muslim shrines but also consult the Quran. Similarly, Muslims would participate in Hindu festivals.

This syncretism, referred to as the Ganga-Jamni tehzeeb in north India, created a socio-religious order which wove together the Hindu–Muslim faith in a patchwork quilt. The result of this was that a Muslim from Bengal had greater cultural affinity with a Hindu of Bengal, rather than a Muslim from Karnataka or even Uttar Pradesh. This was true of all Muslims in all parts of India. Even in matters of religion, each was representative more of her geographical location than the desert of Arabia.

Consequently, successive Muslim dynasties, starting with the Delhi Sultanate (1206–1526), of which Iltutmish was the most successful king, did not look outside India for political or spiritual validation. For them, India was, to turn around the phrase used by Vinayak Damodar Savarkar[57] (the founder of the Hindu Mahasabha), both their punya bhoomi as well as pitru bhoomi—the holy land as well as the fatherland. About Iltutmish (r. 1211–36), Christophe Jaffrelot and Laurence Louer write:

> In 1228-29, he received a delegation from the Abbasid Caliph-al Muntansir and was presented with the Caliphal robe (khilat) and investiture (manshur) signifying the Caliphate's recognition of Iltutmish's rule over India...but Delhi Sultanate remained an independent kingdom since the main sources of his legitimacy did not come from outside India. Indeed, when local orthodox ulama, echoing the Caliphate's recommendations, requested him to give

[56]Ibid., p. 216.

[57]See Q&A, Veer Savarkar.org, available here: http://savarkar.org/en/encyc/2017/5/29/Q-A6.html

> the Hindus the choice of 'Islam or death', he turned to the Sufis... to legitimate his pragmatic decision not to antagonise the Hindus, who were in a majority and may have dislodged Muslims from their position of power if offered such a choice.[58]

The reason why Iltutmish and his successors, across dynasties, were able to ignore the caliphate was because of the Sufis, especially of the Chishtiya order: 'None of the major historical Sufi saints, known as "Shaykhs", ever made the hajj to Mecca and Medina. Their land was India and, as their disciples maintained their dargahs there, they made India sacred for Muslims.'

Nizamuddin Auliya's most famous disciple, the poet Amir Khusro had read in a Hadith that South Asia was the place where Adam descended to earth after being expelled from paradise. Azad Bilgrami, a seventeenth-century Islamic scholar, described India as the place where the eternal light of Muhammed first manifested in Adam, while Arabia is where it found its final expression in the physical form of the Prophet.[59]

The Mughal emperor Akbar sponsored caravans of pilgrims to Arabia for many years, but few commoners undertook hajj. In any case, no Mughal emperor ever went for hajj.[60] They patronized the Sufi shrines, and the Sufis in turn accorded spiritual and moral legitimacy to the emperors. On the strength of this legitimacy, Akbar assumed the position of the leader of the faithful. Akbar even went as far as challenging the Ottomans, who were the caretakers of the holy lands of Mecca and Medina, and considered the leaders of the Islamic world at that time.

'In early September 1579, a group of theologians, including the Shaikh ul-Islam[61], were pressured into signing a text claiming for Akbar a special status of Padshah-i-Islam, beyond that even of a Sultan-i-Adil... one of the epithets used for him was now Mujtahid[62], as also Imam-

[58]Christophe Jaffrelot and Laurence Louer (eds.), *The Islamic Connection: South Asia and the Gulf*, Gurgaon: Penguin Viking, 2017, p. 4.

[59]Ibid., pp. 3–5.

[60]Ibid.

[61]This referred to the most senior Islamic religious leader during Akbar's time.

[62]A person qualified to do ijtihad or interpret the Quran, a privilege then confined to

i-Adil.... Indeed, the challenge was directed in good measure at the Ottomans, who had claimed superior status as the Khalifas of the east, with their conquest of Egypt.'[63]

In addition to challenging the Ottomans, Akbar assumed these grand titles to keep the conservative ulema from interfering in governance, especially in matters pertaining to the treatment of non-Muslims.

Yet, despite this desire for the leadership of the Muslim world, Muslim rulers in India worked towards greater synthesis between Islam and Hinduism. Of course, this was driven by pragmatism rather than altruism, but the effect was that the two communities were able to not only coexist in harmony but also developed several similar customs and traditions.

The pinnacle of this collaboration was suhl-e-kul, a new creed for universal peace and coexistence that Akbar propounded that celebrated what he believed was common to all religions. Suhl-e-kul, also referred to as Din-i-Ilahi, did not live on beyond Akbar's reign, but the idea of mutual respect and peaceful coexistence survived. Even Aurangzeb, his zealousness notwithstanding, did not disrupt the balance between the two communities and neither did his successors. However, the most interesting aspect of this six-and-half-century-long Muslim rule in India, which started with the founding of the Slave Dynasty in 1206 CE was that none declared India an Islamic state and none ruled by Quranic law or Shariah.[64]

Even as late as the nineteenth century, Muslim rulers remained sensitive to the religious sensibilities of the Hindus. William Dalrymple writes of the last Mughal emperor Bahadur Shah Zafar, that 'when a party of two hundred Muslims turned up at the Palace demanding to be allowed to slaughter cows—holy to Hindus—at Id, Zafar told them in a "decided and angry tone that the religion of the Mussalmen did not depend upon the sacrifice of cows".'[65]

---

the caliphs and great imams.

[63]Sanjay Subrahmanyam, *Mughals and Franks: Explorations in Connected History*, New Delhi: OUP, 2011, p. 53.

[64]C. V. Vaidya, *History of Medieval Hindu India, Vol III*, Cosmo Publications, 1926, p. 361.

[65]William Dalrymple, *The Last Mughal: The Fall of a Dynasty, Delhi, 1857,* New Delhi:

Given that the reach and influence of Sufism, not just in South Asia but in most of the Islamic world, was a clear challenge to the ulema, a pushback was inevitable. Sure enough, it came from the Arab world in the form of Taqi ad-Din Ahmad ibn Taymiyyah, the most influential and controversial Islamic thinker, writer, and activist of his era.

Born in Damascus in 1263, Ibn Taymiyyah belonged to the Hanbali school of jurisprudence, the most orthodox of the four Sunni schools (this school was limited to the Arabian peninsula). No mere philosopher, Ibn Taymiyyah was a street fighter and often joined in the jihad that he declared against those he disagreed with.[66] According to him, a literal interpretation of the Shariah was the only way to govern Islamic lands and anyone who contested this was not a true Muslim. Moreover, he believed that jihad should be waged against anyone who claimed to be a Muslim but was not a true Muslim. In 1310, he wrote a treatise titled *Ziyarat al Kubur* in which he condemned the cult of Sufis and Walis. He believed that 'the one who visits the Prophet's grave commits bidah (innovation)'.[67]

Ibn Taymiyyah issued a fatwa for jihad against neo-converts like the Mongols, Shias, and Sufis.[68] This was the first instance in Islamic history that jihad was approved against fellow Muslims, i.e. anybody who disagreed with Ibn Taymiyyah's interpretation of Islam. His extremism caused unease even among the traditional Hanbali jurists, who condemned his pronunciations, leading to his being repeatedly imprisoned. Ibn Taymiyyah died in prison in 1328. But his legacy lived on. Using Ibn Taymiyyah's arguments, four centuries later, Muhammad ibn Abd al-Wahhab (1703–92) changed the future of Islam, not only in Arabia but across most of the world. Driven by a deep hatred for the Ottomans, who controlled Arabia at the time, Abd al-Wahhab set about reforming Islam to rid it of extraneous influences. His teachings converged

---

Penguin Viking, 2006, p. 82.

[66]Ibn Taymiyyah, *Encyclopedia Britannica*, available here: https://www.britannica.com/biography/Ibn-Taymiyyah

[67]Ibid. Since the Prophet's message is considered the final command of Allah, anything that does not conform to his message is considered innovation and hence against Islam. The Quran does not say anything about visiting graves.

[68]Schwartz, *The Two Faces of Islam*, p. 55.

on three main points: 'First, ritual is superior to intentions. Second, no reverence of the dead is permitted. Third, there can be no intercessory prayer, addressed to God by means of the Prophets or saints....' He further condemned those who did not pray at all the prescribed times.[69]

Abd al-Wahhab, says Schwartz, 'made no secret of his opinion that all Muslims had fallen into unbelief and that if they did not follow him, they should all be killed, their wives and daughters violated, and their possessions confiscated. Shias, Sufis, and other Muslims he judged unorthodox were to be exterminated....

'Above all, Ibn Abd al-Wahhab and his followers despised music, which they viewed as an incitement to forgetfulness of God and to sin. Many Sufis, by contrast, used music as a means to heighten consciousness of God.'[70]

On the streets of Arabia the violence of Abd al-Wahhab's ideas became evident during his lifetime; the poison took a few centuries to reach other parts of the world.

Even as the spread of violent Wahhabism started in earnest after the discovery of oil in Saudi Arabia in the twentieth century, the theological argument was carried out of Arabia during Abd al-Wahhab's time by scholars and theologists who visited Mecca–Medina for pilgrimage. That is how, Shah Waliullah, a globally renowned Islamic scholar from Delhi, was exposed to Wahhabi ideas.

Shah Waliullah Dehlavi was born into a family of Sufis of the Naqshbandi order in 1703. Home-schooled in Islamic studies by his father, Shah Abdur Rahim, Shah Waliullah, a prodigy of sorts, started to teach at his father's Madrassa-i-Rahimiya at the age of sixteen. At twenty-eight, he was one of the few Indians who travelled to Arabia for hajj.[71] After the completion of his hajj, he studied with Arab and Persian scholars in the Hejaz province of Arabia, home to both Mecca and Medina.

---

[69]Ibid., pp. 76–77.

[70]Ibid., pp. 69–71

[71]Pilgrimage to Mecca is one of the five pillars of Islam. All Muslims aspire to go for hajj, at least once in their lifetime. In the eighteenth century, the pilgrimage was too expensive and arduous for a large majority of the faithful.

Having been exposed to the thinking and writing of early Islamic scholars like Al-Ghazali and Ibn Taymiyyah, by the time Shah Waliullah returned to Delhi in 1732, his understanding of Islam had changed from that of his father. Though he did not denounce the ways of the Sufis, he criticized the veneration of graves as tantamount to idol worship. Despite this, he tried to bridge the gap between the esotericism of Sufism and the pedantic absolutism of the reformist Islamic movement of Arabia started by Abd al-Wahhab. Hence, unlike the Wahhabis, he continued to regard the Sufis respectfully, even if he didn't encourage reverence of them. He also argued that prayer directed towards Allah was enough and required no intercedence by Sufis.

Waliullah also felt that the Islam followed by Muslims in India had become corrupted over the years because of cohabitation with Hinduism. He believed that this intermingling had made it so that nothing much distinguished the two communities at the social and cultural level.[72] He also felt that the absence of qualified religious teachers and the fact that ordinary Muslims could not understand the Quran (as they didn't know Arabic) were great drawbacks to the proper observance of the faith. The other weakness of the ummah was its moral abjectness and decadence. Even among the religious, Islam was reduced to mere prayer by the clock and nothing else. Waliullah turned away from the Naqshbandi Sufi beliefs of his family and went about trying to reform Indian Muslims, i.e., ridding them of 'un-Islamic' influences and practices.

The first step was to translate the Quran into Persian, the language of the Indian Muslim elite. (In later years, his sons translated it into Urdu.) The second step was to explain to the people, Muslims and non-Muslims alike, how Islam was the answer to all social, political, economic, and moral issues for all time to come. The third step was to present Islam not as a religion, but as a way of life. Saying one's prayers was not enough; a Muslim must also imbibe Islamic life by emulating the Prophet of Islam.[73] Hence, a Muslim must not only behave like one

---

[72]Dalrymple, *The Last Mughal*, pp. 76–78.

[73]Prof. Dr. Nazeer Ahmed, 'Shah Waliullah of Delhi', *History of Islam*, available here: https://historyofislam.com/contents/resistance-and-reform/shah-waliullah-of-delhi/

but should look like one.

To this end, he introduced the books of Hadith for better understanding of the Quran and Shariah. He did this to lay emphasis on the idea of ijtihad (interpretation through reasoning) in addition to taklid—unquestioning acquiescence to the Quran or to a scholar (imam) whom one trusts implicitly on Islamic matters.[74]

However, the option of ijtihad was not available to the ordinary citizenry as they couldn't be trusted with interpreting the texts. Only the learned had the privilege of attempting to interpret Quranic verses with the aid of the Hadith and Sunnah[75]. In any case, the Quran is not an easy document to understand. Written in classical Arabic, its grammar is complicated[76] and the verses are contextual. Hence, unless one also reads about the context of each verse, which demands knowledge of the history of both Semitic religions and the Arabian peninsula, it's not possible to deduce the exact meaning of every verse. The biggest consequence of Waliullah's efforts was the growth of Islamic learning in India, with Madrassa-i-Rahimiya becoming the most sought-after centre for religious education not only amongst Indians but outsiders too.

All Indian Islamic sects (Deobandi, Barelvi, and Ahle Hadith[77]) as well as political movements propounded by people like Maulana Abul Ala Mahdudi (the founder of the Jamaat-e-Islami) and the poet Muhammad Iqbal (who expounded the idea of Islamic exceptionalism) owe their theological development to the vast repertoire of Shah Waliullah and Abd al-Wahhab.

Even though Waliullah tried to combine Sufi beliefs with conservative Islamic practices, his progeny—both biological and ideological—increasingly turned away from Sufism. One of the factors that made the vilification of Sufism possible was the West's efforts to delink Sufi

---

[74]For more on this, see J. M. S. Baljon, *Religion and Thought of Shah Wali Allah Dihlawi, 1703-1762,* Leiden: Brill, 1986, available here: https://www.jstor.org/stable/25212297?read-now=1&seq=3#page_scan_tab_contents

[75]The way of life of the prophets and the examples set by them.

[76]More on this in a later chapter.

[77]These have been dealt with in a later chapter.

philosophy from Islam. Because of its historical prejudice[78] against Islam, the West could not reconcile the sophistication and mysticism of Sufi poetry, especially that of Mevlana Jalaluddin Rumi and Hafez Shirazi, emerging from the Middle East with its perception of the 'desert religion'.

Quoting Omid Safi, a professor of Middle Eastern and Islamic studies at Duke University, Rozina Ali writes in the *New Yorker*, that 'it was in the Victorian period that readers in the West began to uncouple mystical poetry from its Islamic roots. The explanation they settled on, Safi told me, was "that these people are mystical not because of Islam but in spite of it."'[79] This allowed orthodox Muslims (ironically on the authority of the West) to assert that Sufis are not Muslims at all.

To semi-literate Indian Muslims, the objection against Sufism was conveyed in two arguments. One, the playing of music in the dargahs was an un-Islamic innovation. Two, prostration at the tombs and veneration of dead saints was akin to idol worship.

'We neither approve of the music that is played in the dargahs nor the practice of people doing sajda (prostration) at the mazaar (tomb) of the Auliyas. After all, sajda can only be done to Allah,' says Maulana Abdurrahim Nashtar Faruqi of Jamiatur Raza, Bareilly, a trust for the propagation of the ideas of the Barelvi sect. On the surface it appears that the objection to Sufi Islam is superficial but, in reality, it is more fundamental.

Sufism is non-judgemental. It gives agency to the individual in the spirit of the Quran which maintains that faith is between the believer and Allah; it doesn't need a guide in the form of ulema. This challenge to their power is what threatens the ulema. As far as the two above-mentioned objections are concerned, the fact is that the Quran does not forbid music at all. The only mention of forbidden things is made

---

[78]The western prejudice of Islam goes back to the time of Crusades, when, to mobilize foot soldiers, Christian clergy used not just the vilification of the people but religion itself as means to justify waging war against it. Over time, even scholars started believing the image that the clergy had painted of the Muslims.

[79]Rozina Ali, 'The Erasure of Islam from the Poetry of Rumi', *New Yorker*, 5 Jan 2017.

in the chapter Surah Al-Araf[80] in three successive verses. These are:

> O Children of Adam! Dress properly whenever you are at worship. Eat and drink, but do not waste. Surely He does not like the wasteful. (7.31)
>
> Ask, O Prophet, 'Who has forbidden the adornments and lawful provisions Allah has brought forth for His servants?' Say, 'They are for the enjoyment of the believers in this worldly life, but they will be exclusively theirs on the Day of Judgment. This is how We make Our revelations clear for people of knowledge.' (7.32)
>
> Say, 'My Lord has only forbidden open and secret indecencies, sinfulness, unjust aggression, associating others with Allah in worship—a practice He has never authorized—and attributing to Allah what you do not know.' (7.33)

Regarding sajda, Haji Pir Syed Salmi Nizami of the Hazrat Nizamuddin Dargah in New Delhi says, 'Even we know that sajda can only be performed for Allah and no one else. When people bend down in the dargah, it is called kadam-boosi or symbolically kissing the feet of someone exalted. This is a very old, non-religious tradition and stems from love and respect.'[81]

Shah Waliullah died in 1762, at the age of fifty-nine. He had written fifty-one books, both in Arabic and Persian, the most famous of which was *Hujjat Allah al-Baligha* (The Profound Evidence of Allah). Even though the development of contemporary Indian Islam owes itself to the ideas and writings of Shah Waliullah, in his lifetime his ideas were constantly challenged by the tolerance and coexistence that various Muslim kings had painstakingly built over the years.

But in 1857, when the first war of Independence against the British ended in ignominious defeat and the collapse of Muslim power in India, coexistence came under attack. Though the war was symbolically led by the last Mughal emperor, Bahadur Shah Zafar, under whose 'command'

---

[80]Surah Al Araf, Verse 7:31-7:33, translated by Dr Mustafa Khattab (https://quran.com/7).

[81]Interview with the author, New Delhi, 18 November 2018.

Hindus and Muslims fought the British, the truth was that it was largely a Muslim–British affair, which brutally ruptured the delicate balance between Hindus and Muslims that had thrived for nearly seven centuries[82] through mutual tolerance and economic interdependence. Three possible factors worked in tandem to cause this breach.

One, though the sepoys rose against the British quite spontaneously, irrespective of religion, once they were ensconced in Delhi, the radical Muslims, the products of the Madrassa-e-Rahimiya, saw an opportunity to reclaim Muslim power. As a result, fatawa were issued declaring jihad against the British and likening the revolt to an Islamic war. The debilitated Mughal court did not sense the polarizing impact of this call. After all, the early Mughals had labelled their military campaigns jihad to motivate the soldiery. Incidentally, even in today's Indian Army, all pure regiments[83] (as opposed to mixed regiments like artillery or armoured) of the infantry have religious war cries. However, in 1857, overt and frequent references to jihad led to unease amongst non-Muslim sepoys.

Two, since the war was being waged in the name of the Mughal emperor and with the hope of restoring Muslim power, Muslims of all classes and status threw their weight behind the revolt, thereby exposing themselves and their leanings. This was the not the case amongst non-Muslims, where the rich and upper castes either stayed away or covertly supported the British, as they saw this as a war between the Muslim and the British.

---

[82]While the first Muslim dynasty was founded in 1206, Muslim influence on Indian society had started as early as the seventh century when the first Muslim traders landed on the eastern coast of India in 636 CE.

[83]In the Indian Army, most of the infantry regiments are drawn from a single geographical location and are named after that region. For instance, Gurkha, Garhwal, Dogra, Punjab, Kumaon, Sikh, Bihar, and so on. These are referred to as pure regiments. This is a legacy from British India, and is the consequence of the belief that when people of one region are put together there is greater cohesiveness and their fighting ability increases. Similarly, their war cries are reflective of their religious beliefs. For instance, the Dogra war cry is 'Jwala Mata ki Jai', Bihar's 'Bajrang Bali Ki Jai', and the Sikh war cry is 'Jo Bole So Nihal, Sat Sri Akal'.

Three, the British were quick to sense this chasm and worked to widen the rift. This was partly because of their own prejudice borne of centuries of Crusades against the Muslims further fanned by the Evangelical Christians in India; and partly from their own experiences with Muslims in various continents, from North Africa to Asia in the nineteenth century.

'From around the middle of the nineteenth century,' Christopher de Bellaigue writes in *The Islamic Enlightenment*, 'when European colonial interests ran up against Muslim resistance from North Africa to India, it is possible to say that a rolling agenda of conflicts between an expanding Western imperium and the Muslims in its path became inevitable. India's subjugation by the British had produced a situation of almost chronic religious revolt, of which the rebellion of 1857, or Indian Mutiny, was a virulent spasm.'[84]

In addition to the wholesale retributive killings of the Muslims, the British fanned the narrative of Hindu victimhood of several centuries. This narrative continued to get more traction over the years as several right-wing Hindu ideologues emerged from the embers of 1857. The Hindus believed that the Muslims had finally got their comeuppance after several centuries of ruling over them; the Muslims felt let down by their leaders, cheated by their Hindu neighbours, and disillusioned by their faith. They had believed the ulema who told them that, as in the historic Battle of Badr, Allah would intervene to ensure their victory. And so as a defeated people tend to do, they became despondent and inward-looking.

The ulema were quick to turn this to their advantage. They claimed that while the Muslims' cause was just, their faith was weak. Hence, the faith needed to be strengthened. The growth and eventual rise of Sunni Muslim sects like Deobandi and Barelvi were the consequence of this new dependence of the ordinary Muslims on the ulema.

'By the turn of the century,' Bellaigue writes, 'the word "pan-Islamism" had become a portmanteau term to explain the political solidarity that seemed to extend across the Muslim lands in opposition to

---

[84]Bellaigue, *The Islamic Enlightenment*, p. 201.

imperialism. From Cambridge the late-Victorian scholar and Islamophile E. G. Browne deprecated the term as unfairly connoting fanaticism. In his view it was "certainly no more fanatical than Pan-Germanism, or Pan-Slavism, or British Imperialism, and indeed, much less so, being, in the first place defensive, and, in the second, based on the more rational ground of a common faith, not on the less rational ground of a common race".'[85]

The responders in India to this supposed global awakening were the religious scholars and ulema, who had assumed the role of 'rehnumah' or one who shows the way for the community. As a result, ordinary Muslims started shrinking away from the national mainstream, increasingly identifying with the idea of the global ummah.[86] Besides this development, one of the effects of the 1857 revolt was the erosion of the economic and educational foundations of the Muslims. This idea of lost glory and victimhood had a cascading effect on their collective psyche leading to inertia and loss of hope—afflictions that linger on in some way or the other even today.

[85]Bellaigue, *The Islamic Enlightenment*, p. 202.

[86]Addressed in Chapter 8.

3

ONE FAITH, MANY SECTS

Master Nazakat Hussain, a respectable madrassa teacher in the small village of Aharaula, about 20 kilometres from Moradabad, died in 2006. He was eighty-five. His only heir was a nephew, Maulana Hafeez Abu Mohammed. Being the only family member, and a loved one at that, it was natural that Maulana Hafeez would carry out his uncle's last rites, which he did with great devotion. He led his funeral prayer, namaz-e-janaza, too. Such was the reputation of the uncle–nephew duo that the entire village turned up for the funeral prayer.

But as word got around, a mufti, Abdul Mannan Karimi, arrived from Moradabad and declared that the marriages of everyone who had attended the namaz-e-janaza stood annulled.[1] This was because Master Hussain, like Mufti Karimi, had sworn allegiance to the Barelvi sect. The nephew had been part of the Deobandi sect.

Under a Barelvi directive issued nearly a century ago, all non-Barelvi Muslims are held as kafir[2] and hence unworthy of following during namaz[3] (Deobandis have no such restrictions). Whoever follows a non-Barelvi during namaz does so at the cost of their faith or marriage or both, as happened in Aharaula. Around 200 couples, some in their 80s, had to solemnize their nikahs[4] all over again, and perform atonement for committing the sin of offering namaz that was led by a Deobandi.

Recalling this incident, the president of the All India Muslim Women

---

[1]TNN, '200 weddings redone in UP after a fatwa', *Times of India,* 5 Sep 2006.

[2]Infidel.

[3]When men offer namaz in a group (jamaat), one person is supposed to lead the congregation. This person can be an imam or anyone from the group. The rest stand behind him and follow his lead with regard to the chanting of verses.

[4]Islamic marriage contract.

Personal Law Board (AIMWPLB), Shaista Amber, trembles with anger. A news channel at that time had invited her to a television debate with Mufti Karimi, a few clerics from Delhi, and a mufti from Medina, Saudi Arabia.

'They all agreed that what Mufti Karimi had done was wrong, but none criticized him openly on television. He just raved on and on about how he was right and would do this again if required. Finally, when I was asked to speak, I told him that if I was the mufti from Medina and if Mufti Karimi ever entered Medina, I would have him thrown out of the holy city, as he had brought shame not only to Indian Muslims but the entire religion of Islam,' Amber says, recalling the debate.[5]

'I said on television that since you have declared the nikah of hundreds of people invalid simply because they read namaz behind someone you didn't like, clearly your intention is not honourable. Are you going to do halala[6] for these women?'

Her anger and language stunned the other participants, including Mufti Karimi who was livid. Finally, the mufti from Medina spoke. Commending Shaista for her courage, he condemned Mufti Karimi and asserted that only Allah could judge who was a good or a bad Muslim. No human has the right to pronounce another a kafir or infidel. As happens on television discussions, time ran out. Mufti Karimi remained unrepentant. The poor villagers of Aharaula obeyed his diktat. And the Barelvi sect demonstrated its influence.

'Barelvis are extremely dogmatic,' remarks Maulana Kalbe Jawad, a senior Shia cleric, scholar, and member of the All India Muslim Personal Law Board (AIMPLB) based in Lucknow.[7] 'They do not consider Shias to be Muslim and do not even greet a Shia person, unlike the Deobandis, who are relatively more tolerant. Barelvis are also very fond of issuing fatawa at the first opportunity,' he says jocularly, citing the

---

[5]Interview with the author, Lucknow, 15 December 2018.

[6]Halala is a practice by which, to remarry her husband, a Muslim woman is required to marry another man, consummate that marriage, and get a divorce from this temporary husband. There have been incidents of disreputable mullahs offering to temporarily marry women for this. This subject has been dealt with in detail in Chapter 7.

[7]In conversation with the author, Lucknow, 14 December 2018.

example of a directive issued during the hundredth death anniversary commemoration, urs, of its founder, Ahmed Raza Khan Barelvi, which took place in Bareilly in early November 2018.

At a public function during the urs, a cleric from the Marhara dargah aligned with the Barelvi sect, and a professor of AMU, Syed Ameen Miyan Qadri, urged the audience to desist from going to the Ajmer dargah during the urs of Moinuddin Chishti. He told them that the devotees should instead observe the urs in their homes. This directive was issued because the Barelvi clerics hold the caretakers of the Ajmer dargah as bud-mazhab (of bad faith).[8]

'They want people to come only to their dargah. They do not like the idea that dargahs like Ajmer and Hazrat Nizamuddin Auliya draw such huge crowds,' says Maulana Jawad. When I remark that he sounds as if he reveres these dargahs, he replies, 'Yes, Shias believe in the Sufis. Even the Sufi shrines respect Shia sentiments and observe Moharram with full decorum.'[9]

Though they offer no data to support their claim, the Barelvis claim that 80 per cent of Muslims in the Indian subcontinent believe in their creed.

'Barelvi is not a sect, it is the real Islam,' says Maulana Mohammed Shakeel, the principal of Jamiatur Raza, Centre for Islamic Studies, in Bareilly, the primary institution run by the Barelvi sect. 'We are the true Ahle Sunnat wal Jama'at[10] because we follow the 1,400-year-old Shariah in its purest form,' he asserts.

But everybody else, including those who believe in the Deobandi philosophy, also claims to be the Ahle Sunnat wal Jama'at.

'They may claim whatever they want,' shrugs Mohammed Shakeel,

---

[8]Rasia, 'Ameen Miya urges Sunni Barelvi Muslims not to visit Ajmer dargah', *Siasat Daily*, 7 Nov 2018.

[9]Interview with the author, Lucknow, 15 December 2018.

[10]Sunnat means the traditions of the Prophet and jamaat means his community. In the literal sense, the phrase refers to those who follow the lifestyle of Prophet Muhammad and all the earlier Prophets as well the earliest companions of Prophet Muhammad, referred to as Sahabah. Many consider the term Sunni to be a shortened version of Ahle Sunnat wal Jama'at.

insisting that they are the true believers.[11]

In a Hadith[12] associated with Prophet Muhammad he is believed to have told his companions that while the tribe of Bani Israel (the followers of Moses) was divided into seventy-two sects, his tribe would split into seventy-three. One of his companions then asked him how the Muslims would know which of these tribes was the righteous one. He is supposed to have replied that those who followed his creed would be the righteous ones. Hence, those who insist that they are the righteous ones call themselves the followers of Prophet Muhammad's traditions and the creed of his companions.

Since the early years of Islam, and within years of Prophet Muhammad's death in 632 CE, Muslims frequently used this argument to disagree with one another, even resorting to violence. The first disagreement occurred immediately after the Prophet's death on the question of succession. Even as his body was being prepared for burial by his family members, including his cousin and son-in-law, Hazrat Ali,[13] a group of early Muslims led by his closest companion and father-in-law, Hazrat Abu Bakr,[14] met to decide on his succession. The majority believed that the Prophet wanted Abu Bakr to lead the community as the rightly-guided caliph[15] because he had been appointed by the Prophet to lead the prayers in his absence. However, a small but formidable section insisted that the Prophet's only male heir, Hazrat Ali, should lead the bereaved community as he knew the Prophet better than anyone else.[16] This group believed that the Prophet had once said that there

---

[11]Interview with the author, Bareilly, 12 November 2018.

[12]Hadith has been dealt with elsewhere in the book.

[13]He was married to Fatima, the Prophet's youngest daughter with his first wife, Khadija; she was respectfully referred to as Bibi Fatima.

[14]Abu Bakr's daughter, Aisha, respectfully called Hazrat Aisha, was the Prophet's youngest (and some insist most beloved) wife. She was politically the most active and was frequently ranged against Ali. She also led a rebellion against Ali during his caliphate.

[15]As has been noted, only the first four caliphs—Hazrat Abu Bakr, Hazrat Umar, Hazrat Uthman, and Hazrat Ali—are called the rightly guided ones or Rashidun. Their status is exalted and largely undisputed. After their lifetime, the institution of the caliphate became progressively sectarian, hegemonic, and dynastic.

[16]Aslan, *No god But God*, Chapter Five.

was no one better than Ali to lead the community.[17] Another factor in his favour was that Ali was the first man to heed the Prophet's message and embrace Islam.

Arab society, however, was riven by tribal loyalties. Without the unifying presence of the Prophet, old rivalries and loyalties came back to the fore.

Abu Bakr belonged to a rich Meccan tribe that used to be a part of the most influential Quraysh confederacy of Mecca and had many supporters. Since the decision had to be unanimous under the Islamic tradition of ijma (consensus), Abu Bakr became the caliph, and the supporters of Ali accepted it grudgingly, except for a small group which continued to view Abu Bakr as a usurper. Upon Abu Bakr's death two years later, Umar ibn al-Khattab, another companion of Prophet Muhammad, became the caliph. This time the dissent was even stronger, as Umar was nominated by his predecessor upon his deathbed, bypassing ijma and the claims of Ali's supporters. Like Abu Bakr, Umar belonged to another powerful Meccan tribe, also part of the Quraysh confederacy. He was assassinated ten years later by one of the rebels in 644 CE. The age of radicalization and dissent had begun.

Once again, Hazrat Ali's name was proposed by his followers, who had started to call themselves Ahl-e-Bait or Devoted to the House of the Prophet, and once again he was pipped to the post by another companion of the Prophet, Uthman ibn Affan, another member of the Quraysh confederacy. Twelve years later, Uthman's term ended brutally. Protesting several of Uthman's decisions, including the appointment of his relatives in key positions throughout the expanding Islamic world, a group of Muslims revolted against him and laid siege to his house. The siege lasted for a few days as the rebels and his defenders (that included Ali's sons) clashed. Then a handful of Egyptians sneaked into his house and killed Uthman while he was reading the Quran.

---

[17]At the Festival of Ghadir Khumm, when Prophet Muhammad made his last pilgrimage to Mecca, he is believed to have told the congregation: 'Whoever recognises me as his master will recognise Ali as his master'; Vali Nasr, 'Chapter One: The Other Islam', *The Shia Revival: How Conflicts within Islam Will Shape the Future*, New York: W. W. Norton, 2007.

Finally, Ali was elected caliph. But dissension continued to rise. His caliphate was challenged by another contender, Muawiyah, Uthman's nephew and the governor of Damascus.[18] After a long, contentious tussle for power, including a civil war, Ali was forced to negotiate a truce with Muawiyah. Soon after, in 661 CE, he was assassinated by a Kharijite,[19] a member of the first recorded Muslim extremist group.

The Kharijites believed that by agreeing to arbitration with Muawiyah, who was clearly a usurper, Ali had displayed the weakness of his faith and his reluctance to carry out what Allah had ordained. The Kharijites attacked and killed fellow Muslims for not being adequately pious, somewhat akin to the modern-day Taliban. Their reign of terror continued for nearly a decade until they were brutally crushed by Muawiyah, who had taken over the caliphate after Ali's assassination.

A mere twenty-nine years after the death of Prophet Muhammad, the seeds of division that were sown by the election of Abu Bakr as the first caliph had borne fruit in the division of the ummah into the Sunnis and Shias.

The Shias

The group of people that held Ali as the rightful successor of Prophet Muhammad drifted into Shiism, derived from the term Shia'tu Ali or followers of Ali[20]. They had accepted the caliphate of Abu Bakr and tolerated Umar's tenure. But halfway through Uthman's term, given that he was promoting his family members and overlooking their financial profligacy, this group was convinced that the old aristocracy of Arabia, to which the first three caliphs belonged, was deliberately humiliating the Prophet's family and the rightful inheritors of his legacy.

---

[18]Aslan, *No god But God,* Chapter Five.

[19]Kharijites, also called Khwarij, were a group of radical Islamists who terrorized those who disagreed with them. They insisted that only they understood the real meaning of the Quran as revealed by Allah. Kharijite comes from the Arabic word khwarij, which means 'to reject'. These were the people who rejected the Islam being followed in Arabia at that time.

[20]Nasr, *The Shia Revival,* Chapter One.

However, the unbridgeable split occurred when Muawiyah was succeeded by his son Yazid I, removing even the illusion of Islamic morality and the democratic principle of ijma. Yazid I, the villain of the famous Battle of Karbala, in which his army of a few thousand killed most of the members of the Prophet's family including his grandson Husain (Fatima and Ali's younger son) and his companions (totalling seventy-two) in 680 CE, laid the foundation of the Umayyad Caliphate which lasted nearly a century.[21]

In an interesting connection to India, a group of Indian Brahmins devoted to Imam Husain fought alongside him in Karbala. Many were killed. One of the survivors, Rahib Dutt, fled to India after the battle. According to legend, Rahib Dutt brought a strand of the Prophet's hair with him, which is preserved in the Hazratbal dargah of Srinagar. The successors of Rahib Dutt are called Hussaini Brahmins and, to this day, they observe Muharram with mourning and prayer. Hindus who never converted to Islam, Hussaini Brahmins adopted some Islamic practices and beliefs out of love for Imam Husain.[22] (The Indian film actor Sunil Dutt was a Hussaini Brahmin.[23])

Imam Hussain had yet another Indian connection. According to chronicler Mehru Jaffer, there is a legend that one of Hussain's wives was a Persian princess, Shahrbanu, who died very soon after their marriage, well before the Battle of Karbala. She is believed to be a sister of Mihrbanu, one of Chandragupta Maurya's wives. 'It doesn't matter if these are true stories or not. The fact that these legends exist shows that India's connection with Islam was organic and goes back to the time of its revelation. It is not an alien religion as the Hindu right wing would want us to believe today,' she says.[24]

The massacre at Karbala had shocked the young Muslim community, including the group that came to be known as Sunnis. 'The fallen were

---

[21]Ibid.

[22]Nonica Datta, 'The Forgotten History of Hussaini Brahmins and Muharram in Amritsar', *The Wire*, 30 Sep 2019.

[23]Abdul Rasool Syed, 'Hussaini Brahmins and the tragedy of Karbala', *Daily Times*, 21 Sep 2018.

[24]Interview with the author, New Delhi, 8 June 2018.

beheaded; their bodies were left to rot in the scorching heat of the desert, and their heads were mounted on staffs to be paraded through Kufa (the Muslim capital during Ali's caliphate and hence Hussain's city of residence) before being sent to Damascus.'[25] For the Shias, who had reluctantly accepted the first two caliphs, Karbala was the validation of their belief that the ummah had erred in electing Abu Bakr. It 'crystallised'[26] the Shia perspective of Islam. The Shias were convinced that had Ali become the first caliph, Islamic values wouldn't have eroded as had happened during the reign of Muawiyah and his son.

Even the Umayyads were conscious of their religious illegitimacy. Hence, the institution of caliph was shorn of religious authority which now vested in a select group of ulema loyal to the king. They were also under constant pressure from the Shias who believed that Allah had chosen Prophet Muhammad to convey his message because he was more virtuous than ordinary people, and this virtuousness was inherited by his descendants, who should have been his rightful heirs.

As the argument over the legitimacy of the successor grew, Sunnis opposed to the Umayyads veered towards 'another branch of the family of the Prophet, the descendants of his uncle Abbas'.[27] Eventually, a descendant of Abbas, Abu'l Abbas, defeated the last of the Umayyads, Marwan II, and laid the foundation of the Abbasid Caliphate in 749–50 CE.

As Sunni Muslim armies raced across the Middle East, west and north Asia, North Africa, south and east Europe, new empires were established, including the first Shia empire founded by Ali's older son, Hasan's great-grandson in Morocco in 788 CE, which lasted till 974 CE. The most successful and widespread Shia dynasty, however, was the Fatimid, named after the Prophet's daughter, Fatima. Founded in 909, it lasted till 1171. The area under the control of the Fatimid Caliphate extended from Egypt to Persia.[28]

---

[25]Nasr, *The Shia Revival*, p. 41.

[26]Ibid.

[27]Hourani, *A History of the Arab Peoples*, p. 32.

[28]Rafiq Zakaria, 'The Shi'ite Experiment', *The Struggle Within Islam: The Conflict Between Religion and Politics*, New Delhi: Penguin Books, 1990.

Now the rival empires competed for the control of the Muslim mind beyond their borders. The easiest way to accomplish this was through the administration of the two holiest Islamic sites of pilgrimage, Mecca and Medina, which all Muslims aspired to visit at least once in their lifetime. Traditionally, the caliph or Amir ul Momineen, the leader of the faithful, had control of the religious sites. So the Fatimids and the Abbasids frequently clashed over control of Mecca and Medina. Though the Fatimid empire reigned over most of north Africa and parts of the Middle East, including Syria and Iraq between 910 to 1171 CE, it is not clear for how long it had jurisdiction over the holy shrines of Mecca and Medina.

'The institution of the caliphate degraded to such an extent after the assassination of Ali that there was a period when three parallel dynasties claimed it,' says Professor Mohammed Ishaque, head of department, Islamic Studies, Jamia Millia Islamia.[29]

Moreover, to retain religious and moral superiority over their political rivals, each of these dynasts promoted a more puritanical and rigid form of Islam as the true Islam. This mutual intolerance also widened the gap between Sunnis and Shias to the extent that increasingly radical Sunnis started denouncing Shias as un-Islamic or kafirs.

'The difference between Shias and Sunnis started with the dispute over Hazrat Ali's rightful claim to the caliphate,' says Maulana Jawad, 'but over the centuries it became a full-fledged sectarian conflict. Of course, we had some theological differences too. We also do not accept the books of Hadith written by Sunni scholars. And we have our own schools of jurisprudence.'[30]

The fundamental theological difference between the two is about the concept of prophethood and its succession. Sunnis believe that Muhammad was the medium for the transmission of the religion of Islam from Allah to the Muslims. Once the religion had been revealed, the prophethood ended. Thereafter, believers did not need an intermediary between them and Allah as long they followed the Quran and the

---

[29]In conversation with the author, New Delhi, 5 November 2018.

[30]Interview with the author, Lucknow, 15 December 2018.

traditions of the Prophet. The Shias hold that 'people need the help of exceptionally holy and divinely favoured people in order to live in accord with the inner truths of religion'.[31]

They believe that faith has an outer (zahir) manifestation and an inner (batin) meaning. Religion consists of layers of truth leading to absolute Truth. The inner meaning of religion, its esoteric dimension, can be accessed only through interpretation (ta'wil), and that is the domain of the imams and those who are privy to esoteric knowledge. Shias believe that the Quran contains truths that come from the other world. Only the Prophet and the imams, who like Muhammad are blessed with special knowledge concerning things of God, can interpret those truths.[32]

The Shias believe in the institution of imams or Allah's representatives on earth, all of whom descended from the Prophet's family through his daughter Fatima. According to the Shia belief, Ali was the first imam and his two sons, Hasan and Hussain, were the second and third imams respectively. Unlike the Sunnis, the Shias have a well-defined hierarchical clergy from whom they seek both benediction and direction.

'We believe in taklid (unquestioned acquiescence) of a living marjah (religious leader) like Ayatollah Sistani of Iraq or Ayatollah Khamenei of Iran,'[33] says Maulana Jawad.

Eventually, disagreements started afflicting the small Shia community—who make up about 12 per cent of the total Muslim population—the majority of whom live in Iran, India, and Pakistan. The first major disagreement emerged on the question of succession after Imam Jafar as-Sadiq's death in 765 CE. Jafar as-Sadiq was a towering jurist, regarded highly by both the Sunnis and the Shias.

Says Maulana Jawad, 'Even the leading Sunni jurists like Imam Abu Hanifa, who established the Hanafi school of jurisprudence (followed by the majority of South Asian Muslims), and Imam Malik ibn Anas,

[31]Ayatollah Ja'far Sobhani, Reza Shah-Kazemi (ed. and trans.), *Doctrines of Shi'i Islam: A Compendium of Imami Beliefs and Practices*, London: I. B. Tauris, 2001, pp. 96–119.

[32]Nasr, *The Shia Revival*, p. 52.

[33]Interview with the author, Lucknow, 15 December 2018.

who created the Maliki school of jurisprudence were his disciples.'[34] Jafar as-Sadiq, popularly known as Imam Jafari, established the leading Shia school of jurisprudence called Jafari.

Upon his death, a small group of Shias insisted that his successor should be his oldest son, Ismail ibn Jafar, who they believed had been groomed by his father right from his childhood. However, in his adolescence, Ismail was involved in revolutionary activities with some radical Shias against the Abbasid caliph; to escape prosecution by the government, he went into hiding. A few years later, Ismail died. After Imam Jafar's death, his son Musa al-Kazim succeeded him as the next imam; however, those in favour of Ismail insisted that he was not dead but in hiding.

Swearing allegiance to the Imam-in-hiding Ismail ibn Jafar, this breakaway group of Shias came to be known as Ismailis. Even today, 'The Ismailis continue to believe in the line of Imamat, in hereditary succession, continuing from Ismail to His Highness the Aga Khan, who is their present 49th Imam in direct lineal descent from Prophet Muhammad.'[35]

As the salutation 'His Highness' suggests, over the years, the Ismailis became increasingly cult-like and Westernized. In a series of agreements signed with the Portuguese government in 2005, and thereafter in 2008 and 2009, the current leader, Mawlana Hazar Imam, appointed Lisbon as the Seat of Imamat (his government).

'They had an esoteric bent and became immersed in philosophy and mystical practices, eventually breaking with some of the fundamental teachings of Shiism and even Islam,' writes Nasr.[36] Laila Tyabji, an Ismaili, says, 'We are among the most progressive of the Muslim communities. There has always been enormous emphasis on education for both women and men.'[37]

Over the centuries, more groups splintered from the Ismailis, such as

---

[34]Ibid.

[35]The Ismaili Community, The Ismaili.com, available here: https://the.ismaili/about-us/community

[36]Nasr, *The Shia Revival*, p. 76.

[37]In conversation with the author, New Delhi, 22 March 2019.

the Druze in the Levant, Alawis in Syria, Alevis in Turkey, and Bohras in India.

Headquartered in Mumbai, the tightly-knit Bohra community is even more cult-like than the Ismailis. Each member is watched and accounted for through a centrally-issued identification card. The leadership also collects a tax from the people, to be used for their own welfare. However, as the whole process is opaque, there are often allegations of misappropriation of funds.[38] Leadership among the Bohras is hereditary and currently rests with Syedna Mufaddal Saifuddin.

Syedna Mufaddal Saifuddin is called Da'i al-Mutlaq (the ultimate missionary) and his family members are treated as royalty. Journalist-activist Aarefa Johari, who was born in a Bohra family but now identifies as a non-practising Muslim says, 'We have a single Pope-like leader who people revere and all but worship like a second God...the Syedna's family is called the royal family. His children are called shehzadas (princes) and shehzadis (princesses)[39]. Many Bohras declare with unmistaken pride that they have "blind faith" in the Syedna.'[40]

Hence, decisions of the central leadership on all matters are final and unquestionable. For instance, in 2008, the previous leader, Syedna Mohammed Burhanuddin, decreed that communal kitchens would be established for members of the community, which would supply two meals daily to all households. No households were supposed to cook their own food. The idea behind the order was altruistic. One, it ensured that all members of the community, irrespective of their financial or social status, ate the same kind of food. Two, by making the rich pay higher taxes, the community kitchens subsidized food for the less privileged. And, three, they freed women from the daily chore of cooking so that they could 'devote time for religious activities, focus on children's education or even start small businesses'.[41]

While the thought behind this might have been noble, the order took

[38]Pronoti Datta, 'More than one way to cook a goat', *Roads and Kingdoms*, 5 Dec 2017.
[39]The Ismaili leader Aga Khan's children are also referred to as princes and princesses.
[40]Email interview with the author, 9 January 2019.
[41]'Vijaysinh Parmar, '"Community kitchen" gives Bohra women freedom from cooking', *Times of India*, 15 Feb 2012.

away the free will of individuals. This order was followed by another in 2017, in which the Syedna issued a diktat that people must host weddings in official Bohra halls and use only officially-approved caterers and vendors.

'The diktat came out in November or so, right at the start of the wedding season. A lot of people were forced to cancel already planned functions in secular halls and reschedule them (if possible) in Bohra halls. Several people took major financial hits,' recalls Johari.[42]

Recently, the Syedna issued another order, which is 'reportedly unpopular even among loyal community members'. Syedna Mufaddal has 'commanded Bohras to take leave from offices and schools for the ten days of mourning during Moharram...in order to attend prayers. Attendance is monitored by way of smart cards, issued to all practicing Bohras by the Anjuman-e-Shiate-Ali, an organization run by the spiritual leadership that manages community affairs in Mumbai.'[43] The Bohra leadership does not tolerate dissent. Dissenters are ostracized from the community. This ensures that the control of the leadership remains unchallenged.

However, the biggest problem that the Shias have faced did not come from dissenting believers. It came from the Sunnis, who viewed them as political and theological threats. Given their numerical strength and political power, Sunni caliphates like the Umayyad and the Abbasid not only encouraged violence against the Shias but frequently labelled them as heretics or blasphemers. When Ibn Taymiyyah issued a fatwa for jihad against the Shias[44] in the thirteenth century, violence against them got religious sanction.

For self-preservation, the Shias adopted the doctrine of taqqiyah or dissimulation.[45] They started hiding their identity in areas where they were outnumbered by the Sunnis. Often, generations of Shias would live in a region without revealing their true identity. The origins of

[42]Email interview with the author, 9 January 2019.

[43]Datta, 'More than one way to cook a goat'.

[44]Schwartz, *The Two Faces of Islam*, p. 291.

[45]Nasr, *The Shia Revival*, p. 54.

taqqiyah lay in the challenges of early Muslims in Mecca where, out of fear of the dominant Quraysh tribe, Prophet Muhammad's followers were forced to hide their new faith. But as Sunni dominance grew in subsequent years, the doctrine of taqqiyah became limited to Shias in Sunni lands or in times of armed conflicts, for instance, the Mongol invasions in the thirteenth century.

Even today, Shias who work in Saudi Arabia observe taqqiyah. 'When I and my husband lived in Saudi Arabia,' says historian Rana Safvi, 'we pretended to be Sunni to escape discrimination.'[46]

Gradually, Shia populations converged in pockets of numerical strength. For instance, Yemen, parts of Syria, Iraq, and Iran. Outside the Middle East, the majority of Shias live in India and Pakistan.

Incidentally, the founder of Pakistan, Muhammad Ali Jinnah came from a family of Ismaili Shias, though he converted to Ishna-Ashari Shiism.[47] Upon his death, some of his followers claimed that later in life Jinnah had become a Sunni Muslim.[48] An interesting claim to make, given that Jinnah was at best a non-practising Muslim, if not agnostic. Clearly it was difficult for the Sunni Muslim-dominated nation, increasingly under the sway of puritans like the Jamaat-e-Islami, to accept that the father of the nation was a Shia.

As Sunni Islam got increasingly radicalized in Pakistan, violence against Shias increased. According to the South Asia Terrorism Portal (SATP), 2,693 Shias have been killed in Pakistan in a total of 471 incidents since 2001.[49] Almost all of these incidents have been one-sided killings by Sunni extremists.

In India, while the Shia population was spread all across the country, two pockets of density emerged, one on the Deccan plateau abutting the region of north Karnataka–southwest Telangana and another in

---

[46]Interview with the author.

[47]Khaled Ahmed, 'Was Jinnah a Shia or a Sunni?', *Friday Times*, 24 Dec 2010.

[48]Akbar S. Ahmed, *Jinnah, Pakistan, and Islamic Identity: The Search for Saladin*, London: Routledge, 1997, p. 4.

[49]'Shias killed in Pakistan since 2001', South Asia Terrorism Portal, available here: https://www.satp.org/satporgtp/countries/pakistan/database/Shias_killed_Pakistan.htm

Lucknow. This was because of the establishment of the Bahmani kingdom (1347–1526) in the Deccan and the nawabs of Awadh (1732–1856) in Uttar Pradesh.[50] Since Muslims as a whole faced discrimination in some form or the other in post-Partition India, the Shia–Sunni conflict did not go beyond petty rivalry. The violence between the two has been more a consequence of riots and arson during Muharram processions, localized to Lucknow, where the Shia–Sunni population is nearly evenly matched.

During almost every Muharram, the two sides have indulged in heckling and rioting leading to an imposition of curfew. The local administration in Lucknow has also frequently imposed restrictions on taking out the taziya[51] processions on the tenth day of the month of Muharram, referred to as Ashoura. Sociologists argue that this has more to do with political and economic rivalry than religious discord. Since the royalty in Lucknow was Shia, the community enjoyed royal patronage. However, after the deposition of Nawab Wajid Ali Shah in 1856, select Sunnis were awarded landholdings by the British and consequently emerged as powerful taluqdars.[52] The emergence of conservative Sunni sects like the Deoband and Barelvi added a religious angle to the traditional political–economic rivalry.

Sunnis accuse Shias of being heretic or, worse, kafir. Conservative Sunnis have frequently spread canards about Shias to reinforce prejudice about them. For instance, a few members of my family insisted on not drinking water in a Shia's house because they 'spit in the glass before serving water'. Even going out to watch the taziya procession during Muharram was forbidden as sinful. Meanwhile, to rile the Sunnis, the Shias started abusing the first three caliphs—Abu Bakr, Umar, and Uthman—held sacred by the former. Of late, however, there have been efforts to bridge the Shia–Sunni divide in India.

The Sunni Way

Perhaps because of their numerical strength worldwide and unity of

---

[50]Nasr, *The Shia Revival*, p. 79.

[51]Taziyas are elaborately decorated replicas of the tomb of Imam Hussain.

[52]Kunaal Sharma, 'Ending Lucknow's unholy hatred', *Hindu Business Line*, 13 Jul 2015.

belief, Sunnis did not splinter into too many rival groups globally. The only worldwide faction of some agency and clout is Ahle Hadith, an offshoot of Salafism that emerged from the Wahhabism of Saudi Arabia.

According to the current amir of Ahle Hadith's India chapter (founded in 1906), Maulana Asghar Ali Imam Mahdi Salafi, 'Ahle Hadith only follows the path of the Prophet through Quran and his Hadith. Both of these make it absolutely clear what being a Muslim is and what a Muslim must do to stay on the path of righteousness.' He further says, 'It is only when one tries to apply one's mind to what is clearly stated in the Quran and Hadith or tries to interpret it that distortions occur. That is how different sects have emerged, because they have tried to interpret the Quran and Hadith.'

Maulana Asghar Ali says that believers of Ahle Hadith refer to all the imams of Islam who have written books on Sunni jurisprudence whenever they are in doubt. 'Why must we limit ourselves to just one book of law or the version of just one imam and follow it blindly, when we can refer to all of them and decide what is best for us based on them,' he points out.[53]

In this respect, Ahle Hadith is distinct from both the Barelvi and the Deobandi sects, which follow the Hanafi school of jurisprudence[54]. Ironically, despite these seemingly similar roots, the sectarian scuffling between the Deobandis and the Barelvis in the Indian subcontinent has been unparalleled, with both sides going so far as to calling one another kafir. Not only have they separated their mosques, the Barelvis frequently issue fatawa against both the Deobandis and Ahle Hadith.

Maulana Asghar Ali says, 'Hakim Ajmal Khan[55] is on record saying in a public speech that if one was to put all the fatawa issued by muftis across the world in the 1,400-year-old history of Islam on one hand and those issued in India against Muslims on the other hand, the latter would form a higher pile. Since we have issued no fatwa against other

[53]In conversation with the author, New Delhi, 10 January 2019.

[54]The Islamic schools of jurisprudence have been dealt with in Chapter 4.

[55]A physician of Unani medicine, founder of Tibbia College and co-founder of Jamia Millia Islamia in Delhi, Hakim Ajmal Khan was also closely associated with M. K. Gandhi during the freedom struggle.

sects, all of them have been issued by the other two, and mainly by the Barelvis.'

While the Ahmadiyyas[56] call themselves an Islamic sect, all Muslims (both Sunnis and Shias) insist that they cannot be called one because they have refused to accept the very fundamental principle of Islam: khatm-e-nabuwat (the end of prophethood). The Ahmadiyyas do not consider Muhammad the last prophet. This puts them beyond the pale. According to the Quran, Muhammad is the last prophet and there is no contesting this issue.

In popular perception, the difference between Deobandis and Barelvis appears to hinge on the Deobandis' disapproval of visiting the shrines of Sufis and Auliyas, whereas Barelvis revere them. But according to Maulana Abdurrahim Nashtar Faruqui of Raza Foundation, Bareilly, the difference between the two sects is fundamental and theological, and therefore unbridgeable.

'The Deobandis say that Allah is capable of lying. For us it is unacceptable to accuse Allah of lying or to attribute any negative characteristics to him.' They also say that if thoughts of Prophet Muhammad come up during namaz, that is a terrible thing. 'These two [beliefs] are reasons enough for them to be cast aside as non-believers,' he concludes.[57]

Armed with these two contentious claims, Ahmed Raza Khan Barelvi, who founded the Barelvi sect in the early twentieth century, went to Mecca in 1906. He convinced a group of Arab and Turk ulema to issue a fatwa known as 'Husamul Haramain' or sword of the faith against disbelievers, declaring the leading scholars of Darul Uloom Deoband as kafir. And that is where the conflict began.

---

[56]Like all other sects, the Ahmadiyya sect started as a reformist, puritan movement meant to cleanse Islam of external influences in the late twentieth century. At some point, its founder, Mirza Ghulam Ahmad (1835–1908), started to call himself the divinely ordained Mahdi, who, according to some Islamic beliefs, is supposed to come just before qayamat, or the end of the world. The sect has largely remained localized to the Punjab province of the Indian subcontinent.

[57]In conversation with the author, Bareilly, 11 November 2018.

Holding the Turf

Despite being a sect that claims the allegiance of 80 per cent of South Asian Muslims, Dargah Aala Hazrat[58], the tomb of Ahmed Raza Khan Barelvi, is housed in a small, nondescript building.

'Your car cannot come here,' I was told by the person who was explaining how I could get there. 'You will have to take a rickshaw or walk from the main road.'

I started walking. The lane, lined with shops selling a whole variety of items from milk products to groceries, became narrower and more uneven. Smaller lanes started to sprout on either side, adding to the confusion. Finally, I spotted a cycle rickshaw squeezing its way towards me. After a jerky ten-minute ride, the cycle rickshaw stopped at an opening of sorts where the lane bifurcated. The shops here displayed rose petals and white sugar candies. I had reached my destination, it seemed. Disembarking from the cycle rickshaw I looked around. There was no dargah in sight, no crowd jostling to get in, no rows of lined-up footwear, and hardly any beggars.

I wondered if I had been tricked. Spotting my confusion, a shopkeeper helpfully called out. 'You can leave your shoes here.'

'But where is the dargah?' I wanted to know.

He pointed to the receding backs of two women who had just entered a doorway to his right.

Is that the dargah? I insisted.

He nodded.

Buying a small bag of rose petals, I took off my shoes and hurried behind the two women. The narrow doorway with black shutters opened into a closed corridor that led to a small ante room. Placed perpendicular to each other were two tombs; at the foot of each, the women who had preceded me were sitting. The stillness of the room forbade speech. I looked from tomb to tomb trying to judge by their grandeur which could be the grave of Ahmed Raza Khan Barelvi.

By this time the women had stopped their ministrations and were

[58]Aala roughly translates to best or incomparable. Ahmed Raza Khan is reverentially referred to as Aala Hazrat.

looking at me. One of them beckoned me close with a gesture. She pointed towards the curtain in the middle of the room, which I hadn't noticed.

'Pull the curtain slightly aside and extend your hand,' she whispered.

I drew the curtain aside and exposed an iron grille. On the other side of the grille was a bigger hall. At the head of the room I spotted an elaborately decorated tomb under a canopy. An elderly man was sitting next to the grille with several baskets of rose petals. My brashness surprised and alarmed him. He quickly grabbed the bag of petals from me and hissed, 'Draw back the curtain.'

Taken aback, I meekly obeyed and stepped back. But curiosity got the better of me. Drawing the curtain apart a wee bit, I peered in once again. There were a few men on the other side of the grille. Barring two or three, who appeared to be visitors, the rest seemed to be caretakers, involved as they were in various chores. The elderly man noticed my insolence and nearly lunged at the grille. I quickly pulled back. The women were staring at me, their expressions a mix of horror and amusement.

I hung around that cloistered room trying to figure out what to do next. I felt no urge to sit there and hug the tombs like the two women. I didn't even know whose tombs they were and why they deserved reverence, given that the main tomb was out of bounds for women.

Several dargahs forbid women from entering the main shrine. Some argue that it is because menstruating women are deemed impure and their presence defiles the sanctity of the shrine. Others insist that the restriction stems from the Islamic injunction of purdah or the segregation of the sexes. This argument is based on the notion that the spirit of the departed saint remains in the vicinity of the tomb. Hence, the presence of a 'na mehram'[59] woman inside the shrine is against the principles of purdah.

When I was growing up, my family observed no such regulations.

[59]A mehram is a person with whom marriage is forbidden, for instance, parents, siblings, first uncles and aunts, one's own children or those the woman may have suckled. A woman does not observe purdah in their presence. Conversely, a na mehram is a person with whom marriage is permissible, hence women need to observe segregation from everyone who falls into this category, starting from one's first cousins to the rest of the world.

The only restriction was on the 'days' women menstruated. During our family picnics to Fatehpur Sikri with my grandfather, my aunts sometimes made excuses for not visiting the shrine of Sheikh Salim Chishti, which was always our first stop. My aunts were adults and they could be left behind while everyone else went inside. However, when my cousin and I reached puberty, nobody would heed our excuses if we happened to go to Fatehpur Sikri during our periods—imagine feeling well enough for the picnic but not for saying a quick prayer at the shrine! For such occasions, my mother had a piece of advice for me: 'Ask Sheikh sahib for forgiveness in your prayers. He will understand that you entered the shrine because you had no choice.' That was the Islam of my childhood!

In Bareilly, they took no such chances—the segregation began right at the entrance.

'We discourage women from coming to the dargah,' explains Maulana Faruqui, whose office overlooks the dargah. In addition to being an informal spokesperson of the Imam Ahmed Raza Trust which runs the dargah, Faruqui edits its monthly publication called *Mahanama Sunni Duniya*; he is also one of directors of Jamiatur Raza Centre for Islamic Studies, which is run by the trust.

He offers an entirely new argument against women coming to dargahs. 'You see, wherever women go, they create a whole marketplace because they indulge in a lot of shopping. You would have noticed rows of flourishing shops at other dargahs, which encourages all kinds of people and activities. The whole experience of the dargah is reduced to a spectacle. We don't want that to happen here,' he says.

'Why doesn't this logic apply to men?' I want to know.

'Men are careful spenders unlike women, because they are conscious of the hard work they put in to earn money. Whoever earns will not spend as carelessly as those who don't earn,' he says casually, and then noticing my perturbed expression quickly adds, 'Even my son is a spendthrift. He doesn't think twice before making a purchase.'

Finally, he offers a weak excuse: 'I know not everyone will agree with me.'[60]

---

[60]Interview with the author, Bareilly, 11 November 2018.

Ahmed Raza Khan (who added Barelvi to his name to indicate his place of birth which subsequently became the name of the movement) was born in 1856 into a Pashtun family that had immigrated to India from Afghanistan. His adolescent years were spent watching the aftermath of India's First War of Independence in 1857, in which the Rohillas of Bareilly under Khan Bahadur Khan Rohilla played an active role. Khan Bahadur Khan was eventually hanged in public after the British crushed the revolt. Ahmed Raza Khan heard stories about large-scale massacres of Muslims by the British and probably saw the abjectness of Muslims around him. They were a defeated people, powerless and susceptible to the influences of other religions. Moreover, with British power sweeping unchecked across India, it was normal for many people to convert to the faith of the rulers to secure not just life but a future too! This deeply worried Ahmed Raza Khan as it did a few others.

'Once the rebellion was crushed, the British turned their attention towards the Muslim ulema who were viewed as thought leaders,' Maulana Mahmood Madani, general secretary, Jamiat Ulama-i-Hind told me in his office at ITO, New Delhi. 'The purpose was two-fold. One, by removing the ulema, the British hoped to remove those who could provide moral guidance to the beleaguered community; and two, it would remove the primary obstacle in the way of their missionary work. Hence, they carried out wholesale slaughter of the religious leaders.' According to him, over the next few years, the situation had deteriorated to such an extent in some districts that the Muslim dead were buried without janazas (funeral processions) and namaz-e-janazas. 'There was no one left to carry the bier,' he said.[61]

'Not only was the Muslim government thrown out but a multitude of Muslim leaders and scholars were beheaded, gunned down, and even hanged,' Maulana Muhammadullah Khalili Qasmi, spokesperson and head of the internet department, Darul Uloom, Deoband, told me in an email interview. 'The Muslim monuments, mosques, madrassas, and institutions were razed and set ablaze. Nearly all the Muslim educational places which used to survive on the endowments of Muslim rulers and

---

[61]In conversation with the author, New Delhi, 15 November 2018.

nawabs ceased to exist. The entire Muslim culture and Islamic heritage was on [the] verge of...perishing.'

While most of the people were worried about staying alive, 'There were few fortunate ulema who escaped the deadly reprisal.... They did not sit back quietly. Though they were defeated on the battlefield, they did not spare hope to preserve the Muslim honour and Islamic heritage entrusted to them by their elders and ancestors. So, they planned to start an Islamic seminary (madrassa) in Deoband with public contributions and cooperation,' Maulana Muhammadullah explained.[62]

From their perspective, this was of critical importance because India had been the crowning glory of Islam for many centuries. Eventually, one Muslim scholar found a willing pupil and started teaching him about Islam under a pomegranate tree in 1867, about 150 kilometres north of Delhi in Deoband. Gradually, more students joined. Some local Muslims collected funds to run the madrassa 'to save the religion of Islam'[63].

Once both numbers and funds increased, the locals decided to invite Maulana Muhammad Qasim Nanautavi[64]—a reputed scholar of Islam who had escaped British reprisals—to establish a proper centre of Islamic learning in Deoband. Nanautavi, along with his junior colleague Rashid Ahmad Gangohi[65], and several others like Syed Muhamad Abid Deobandi, Maulana Muhammad Yaqub Nanautavi, Maulana Rafiuddin Deobandi, Maulana Zulfiqar Ali Deobandi, and Maulana Fazlur Rahman Usmani Deobandi established Madrassa Arabi Deoband. As the number of pupils increased, the madrassa moved from the smaller mosque to the larger one in Deoband, until it was able to raise adequate funds to create

---

[62]Email interview with the author, 6 March 2018.

[63]Maulana Mahmood Madani, in conversation with the author, New Delhi, 15 November 2018.

[64]Originally from Saharanpur town in Uttar Pradesh, Maulana Nanautavi studied at Madrassa Ghaziuddin Khan (also known as Delhi College) in the walled city of Delhi. The madrassa eventually grew into the present-day Zakir Husain College. Nanautavi was one of the rebels of the 1857 revolt that was considered a jihad. He operated in Thana Mandi and Shamli towns of UP. After defeat of this jihad, he went back to propagation of Islam.

[65]He also studied at Delhi College.

its own infrastructure. Land was procured and a full-time madrassa was established, which eventually grew into Darul Uloom, an Islamic seminary akin to an Islamic university in terms of its curriculum and student strength.

But with scholars like Nanautavi, Gangohi, and Muhammad Ashraf Ali Thanawi[66] at the helm, merely educating Muslim children was not going to be the aim. As the institution grew, so did its ambition. And saving the religion of Islam meant chiselling out a puritanical faith by ridding it of extraneous influences. For instance, in India, after centuries of cohabitation with Hindus, Muslims—a majority of whom had converted from Hinduism or animism—had reverted to the culture and superstitions of their ancestors[67]. Even though they called themselves Muslims, and intellectually accepted the concept of tawheed[68] or unity of God, emotionally they couldn't help but cling to holy symbols and

[66]Thanawi had become so renowned a scholar that, even during his lifetime, his lectures on Islam were frequently compiled and published. Even today, his book *Bahishti Zewar* (Heavenly Ornaments) forms part of a Muslim woman's trousseau, handed down from mother to daughter. My mother's well-thumbed and frequently-referred-to hardcover is now a mess of loose pages held together by staples.

[67]Even today, do-gooder Muslims believe that it is their religious duty to ensure that illiterate Muslims (and poor converts) are given a proper Islamic education. 'It pains me to see that these blighted vegetable and fruit vendors are Muslims only in name. They can't even recite the Kalimah properly,' a lady who tried to rope me into her group of 'evangelist' Muslims told me. Her Islamic 'kitty group' has hired a hafiz who conducts free Quran classes for the children of these daily wagers. One of the recurring complaints of these well-meaning ladies is that neither the children nor their parents have much interest in religious education. 'They have money to send their children to schools and also pay for private tuitions, but when it comes to Quranic education, they tell me that they can't afford to pay a maulvi,' she said in an attempt to convince me that we should pay for the maulvi.

[68]Tawheed is the first fundamental precept of Islam. It means that there is only one god and that is Allah. He does not have any partner or peer. In practice, it means that a Muslim can only pray to Allah and no one else. Praying to anyone else would amount to shirq, the gravest of all sins. Shirq means sharing Allah's godliness with others. This is why it is said that a true Muslim prostrates only before Allah and no one else. This strict adherence to monotheism is what distinguishes Islam from the two other Semitic faiths, Judaism and Christianity, despite a shared history and near common geography.

even human beings who appeared to offer some sort of panacea for their insecurities.

Hence, most of the Muslims in the Indian subcontinent relied excessively on Sufis and pirs. Such was the preponderance of this faith that the Indian landscape became dotted with innumerable mazars—on the roadsides, in the fields, and even inside homes. For instance, as I have mentioned earlier, the house that I grew up in had a small mazar, dedicated to one Sayyid Badshah. While some people keep a respectful distance from these mazars, not taking any chances with the spirit who was believed to reside there, a large number of Muslims, especially the poor and the illiterate, regard them as places of veneration, an idea that has spawned its own set of rituals and festivals.

Having been brought up and educated in the schools of Islamic theology and philosophy that emerged out of the Arabian peninsula, Egypt, and Persia, people like Nanautavi and Thanawi were appalled at the state of the Indian Muslims and what they saw as the weakness of their faith, just as Shah Waliullah nearly a century ago. The biggest challenge they faced was articulated by Allama Iqbal in his twin long poems titled *Shikwa* and *Jawab-e-Shikwa*[69], albeit several years later. In *Shikwa*, Iqbal pointed out:

Humse pehle tha ajab tere jahan ka manzar
Kahin masjud the pathar, kahin mabood shajar
Khugar-e-paikar-e-mehsoos thi insaan ki nazar
Maanta phir koi andekhe khuda ko kyunkar

(Before our time, a strange sight was the world you had made
Some worshipped stone idols, others bowed to trees and prayed
Accustomed to believing what they saw, the people's vision wasn't free.
How then could anyone believe in a God he couldn't see?)[70]

---

[69]*Shikwa* was written in 1909 as a devout Muslim's plaintive plea to Allah and *Jawab-e-Shikwa* was written in 1913 as Allah's response to the Muslims.

[70]Translation from Khushwant Singh, *Shikwa and Jawab-i-Shikwa: Iqbal's Dialogue with Allah*, New Delhi: OUP, 1991.

This supposed limitation of a Muslim's understanding of his own religion was compounded by the fact that year after year more people were embracing Islam and learning about their faith from half-learned mullahs and neighbourhood pirs, thereby causing further distortions, or what is termed as adding bid'ah[71], to the faith that was perfected by Prophet Muhammad in Medina[72].

On its website, Ahle Hadith lists that one of its objectives is to 'oppose polytheism, innovations in religious matters (bidat), blind imitations and reject many practices prevalent among the mystics (Sufiyas) of this day as un-Islamic accretions.'[73] These are objectives it shares with all Islamic reformist movements.

Like the Wahhabi and Barelvi movements, Ahle Hadith also claims to be following the true form of Islam as revealed to Prophet Muhammad. Its website says 'Ahle Hadeeth exist (sic) with the existence of Islam. In every part of the world wherever is Muslim population. They exist in India from time Muslims came to the country (sic).'

As each lays claim to the truth, it becomes imperative for them to denounce others as misguided or even un-Islamic. Yet, at the heart of this conflict lies—what one senior Kashmiri bureaucrat described to me nearly a decade ago when Islamic sectarianism was threatening to invade Kashmiri streets as in Pakistan (where extremist groups aligned to either the Deobandi or Barelvi sects frequently spill each other's blood on the streets)—the battle of the pulpit.

He said, 'They all make competing claims to garner more followers, more funding, mainly from Saudi Arabia, and to wield more political influence.'[74] He had a point. While the Barelvis claim the adherence of 80 per cent of South Asian Muslims worldwide, the Ahle Hadith say that in India alone '25 to 30 million Muslims' believe in their creed.

---

[71]Religious innovation, i.e. practices that were not integral to Islam but were added subsequently, either deliberately or through ignorance.

[72]Medina was the city Prophet Mohammad escaped to (Hijrah) from Mecca and where he established Islam. It is regarded as the only true Islamic state by Muslims, hence an ideal worth aspiring to or emulating.

[73]See here: https://www.ahlehadees.org/markazi-jamiat-ahle-hadees-hind/

[74]Pravin Sawhney and Ghazala Wahab, 'Battle of the Pulpit', *FORCE*, May 2011.

The Seat of Deobandis

The Deobandis on the other hand make no overt claims of popularity and strength. This is probably because their intellectual influence on the Muslim mind is the strongest, not merely through Darul Uloom, but also through the literature they produce. From a nondescript beginning in 1867, the sprawling Darul Uloom complex is a mini township today. It has the capacity to teach 5,000 resident students at a time, an activity that also fuels the economy of the Deoband village. And yet it continues to be a work in progress.

As I exited the national highway and drove through the huge gates of the Darul Uloom complex, I was overwhelmed by its expanse. There were residential buildings on the left of the road and a vast open ground on the right on which construction of a new complex was underway. Further down the road, the buildings started to hem in closer and the road narrowed as another gate loomed. This gate led to a street of sorts with a huge mosque in front, a bazaar along its periphery, and more construction activity on the far right. I was asked to come to the mehmaan khana (guest house), which was on a narrow street behind the mosque.

As I continued down the narrow road bustling with scholars in kurta pyjamas, another gate appeared. This was more of an architectural feature akin to the Mughal city gates. From a distance it appeared that the car wouldn't be able to squeeze through its narrow opening, but it miraculously did. This led to a small courtyard surrounded by double-storeyed buildings. At the far end was another sandstone gate. Flanking the gate were small rooms marked as vocational training centres. A tailoring class was in progress in one of the rooms.

The gate opened into another narrow lane, with shops on the left and other buildings on the right. The first of these, a three-storey one, was the mehmaan khana, where Maulana Muhammadullah Khalili Qasmi, who had earlier answered some of my questions via email, was waiting to receive me. 'I have got one of the guest rooms opened for you in case you wish to rest,' he said in English as he led me up the flight of stairs. I declined. We sat down in a living room of sorts, a narrow hall with sofas and tables. In a few moments, tea arrived accompanied by biscuits. 'We will have lunch here after your meeting with the mohtamim (the rector),'

Maulana Qasmi informed me helpfully, lest I filled up on biscuits.[75]

As we waited for the rector to summon us, he filled me in on the institution. 'While 5,000 students study here at a time, about 2,000 of them pass out every year, of which only a handful are foreign students.' A large number of foreign students used to attend Darul Uloom but this is no longer the case because of government restrictions. The few foreign students are from Afghanistan, who are permitted to study here under the law. While no Pakistani studies in Darul Uloom, several of its alumni migrated to Pakistan during and after Partition and opened chapters there. In India, 3,000 madrassas are affiliated to Darul Uloom through its madrassa board called Raabta Madaris.

'Everything, education, boarding, and food are free, though some students pay for their food,' said Maulana Qasmi. Darul Uloom runs entirely on zakat (obligatory charity by Muslims). 'Since only the poor are entitled to receive zakat, those who can afford to, pay for their food,' he explained. The majority of the students come from impoverished backgrounds. Darul Uloom regards itself as a premier school of Islamic studies hence it has no bilateral agreements with any other Islamic institution, including the famed Al-Azhar of Egypt. 'Those who complete their doctoral studies at Darul Uloom are as good as the best in the world,' Maulana Qasmi claimed.

Finally, we received word that the mohtamim Mufti Abul Qasim Nomani was ready for us. His office complex was a short distance away. It was as nondescript as the rest of the buildings on the campus. The visitors' room on the first floor was large and had several sofas in it. Within moments of our entering the room, Mufti Nomani strode in briskly. A reedy man in his seventies, attired entirely in white with the exception of a grey-and-white chequered scarf on his shoulders, Mufti Nomani exuded no airs that denoted his power or position. He settled down on a sofa and smiled broadly, looking like an indulgent patriarch rather than a religious leader with rigid, unswerving views.

Pleasantries over, he nudged gently, 'You have some questions I believe.'

---

[75]Interview with the author, Darul Uloom, Deoband, 23 November 2018.

I asked him why Deoband was synonymous with Islamic extremism.

'It is nothing but propaganda which was started by the British to weaken the Indian freedom struggle by creating fissures in the movement. After all, the ulema of Deoband were at the forefront of the freedom struggle. We worked alongside Gandhiji,' he explained. According to him, the British were facing trouble in Arabia because of the Wahhabi hardliners who were trying to establish their control over the whole country. The British termed them extremists and bigots. Hence, when they were faced with ulema in India, they equated them with religious leaders in Arabia and the perception grew that the Deobandis were ideologically similar to Wahhabis.

Even though Wahhabism as a reformist movement started in the mid-eighteenth century, and had started forcing its extremist beliefs on the Arabian people, it came to the world's notice in 1925, when people claiming allegiance to the sect razed to the ground the house and mosque built by Prophet Muhammad. Their objection was that Muslims had started to revere these as holy places, which amounted to idol worship, hence bid'ah.[76] Earlier, in 1924, the Wahhabis had entered into an agreement of coexistence with Abdul Aziz ibn Saud, who after a twenty-three-year-long campaign had managed to unite the warring tribes of Arabia and had fashioned a nation after his name—Saudi Arabia.[77] (More on this in the next chapter.)

'Are they not similar?' I asked.

'This is a complex question. We are similar as far as our core religious beliefs are concerned. But unlike the Wahhabis, we are not intolerant of differing views. We encourage discussion. Most importantly, we believe in moderation, because the Quran itself urges us to be moderate,' he said.

To further underline the difference, Mufti Nomani gave the example of Maulana Shabbir Ahmed Usmani's 1925 visit to Saudi Arabia at the invitation of Sultan Abdul Aziz ibn Saud to debate the position of tombs

[76]George S. Rentz, *The Birth of the Islamic Reform Movement in Saudi Arabia: Muhammad Ibn Abd al-Wahhab (1703/4-1792) and the Beginnings of Unitarian Empire in Arabia,* London: Arabian Publishing Ltd., 2004, p. 139.
[77]Schwartz, *The Two Faces of Islam,* Chapter 4.

and heritage sites associated with the Prophet under Islamic law. The Wahhabis, whose unforgiving version of Islam was accepted as the Saudi state religion, were determined to destroy all tombs as they considered them un-Islamic. They wanted to stop the practice of Muslim pilgrims at Mecca and Medina visiting and praying at these sites.

According to Mufti Nomani, 'It was because of Maulana Usmani's efforts that the Wahhabis did not destroy Islamic heritage sites.'

Maulana Nomani pointed to the absence of terrorists in India who claim allegiance to Deoband. 'This is the centre of our learning. If we were teaching extremist thinking, wouldn't there be Indian extremists? After all, almost all our students are Indian,' he said, refusing to comment on the Taliban or extremists in Pakistan. 'These are region-specific and politically motivated issues.'

I then asked him about the Barelvis calling the Deobandis kafir.

'That is the foundation of their existence. The Barelvis' identity is based upon their hatred of other Muslims. If they didn't do that, they would have no reasons to exist.'

But how did Ahmed Raza Khan manage to impose a fatwa against Deoband scholars like Nanautvi, Gangohi, and Thanawi?

'Do you know that the fatwa doesn't hold any longer, that it was revoked?' Mufti Nomani countered. 'Ahmed Raza Khan picked up a few lines out of context from our different books, highlighted them, and took them to Arabia. At that time, the caliphate was with the Turks. Their officials in Mecca could not understand Urdu, so Ahmed Raza Khan translated those lines into Arabic, which were further translated into Turki. Who knows what he said? Based on his translations, the fatwa was issued. However, the Turk ulema realized their folly of issuing the fatwa without representation from Deoband. They sought clarification from us. Maulana Khalil Ahmed Saharanpuri represented our case to them and the fatwa was revoked. After all, only I can talk about my faith, others cannot.'

According to him, the Barelvi allegations are simplistic and non-intellectual. As Islamic thought started to grow, several schools of thought emerged, of which the Ashari and Maturdi schools of the tenth century were the most popular and became the basis on which Islamic creed was formulated. These thinkers started debates on the nature of divinity, revelations, asking if that alone should be the basis of faith or whether believers should apply rational thought to the revelations.

'One of the issues that was fiercely debated was the nature of God, leading to the theory of possibility,' Mufti Nomani explained. 'If Allah is all-seeing, all-knowing and capable of everything and if nothing happens without Allah's will, then even the bad that happens, happens because of his will.... Now he may be allowing bad things to happen for reasons beyond our comprehension, but that does not mean that he is not capable of stopping them from happening. The comment on Allah being capable of lying was made in a similar context by one of the theologians. But the Barelvis reduced this debate to a single line: that our books say that Allah lies,' he said, murmuring 'Nauozobillah' under his breath. Muslims utter 'Nauozobillah' seeking forgiveness from God if they are forced to say something disrespectful about Allah.[78]

The issue of namaz was similar. One pays obeisance to Allah by offering the namaz. Hence, one should only think about Allah during namaz. If one's mind gets distracted and worldly thoughts occur, it is not an issue because none of these are objects of one's prayer.

The other points of contention between the two groups involve the qualities and capabilities of the Prophet himself. Like the Wahhabis, the scholars at Deoband believe that Prophet Muhammad was a human being of exceptional qualities and personal character who was made more special because Allah chose him to be the last prophet of Islam. But there was no doubt he was human.

The Barelvis, on the other hand, believe that Prophet Muhammad was no ordinary human being that Allah created from dust like everybody else. He was created from Nur, the celestial light. And Allah blessed him with the ability not only to see the past but also know the future. 'We believe that the Prophet had knowledge over things we don't,' Maulana

---

[78]'Do the scholars of Deoband believe that Allah can lie?', Darul Ifta, 24 Sep 2013, available here: https://daruliftabirmingham.co.uk/do-the-scholars-of-deoband-believe-that-allah-can-lie/

Faruqui of the Raza Trust had told me earlier.[79] What's more, he was both haazir and naazir (omnipresent and omniscient)[80].

Today, the Barelvi sect considers the Deobandi sect its biggest adversary. However, when Ahmed Raza Khan started his movement, the immediate aim was to curtail the influence of Sufis[81] and rid the dargahs of what he considered un-Islamic practices of music (qawwalis) and going into a trance (haal). In that respect, he was closer to the Wahhabi and Deobandi approaches to Islam than he would have liked.

Maulana Faruqui had said to me that the Barelvis don't object to people going to dargahs. 'We only object to the tamasha (spectacle) that goes on there.' This is exactly what the Deobandis claim, too. According to *The Maslak of Ulama of Deoband*:

> ...the Auliyaa and Sufia are like the soul of the Ummat.... the Ulama of Deoband regard Muhabbat and honour for them to be incumbent for the preservation of Imaan. However, excessiveness in Muhabbat should not lead one to deitise them. Whilst respect and honour for them is necessary it should not be translated into acts of worship, where people prostrate at their graves, circumambulate around their graves... Their graves should not be made venues of festivities. Singing and dancing should not be a part of their remembrance occasions.[82]

And therein lies the irony. While the Barelvi movement was started to cleanse the dargahs of un-Islamic practices, it ended up creating a personality cult which, unlike the Islamic practice of ijma, is hereditary. Ahmed Raza Khan, or Aala Hazrat, was succeeded by his son, Hujjatul Islam, in 1921. After his death, his son, Muffasir-e-Azam, became the leader of the sect in 1943, followed by his son, Tajushariya, in 1981. None of these are given names; these are self-assumed, exalted titles. For

[79]Interview with the author, Bareilly, 11 November 2018.

[80]Maulana Yusuf Ludhyanwi, *Differences in Ummat and Sirat-e-Mustaqeem*, Deoband Publication, pp. 17–21.

[81]The issue of why all reformist Islamic sects had problems with Sufism is dealt with in Chapter 2.

[82]Maulana Qaari Muhammad Tayyib, *The Maslak of Ulama of Deoband*, Karachi: Zam Zam Publishers, 2010, p. 12.

instance, Hujjatul Islam means proof of Islam. Muffasir-e-Azam means interpreter of the world. Tajushariya means the crown of Shariah.

Tajushariya institutionalized the sect by creating the Imam Ahmed Raza Trust in 2000. The trust runs the Jamiatur Raza Centre of Islamic Studies, publishes books, and works towards 'Islamic reforms', according to Maulana Shakeel, the principal of the Jamaitur Raza. Tajushariya passed away in 2018, and has been succeeded by his son, Maulana Asjad Raza Khan.

In the summer of 2018, I had called Maulana Asjad Raza Khan on his mobile. He answered the phone and fixed a meeting with me in Bareilly two weeks later. However, I had to postpone my visit by a few months. When I called to inform him about this, he told me quite pleasantly to get in touch whenever I was in Bareilly. In the meantime, his father, Tajushariya, passed away and he became the head of the sect. When I tried calling him in the autumn of 2018 to fix a meeting, he did not answer his phone. Finally, somebody answered on his behalf and I was told to meet Maulana Faruqui and Maulana Shakeel.

During my meeting with Maulana Faruqui, I repeatedly requested him to arrange a meeting with Maulana Asjad Raza Khan. But he continued to stonewall me for a time. Finally, as I refused to relent, he called Maulana Asjad Raza Khan in my presence and told him that I wanted to pay my respects to him—haaziri dena chahateen hain. I interrupted, saying that I wanted to talk to him about the Barelvis and not merely pay my respects. Once he finished the call, Maulana Faruqui informed me that every evening Maulana Khan had an open house for his followers, and I could go to that if I wanted. He looked visibly uncomfortable while conveying this to me. I thanked him but chose not to go to the open meeting.

◆

Notwithstanding the ongoing strife between the two schools of Sunni Islam, most Sunni Muslims, even in the Indian subcontinent, do not identify themselves as either Barelvi or Deobandi. Maulana Dr Saeedur Rahman Azmi Nadvi, mohtamim of Darul Uloom Nadwatul Ulama of Lucknow, confirmed this in a conversation with me. 'The majority of

Muslims in India do not identify themselves as Deobandi, Barelvi, or Ahle Hadith. It is only when somebody wants to pursue Islam as a vocation that he or she is drawn to these sects. As it is important for these sects to have numbers on their side, their ulema reach out to people in their areas, mainly the poor and vulnerable, to tell them that only they can show them the path of true Islam,' he says.[83]

Most Muslims follow the traditional practices of their families. For instance, my family, including the conservative members, did not identify with any sect. Now that some of them consult mullahs on a regular basis, a sense of exclusivism has crept in. Some disapprove of the practice of going to dargahs, and a few have started to speak the language of the Barelvis.

Darul Uloom Nadwatul Ulama is a non-sectarian Islamic seminary which also started in the early twentieth century. Located next to Lucknow University, it has a capacity of 3,000 resident students, of which 300 seats are earmarked for foreign students, mainly from countries such as Nepal, Thailand, Malaysia, China, Indonesia, and even the United Kingdom. They also have a network of 300 madrassas worldwide. The most interesting part about Nadwa is that unlike seminaries run by the Deobandi and Barelvi, education here is not free. Each pupil is charged a monthly fee of ₹1,100.

Mufti Mohammed Sarwar Farooqui, head of the research department at Nadwa, justifies the fees. 'We are producing extremely learned and Islamically-sound, non-parochial ulema. Why shouldn't we charge them for this education?' he asks.[84] Nadwa combines Islamic education with regular liberal arts subjects as well as general sciences. Hence, quite a few of their students are able to successfully transition into the mainstream, including into the Indian administrative services.

In the last few years, as sectarian violence among Muslims has increased in other parts of the world, an awareness has started to grow among the Indian ulema that too much focus on puritanism and exclusivism could lead to violence and killings in India too. The rise of the

[83]In conversation with the author, Lucknow, 15 December 2018.
[84]Ibid.

Hindu right wing has been another factor that has prompted attitudinal changes. Sectarian Hindu organizations have also been reaching out to 'amenable' Muslims to further divide the beleaguered community. For instance, one Shia group broke ranks with other Indian Muslim organizations in 2018 to assert that it supported the construction of a Ram temple at the site of demolished Babri Masjid.[85]

Given these various pressures, all three major Sunni sects have been making efforts to reach out to each other, and have held their peace with the Shias. Even if there is no way to completely ignore their differences, they can at least stop labelling one another as un-Islamic, especially when targeted violence against Muslims has been on the rise since 2014.

'We started this process of bringing everyone on the same platform for the first time when we held an international conference against terrorism in 2006,' says Maulana Asghar Ali of Ahle Hadith.[86] Thereafter Jamiat Ulama-i-Hind organized a few meetings with representatives from other groups. 'We are trying to bring all sects together and the first step towards that is attending each other's functions,' says Maulana Madani.[87] Maulana Jawad concurs. 'Opportunistic politics fanned sectarianism over the years. However, today there are more reasons to be united despite our differences. After all, the core belief of all Muslims is the same,' he says.[88]

Now if only they could collectively address the issue of radicalization, which comes in the way of independent and progressive thinking, they would make a meaningful contribution to the lives of Indian Muslims. Given that there is no 'one' truth in Islam, it wouldn't really hurt the ulema to accept that perhaps there could be many ways to interpret Quranic injunctions, as long as the 'core belief' remains in place. After all—to appropriate Faiz Ahmed Faiz's verse—Aur bhi dukh hain zamane mein mazhab ke siwa (There are more worries in the world than religion.)[89]

---

[85]'Willing to donate Muslim part of Ayodhya land for Ram temple: Shia Waqf Board tells SC', *Hindustan Times,* 13 Jul 2018.

[86]In conversation with the author, New Delhi, 10 January 2019.

[87]In conversation with the author, New Delhi, 15 November 2018.

[88]Ibid.

[89]The original verse is 'Aur bhi dukh hain zamane mein mohabbat ke siwa' (There are more worries in the world than love alone).

4

ISLAM, TABLIGH, AND JAMAAT

Observing the full forty-day mourning after my grandfather's death in 1985 required, in addition to patience, imagination to ensure there was at least one communal activity every week in which family members and visitors could participate in remembrance of the deceased.

Since he died in our home, my mother had to shoulder most of the responsibility of hosting these memorial services, which ranged from a group recital of the Quran, called Quran Khwani, to sessions of Islamic preaching called milad, in which learned people with expertise in religious recital were invited to deliver sermons on Islam. The milad was an all-men or all-women affair, never a mixed one, though in all-men sessions, women could listen to the sermons from behind the curtains. Milad combined sermons with poetry in praise of Prophet Muhammad and concluded by sending a greeting to the Prophet, called salaam, and by reciting specific verses called durood—this sends blessings to the Prophet and his family.

Revisionist Islamists like the Wahhabis and Deobandis (in India) consider these post-death mourning rituals as unnecessary and even un-Islamic. The milad, for instance, is considered bid'ah or an innovation.[1] But in those days, nobody in my family, and perhaps in other families too, had heard the term bid'ah. What's more, even the neighbourhood hafizji, who presided over most of these rituals, was unaware of the concept of

[1]The Deobandi as well the Salafi/Wahhabi school favour Tablighi Jamaat's ijtima over milad, which comprises sessions of conservative Islamic preaching without poetry or music. Some of the ijtimas are organized on a very large scale. They are advertised in advance and sometimes carry on for a couple of days. For instance, the ijtima in Bulandshahr in December 2018, which was followed by an incident of rioting by Hindu right-wing activists, and led to the killing of the police officer Subodh Kumar Singh, was held over three days and was attended by nearly 10 lakh Muslims.

innovation in Islam. What mattered to everyone was the intent, which, for those forty days, was driven by love for my grandfather. Such was the power of sentiment that neither I nor my siblings complained that we had been denied the television, for example. There was to be no entertainment for the period of mourning; only essential activities were undertaken, like school for the children, and office and housework for the adults.

The solemnity of the mourning apart, these rituals exposed me to yet another side of Islam, one I hadn't encountered before. Returning from school one afternoon, I found a group of women huddled together in the room designated for these rituals. Though I was not expected to join this purely adult assembly, curiosity got the better of me. Once I had changed into what had become my 'home staple'—a sleeveless midi dress that ended at my knees—and was done with my lunch, I entered the room.

At the far end, facing the door and me, three women were perched on a low couch and addressing a group of over twenty earnest ladies, heads dutifully covered, seated on dhurries on the floor with their backs to me. Though I was only thirteen, I immediately became conscious of the inappropriateness of my attire and attempted to step back.

'Stop where you are,' the leader of the three women ordered. The entire room of women, including my mother, turned to look at the object of that command. I could tell from my mother's expression that she was disappointed to see me. But she didn't know what to do. Should I be asked to come in or leave?

The sermonizer made the decision. I was to remain standing where I was, as an exhibit. 'Look at those two braids resting on her shoulders,' she told her audience, nearly shrieking. 'On the Day of Judgement, two poisonous snakes will dangle on her shoulders. Look at those bare arms. On the Day of Judgement, the skin will be peeled off those naked arms.' By now her voice was almost guttural with emotion. Before she could turn her attention to my legs, my mother interrupted her.

'You should not talk about my daughter like that. She is just a child.'

Since my mother was the paymaster for the day, the sermonizer quickly apologized. 'I didn't realize that she was a child. Of course, these rules do not apply to children, only to adults.'

With this, the matter was settled. I was asked to leave and the sermon continued. I later found out that before arriving at the topic of the Day of Judgement, the lady had spent a good amount of time describing the conditions of the graves and what sort of worms would feast on which part of one's body.

Kabar ka manzar, or description of the grave, is one of the favourite whips with which the mullahs try to keep the flock under control. Perhaps that's the reason why the famous Urdu writer Ismat Chughtai didn't want to be buried. 'I am afraid of [the] grave. So, I have willed to be cremated. My body, mind and heart belong to me and whatever I want will be done,' she wrote to a fellow writer.[2]

When I was growing up, the 'horror of the grave' was one of the subjects that the mullahs spoke of passionately or wrote about in small booklets that one could buy from shops adjoining mosques or dargahs. Once the internet arrived, this formed part of forwarded emails among Muslims. Today, YouTube is the favoured medium. The source of these vivid descriptions is not the Quran, but ancillary texts written several centuries after the death of the Prophet.

'Why did you call those ladies over?' I asked my mother once the milad was over.

'This one was a bit rabid,' my mother agreed. 'But not all are the same. Some are really good. They give very useful information about Islam and how a Muslim should lead her life. Even if we don't follow it in its entirety, it's good to hear these things. They are motivating.'

I wanted to know if there were things that my mother didn't know about Islam.

'How can I know everything when scholars have spent their lives studying Islam and still remain unsure?'

Even now, my mother feels that she doesn't know enough about Islam. And she is not the only one. And this doesn't apply only to the theoretical and esoteric aspects of Islam, which do not impact one's daily life. The problem is that a lot of Muslims feel that they

---

[2]Noor Shah, 'Ismat Chughtai—her life and ideals', *Milli Gazette,* 1–15 Feb 2005.

don't know enough to even lead a regular life, despite following the tenets of Islam and abstaining from the forbidden. While some Muslims have always felt insecure about not being good enough, today, a large number, including the educated, are afflicted by self-doubt. There are two reasons for this.

One, the bar for being a good Muslim has been raised very high. As Maulana Mohammed Shakeel, principal of the Jamiatur Raza, Bareilly, says, 'The only purpose of a Muslim's life is prayer and preparation for his afterlife (aakharat). Of course, as long as he is in this world, he has some societal obligations, too, but these must be fulfilled within the boundaries of Islam.'[3]

General secretary Jamiat Ulama-i-Hind, Maulana Mahmood Madani adds, 'It is true that there is restriction of free will in Islam, because an individual must follow the will of Allah, but the reason it appears that there are a lot of don'ts in Islam is because people do not understand the pleasure of submission. This joy is better than exercising free will. It has to be experienced to be understood.'[4] Since one needs to submit and not exercise free will, there is a constant need to get validation that one is submitting correctly.

And, two, the extremely dogmatic version of Islam that is being disseminated worldwide by Saudi-inspired clerics negates everything that Indian Muslims have traditionally believed about their religious practices. As we've seen, the process started with the return of Shah Waliullah to Delhi, but his reach was geographically limited. Today, the internet can bring this version of Islam to an individual's mobile phone. While it piques one's interest, it also raises questions in the minds of those who seek constant self-improvement in their religious observance.

Some turn to public events like ijtima, others watch television or YouTube preachers. One of the very well-known South Asian Islamic preachers in recent times is Zakir Naik. He was accused of spreading religious intolerance, fled to Malaysia, and has been declared an absconder

[3]Interview with the author, Bareilly, 12 November 2018.

[4]Interview with the author, New Delhi, 15 November 2018.

by Indian investigation agencies. The case now includes charges of money laundering.[5] An Indian by birth, Naik claims an audience of nearly 200 million worldwide through his television channel, Peace TV. Naik portrays the image of a modern, accessible Muslim who wears western clothes and speaks in English. Yet, what he says comes from a primitive, almost tribal, form of Islam, which subtly conveys a message of intolerance towards other religions by emphasizing the primacy of Islam over other religions. He does this by engaging in televised debates with people from other religious groups or in the format of answering questions on comparative religion in the presence of a live audience. In this lies his appeal. He tells his followers, a multitude of insecure people needing assurance about their greatness, that Islam is the one true religion, superior to all others.[6] It is not enough for them to practise their faith; they also need to hear from supposed 'experts' that they are on the best available path to salvation.

Those who do not tune into Naik's lectures seek direction from other ulema in the form of fatawa or advice. The Darul Uloom Deoband, which disapproves of Naik on the ground that he is too radical, has a separate website where it receives questions from its followers and replies to them. These questions range from the ridiculous to the absurd. For instance, a few years ago, somebody wanted to know if a Muslim could travel by the now defunct Kingfisher Airlines because its owner also ran a company that produced alcoholic beverages. Another person wanted to know if it was permissible to buy second-hand goods which were bought on loan by its original owner who had interest paid on them?[7] Islamic law forbids earning from interest.

The religion of Islam has two primary sources: the Quran as

[5]'Zakir Naik case: ED attaches assets worth ₹16.40 crore under PMLA', *Indian Express*, 19 Jan 2019.

[6]'Is the Islam True Religion If Yes, How Answered By Dr Zakir Naik', YouTube, 5 Mar 2012, available here: https://www.youtube.com/watch?v=oZ-N5MJhiRc; 'If Islam is the best religion, Why Muslims are the worst?—Dr. Zakir Naik', YouTube, 7 Sep 2013, available here: https://www.youtube.com/watch?v=pDJbznuqCLU

[7]Ask a Question, Website of Darul Uloom Deoband India, available here: http://www.darulifta-deoband.com/home/en

revealed by Allah through Archangel Gabriel to Prophet Muhammad over a period of twenty-three years through the process referred to as wahy[8] (divine revelation); the second source is the teachings of Prophet Muhammad by way of speech and action. The art of offering namaz, the manner of fasting during Ramzan, and the way of undertaking hajj in the Islamic month of Dhu al-Hijjah are all examples of the Prophet's Sunnah (teachings) and form part of the Hadith, which, as has been noted, is a compendium of the Prophet's life and times. Between the two, they comprise the entire range of Islamic laws on marriage, divorce, inheritance, trading, etc. They include a list of the permissible and forbidden. They also mention a range of punishments for different sins. Yet, over the centuries, Muslims have felt that these instructions are not enough to lead an Islamic life. Why do they need frequent validation?

Mufti Mohammed Sarwat Farooqui, head of the research department at Darul Uloom Nadwatul Ulama, quotes a Quranic verse before answering.

'He also created' horses, mules, and donkeys for your transportation and adornment. And He creates what you do not know.[9]

'Does this mean that these are the only means of transportation available to Muslims? Should Muslims not travel in cars, trains, or airplanes?' he asks. 'The Quran has given broad guidelines for us. But as the world changes and Muslims are confronted by new challenges every day, they need someone to guide them.'

A trait common to especially devout Muslims is that they prefer the judgement of someone deemed more religiously adept than themselves on a variety of issues; hence the ever-growing industry of fatawa. Never mind that Prophet Muhammad, in his last sermon given in Mecca in 632 CE, told his followers, 'I leave behind me two things, the Quran and my example, the Sunnah, and if you follow these you will never go astray.'[10]

---

[8]Mufti Mohammed Shafi, *Maariful Quran*, p. 1.

[9]Surah An-Nahl, Verse 16:8, translated by Dr Mustafa Khattab (https://quran.com/16).

[10]'Prophet Muhammad's Last Sermon: A Final Admonition', IslamReligion.com, available here: https://www.islamreligion.com/articles/523/prophet-muhammad-last-sermon/

When the Meccans denounced his claims of prophethood and asked him to produce a miracle to prove himself, he is recorded as having proclaimed, 'Before me every Prophet was given a miracle and they practiced it in their lifetime. Isa (Christ) cured the sick and revived the dead. Musa (Moses) was given the cane and I have been given the permanent miracle of the Quran which will remain till the Hour is established.'[11] The Quran—a book so lyrical and mystical that each reading yields a new meaning—was the miracle that Allah gave to Prophet Muhammad.

The seeking of fatawa is a very unique Islamic practice which has no parallel in any other religion. The fatwa is a non-binding piece of advice given by ulema who are authorized to do so. By qualification, he must be a mufti or an expert on Islamic jurisprudence, called figha, an interpretive and codified derivation of Shariah, which comprises basic rules and punishments mentioned in the Quran. Even though fatawa are frequently sought and given by local unqualified mullahs, they have no religious validity. Of course, one can argue that no fatwa has religious validity because it is non-binding, but when issued by a designated authority, it is usually taken seriously. Another aspect of the fatwa is that it can only be sought by the person needing that advice personally. It cannot be sought by a third party out of academic interest. A case in point is journalists seeking fatawa from obscure maulvis for the sake of writing an article! Nor can an imam voluntarily issue a fatwa on a political matter, such as the fatwa of the imam of Delhi's Jama Masjid asking Muslims to vote for a particular political party.[12]

Since fatawa are the raison d'etre of most muftis, they take this role very seriously. Ulema from all over India gather in the Islamic Fiqh Academy in Delhi to confabulate on issues pertaining to Islam and Muslims. Sometimes these discussions form part of the classroom training for aspiring muftis, and sometimes they become subjects for seminars; papers from these seminars are disseminated to different Islamic seminaries.

[11]Dehlvi, *Sufism*, p. 408.

[12]For more on this, see Chapter 6: Minority Politics.

Sects like Ahle Hadith also run a training centre called Darul Ifta, which conducts year-long courses on the technicalities of issuing fatawa. According to the amir of Ahle Hadith, Maulana Asghar Ali Imam Mahdi Salafi, the reason fatawa are complicated is because they are supposed to be the 'considered opinion' of experts based on the Quran, Shariah, Hadith, past precedents, as well as the socio-economic environment of the fatwa-seeker. They cannot be issued either in isolation or verbally. 'The fatwa has to be issued in writing only,' he said.[13] One question can have multiple answers depending on who you ask and under what circumstances.

In essence, the issuing of a fatwa incorporates all the earliest Islamic traditions of ijtihad (interpretation), ijma (consensus), raye (personal judgement or opinion) and qiyaas (analogical reasoning). Of course, this privilege of interpreting the Quran is the domain of a select few. Ordinary Muslims are only supposed to offer taklid (unquestioned acquiescence) to a chosen school of Islamic jurisprudence, for instance, the Hanafi, which is more prevalent in India. This is so because it is believed that the imams who established jurisprudence understood Islam better. Justifying the necessity and importance of taklid, a Deoband publication writes:

> The meaning of Taqleed is to accept the ruling of some reliable and trustworthy person's research without making any investigation into the matter, seeking proofs.... To leave aside the research of the experts of Shariah and for a layman to seek for every ruling by contemplating on the Qur'aan Majeed and Hadith is like the similitude of a person who has a very complicating (sic) illness and he deems it to be below his dignity to refer to the experts in the medical field. So in order to alleviate and solve his problem he purchases the best and most authentic books on the subject of medicine and he relies on his own understanding and research of these books and seeks a cure for his illness. I am quite certain that no intelligent person will resort to such foolishness.[14]

---

[13]Interview with the author, New Delhi, 10 January 2019.

[14]Ludhyanwi, *Differences in Ummat and Sirat-e-Mustaqeem*, p. 14.

All this flies in the face of how Islam was originally designed to be. As a religion, it was meant to be simple to understand and follow and essentially rested on five pillars. It was designed to obviate the need for any intervention or mediation by the clergy, which is why Sunni Islam has not had a formal priestly hierarchy since the end of the caliphate. As the Quranic verse Al-Qamar makes clear: 'And We have certainly made the Quran easy to remember. So is there anyone who will be mindful?'[15]

But no religion is created by prophets alone. The prophets only propagate an idea. In the case of Islam, the Prophet transmitted the Quran from Allah to the Muslims.

Soon after the death of Prophet Muhammad, first his closest companions, and thereafter Islamic scholars, realized that the Quran and Sunnah, which they had inherited from the Prophet, were not enough for the establishment of Allah's kingdom on earth. More, and much more, was required. While the Quran was the word of Allah and included broad guidelines on Islamic law in the form of Shariah, Sunnah was the manner in which various prophets, starting with Adam, put Allah's directives into practice through prayer, pilgrimage, and fasting. These religious practices were not unique to Prophet Muhammad. He only continued what his predecessors had been doing. After all, pilgrimage to Mecca had been established by Abraham.

Gradually, Islamic scholars started adding layer upon layer of complexity with newer texts, such as the Hadith and fiqha, to the faith that was meant for all, irrespective of their literacy or intellectual level. Maulana Madani says, 'Islam implies only two things—Iman (faith) and Amal (action). One's belief in Islam is complete by Iman alone, which means accepting that there is only one God, Allah, and Muhammad is his messenger. Amal involves a list of dos and don'ts, and is secondary to faith.'[16]

Despite this, Darul Uloom, which shares a symbiotic relationship with Jamiat Ulama-i-Hind (the early muftis who emerged from Darul

---

[15]Surah Al-Qamar, Verse, 54:17, translated by Dr Mustafa Khattab (https://quran.com/54).

[16]Interview with the author, New Delhi, 15 November 2018.

Uloom formed the Jamiat as a sociopolitical organization in 1919. As alumnis, these muftis wield enormous influence over the senior faculty of Darul Uloom, including the appointment of the vice chancellor[17]), insists that ordinary people cannot understand and interpret the religion without an expert's guidance. In a Darul Uloom publication *Ma'ariful Quran*, Maulana Mufti Mohammed Shafi writes:

> It is regrettable that a dangerous epidemic has overtaken Muslims lately whereby many people have started taking the sole reading ability of Arabic sufficient for the tafsir (interpretation) of the Qur'an. As a result, anyone who gets to read ordinary Arabic starts passing out opinions in the domain of Qur'anic exegesis. Rather, it has been noticed on occasions that people having just passable familiarity with the Arabic language...take it upon themselves to engage in explaining the Qur'an...even going to the limit of finding faults with classical commentators.... It should be understood very clearly that this is a highly dangerous pattern of behaviour which, in matters of religion, leads to fatal straying. ...should a person simply learn the English language and go on to study books of medical science, he would not be acknowledged as a physician by any reasonable person...and certainly not trustworthy enough to take care of somebody's life unless he has been educated and trained in a medical college. Therefore, having learnt English is not all one needs to become a doctor. [18]

The medical analogy appears to be a favourite argument at Darul Uloom, perhaps because health and illness are universal concerns. However, to be fair, Maulana Shafi does have a point. Forget ancillary Islamic texts like the Hadith and fiqha, the Quran itself is a complex book, full of allegories and references to the history of Arabia and the Semitic religions that preceded Islam. Moreover, since the verses were revealed to the Prophet over a period of twenty-three years (according to Islamic history), many

[17]About us, Jamiat Ulama-i-Hind, available here: https://www.jamiat.org.in/masters/jamiat_about/

[18]Mufti Mohammed Shafi, *Maariful Quran*, p. 42.

of them were in response to a particular situation that arose at that time, especially the verses pertaining to jihad. There are multiple verses on the same subject, such as divorce and the veil, that appear in different places, the subsequent verses giving further instructions.

As the rector of Darul Uloom Deoband Mufti Abul Qasim Nomani points out, 'Some Quranic verses were circumstance-specific and were rendered redundant when the circumstances changed. Hence, these must be read within their context.'[19] He argues that this is the reason only those with expertise in Quranic exegesis should attempt to interpret it. To further emphasize his point, he gives the example of the so-called sword verses, some of which talk of unleashing unforgiving violence against both the disbelievers as well as the hypocrites.

'These verses on jihad cannot be taken out of context and held as applicable for all time to come,' he says. 'The jihad verses came with very strong conditionalities. Not everyone can declare a jihad and nor can it be declared in all circumstances.' According to Mufti Nomani, jihad can only be declared by the leader of the ummah or an Islamic state. And once declared, it is incumbent upon all Muslim residents of that state to participate. There is no room for free will or individual decisions. 'Jihad cannot be declared by an individual against other individuals,' says Mufti Nomani. 'Moreover, in the Indian context, no jihad can be declared here as it is a dar-ul-aman (land of peace) for Muslims.'[20]

The complexity of Quranic verses is further compounded by the fact that the Quran was an oral treatise during the lifetime of the Prophet. As we have seen, Allah revealed the verses, one at a time, to him through Archangel Gabriel. Being unlettered, Prophet Muhammad memorized the verses. He would repeat the revealed verses to his companions who in turn would try to memorize them. Most early Muslims knew at least some verses of the Quran by heart. According to Islamic belief, once a year, in the month of Ramzan, Archangel Gabriel used to run through all the revealed verses with the Prophet to obliterate the possibility of

[19]Interview with the author, Darul Uloom, Deoband, 23 November 2018.
[20]Ibid.

error. Apparently, towards the end of his life, when the entire Quran had been revealed, the Prophet went over all the verses twice with Gabriel.

While the popular belief is that thousands of Muslims had memorized the Quran in its entirety during the Prophet's life, a scholar of the history of the Quran, its collection and transmission, Shehzad Saleem has pointed out that while many knew several verses of the Quran, only four had memorized the complete Quran in the Prophet's lifetime. These hafiz[21] of the Quran were Abu al-Darda, Mu'adh ibn Jabal, Zayd ibn Thabit, and Abu Zayd[22]. In addition to memorizing, several people wrote down the verses they heard on whatever surface was available to them, from leaves and rocks to bones. Consequently, some verses were available in a rudimentary written format.

The first attempt to compile the Quranic verses was made during the caliphate of Abu Bakr (632–634 CE) after the Battle of Yamamah, in which several people who had memorized Quranic verses perished. The worry was that if it remained an oral tradition, over time, the Quran might cease to exist. Hence, upon the advice of Umar (who succeeded Abu Bakr as caliph) Abu Bakr tasked Zayd ibn Thabit to 'write' the Quran. This was challenged by a few people, including Thabit himself, who argued that if the Quran was meant to be written down then the Prophet would have ordered this in his lifetime.[23]

Eventually, pragmatism won over the doubters. What if everyone who remembered the verses died in battle over the next few years? What if those who were able to remember it now forgot parts of it as they aged? What if distortions crept in over the years owing to misunderstanding, mispronunciation, or differences of accents, especially when the religion was expanding rapidly beyond the confines of Mecca and Medina?

---

[21]As we've noted, hafiz is a person who has done hafz or memorized the Quran.

[22]'Collection of the Qur'an: A Critical and Historical Study of Al-Farahi's View', Al-Mawrid, available here: http://www.al-mawrid.org/index.php/books/view/collection-of-the-quran-a-critical-and-historical-study-of-al-farahis-view; Dr Shehzad Saleem, Topic 1 - Part 1/3: Towards a New Inquiry| History of the Quran| YouTube, 18 Aug 2016, available here: https://www.youtube.com/watch?v=4sNWx-SSvc8

[23]Mufti Mohammed Shafi, *Maariful Quran*, pp. 23–24.

While writing the Quran, Thabit did not rely on *his* memory alone. He tested each verse with others who had memorized it and only wrote it down after it had been corroborated by multiple sources. The Quran was written neither chronologically nor thematically. It is believed that once the full Quran was revealed, the Prophet advised his companions about the sequence of verses and the manner in which the holy book was to be recited.[24] Thabit followed this same sequence. He created only one copy of the Quran which was handed over to Abu Bakr. There was no other version and people continued to recite the verses from memory. After Abu Bakr's death, this copy was inherited by the next caliph, Umar, after whom it came into the possession of his daughter, Hafshah, who was also one of the wives of the Prophet.

During the reign of the third caliph, Uthman, Islam had spread well beyond the Arabian peninsula. In the west, Muslims had reached North Africa, and in the northeast, they were waging jihad in Armenia. In the course of the Armenian campaign, one of the commanders of Uthman discovered that his troops, who included soldiers from Syria, Iraq, and Yemen, were not only reciting Quranic verses differently, they were charging each other with being kafir!

When he reported this to Uthman, the latter realized that ethnic differences among the followers of Islam led to each group reciting the Quran differently. Consequently, he requested Hafshah for the written version of the Quran so that copies could be made and provided to all who professed Islam. A committee of four scholars was formed, including Thabit who wrote the original version, to make several copies of the Quran, uniting differences of accents and pronunciations. While Thabit belonged to the Ansar tribe, the other three were from the Quraysh, the powerful Meccan tribe. Uthman and his two predecessors belonged to tribes that formed part of the Quraysh.

'Therefore, Sayyidna Uthman said to them: "When you and Zayd differ in respect of any portion of the Qur'an (that is, differ as to how

---

[24]Ghazala Hassan Qadri, 'The History And Compilation Of The Holy Quran', Minhaj-ul-Quran International, 20 Dec 2007, available here: https://www.minhaj.org/english/tid/2929/The-History-And-Compilation-Of-The-Holy-Quran.html

a certain letter should be written) you write it in the language of the Quraysh because the noble Qur'an has been revealed in their very language."'[25]

A total of seven copies were made and sent to Mecca, Syria, Yemen, Bahrain, Basra, and Kufa. One copy was kept in Medina for reference. However, as literacy rates were low, the practice of oral recitation continued. Once the Quran was written and distributed, the original version was destroyed so that the Uthmanic version was held as final. This, perhaps, was not the most sensible thing to do. Apart from the destruction of Islamic heritage, this also meant that there was no way to quell the doubts that arose later about the accuracy of the Uthmanic copies, since these were the basis of all the future editions of the Quran.

As Shehzad Saleem has pointed out in a series of lectures 'Towards a New Enquiry: History of the Holy Quran' on YouTube[26], not only are there five different versions of the Quran in the world today, with minor differences of grammar, which causes some discrepancies in interpretation, the seven copies of the Quran that were made under Uthman's command have about sixty variations between them. Some are inconsequential, but there are instances where the positive has been rendered negative by the addition or deletion of a syllable or the placement of a punctuation mark. Moreover, in some copies, the sequence of the verses differs from others.

Shia cleric Maulana Kalbe Jawad gives an example of an Urdu sentence—Roko mat jaane do—to illustrate these differences in meaning. 'If you put a pause after the first word, "roko, mat jaane do", the meaning becomes "stop, don't let him go",' he says. 'However, if you put it after the second word then it becomes "roko mat, jaane do". The meaning changes, now it means "don't stop, let him go".'[27]

These issues arose because the earliest versions of the Quran were written down without any punctuation or diacritical marks.

---

[25]Mufti Mohammed Shafi, *Maariful Quran*, p. 28.

[26]Shehzad Saleem, History of the Holy Quran, last updated 11 May 2018, available here: https://www.youtube.com/playlist?list=PL7oYOZNO0kHwDzi9P4UmSremVOVKzku7s

[27]Interview with the author, Lucknow, 14 December 2018.

Once punctuation marks were introduced in later years, differences in the interpretation of certain verses arose. While these could have been genuine scribal errors, doubts persisted. Some Shias, for instance, believed that the Uthmanic version was not entirely faithful to the Quran as revealed to the Prophet, with some ultra-conservative elements within the Shia religious hierarchy holding that Uthman made deliberate changes to the holy book.

'The majority of Shias do not believe that deliberate intervention was made while writing the Quran,' says Maulana Jawad. But the Shias believe in a different history of the recording of Quranic verses. According to the Shia version, the Quranic verses were first collected by Prophet Muhammad's cousin and son-in-law, Ali, after the former's demise. However, when he presented this collection to the rest of the companions, they refused to accept it as correct.[28] This narration fits in well with the Shiite view of persecution at the hands of the early companions of the Prophet.

Once the printing press was invented, the first copy of the Quran was printed in Hamburg in 1701. But no Muslim would accept the printed copy and the Quran continued to be transcribed by hand. Thereafter, a few copies were printed in St Petersburg in 1787, but it wasn't until 1828, when a press in Iran printed a few copies of the Quran, that Muslims started accepting industrial production of the holy book[29]—yet another example of how Muslims have been reluctant to accept change and modern technology, holding it to be un-Islamic. Perhaps this is the reason why, amongst all religious groups, they remain one of the least educated in the modern arts and sciences and most reluctant to enter the realm of scientific inventions. The popular belief is that if Allah wanted it, he would have communicated it to the faithful.

The early decades after the death of the Prophet were spent in the consolidation and expansion of Islam. This required unprecedented physical effort. It also required the caliphs to convince the growing

---

[28]Saleem, History of the Quran, available here: https://www.youtube.com/watch?v=4sNWx-SSvc8

[29]Mufti Mohammed Shafi, *Maariful Quran*, p. 36.

ummah that decisions being taken by the leadership had the sanction of the Prophet in principle. Hence, out of both love and necessity, the companions started to recall incidents from the Prophet's life and purported conversations with him when he was alive to validate subsequent laws and policy decisions. As we have seen, this collection of memories formed part of the historical record of the Prophet's life and times and came to be known as Hadith.

'There are three categories of Hadith,' says Professor Mohammed Ishaque. The first one was Hadith-e-Qauli, which recalled the Prophet's conversations and comments on issues; the second was Hadith-e-Amal, the memory of his actions, whether he condoned something or punished someone; and the third was Hadith-e-Takrir, which was interpreted as his silent approval. These refer to occasions when he witnessed something but did not react to it, either in protest or in acquiescence. Since he didn't react, it was assumed that he did not find that action or speech objectionable.

'But another way of looking at it is that by not vocally supporting a particular action or speech he was conveying the message that while he was not opposing it, he didn't approve of it either,' Professor Ishaque points out.

Gradually, narrating incidents from the life of the Prophet became fraught with complications. Those with a passing connection to the people who had known him, and those with no connection at all, started narrating their memories of the Prophet, sometimes to demonstrate their intimacy with him and sometimes to justify their actions. Over the next two centuries, the situation deteriorated to such an extent that people started making up stories.

It was under these circumstances that a few Islamic scholars like Imam Bukhari and Imam Muslim among others started the process of sifting through thousands of these Hadiths nearly two and half centuries after the death of the Prophet.

Describing the process of categorization of the Hadith, Professor Ishaque says, 'Hadiths are man-made. They cannot be without error.'[30]

[30]In conversation with the author, New Delhi, 5 November 2018.

Imams Bukhari and Muslim divided the Hadith into four categories. Sahi Hadith referred to those they found accurate primarily because of the credentials of the people who were the original source for them—for instance, Prophet Muhammad's family members (mainly his wives) and closest companions. The second category was Hasan Hadith, which were found to be less accurate because of the long chain of narration or narration by secondary sources. The third category was Zaeef or weak Hadith, whose veracity could not be established without doubt. The last category was Mousi or fictitious Hadith.

Based on these categorizations, Muslim scholars created a compendium of six Hadith books called Syah-Satta[31] which gradually attained the stature of holy books. 'This is not only incorrect but un-Islamic too,' says Professor Ishaque. 'Islam came to us through two sources alone: Quran and Sunnah. Even if we want to read the Hadith, it has to be done in consonance with the Quran and Sunnah. Anything mentioned in the Hadith which goes against the spirit of the Quran cannot be accepted.'[32]

Professor Ishaque has a point. Given that the Hadith were being compiled a few centuries after the death of the Prophet, his family members, and his companions, it is unrealistic to believe that distortion of memories or individual interests didn't play a role in their telling and retelling across generations.

A scholar of Islam and author of the book *Islam: A Comprehensive Introduction*[33], Javed Ahmad Ghamidi went a step further when he told a television audience that the Hadith was merely a historical record of the Prophet's life. 'Isse deen mein na ek tinke ka izaafa hota hai na kami hoti hai. Deen pura ka pura Quran aur Sunnat mein maujood hai.'[34] (Not even a straw is added or removed from Islam by Hadith. The entire

[31]Syah-Satta books comprise *Sahi Bukhari, Muslim Sharif, Tahmizhi Sharif, Abu Daood, Nasa-e-Sharif* and *Ibn-e-Maja.*

[32]In conversation with the author, New Delhi, 5 November 2018.

[33]This is the English translation (rendered by Shehzad Saleem) of the original book *Mizan*, published by the Al-Mawrid Foundation.

[34]Javed Ahmad Ghamidi, Is it compulsory to believe in Hadith?, YouTube, 29 Aug 2016, available here: https://www.youtube.com/watch?v=xI5WAXSEYs8

Islamic faith is complete in the Quran and Sunnah.)

To emphasize his point, he gave the example of two narrators of the Hadith. The first is Abu Bakr, who was Prophet Muhammad's closest friend and the first caliph. He accompanied the Prophet during Hijrah in 622 CE and remained by his side in all the battles that he waged right till the Prophet's death in 632 CE. Abu Bakr recounted only thirty-four Hadiths.

'On the other hand was Abu Huraira who embraced Islam only after the victory of Mecca in 630 CE.[35] Yet, he has recounted thousands of Hadith,' said Ghamidi.[36]

Despite this historical background, contemporary Muslims accord such significance to the Hadith that even people like Mufti Nomani hold them sacred: 'Hadith and Sunnah are one and the same thing. There is no difference between the two.'[37] Minor ulema like Mufti Wasim, an alumnus of Darul Uloom who heads a mosque in Greater Noida and advises the local Muslim community on Islamic matters, considers the Hadith to be complementary to the Quran and refers to them collectively as Quran-Hadith.

Today, most of the Islamic injunctions pronounced by the mullahs through fatawa, and even Muslim Personal Law, including the infamous triple talaq, trace their origin to the Hadith and not the Quran.

The Syah-Satta comprises the Sunni books of Hadith. Shias have their own set of Hadith in the form of four books—*Usooli-e-Qaafi*, *Tehzeeb*, *Istibsaar*, and *Man La Yahzarohul Faqih*. 'But Shias refer to these only for direction. They don't follow them blindly,' qualifies Maulana Jawad, adding, 'Shias believe in the taklid of the living marjah or a religious leader like Ayatollah Sistani and Ayatollah Khamenei.'[38] This reduces their dependence on the Hadith, because when they have doubts about their Muslimness, they ask the Ayatollahs. Moreover, the smaller Shia sects like the Ismailis and the Bohras have a singular religious

[35]Prophet Muhammad died in 632 CE, so Abu Huraira knew him for barely two years.

[36]Ghamidi, Is it compulsory to believe in Hadith?

[37]Interview with the author, Greater Noida, 15 October 2017.

[38]Interview with the author, Lucknow, 15 December 2018.

head to guide the community; they not only interpret Islam for them but also dictate laws.

Hence, while Sunni Muslims need the Hadith to chart the course of their lives, Shias rely on the living marjah. For both, living as per the Quran and Sunnah does not instil adequate confidence for securing their afterlife.

Islamic texts do not end here. Even as some imams were labouring over the Hadith, another set of scholars was pondering the theological and metaphysical aspects of Islam. By the mid-ninth century, they were debating the nature of the Quran—was it a book created by Allah and revealed to Muhammad, or was it an uncreated book, coeval with Allah?[39] With these questions arose the issue of the stature of the Quran, Prophet Muhammad, and those who preceded him. As the deliberations deepened on the 'uncreated' nature of the Quran, the Shariah (the manner in which a Muslim must lead her life) became rigid.

Based on their understanding of the nature of the Quran and Shariah, imams started to codify Islamic laws or jurisprudence. And once again, consensus was difficult to come by. Hence, while Sunni imams created four schools of Islamic jurisprudence—Hanbali[40], Hanafi[41], Maliki[42], and Shafi[43]—the Shia imams created Jafari[44], Ismaili, and Zaidi[45]. As mentioned earlier, Imam Hanafa, who established the Hanafi school, and Imam Malik who established the Maliki school, were disciples of Shia Imam Jafar as-Sadiq, who established the Shia school of law called Jafari. Hence, despite the common source material, differences emerged in their interpretation.

In the last fifty decades, there have been four issues on which

---

[39]Aslan, *No god But God*, Chapter 6: This Religion Is a Science.

[40]Followed in the Arabian peninsula.

[41]This is the largest school of Islamic law among Sunnis and is followed by most of the region that was under the Ottoman empire, which, in addition to Turkey, included parts of Europe, Mongolia, South Asia, and China.

[42]Prominent in Africa and adjoining parts of the Middle East.

[43]Followed mainly by the Muslims of the Malabar coast of India.

[44]Followed by the majority of Shias.

[45]Followed by the Shias of Yemen.

Muslims disagree—jihad (addressed earlier in the chapter); seventy-two houris in paradise for martyrs or those who participate in jihad; consumption of alcohol; and hijab (addressed in Chapter 7: Women).

As political resistance, for instance in Palestine, started to get defined as jihad so as to mobilize foot soldiers, the leaders of the movement frequently referred to Quranic verses from Surah Waqiah that describe the pleasures of paradise for the believers. One of the pleasures mentioned are houris or 'fair women' like pearls with 'beautiful eyes'.

Describing paradise as 'the Gardens of Bliss', Surah Waqiya says, 'They will be a multitude from earlier generations, and a few from later generations. All will be on jewelled thrones, reclining face to face. They will be waited on by eternal youths, with cups, pitchers, and a drink of pure wine from a flowing stream, that will cause them neither headache nor intoxication. They will also be served any fruit they choose, and meat from any bird they desire. And they will have maidens with gorgeous eyes, like pristine pearls, all as a reward for what they used to do.[46]

Imposing their own fantasies upon the verse, various Islamic scholars, put a number to the houris, from seventy to seventy-two, and made them eternally virgin. Radical organizations later turned 'eternally virgin' houris into a reward for martyrs instead of all Muslims. Scholars like Al-Suyuti (1445–1505) described the sensual pleasures of paradise in rapturous details.[47]

The source of these claims are not Quranic verses but ostensibly the Hadith, even though several were dismissed as false even when they were recorded. Some, according to Professor Ishaque, insisted that at least one of them was indeed true and was attributed to the Prophet. But a Hadith, no matter how true, is not a Quranic verse, and as he adds, they have to be read in the spirit of the Quran. Hence, most Islamic scholars, as well as practising Muslims, tread cautiously around such claims. The widely accepted explanation is that the houris in the Quran refer to the earthly wives of the men in question, who would be restored to their youthful charm, making them irresistible.

---

[46]Surah Waqiya Verse 56:12-40 (https://quran.com/56)

[47]For more on this, see Ibn Warraq, 'Virgins? What Virgins?', *The Guardian*, 12 Jan 2002.

Some provide yet another interpretation of the verses by quoting a verse from another chapter, Surah Fussilat, which promises the believers that: 'We are your supporters in this worldly life and in the Hereafter. There you will have whatever your souls desire, and there you will have whatever you ask for.[48]

Scholars such as Ghamidi argue that one has to understand paradise as a concept[49] and not as a literal place; it is the least important aspect of what Allah has promised believers in the Quran. According to him, paradise is a place where one will have 'no regrets of the past and no insecurities of the future because all realms will coalesce to form a continuum'. He further says that the concept of sin would cease to exist because desires would become meaningless, given the all-around abundance and satiation. However, for those who could not understand the sublimity of paradise, a few verses with literal descriptions of paradise were revealed, but they did not suggest any debauchery.

Interestingly, in 2000, a German author writing under the pseudonym Christoph Luxenberg published *Die Syro-Aramäische Lesart des Koran* which was translated into English in 2007 as *The Syro-Aramaic Reading of the Koran: A Contribution to the Decoding of the Language of the Koran.* Luxenberg concluded that the language of the Quran was not entirely Arabic and 'that parts of Islam's holy book are derived from pre-existing Christian Aramaic texts that were misinterpreted by later Islamic scholars who prepared the editions of the Koran commonly read today'.[50]

Hence, by combining Aramaic with Arabic in his reading of the Quran, Luxenberg translates houris as white raisins. Reviewing his book for *The Guardian*, Ibn Warraq writes:

> Luxenberg's new analysis, leaning on the Hymns of Ephrem the Syrian, yields 'white raisins' of 'crystal clarity' rather than doe-

---

[48]Surah Fussilat, Verse 41:31, translated by Dr Mustafa Khattab (https://quran.com/41).

[49]Javed Ahmad Ghamidi, Why should men get Houris and Women only their husbands in Heaven, 29 August 2016, available here: https://www.youtube.com/watch?v=UKqd5Di9eYs

[50]Alexander Stille, 'Scholars Are Quietly Offering New Theories of the Koran', *New York Times,* 2 Mar 2002.

eyed and ever willing virgins—the houris. Luxenberg claims that the context makes it clear that it is food and drink that is being offered, and not unsullied maidens or houris.[51]

Mainstream Muslim scholars have not taken Luxenberg's theory seriously. The idea that the Quran could have been 'revealed' in a language that was not classical Arabic does not sit well with the notion that Arabs were the people chosen to receive the religion of Islam.

The other reason why it is difficult to accept that houri could have meant anything other than a beautiful woman is because in the Arab society to which Prophet Muhammad was preaching, women were treated as objects meant for the fulfilment of sexual desires. A rich Arab not only had multiple wives, but several concubines and slave women. Hence, when the Quran sought to restrict the number of wives a Muslim man could have, perhaps the promise of paradise was meant to mollify him.[52] After all, Quranic verses were 'revealed' over a period of time and in response to emerging situations. This explains the rapturous language early Muslim scholars employed in describing the sensual pleasures awaiting the believers. Women needed no such temptation, and hence no such promise was needed to be made to them. Women were offered 'fulfilment of all desires' in Surah Fussilat and that was considered sufficient.[53]

The need to mollify the new converts to the faith could also explain the ambiguity of instructions on other issues, such as intoxicants. Many Muslims, who enjoy a drink or two, insist that Islam does not explicitly forbid alcohol; at least not as explicitly as it forbids pork. In their defence, they quote three Quranic verses in the sequence of their revelation.

---

[51]Warraq, 'Virgins? What Virgins?'.

[52]Surah Nisa, Verse 4:3 says: If you fear you might fail to give orphan women their due rights if you were to marry them, then marry other women of your choice—two, three, or four. But if you are afraid you will fail to maintain justice, then content yourselves with one or those bondwomen in your possession. This way you are less likely to commit injustice. Translated by Dr Mustafa Khattab (https://quran.com/4).

[53]Javed Ahmad Ghamidi, Why should men get Houris and Women only their husbands in Heaven, 29 August 2016, available here: https://www.youtube.com/watch?v=UKqd5Di9eYs

The first verse says:

> They ask you O Prophet about intoxicants and gambling. Say, 'There is great evil in both, as well as some benefit for people—but the evil outweighs the benefit.' They also ask you O Prophet what they should donate. Say, 'Whatever you can spare.' This is how Allah makes His revelations clear to you believers, so perhaps you may reflect.[54]

The second says:

> O believers! Do not approach prayer while intoxicated until you are aware of what you say.[55]

And the third is:

> O believers! Intoxicants, gambling, idols, and drawing lots for decisions are all evil of Satan's handiwork. So shun them so you may be successful.[56]

They further argue that the verses on dietary restrictions make no mention of intoxicants. For example, this verse from Surah Baqarah:

> He has only forbidden to you dead animals, blood, the flesh of swine, and that which has been dedicated to other than Allah. But whoever is forced (by necessity), neither desiring (it) nor transgressing (its limit), there is no sin upon him. Indeed, Allah is Forgiving and Merciful.[57]

However, the ulema use the first three verses to emphasize that intoxicants were indeed forbidden in Islam. As the Arabs were big drinkers, they argue that Allah slowly eased the believers into giving up intoxicants.[58] Islamic scholar and former chancellor of Darul Uloom Nadwatul Ulama, Sayed Abul Hasan Ali Nadwi, popularly known as Ali

---

[54]Surah Baqarah, Verse 2:219, translated by Dr Mustafa Khattab (https://quran.com/2).
[55]Surah Nisa, Verse 4:43, translated by Dr Mustafa Khattab (https://quran.com/4).
[56]Surah Maidah, Verse 5:90, translated by Dr Mustafa Khattab (https://quran.com/5).
[57]Surah Baqarah, Verse 2:173, translated by Dr Mustafa Khattab (https://quran.com/2).
[58]Huda, 'Understanding Islam's Stance on Alcohol', *Learn Religions*, 7 Aug 2019, available here: https://www.thoughtco.com/why-is-alcohol-forbidden-in-islam-2004329

Mian, wrote in his book *Islam and the World*, 'The wealth of expressions contained in the Arabic language for the "Daughter of Vine" and the delicate variations of meaning these expressions convey, reveal how passionately the Arabs were in love with it.'[59]

However, the biggest source for prohibiting alcohol is not the Quran but the Hadith. Several narrations, including those attributed to the Prophet's wife Aisha, and listed as sahi or accurate, say that Prophet Muhammad told some people who needed clarification on the kinds of wines that were forbidden, that, 'Every drink that causes intoxication is forbidden.'[60] He is further reported as having told some of the believers: 'He who drinks wine in this world and dies while he is addicted to it, not having repented, will not be given a drink in the Hereafter.'[61]

Conservative Muslims argue that wines were forbidden because they were a source of several evils including sexual profligacy and violence. Ironically, they are believed to be the drink of choice in paradise. Even more ironical is the fact that many Muslims who do not drink alcohol citing the Quran and Hadith consume drugs, tobacco, and even cough syrups, claiming that only drinking is expressly forbidden and other forms of intoxication are not. They take recourse in the word 'khamr' mentioned in the verses pertaining to intoxicants quoted above. Khamr is the root word, from which grapes and dates are drawn. Hence, many scholars, including jurists from different schools of Islamic jurisprudence, argue that as long as alcohol is produced by sources other than grapes and dates, it is permissible. In the same vein, chemically-produced alcohol, like ethanol, is not objected to.[62]

Interestingly, in 2014, Saudi author Abdullah bin Bakhit claimed in a tweet that 'I did not find anything in the Holy Quran that forbids

---

[59]Sayyed Abul Hasan Nadwi, *Islam and the World*, Academy of Islamic Research and Publication, Nadwatul Ulama, 3rd edition 2013, p. 38.

[60]'Every Intoxicant is Khamr and Every Khamr is Forbidden', The Book of Drinks, available here: http://www.sahihmuslim.com/sps/smm/sahihmuslim.cfm?scn=dspchaptersfull&BookID=23&ChapterID=844

[61]Ibid.

[62]'Alcohol: Its kinds, usage and Rulings', available here: https://www.central-mosque.com/index.php/General-Fiqh/alcohol-its-kinds-usage-and-rulings.html

alcohol. And there is no punishment too'.[63]

For those who seek, perhaps the answer lies in the Quran itself. According to Verse 33 of Surah Araf,

> Say, 'My Lord has only forbidden open and secret indecencies, sinfulness, unjust aggression, associating others with Allah in worship—a practice He has never authorized—and attributing to Allah what you do not know.'[64]

Interpreting this verse, Ghamidi says that Allah has given broad guidelines about what is permissible and what is not. An individual is the judge of her own conduct. As long as one does not indulge in immoralities or oppression of others, Allah puts no restrictions upon you.[65]

Tablighi Jamaat

If life as Muslims were made so easy and everyone was allowed to be the judge of their own conduct, where would the proselytizers go? Despite explicit messages from the Quran giving agency to Muslims to judge right from wrong for themselves, there were always those who claimed that they had a better understanding of Islam and Allah's message. Starting with Ibn Taymiyyah (1263–1328) and Abd al-Wahhab (1703–1792), puritanical and humourless Muslims sought to put Islam in a straitjacket, forbidding everything that could be a source of pleasure. Entertainment was considered the gravest of sins. Maulana Mohammed Shakeel, the principal of Jamiatur Raza, Bareilly, told me categorically, 'Entertainment is not allowed without prayer.'[66]

India, with one of the largest Muslim populations in the world, could not have remained unaffected by these proselytizing missions aimed at dragging ordinary believers onto the path of righteousness.

---

[63]'Nothing in the Quran Says Alcohol "is Haram": Saudi Author', *Morocco World News*, 23 Dec 2014.

[64]Surah Araf, Verse 7:33 (https://quran.com/7).

[65]Javed Ahmed Ghamidi, Is Music Haram in Islam, YouTube, 14 Jul 2016, available here: https://www.youtube.com/watch?v=5ESqPXKi3f8

[66]Interview with the author, Bareilly, 12 November 2018.

Given the intellectual capital that Indian Muslims had accrued over the centuries, it was only fitting that new interpretations of the ancient message emerged from India.

Interestingly, all conservative 'reformist' movements—including sects like Deobandi and Barelvi that were followed by mass proselytizing movements like the Tablighi Jamaat and Jamaat-e-Islami—started in the area abutting Uttar Pradesh and Delhi. As noted earlier, this region was the crucible of syncretism or Ganga-Jamni tehzeeb, so named after the two major rivers which merge at Allahabad, recently renamed Prayagraj by the Uttar Pradesh state government helmed by its Hindu right-wing chief minister. This is also the region, which for a large part of its medieval and modern history was the seat of Muslim power, the social-cultural pinnacle of which was reached during Mughal emperor Akbar's reign.

The reformists didn't only want to rid Islam of Indian influences, but Turkish and Persian ones too. Unless it was Arabic, it was not good enough. In this they were echoing the thoughts of the third caliph Uthman, who said that since the Quran was revealed in the language of the Quraysh, that dialect of Arabic should take precedence over others. However, for want of resources and committed foot soldiers, these efforts at regressing Indian Islam remained localized to north India till about a few decades ago.

The situation began to change towards the closing decades of the last century when money started to pour into these institutions and movements, giving them not only mobility but motivation too. Before we dig further into this, we must learn to distinguish between organizations like Deoband and movements like Jamaat-e-Islami. As mentioned earlier, Darul Uloom Deoband started as a movement to protect the Islamic faith which appeared to be on the verge of extinction in the Delhi–UP region following the British reprisals of 1857. Gradually, it increased its mandate to the reformation of all Indian Muslims and to rid them of extraneous (i.e. Hindu) influences. To start with, they wanted to create a distinct Muslim identity. A document published as the creed of the founders of Darul Uloom states:

> For the reformation of the locals, Hadhrat[67] (rahmatullahi alaih) paid great attention to the rectification of social dealings and behaviour, because the brotherhood of Deoband was generally involved in customs of ignorance. Marriage to widows was initiated, a practice which previously was regarded as extremely degrading and disgraceful to such an extent that even the mention of it would result in the drawing of swords. The womenfolk of the affluent were encouraged to discard the dress of Hindus, which was common amongst them.... Rectification was effected with regard to the various customs regarding marriage, times of grief, etc.... The result was that the (Muslim) residents were placed on the path of becoming an Islamic society. This was achieved not by admonishing lectures and sermons, but rather by means of practical demonstration. A written pledge was taken from the responsible people of the community and they signed and endorsed it, after they were made to understand. Good social dealings were thus initiated and spread. This demonstrated that one of the objectives of the Daarul Uloom was to rectify and reform the society.[68]

However, it did not approach this by undertaking door-to-door proselytization. Instead, the Darul Uloom imparted religious education and laid down dos and don'ts. It focussed on the creation of an Islamic seminary somewhat akin to Al-Azhar of Egypt, where the ulema could be taught. The idea was that these learned ulema would return to their respective communities to impart the learning they had imbibed, thereby creating a cascading effect of puritanism.

Since the Islam taught at Darul Uloom bore the stamp of its founders, their successors and teachers, (who were inspired by the Wahhabi/ Salafi view of Islam) and their interpretation, Deoband gradually turned into a Sunni Islamic sect, which spawned proselytizing movements like the Tablighi Jamaat and Jamaat-e-Islami, neither of which involve themselves in interpretative Islam, focussing only on

---

[67]Muhammad Qasim Nanautavi, one of the founders of Darul Uloom, Deoband. More on him and Darul Uloom in the section Divided Ummah.

[68]Tayyib, *The Maslak of Ulama of Deoband*, p. 31.

orally preaching the practice of the religion.

Islam has no prescribed dress code for either of the sexes. As long as one is modestly attired and does not draw attention to one's body or assume an air of arrogance about one's appearance, one can wear anything. While conceding that 'Islam does not require a Muslim to dress in a particular way', Maulana Mahmood Madani insists that, 'The Prophet had ordered that one should not adopt the identity of other religions.'[69]

He refers to the advice given to the Muslims of Mecca in 629 CE to distinguish themselves from the majority Quraysh population of the city. As has been noted, Prophet Muhammad was leading an army of Muslims towards Mecca from Medina against the Quraysh, after the latter violated the Treaty of Hudaybiyyah.[70] Since there were a few Muslims in Mecca as well, they were asked to distinguish themselves so in case of war, they would be spared. According to Islamic scholar Javed Ahmad Ghamidi[71], one way they did this was with the greeting 'As Salaam Aleikum'[72] to which the Muslim would respond, 'Walekum as Salaam'.

The advice regarding attire was time and circumstance-specific, and in no way pertained to a particular way of dressing. Yet, Muslims in India have always found some argument or the other to justify a distinctive appearance. For example, a scholar of Barelvi persuasion, Maulana Mohammed Shakeel, told me, 'We need to look like Muslims because if we die among strangers how would they know whether we have to be buried or cremated.'[73] How indeed!

Of the two Darul Uloom-inspired proselytizing movements, given its non-complicated, non-intellectual focus, Tablighi is a worldwide phenomenon that has a bottom-up approach working mostly with poor

---

[69]In conversation with the author, New Delhi, 15 November 2018.

[70]The Treaty of Hudaybiyyah was agreed in 628 CE between Muhammad and the Quraysh. It called for a ten-year truce. However, in early 629 CE, a group aligned with the Quraysh killed a group aligned with the Muslims, thereby ending the truce.

[71]Ghamidi—Identity of Muslim, 28 July 2009, available here: https://www.youtube.com/watch?v=HzFBhHlUZxA

[72]'Peace be upon you'. The response walekum salaam means 'and peace be upon you too'.

[73]Interview with the author, Bareilly, 12 November 2018.

and semi-literate people. For example, the conversion of black prisoners to Islam in the United States is attributed to the Tablighis who have been regulars in the penitentiaries as spiritual volunteers and do-gooders.[74]

The Tablighi Jamaat was founded in the late 1920s by Maulana Muhammad Ilyas Kandhalwi by putting together a group of fresh graduates from Darul Uloom Deoband. He took them on a proselytizing mission to other parts of north India, particularly the Mewat district of Haryana. The mission had two purposes: one, self-improvement; and two, the improvement of others. Even today, this is the mission statement of the Tablighi Jamaat. They not only strive to turn themselves into a version of the Muslim who lived in Medina during the Prophet's lifetime, they also reach out to others, through a process called da'wah, which means invitation. They are seldom satisfied with polite regrets to their invitations because that implies failure. As an evangelical group, soul-harvesting adds credit to their accounts which would go a long way in reserving a berth for them in paradise.

Incidentally, members of the Tablighi Jamaat have frequently come under a cloud. In the last decade, individual terrorists indicted in the US such as Richard Reid (the shoe bomber), Jose Padilla (the dirty bomber), and Lyman Harris who tried to blow the Brooklyn Bridge were all found to have been members of the Tablighi Jamaat at some stage.[75] In Europe and North Africa, a large number of terrorists arrested for the Casablanca blasts of 2003 were also found to have had connections with the local chapters of the Tabligh. Yusef Fikri, the leader of the Moroccan terrorist organization At-Takfir wal-Hijrah, who was sentenced to death for his role in the Casablanca attack by the Moroccan authorities, was also a member of the Tablighi Jamaat. However, in India, despite frequently coming under suspicion and temporary detention of the travelling parties of Jamaatis, no member has been found to be involved in any terrorist activity. Yet, suspicion remains but in India it is largely driven

[74]Wahab, 'In the Name of God'.

[75]Nicholas Howenstein, 'Islamist Networks: The Case of Tablighi Jamaat', United States Institute of Peace, 12 Oct 2006.

by right-wing prejudice than any real evidence.[76]

But the Jamaatis remain unmindful of this. The glory of the religion would not be possible unless spread through personal examples and sacrifices. After all, if everyone minded their own business and adhered to the Quranic verse of 'for you your religion for me my religion', Islam wouldn't have spread so rapidly across the world. Hence, focussing on a regressive form of Islam, Kandhalwi emphasized that Muslims should restrict themselves to a religious education and shun modern subjects. He preached the complete segregation of the sexes to such an extent that even a Muslim woman's voice was not supposed to be heard by men who were not blood relations.[77]

Ignoring social and charitable work, the Jamaat concentrates on the religious obligations of individual Muslims.[78] To avoid attracting attention or controversies, the Jamaat tries to remain apolitical and largely invisible outside the religious realm. The only evidence of its existence are its followers in trademark 'Muslim' dress—thick moustacheless beards, skullcaps, long kurtas and short pyjamas which end above the ankles—politician and former Member of Parliament Arif Mohammed Khan mocks this sort of attire as 'bade bhai ka kurta, chhote bhai ka pyjama' (elder brother's kurta and younger brother's pyjama).[79]

Today, it is a large and growing movement with an unaccounted number of active and passive members. Like the Rashtriya Swayamsevak Sangh (RSS), its administrative and financial details are opaque. It claims to have no records of its membership or funds, both of which, according to its office-bearers, are entirely voluntary.[80]

---

[76]S. Gurumurthy, 'Tablighi Jamaat: Its Other Evil Side', Vivekananda International Foundation, 2 April 2020.

[77]Wahab, 'In the Name of God'.

[78]Ibid.

[79]Arif Mohammed Khan rose to fame when, as Congress MP, he defended divorcee Shah Bano's right to compensation from her husband in opposition to the Muslim ulema. He said this to me when we spoke in his New Delhi home on 7 October 2017.

[80]Satyendra Tripathi, 'Mainstreaming of RSS is complete: Why not declare RSS a political party?', *National Herald*, 19 Jul 2019 and Ashwaq Masoodi, 'Inside the Tablighi Jamaat', *Mint*, 16 Sep 2013.

Tablighi Jamaat carries out its evangelical activities in a two-pronged manner. The first prong is the organization of periodic ijtemas or religious congregations—these take place over a few days at different locations at which senior members of the movement give sermons. The major ijtemas to be held in the year are announced by the Tablighi Jamaat's headquarters in Delhi through its YouTube channel.[81] The destinations are as diverse as Tamil Nadu, Karnataka, Rajasthan, Himachal Pradesh, Uttar Pradesh, and Delhi.

Ijtemas are funded and organized by local members of the Jamaat. Depending on their timing, as well as the scale, the 'now India-led'[82] leader of the worldwide Tabligh movement, Maulana Saad, attends them and gives his bayaan (loosely translated as sermon). His deputies stand in for him in case he is unable to attend. The primary audience of the ijtemas are Muslims who attend voluntarily.

The unwilling are targeted through the second prong, described vividly by a Moradabad-based exporter, and an occasional Tablighi, Salim Khan, 'The Tablighi members watch out for young boys who have finished their board examinations. It is not difficult to find out from the neighbourhood mosque as to which boys have taken the examination that year. Once the holidays begin, they start visiting those houses, urging the fathers to send their young sons to the mosque. Since it is such an innocuous request, and since most Muslims in any case pray at the neighbourhood mosque at least once a week, the youngsters do come. Gradually, for want of anything else, they listen to the sermons as well.'[83] However, the real initiation happens when the youngsters are persuaded to accompany a travelling party of Tablighis on a proselytizing mission.

---

[81]The YouTube channel has since been disabled following the COVID-19 pandemic.

[82]Till a few years ago, the nucleus of the worldwide movement was the Delhi headquarters located at the Banglewali Masjid near the Nizamuddin dargah. But the group had a three-way split on the issue of succession, when the centres in Pakistan and Bangladesh refused to accept Maulana Saad as their leader. Currently, different Tablighi centres across the world swear allegiance to one of the three headquarters—India, Pakistan, and Bangladesh.

[83]Wahab, 'In the Name of God'.

For Salim Khan, the initiation happened at the age of fifteen and almost had an air of adventure. 'It was the first time in my life that I was travelling outside Moradabad without my parents. A few of my friends also came along, so it was like an excursion. We visited villages, bathed at the tubewells, and ate sugarcane in the fields.' The group went to a small place called Joya close to Amroha for a three-day proselytizing trip.

During such trips, the Jamaatis stay at the local mosques, do all their own chores, like washing clothes, cooking, and cleaning. The rest of the time is spent either in prayer or walking through the neighbourhood, persuading the locals to come to the mosque for bayaan.

A regular day of the travelling Jamaati starts at 3 a.m. with a special prayer session called tahajjud, after which those who want to are allowed to go back to sleep while the rest continue to pray. Everyone is required to get up by five in the morning for fajr, the first prayer of the day. This is followed by religious education or taalim for about twenty minutes. Then there is another prayer after sunrise called ishraq after which breakfast is served. For the next hour, the Tablighis are free to either rest or go out in the neighbourhood with a guide to invite people to the mosque. More rest follows for an hour and a half, which doubles as personal time. At 10, a group meeting is held to discuss the plans for the next twenty-four hours. Called mashwara or deliberation, at this meeting all members of the visiting Jamaat are free to give suggestions on how best to rope in more and more local people. After the meeting, it is back to taalim for two hours which culminates in lunch just before the zuhar prayer after noon. Since many local people come to the mosque for the afternoon prayers, they are requested to meet with the amir of the visiting Jamaat delegation for a twenty-minute bayaan. Some rest is followed by more taalim at 3 p.m., both through religious books and a Tablighi Jamaat primer called the 'Six Numbers' which was evolved by Maulana Ilyas and fine-tuned by Maulana Zakaria Kandhalwi in the book *Fazail-e-Amal*.

The primer lists six principles that all Tablighi members must adhere to. Based on the basic principles of Islam, in the hands of the Tablighis, they have acquired a missionary objective. The six principles are:

1. Kalimah, which is an article of faith for all Muslims and proclaims that there is no God but Allah and Prophet Muhammad is His messenger.
2. Salat (Arabic for namaz) are the five compulsory daily prayers: fajr, zuhar, asar, maghrib, and isha. However, Tablighis have added additional prayers to the mandatory ones.
3. Ilm and zikr literally mean knowledge and preaching of Islam. Zikr usually happens in the mosque after the namaz when a senior member of the Tabligh sermonizes to the assembled congregation.
4. Ikram-i-Muslim enumerates the responsibilities of Muslims towards co-religionists.
5. Ikhlas-i-Niyat refers to reforming oneself so that one leads a pious life in the service of Allah without any personal desires and ambitions.
6. Tafrigh-i-Waqt involves devoting time and effort to leading a life of piety and inviting and encouraging others to do the same by travelling not only within the country but outside as well.

This session, which begins at 3 p.m., continues for over an hour after which the Jamaatis just have time to have a quick tea before the asar prayer, which is again followed by a bayaan and more neighbourhood visits to invite people to come to the mosque to listen to the sermons during the next prayer, maghrib. Bayaan continues for nearly an hour with any locals who have heeded the call and come to the mosque. Post dinner is the isha namaz after which the group breaks off and goes on individual proselytizing rounds in the area focussing on those who did not attend the bayaan. By 10 p.m., it's lights out.

At the city level, the Jamaat is dominated by the elders, buzurgwan, who form the shura. They appoint the amir for that city from among themselves on a rotational basis. This body decides the travel plans of the Jamaat (called chilla) and organizes funds through voluntary donations. Committed Jamaatis who are themselves unable to travel donate money to the chilla. In addition, each travelling member meets his own expenses. The chilla can be for three days, forty days, or four months. Only those Jamaatis who have travelled for four months at a stretch within the country, leaving their homes and businesses, are eligible to travel abroad. However, these are not rigid rules. Those who can pay for their passage and accommodation and perhaps sponsor fellow Tablighis can travel abroad for the propagation of Islam.[84]

Like Salim Khan, Umer also encountered the Tablighi Jamaat in the mosque he used to frequent during his university years in Benares. 'The Tabligh has been a big influence on my life,' he says. 'I have participated in several short-term Jamaat activities. It is my desire to go on a forty-day chilla (proselytizing trip) with them.'[85] Given that the Jamaat expects its volunteers to not only give their time, but also their money, its sway over its adherents can only be imagined.

'Tablighi Jamaat is doing good work by motivating the youth towards Islam, but there are a few issues with the way it works,' says Umer. According to him, young boys, barely a few months into the Jamaat, start behaving like local leaders even without an adequate understanding of Islam. 'They become aggressive and overtly critical of those who are less religious or those who refuse to heed their calls. This heaping of guilt on the uninterested is not right,' he says.

But those convinced of their righteousness seldom care for such niceties.

Jamaat-e-Islami

The Jamaat-e-Islami, on the other hand, is essentially a subcontinental sociopolitical movement founded by Maulana Sayyid Abul A'la Maududi[86] in 1941. It started as a political alternative to the Muslim League, whose members Maulana Maududi considered pretenders and not Islamic enough. He feared that Muhammad Ali Jinnah's vision would kill the idea of an Islamic state, because neither Jinnah nor his acolytes were true Muslims.

---

[84]Wahab, 'In the Name of God'.

[85]Interview with the author, New Delhi, 18 August 2019.

[86]He was born on 25 September 1903 in Aurangabad, then part of the State of Hyderabad. He died on 22 September 1979 in New York, United States.

Maududi also opposed the ulema of Deoband, who had formed an umbrella organization called Jamiat Ulama-i-Hind, and were working alongside the Congress party against the British. In response to the call for a separate nation for Muslims, Jamiat Ulama-i-Hind had proposed the concept of composite nationalism. According to Maulana Mahmood Madani, composite nationalism envisaged Hindus and Muslims living together as one people but with separate institutional structures to manage their religious and personal affairs.[87]

However, once it was clear that the Muslim League was the primary opponent to the Congress party, the Jamaat-e-Islami started to work with it, providing the party with street power. Eventually, when India was partitioned, Maududi opted for the Muslim homeland, devoting the rest of his years towards turning Pakistan into an Islamic state and he was largely successful in his efforts. The 1956 constitution of Pakistan incorporated suggestions towards Islamization made by Maududi. Thereafter, the Jamaat-e-Islami played an important role in Pakistan's politics, especially during and after General Zia-ul-Haq's term; it continues to do so. In fact, it was the Jamaat's agitational street politics that pressured the Pakistan government to declare the Ahmadis, a small Islamic sect largely based in Pakistan, un-Islamic. This paved the way for frequent violence against the miniscule group, which continues till today.

In India, the party had to re-establish itself in 1947. Not only was 'Hind' suffixed to its name, it also changed its mandate from political to socio-religious. But even in the realm of socio-religious emancipation of Muslims lies an undercurrent of exclusionary politics, which Maududi believed was integral to Islam. This is the reason that Jamaat-e-Islami Hind has often been equated with the RSS. It was banned for nineteen months in 1975, and later in 1992, along with the RSS. The editor-in-chief of Jamaat-e-Islami's publication, *Radiance Viewsweekly,* and a member of the central shoora (committee) of the organization, Ejaz Ahmed Aslam, dismisses those bans as 'policeman's justice'.

Explaining Maududi's vision, he says, 'Maududi propounded the idea of "Khilafat se Mulkiyat", which means from caliphate to nation-

[87]Interview with the author, New Delhi, 15 November 2018.

state. And that is what we worked towards. He believed that Islam is a religion not only for Muslims, but for the entire humanity. It promises salvation for all humanity through the long chain of prophets, from Adam to Muhammad.'[88]

Maududi's vision was not only grandiose but hugely ambitious. He believed that Islam was not merely a religion, but a nation state in itself. Hence, politics was integral to Islam. Moreover, it was incumbent on all Muslims to convince others to embrace the faith. Once this was done, India would become a truly Islamic state, similar to the one founded by Prophet Muhammad in Medina. The Islamic state of Maududi's dreams was not simply a country of Muslims run by Muslims. It was one that would be governed by the law of Allah, without human innovation. He wanted Shariah to be imposed both in letter and spirit, because it was the law for all humanity for all time to come. Furthermore, since he considered Islam to be a nation state, he supported equating apostasy and blasphemy with treason. This position has been the cause of a lot of violence and social discord in Pakistan.

Maududi was conscious of the impossibility of his vision. Even at his most optimistic, he felt that there was only a 60 per cent chance of India becoming a true Islamic state. Hence, to reach the 100 per cent mark, Muslims first needed to strive harder to become 'true Muslims', instead of remaining 'partial Muslims', who

> Profess faith in God and the Messenger and declare Islam as their religion; but then they confine this Islam to only a part of their lives...they extensively perform worship rituals like Prayers, use of rosary, remembrance of God's name.... They are very particular in conforming to outward piety in matters like food, dress and other external social, cultural customs....
>
> But beyond these conventions their lives are not ruled by God. If they love, they love for the sake of their own selves, their country, their nation, or for anything else, but not for Allah... Their relations with their businesses, their wives and children, families, societies—will all be to a great extent unaffected by Islam and based

[88]Interview with the author, New Delhi, 9 November 2018.

> on secular considerations... When such people establish cultural, educational and political norms and institutions, these have nothing to do with Islam, even though they may seem Islamic.[89]

In the same chapter Maududi laments that

> Because of the preponderance of such 'Muslims' in Muslim society, power and world leadership largely passed into the hands of rebels against God. For these 'Muslims' have been content merely with ensuring that they enjoy the freedom to live religiously within the narrow confines of their private lives.
>
> God never desired to have such 'Muslims'. Nor did He send His Prophets or reveal His Books to create them.

As opposed to such nominal Muslims, true Muslims are those

> Who completely merge their personalities and existences into Islam. All the roles they have become subordinate to the one role of being Muslims.... Their feelings, their desires, their ideologies, their thoughts and opinions, their likes and dislikes, all are shaped by Islam. Allah's guidance holds complete sway over their hearts and minds.... Neither their loves nor their hatreds are independent of Islamic criteria.... If they give anything to anybody, it is because Islam requires it to be given. If they withhold anything from anybody, it is because Islam wants it to be withheld.'[90]

While Maududi became a cult figure[91] of sorts in his lifetime, his legacy of marrying Islam with politics, while idealizing only one type of Muslim as true, has endured and has inspired Islamic reformation and revivalism from north Africa to Central and South Asia. Scholars like Vali Nasr argue that Maududi's writings on political Islam (he wrote seventy-three books), including on jihad, that were translated into different languages, provided the impetus for movements like the Muslim Brotherhood and

---

[89]Maulana Sayyid Abul A'la Maududi, *Fundamentals of Islam*, New Delhi: Markazi Maktaba Islami Publishers, 2014, pp. 114–16.

[90]Ibid.

[91]Vali Nasr, *Mawdudi and the Making of Islamic Revivalism*, New York, Oxford: OUP, 1996.

later the Iranian Revolution. His books remain the biggest revenue generator for Jamaat-e-Islami even today. Says Aslam, 'We sell books worth ₹5 crore every year.'

Indeed, the sprawling Jamaat-e-Islami Hind's central headquarters in Delhi's Abul Fazal Enclave has to be seen to be believed for its sheer size. It houses a hospital, a small dispensary, a guest house, a polytechnic, a library, and a mosque in addition to the Jamaat's administrative buildings and those of its student body, Student's Islamic Organization of India. On the periphery of the complex is a bookshop, a section of which has been set aside for those who wish to sit and read.

The day I visited the bookshop, the two cashiers were extremely busy. Some 250 booklets, about sixty pages each, on the duties and responsibilities of a Muslim, had been ordered by a philanthropist for free distribution in one of the neighbourhood madrassas. Since it was a big order, the cashiers had no time for anyone else. 'Madam, please wait,' the cashier told me before going back to counting the booklets.

I wandered around inside the shop. In addition to a few adults, there were two boys, barely ten years old. Dressed in long kurtas and short pyjamas with skullcaps fitted on their heads, the two boys were sitting in the reading area, browsing through booklets. The boys had been sent by their poverty-stricken parents in West Bengal to study at a madrassa run by the Ahle Hadith sect of Islam. They not only get free education, boarding, and lodging, they also get a nominal monthly stipend, half of which they are required to spend on religious books. The booklets that the boys were browsing through were in Urdu.

'Can you read Urdu?' I asked.

'Yes,' replied one of the boys. 'That is the first thing we learn here, the language of the Muslims.'

Since when has Urdu become the language of the Muslims? I wondered to myself. The answer was provided by Abdur Rahim of the Jamaat-e-Islami's Karnataka unit based in Bengaluru.

'Well, the language of Islam is no doubt Arabic, but the language of Indian Muslims is Urdu,' he says[92] in impeccable Urdu without any

[92]Interview with the author, Bengaluru, 19 February 2019.

hint of a south Indian accent or the inflection of Daccani Urdu.[93] It then occurred to me that Aslam, the editor-in-chief of *Radiance Viewsweekly*, who is Tamil, spoke perfect Urdu, perhaps even better Urdu than the old residents of Delhi or Lucknow. Just as Tablighi Jamaat has an Indian Islamic dress of long kurta and short trousers, Jamaat-e-Islami has a 'Muslim' language—Urdu—which is the identity of the organization.

Though Rahim could not explain how north Indian Urdu became the language of all Muslims, this was one of the means that Maududi employed to create a class of true Muslims. Maududi belonged to a family of minor nobles of Delhi who used to work in the Mughal courts and traced their ancestry to the family of Prophet Muhammad's daughter Fatima. In his 1996 book, *Mawdudi and the Making of Islamic Revivalism*, Vali Nasr writes that like most Muslim nobility of Delhi, Maududi was extremely proud—even arrogant—about the class he belonged to and the purity of his language which he thought reflected his erudition. Even though he spent his formative years in Hyderabad, he did not allow that to impact his speech. This is the tradition that the Jamaat upholds, to the extent that its office-bearers now believe that language is part of religious identity.

Rahim argues that not only is Urdu part of Islamic identity, but that this identity is integral to being a Muslim. 'What is the point of modernity without identity?' he asks. Like the headquarters in Delhi, the office complex in Bengaluru, just a few minutes from the famous Cubbon Park, houses multiple institutions—from an Islamic travel agency that facilitates hajj, to a clinic, a NEET coaching centre,[94] interactive lecture halls where discussions are held on Islam, and an Islamic helpline which responds to calls on Islam.

'A large number of calls come from our Hindu brothers and sisters,' Rahim says with a touch of pride. 'One of our roles is da'wah [invitation to embrace Islam]. After all, Islam is the religion for all humanity.'

Conspicuous at the Bengaluru complex were women (there were

[93]Urdu spoken on the Deccan plateau, including in Hyderabad.

[94]National Eligibility Cum Entrance Test. This is conducted for admission to medical colleges.

very few at the Delhi complex), scores of them, covered head to toe in burkhas. While some had their faces exposed, many wore a face mask too that left only their eyes visible. These were medical aspirants who were leaving after attending the coaching class for NEET provided at a subsidized rate by the Jamaat-e-Islami.

'Why are all of them dressed in similar burkhas?' I asked.

'That's the uniform here,' Rahim clarifies.

'Uniform? At a coaching centre?'

'Our primary objective is reformation of the Islamic society. We have to first make ourselves true Muslims before we can ask others to embrace Islam.'

Jamaat-e-Islami Hind is punching well above its weight. It has only 13,000 full-time members and 70,000 workers. Even though it started as a north Indian organization, today it has a greater presence in south India, which also produces the largest number of office-bearers. Interestingly, they all look and sound the same. Any regional peculiarities have been obliterated. Unlike any other Islamic organization, the Jamaat's members are largely professionally qualified people. For instance, the head of the Karnataka chapter is a practising urologist. The current amir of the organization, Syed Sadatullah Husaini, is an electronics and telecommunications engineer. When people like them hold a discourse, the weight of their secular qualifications has a salutary effect on their listeners—their professional standing helps motivate those who aspire to become a 'true' Muslim—those who are as similar as possible to the seventh-century Medinan Muslims whose obedience to the Prophet was unflinching even in the face of death.

The pervasiveness of the Jamaat-e-Islami comes not only from its members, but also from the influence it wields over educated Muslims, even those who are unaffiliated. Most shops selling Islamic literature are flooded by Jamaat-published books, from basic primers to handbooks on being a true Muslim. Sold for as little as ₹10, it is common for people to buy them in bulk for free distribution at mosques, orphanages, and madrassas as part of their zakat obligation. Busy parents also buy them to help inculcate Islamic values in their children.

Since most proselytizers, even of the Tablighi variety, do not have their own literature to rely on when they go preaching or to deliver sermons at ijtemas, they refer to Maududi's texts. At an all-women ijtema that I attended in Delhi, the speaker, completely covered in a burkha inclusive of a face mask, claimed to be a self-taught, independent proselytizer, unaffiliated to any organization. Yet, she was regurgitating paragraphs on the importance of the Quran from Maududi's writings. What's more, the copy of the Quran which she held up as an exhibit while talking to the assembled women was a Jamaat publication with commentary by Maududi. Clearly, the Jamaat's capture of the Muslim mind, especially those of the young, is greater than that of any other 'reformer's'.

The consequence is that a uniform class of Muslims is emerging where regional diversities were once seen. These differences are now regarded not only as inappropriate but un-Islamic too. After all, Allah desired only one kind of Muslim, those who looked and lived like the Arabs. This is why Allah chose to reveal his religion to them.

The first impact of this homogenization has been on the language—Persian influences are being erased and Arabic is being brought in haphazardly. Hence, Ramzan has become Ramadan, namaz is now salat and roza is sawm. Among these changes is the modification of Khuda Hafiz to Allah Hafiz. While Khuda is a generic name for God, Allah is the name by which Arabs refer to God. Hafiz means protection. When used together as a farewell greeting, it means 'may you go under God's protection'. But revisionist Muslims are not happy with the generic Khuda. Hence, they have replaced it with the more Islamic, rather, more Arab, Allah, even though the closest Arabic farewell would be Fi Aman Allah, which means 'May you be in the custody of Allah'.

'This is what happens when illiterates become custodians of faith,' laments Zafarul Islam Khan, former chairperson, Delhi Minorities Commission, and editor of the *Milli Gazette*. 'The puritan Bangladeshis started using Allah Hafiz to show their closeness to Saudi Arabia. From them the Pakistanis, during Zia-ul-Haq's term, picked it up. And Indian Muslims, who suffer from a complex, copied it immediately. It is plain silly and makes us sound ridiculous. If you have to copy the Arabs, then say what they say. No Arab says "Allah Hafiz".'[95]

However, since Arabic is still not spoken by Indian Muslims, they have struck a compromise by adopting Urdu, which is written in a similar script as Arabic. 'Till a few years ago, the khutbas[96] which used to be in the local languages are now issued in Urdu,' observes Javad Basith, a retired businessman who calls himself a pure Bangalorean, his family having lived in the city for nearly two generations.

Basith inherited his progressive thinking from his parents. According to him, his parents were not exceptional for their time. But things are no longer the same. 'Constant, in-your-face preaching in the form of neighbourhood ijtemas, is drawing more people towards conservative religion and from there to Arabized Islam because that is what the young with little sense of history believe to be true,' he says.[97] While adults are inveigled through ijtemas or 'Islamic kitty parties', children are roped in through innovative Islamic summer camps. Most parents look for opportunities to enrol their children in some activity during the long summer vacations. What could be better than a religious camp where children spend a few hours every day learning about Islam? With a meal thrown in, these camps are hard to say no to.

◆

The process of Arabization of Sunni Islam began after 1979, when three landmark events shook the Saudi government.[98] The first was the Iranian Revolution, whose reverberations were felt among the Shia population of Saudi Arabia. The second was the seizure of the Grand Mosque of Mecca in December when Wahhabi extremists tried to overthrow the Saudi monarchy. And the third was the Soviet invasion of Afghanistan.

While the first and second events presented a challenge, the third offered an opportunity to the House of Saud to wean the US away from Iran and bring it closer to Saudi Arabia, adding a more durable

[95]Interview with the author, New Delhi, 16 February 2018.

[96]A religious sermon given by the imam after Friday afternoon prayers.

[97]Interview with the author, Bengaluru, 19 February 2019.

[98]Nabil Mouline, 'Can the Saudis Break Up With Wahhabism?', *New York Times*, 3 Jul 2018.

dimension to its hitherto energy-driven relationship with Washington. With the ongoing Teheran hostage[99] crisis and the Soviet push into Afghanistan, the US was more than happy to align itself with Saudi Arabia if it could lead to containing both the Iranian influence in the Middle East and the Soviet advance in South Asia. Meanwhile, with the powers vested in the clergy in Iran, it had started funding Shiite groups in the neighbourhood, including in Saudi Arabia.

'The Saudis launched an ideological offensive and said, "Now we are exporting our own ideology. We will show the hardliners in our own country what we are capable of achieving." Then, they started promoting Wahhabism through intermediaries and organizations like the World Muslim League in different countries throughout Asia, Africa, and parts of Europe,' Professor Susanne Schröter, Director, Frankfurter Research Center for Global Islam, said in an interview to *Deutsche Welle*.[100]

It started with support to the Islamist fighters, mujahids, resisting the Soviet Army in Afghanistan under a trilateral agreement between the US, Pakistan, and Saudi Arabia. But once the radical Islamic forces were unleashed, they could not be held back. Besides, the Saudi government also realized the value of promoting Wahhabi Islam abroad as it kept the conservative Saudi clergy happy and out of the way of the monarchy. It was a happy state of coexistence, based on the spirit of the 1744 agreement between Muhammad bin Saud and Abd al-Wahhab. That agreement split the caliphal roles into two—while political authority rested with Saud, the religious was al-Wahhab's domain. They didn't interfere with each other.

Says Schröter, 'There has been a dramatic development towards radicalism over the past three decades. It is perfectly clear that this development has been encouraged by Saudi money. Moreover, young

---

[99]In November 1979, Iranian students devoted to Ayatollah Khomeini laid siege to the US embassy in Teheran, holding ninety people hostage. The crisis ended in January 1981 with the release of all hostages. In return, the US had to release Iranian assets and accounts which it had frozen after the revolution. See more here: 'Iran Hostage Crisis Fast Facts', CNN.com, 15 Oct 2020.

[100]'Saudi Arabia exports extremism to many countries—including Germany, study says', DW.com, 9 July 2017.

intellectuals have been recruited with generous scholarships at Saudi universities. These people return to their homes after having studied at Saudi universities and suddenly carry out Wahhabi missionary work in all their home countries.'[101]

In India, Saudi money, disparagingly referred to as 'petro dollars', started coming in by the late 1980s. These were channelled into madrassas in the remotest corners of India teaching the Wahhabi/ Salafi version of Islam, wiping out the traditional ways of imparting Islamic education. While earlier the pupil had to come to the madrassas, now madrassas went to the pupil.

Assamese filmmaker Shahnaab Alam remembers the sudden mushrooming of Darul Uloom-sponsored madrassas in and around Guwahati, his home town. Even the foot soldiers of Tablighi Jamaat started carrying out their proselytizing missions in these parts, roping in more and more local youth.

'Two of my cousins joined the Tabligh and were transformed overnight,' recalls Alam.[102]

In the early years, the Saudi government was not discriminatory about the recipients of its generosity. Shaista Amber, the founder-president of the All India Muslim Women's Personal Law Board, recounted the story of her early struggle. In 1996, she had wanted to build an intercommunity mosque in Lucknow where people of all sects and sexes could pray. She approached Maulana Abul Hasan Ali Hasani 'Ali Mian' Nadwi, then chancellor of Darul Uloom Nadwatul Ulama of Lucknow for assistance. Ali Mian promised to help her get funding from Medina. Amber claims that the Saudi government sent the requisite amount to Nadwa to be given to her for the mosque but the money was siphoned off by some middle-level Nadwa officials.

'I complained to Ali Mian,' she recalls, and he was extremely pained by the dishonesty of his own staff, but helpless to hold them accountable. 'Thereafter, he requested the Saudi ambassador to India,

[101]Ibid.

[102]Telephonic interview with the author, 10 March 2019.

who was attending a function at Nadwa, to support me,' she says.[103]

In addition to funding religious education, the Saudi influence is also seen in the Indian Muslim diaspora in the Middle East.

'My maternal uncle and his wife used to work in Saudi Arabia. Whenever they returned to Guwahati during their annual holidays, we used to notice subtle changes, not only in their personality, by way of their clothes and language, but also in their attitude towards Islam,' remarks Alam.[104]

Gradually, they started influencing other family members, telling them that what they had been practising as Islam was not right. 'Hence, traditional religious activities like Darz[105] were frowned upon,' he says. Today, the traditional mekhla chador[106] of Assam is being replaced by so-called Islamic dresses like salwar-suits or shararas (floor-length skirts) complete with the hijab.

The reason Saudi Arabia has been so successful in exporting its version of Islam is the exalted position the country enjoys in the minds of Muslims solely because of the presence of Mecca and Medina in that country. Recognizing this, King Fahd, upon succeeding his father, assumed the title 'Custodian of the Two Holy Mosques' in 1986. And thereafter, for Muslims worldwide, Saudi Arabia became the last word on Islam. For Indians particularly, the region was conflated with religion.

In Islamic traditions, the caliphs controlled the hajj pilgrimage because the shrines were their responsibility. When the Ottomans assumed the caliphate after defeating the Abbasid empire, they controlled the mosques in Mecca and Medina through their local regents. The revenue from the pilgrimage also accrued to them. However, after the defeat of the Ottomans in Word War I, and the end of caliphate, the Saudi government, with the support of, first, Great Britain, and later the US (after the discovery of oil in 1938), took control of the Islamic religious sites, making them an integral

---

[103]Interview with the author, Lucknow, 15 December 2018.

[104]Telephonic interview with the author, 10 March 2019.

[105]Darz is the community reading of the Quran followed by a feast.

[106]A two-piece unstitched garment draped like a saree.

part of the country. This fit well with the Islamist narrative that Arabs are the chosen people because Allah selected them to receive the last Prophet of Islam, Muhammad.

In the eyes of many, successive Saudi regimes have caused the greatest harm to Muslims across the globe.[107] They have radicalized thousands of innocent people, besmirched the name of Islam, which is now often seen as synonymous with terrorist violence, and imperilled the lives of millions, both Muslims and non-Muslims alike, because of their political opportunism and selfishness. Today, the biggest victims of violence at the hands of the Muslims are other Muslims, all in the name of the puritanical Islam peddled by the Saudi government through its Faustian compact with Wahhabi Islamists.

Of course, there is a growing consciousness that there is nothing Islamic or noble about Saudi Arabia, but the emotional attachment to Mecca and Medina prevents people from holding the House of Saud accountable. To save the future of Islam and that of its adherents, this needs to change.[108]

At every stage of its evolution, Islamic history was full of debate and disagreements among its thinkers and theologists. Yet, over the years, Islam started to stultify into an extremely conservative and intolerant religion, one which frequently turned against its own. As Professor Ishaque points out, 'While religion is absolute, its understanding can vary. It will cause no harm if Islamic thought is revisited.'[109] After all, the purpose of Islam was to civilize the human race through a set of moral principles and doctrines. It was an advisory to life, which would fail in its objective if it didn't adapt to the modern world.

---

[107]'Analysis: Saudi policies increasingly hurt Muslim causes worldwide' *TRT World*, 10 January 2020.

[108]'Saudi Policies May Provoke Muslims in the World to Boycott Hajj', *Albawaba News*, 8 July 2019.

[109]In conversation with the author, New Delhi, 5 November 2018.

5

INSECURITIES OF MUSLIMS IN INDIA

The centre table was some distance away. I looked around for something on which to place my glass so I could eat the kebab on the small plate that I was holding in my other hand. Swiftly and suddenly, my host appeared with a low, three-legged stool and placed it next to my chair.

'There you go,' he said cheerfully.

The year was 2010. I was at the home of a serving colonel of the Indian Army in Mhow along with a few of my colleagues. After a full day of interaction at various training institutes of the army, one of the faculty members had invited us home for dinner. It was a pleasant winter evening in early December. The breeze was cool so he had left the window open, and I could see the moon through it.

As the evening progressed, the conversation moved from the military to music. Inspired by the three-legged stool, the sight of the glimmering moon, and the general conviviality, I mentioned a nazm[1] that Urdu poet Kaifi Azmi had recited at my parents' home on one such evening over two decades ago.

'Do you remember it?' the host asked.

I did.

Raat, jab mere hathon ke nazdeek tha mahtaab
Aur main ek dost ke ghar baitha pee raha tha sharaab
Kya haseen bazm thi, kya haseen sham thi
Door tak chandni, door tak gardish-e-jaam thi
Chaand utra zameen par mujhe bekhabar dekh kar

[1]A form of poetry in which only one thought is conveyed, unlike a ghazal, in which each couplet can convey separate ideas.

Aur chupke se aaya uss tipahi ke paas
Ghoont pee kar maine jahan rakh diya tha glass
Mud ke dekha toh hua dil to pech-o-taab
Chaand chori se pee gaya tha saari sharaab[2]

I recited the last line with a bit of a dramatic flourish, as Kaifi Azmi would have done. There was applause. It had barely subsided when the host came over to sit next to me. Leaning across, he said, 'We were talking about future threats a while back.' I was surprised that we were back to military matters.

'One of the threats that we are looking at is Ghazwa-e-Hind.'

My interest was roused. What is that?

'Look it up,' he advised. 'The internet is full of it.'[3] I noticed only later that he said this in a private conversation with me. The others were not party to it.

Several weeks later, my attention was drawn to Ghazwa-e-Hind once again by an email forwarded to me (along with several others) by a retired army officer. For some reason, I was added to the list of recipients even though I didn't know most of them.

The mail explained that the unresolved Kashmir issue was a mere ruse. That Pakistan would not stop bleeding India through a thousand cuts because it was driven by the prophecy of 'Ghazwa-e-Hind'. Finally, I turned to Google. The internet was indeed full of it. Based on some Islamic prophecy, it was believed that Ghazwa-e-Hind would be that decisive war in which the army of the believers would rise in the west to invade India and convert it into Dar-ul-Islam (land of Islam or peace, as Islam means peace) from the present Dar-ul-Harb (land of non-believers, hence conflict).

---

[2]One night, when the moon was within touching distance of my hand/ And I was sipping wine with a friend/ It was a beautiful gathering and a beautiful evening/ The moonlight was all around us, as was the effect of the wine/ Finding me distracted, the moon quietly crept up to the three-legged stool where I had placed my glass after a sip/ When I turned to pick up my glass again, I discovered, much to my chagrin, that the moon had polished off my wine. (Translation by the author.)

[3]In conversation with author, Mhow, December 2010.

Given Pakistan's historic hostility towards India, and the fact that some Indian Muslims cheer the victories of the Pakistani cricket team, the concern, according to this theory, is that Pakistan will be at the helm of this army. Indian Muslims, being fifth columnists, will rise in its support. Forewarned, we now have to be forearmed.

A couple of years later, I met the then recently retired home secretary, G. K. Pillai, for an interview. Towards the end of the conversation, I asked him if he was aware of something called Ghazwa-e-Hind or if it was ever discussed in internal security meetings of the Ministry of Home Affairs. He hadn't even heard the term. I concluded that if the home secretary was not aware of it then clearly it couldn't be a credible threat.

That the internet was full of this conspiracy theory is understandable, but for a serving military officer to mention it could only mean two things—prejudice or a desperate attempt to sound knowledgeable. Of course, a combination of both is also possible. Be that as it may, at the time I first heard of it, on the basis of the evidence available to me, Ghazwa-e-Hind seemed to belong to the realm of fear-mongering conspiracies related to Islam, usually propagated by Hindu right-wing ideologies. However, right-wing Hindus are not the only people who have discovered the uses of this supposed threat. Outside India, it has periodically been used by extremist groups to rally the Muslims. They present it as a Muhammadan prophecy whose time has come. Interestingly, the target is not always the whole of India, despite its name.

In his research paper for the US-based Hudson Institute, former Pakistan diplomat Husain Haqqani wrote, 'Lashkar-e-Taiba has often spoken of Ghazwa-e-Hind as a means of liberating Kashmir from Indian control. The group's founder, Hafiz Muhammad Saeed, has declared repeatedly that "if freedom is not given to the Kashmiris, then we will occupy the whole of India including Kashmir. We will launch Ghazwa-e-Hind. Our homework is complete to get Kashmir".'[4]

This clearly doesn't sound like the war Prophet Muhammad would have prophesied, or even something that the faithful outside

[4]Husain Haqqani, 'Prophecy & the Jihad in the Indian Subcontinent', Hudson Institute, 27 Mar 2015.

Pakistan would be interested in. He further writes, 'Although the idea of Ghazwa-e-Hind as a war against the contemporary Indian state has not been universally accepted, it continues to feature in the jihadist discourse.'[5]

I continue to come across references to Ghazwa-e-Hind in articles and essays written by Indian security experts. In an article published in February 2018, an expert wrote:

> There is yet another reason why Pakistan will continue to trouble India as an enemy nation in the years to come. Not many people in India and elsewhere are aware that many Pakistani ulema, clerics, professional scientists, army personnel and defence experts are actively engaged for years, allegedly citing [a] Hadith, in constantly spreading the ideology of 'Ghazwa-e-Hind', that means conquest of India. Ghazwa means a war to kill Kafirs and Hind is the part of the land of Kafirs today known as India. These people keep on poisoning the minds of Pakistani masses to be ready for the day when the idolaters of the Hind (Hindus) will be conquered and wiped out from the face of the Indian subcontinent.[6] (sic)

Yet not many Indian Muslims are aware of this prophecy (much less preparing for it) or care for it much. The reason is that Ghazwa-e-Hind is a propagandist's tool used by extremists on both sides—Muslims as well as Hindus—based on an entirely unverifiable comment attributed to the Prophet recorded a few centuries after his death. Even conservative Islamic scholars say that it is based on a 'zaeef'[7] (weak) Hadith that has not been corroborated.

Explaining Ghazwa-e-Hind, Ejaz Ahmed Aslam, says, 'All the wars, expeditions in which Prophet Muhammad participated, were called Ghazwa. The expeditions which he ordered but did not participate in

---

[5]Ibid.

[6]Dr Jaipal Singh, 'Terrorism, Ghazwa-e-Hind and Pakistan', Boloji.com, 11 Dec 2020, available here: https://www.boloji.com/articles/50148/terrorism-ghazwa-e-hind-and-pakistan

[7]The types of Hadith as well as their significance have been dealt with in the previous chapter.

were called Sariyyah. Given this, there can be no more ghazawats [plural of ghazwa] any longer. This alone points to the fallacy of this supposed prophecy.' [8]

'In that case, how did this theory originate?'

'There is a Hadith, a weak one, which says that the Prophet had once remarked that "good winds are blowing from India". This was taken by some to mean that the conditions are opportune to wage a successful jihad against India. There are two flaws in this. One, there is no way to authenticate if indeed the Prophet said this; and, two, even if he did, there is no way to know what he meant.'

Central to the Hindu right wing's belief in Ghazwa-e-Hind, or a pan-Islamic conspiracy of invading India to turn it into a Muslim country, is a letter written in the eighteenth century by Shah Waliullah Dehlavi, the renowned Islamic scholar from Delhi.[9]

Shortly after the Battle of Plassey in 1757, which signalled the beginning of the decline of Muslim power in India, the Marathas had started to systematically dislodge Mughal governors from several north Indian provinces. By the late 1750s, they had reduced the Mughal emperor, Alamgir II (the great-grandson of Aurangzeb), to the status of a vassal. The political powerlessness of the Muslims impacted many aspects of their lives—economic, religious, and military.

Shah Waliullah was dismayed by the pathetic state that Muslims, who once ruled not only India, but also much of other parts of the world, had been reduced to. Convinced that once political power was restored to the Muslims, the glory of Islam would be assured, he wrote a letter to Ahmad Shah Abdali, urging him to wage war against the Marathas. There is no record of Ahmad Shah Abdali having received this letter or deciding to attack the Marathas (in the Third Battle of Panipat) on receipt of this letter for the glory of Islam.

According to Professor (Dr) Nazeer Ahmed:

> In 1758, the Maratha armies occupied Lahore and evicted Timur, son of Ahmed Shah Abdali.... Three years later, in 1761, Ahmed

[8]In conversation with the author, New Delhi, 9 November 2018.

[9]For a brief history of Shah Waliullah, see Chapter 2.

> Shah crossed the Indus and took Lahore. A large Maratha army advanced from Delhi and met him on the plains of Panipat. The decisive battle, commonly known as the Third Battle of Panipat, was fought on June 14, 1761. In the desperate clash of arms, over 150,000 Indian soldiers perished, and the Afghans were victorious.[10]

In further proof that this was not a Hindu–Muslim contest for the seat of Delhi, the Maratha army comprised several Muslims, including the commander, Ibrahim Khan Gardi, and Abdali's forces were joined by two Indian nawabs, the Rohillas and Shuja-ud-Daula of Awadh. Moreover, he had bought the neutrality of the Jats and the Rajputs who did not come to the Marathas' assistance.

Moreover, after carrying out a wholesale massacre of Indians, Hindus and Muslims alike, and collecting his booty, Abdali rode back to where he came from. He had no interest in either restoring Muslim power in India or the glory of Islam.

The British, on the other hand, had interests in India, which escaped the attention of Waliullah. The weakened Marathas strengthened the British. Another interesting detail about Waliullah and his successors was that they abhorred the Mughals for their syncretic faith, attitude towards non-Muslims, and their disdain for the ulema. Abdali was no better, according to Waliullah, even surpassing the Mughals in debauchery. So, it is difficult to understand why Waliullah would want one debauch to restore the power of another.

Yet, the letter became the defining proof for the Hindus' suspicion of the Muslims. It was frequently put forward as evidence of the Muslims' unpatriotic temperament. In his book *Terrifying Vision: M. S. Golwalkar, the RSS and India*, Jyotirmaya Sharma writes about Golwalkar's views:

> ...the Muslims in India did not see the creation of Pakistan as a final event. Rather, it was for them a first step towards establishing an Islamic empire....

He accuses them of turning their attention to places outside the country

---

[10]Prof. Dr. Nazeer Ahmed, 'Shah Waliullah of Delhi', *History of Islam*, available here: https://historyofislam.com/contents/resistance-and-reform/shah-waliullah-of-delhi/

and directing their prayers to that destination. Neither do they consider any place within this land sacred.... Using a dark and threatening phrase, he calls them ghar ke baaharwaley or those who are not part of our home....[11]

Madhav Sadashiv Golwalkar was the second chief of the RSS with a tenure spanning thirty-three years (1940–73). In 1966, his speeches were compiled into a book *A Bunch of Thoughts*, which became the guiding principle of the RSS. Even though Keshav Baliram Hedgewar had established the organization in 1925, the credit for its consolidation and expansion goes to Golwalkar, who steered its political and social course.

The animosity of Hedgewar and Golwalkar towards the Muslims was partly the result of their early experiences and partly due to a growing Hindu consciousness. In his 1996 book, *The Hindu Nationalist Movement and Indian Politics*, Christophe Jaffrelot narrates an incident from 1924 in Nagpur where a Hindu–Muslim clash during a religious procession led Hedgewar to conclude that small numbers of Muslims were able to overwhelm Hindus because the latter were 'disorganized and panicky'.[12] This fit in well with the growing narrative of Hindu weakness or cowardliness[13] which led to their subjugation by a foreign power. Hartosh Singh Bal writes:

> Among the most popular explanations, propounded by figures ranging from Vivekananda to Dayananda Saraswati, was that Indian history had seen a steady decline from a glorious Hindu past. Having lost touch with this past, the Hindus were easy prey to foreign invaders, whether they were the Muslims or the British.[14]

---

[11]Jyotirmaya Sharma, *Terrifying Vision: M.S. Golwalkar, The RSS, and India*, New Delhi: Penguin Viking, 2007, pp. 82–83.

[12]Christophe Jaffrelot, *The Hindu Nationalist Movement and Indian Politics*, London: C. Hurst & Co, 1996, p. 34.

[13]In his series of articles for *The Tribune* in 1924, Lala Lajpat Rai wrote (referring to Mahatma Gandhi), 'Mahatmaji himself said that the average Mussalman was a bully, and the average Hindu a coward', *The Hindu-Muslim Problem: A Plea for Mutual Co-Operation* (http://www.columbia.edu/itc/mealac/pritchett/00islamlinks/txt_lajpatrai_1924/13part.html)

[14]Hartosh Singh Bal, 'How an inability to stomach Gandhi's overtures to Muslims led Hedgewar to set up the RSS', *The Caravan*, 10 June 2018.

Consequently, Hedgewar took it upon himself to not only organize but also impart quasi-military training to them. He got together a group of 100 volunteers or swayamsevaks and led a Ganesha procession through a Muslim area up to the mosque in the locality. As expected, the local Muslims came out to protest and the disagreement turned into a riot that lasted for three days. Eventually, the Muslims were forced to retreat and leave Nagpur.[15]

This small victory validated Hedgewar's reasoning that all that the Hindus needed to defeat the Muslims was organization and military training. It's another matter that what he eventually ended up doing was laying the foundation for prejudice and sectarian violence on a hitherto unprecedented scale in post-Independence India. As the late Asghar Ali Engineer recorded in his 2004 volume, *Communal Riots After Independence: A Comprehensive Account.*

> The Sangh Parivar (a collective term for the RSS and its affiliated organizations like the Vishwa Hindu Parishad, Bajrang Dal etc.) not only instigated riots and but also led the rioting mobs on more than one occasion.[16]

But to return to Hedgewar's philosophy of Hindu exclusivism, Akshaya Mukul writes in *Gita Press and the Making of Hindu India*:

> The founder of the RSS, K. B. Hedgewar, put forward his own concept of nation: 'It is not merely some piece of land that is called a Nation. A Nation is formed by people who have held the same thoughts, the same customs, the same culture and the same traditions since long time past.'[17]

---

[15]Tapan Basu, Tanika Sarkar et al, *Khaki Shorts and Saffron Flags: A Critique of the Hindu Right*, Hyderabad: Orient Longman, 1993, pp. 19–20.

[16]Engineer based his book entirely on media reports because, 'The Home Ministry, Government of India, treats its records as secret and had declined our request to provide us with information. We had no other recourse but to rely on the newspaper reports.' Engineer, *Communal Riots After Independence*, p. 7.

[17]Akshaya Mukul, *Gita Press and the Making of Hindu India*, New Delhi: HarperCollins Publishers, 2015, p. 228.

Diversity certainly did not appeal to him. However, the credit for transforming the idea of a monolithic Hindu identity into a philosophy and providing intellectual heft to the sentiment of defeating the Muslims goes to Vinayak Damodar Savarkar. Savarkar propounded the concept of militant Hindu nationalism and coined the term Hindutva in a booklet by the same name. First published in 1923 as *Essentials of Hindutva*, it was republished five years later as *Hindutva: Who Is a Hindu*?

Quoting from the book, Pankaj Mishra writes in *Age of Anger*:

> 'Nothing makes the Self conscious of itself,' Savarkar wrote, 'so much as conflict with [the] non-self. Nothing can weld peoples into a nation and nations into a state as the pressure of a common foe. Hatred separates as well as unites'.[18]

According to Mishra, none of these were original ideas. Savarkar borrowed liberally from the Italian revolutionary Giuseppe Mazzini (1805–72), who not only emphasized using religion to mobilize the public for political purposes but also promoted a revision of history to meet political objectives. Of Mazzini, Mishra writes, 'Mazzini brought God back into the political frame, identifying Him with national sovereignty: "We must convince men," he wrote, "that they are all sons of one sole God, and bound to execute one sole law here on earth.... Ours was not a sect but a religion of patriotism," he clarified. "Sects may die under violence; religions may not".'[19]

'Mazzini,' also 'blithely revised history: the Roman Empire, he claimed, had been the "most powerful nationality of the ancient world".'[20]

Savarkar and other Hindu ideologues like Lala Lajpat Rai and Bipin Chandra Pal were taken over by Mazzini's zeal and conflation of religion with nationalism.

'Lala Lajpat Rai explicitly identified Mazzini as the founder of a new religion, whose creeds of nationality, liberty and unity were to be

[18]Pankaj Mishra, *Age of Anger: A History of the Present*, New Delhi: Juggernaut, 2017, pp. 225–57.

[19]Ibid.

[20]Ibid.

practiced with blood and martyrdom.'[21]

Applying Mazzini's template to India, Savarkar identified Muslims and not the British as the enemy for four probable reasons.

The first was the loss of power. Just as the Muslims found themselves powerless and victimized after 1857, some sections of Hindus, especially the Brahmins, had felt the same sense of powerlessness with the arrival of the Muslims. The invaders didn't bother them so much; they came, plundered and went away; in fact, the invaders came in handy when the narration of cruelty had to be built. However, those who stayed back to make India their home, founded new empires, and created their own kind of social structure were the disrupters, as they co-opted the local Hindus, mainly non-Brahmins—in their enterprises, and perpetuated the powerlessness of the Brahmin class.

This is the reason the Hindu right-wing movement in India, whether the Hindu Mahasabha (whose member Nathuram Godse assassinated Mahatma Gandhi[22] on 30 January 1948) or the RSS, has been spearheaded by Brahmins, the caste that was the first to adopt an English education and a westernized lifestyle because they suffered from what V. S. Naipaul called an 'amalgam of self-adoration and self-contempt'.[23] A consequence of this was the deliberate vilification of the Muslims propelled by social and economic insecurities.

Savarkar's mission to 'Hinduize all politics and militarize Hindudom', was inspired by Hitler and the Nazis.

'A Nation is formed,' Savarkar wrote in 1938, 'by a majority living therein. What did the Jews do in Germany? They being in minority were driven out from Germany.'[24] Admiration for Nazi Germany was widely shared among Hindu nationalists at the end of the 1930s. In his manifesto, *We, or Our Nationhood Defined* (1939), Golwalkar, sarsanghchalak of the RSS from 1940 to 1973, asserted that India was Hindustan, a land of

[21]Ibid.

[22]Vinay Lal, 'Nathuram Godse, the RSS, and the Murder of Gandhi', Manas, UCLA Social Sciences, available here: http://southasia.ucla.edu/history-politics/hindu-rashtra/nathuram-godse-rss-murder-gandhi/

[23]Mishra, *Age of Anger*, p. 375.

[24]Akshay Jog, 'Veer Savarkar, Nazi, Hitler & Jews', *Organiser*, 25 Feb 2020.

Hindus where Jews and Parsis were 'guests' and Muslims and Christians 'invaders'.[25]

The second reason Muslims were targeted was because with the collapse of the Mughal Empire and British reprisals after the revolt of 1857, Muslims, as a community, were considerably weakened and insecure. They were an easy enemy to take on.

Three, given the global rivalry between Christianity and Islam, there was a case for Hindu–British partnership against the Muslims. And, four, the long history of Muslim rule, running into several centuries, had greater potential for revision and distortion to build the narrative of unending Hindu victimhood.

'To this end', writes Mishra, 'Savarkar built a lurid narrative of Muslims humiliating Hindus; but he also played up Muslims' "fierce unity of faith, that social cohesion and valorous fervour which made them a body so irresistible". He gushed enviously about the Prophet and the world dissemination of Islam through a deft use of the "sword"...'[26]

One of the recurring themes of militant Hindu nationalism, which became a symbol of Muslim intolerance and Hindu victimhood, was the claim that between the thirteenth and eighteenth centuries over 60,000 Hindu temples were destroyed by the Muslim rulers. There is no conclusive evidence to support this number. And even though the right wing holds this as an absolute truth, credible historians have exposed it as being fallacious.

In his essay 'Temple Desecration and Indo-Muslim States', historian Richard M. Eaton argues that in ancient and medieval India, temples were closely linked to the ruler of the region, and, hence, were symbols, more of political power, than religious piety. Because of this, the desecration or destruction of temples was commonplace in India as a mark of victory by invading kings much before the arrival of Muslims in the subcontinent. In fact, once the Muslims assumed power in parts of India, they often did

---

[25]Mishra, *Age of Anger*, p. 375.

[26]Ibid.

the exact opposite by becoming benefactors of temples.[27]

'Between 1590 and 1735', Eaton writes, 'Mughal officials repeatedly oversaw, and on occasion even initiated, the renewal of Orissa's state cult, that of Jagannath in Puri. By sitting on a canopied chariot while accompanying the cult's annual car festival, Shah Jahan's officials ritually demonstrated that it was the Mughal emperor, operating through his appointed officer (mansabdar), who was the temple's—and hence the god's—ultimate lord and protector'.[28]

Eaton points out that from the time of the Delhi Sultanate, Muslim rulers relied extensively on the benediction of Sufi saints, primarily of the Chishtiya order, a practice that was continued by the Mughals. Given this, and the fact that most of their military commanders were local Rajputs, they had no reason to indulge in the wanton destruction of temples.

According to Eaton, the primary source for the figure of 60,000 temples is the hagiographic writing of Persian chroniclers whose job it was to raise the profile of their benefactor kings in the eyes of the larger Muslim world. In their perception, the image of a mujahid (God's warrior) or butshikan (destroyer of idols)[29] would have helped raise the stature of Indian Muslim rulers in the eyes of the caliphs.

By studying 'evidence found in contemporary or near contemporary epigraphs and literary evidence spanning more than five centuries (1192–1729)', Eaton has identified 'eighty instances of temple desecration whose historicity appears reasonably certain'.[30]

---

[27]David Gilmartin and Bruce B. Lawrence (eds.), *Beyond Turk and Hindu: Rethinking Religious Identities in Islamicate South Asia,* Gainesville, Florida: University Press of Florida, 2000, p 246, available here: https://static1.squarespace.com/static/56d748571d07c0ad6dd87e74/t/5b9891af2b6a28301fa39e3f/1536725435393/Beyond+Turk+and+Hindu+-+Rethinking+Religious+Identities+in+Islamicate+South+Asia.pdf

[28]Ibid. p. 262.

[29]The importance of idol destruction stems from Prophet Muhammad's cleansing of the Kaaba when he returned to Mecca in order to rid it of pagan religions and claim it as the nucleus of Islam.

[30]Gilmartin and Lawrence, *Beyond Turk and Hindu*, p. 257.

However, historicity means little in the face of belief. Hence, once the Muslim was identified as the enemy, the next step was to vilify him by portraying him as a threat to the nation as well as a subhuman, uncivilized creature unfit for an ancient civilization like India. This was done both blatantly and insidiously. For instance, Pandit Deendayal Upadhyaya, the ideologue and founding member of the Bharatiya Jana Sangh (the forerunner to the BJP), recounted an incident pertaining to M. S. Golwalkar in a lecture delivered on 24 April 1965 in Bombay:

> Once during a conversation between Shri Vinobaji and the Sar Sanghachalak of Rashtriya Swayamsevak Sangh, Shri Guruji (M. S. Golwalkar), a question arose as to where the modes of thinking of Hindus and Muslims differ. Guruji said to Vinobaji that there are good and bad people in every society. There can be found honest and good people in Hindus as well as in Muslims. Similarly rascals can be seen in both the societies. No particular society has a monopoly of goodness. However, it is observed that Hindus even if they are rascals (in) individual life, when they come together in a group, they always think of good things. On the other hand when two Muslims come together, they propose and approve of things which they themselves in their individual capacity would not even think of. They start thinking in an altogether different way. This is an everyday experience. Vinobaji admitted that there was truth in this observation but had no reasons to explain it.[31]

This thought is once again influenced by Christian Europe, whose Islamophobia goes back to the seventh century.

'The Western horror of Islam began with its early, rapid expansion, which seemed irresistible', Stephen Schwartz explains, 'and its terrifying reputation was strengthened by the later victories of Islamic arms during the Crusades, the Arab conquest and Christian reconquest of Spain, the Ottoman invasions of the Balkans and Central Europe, and maritime

---

[31]Deendayal Upadhyaya, Lecture—3rd, *Deendayal Sansar*, 24 Apr 1965, available here: https://deendayalupadhyay.org/leacture3.html

conflicts between Christian states and Muslim navies from Morocco to Cyprus.'[32]

An immediate consequence of this was the vilification and denigration of Islam as a desert cult and Prophet Muhammad as a 'desert bandit'[33]. On the other hand, the Quran not only does not denigrate the prophets of Judaism and Christianity, it honours them as its own, since Islam's theological history comes out of the book of Genesis in the Bible. Prophet Muhammad is believed to have been a descendant of Abraham, one of the most revered and frequently mentioned prophets in the Quran. What's more, an early Quranic verse in Surah Al-Anam forbids Muslims from insulting gods of other religions.[34]

This is the reason even the most radical Islamist does not denigrate icons of other religions, a concession he does not get in return. Hence, the hurt, rage, and sometimes violent outbursts towards those who deliberately mock Prophet Muhammad. In this sense, many Muslims do not understand the civilizational notion of freedom of expression.

Incidentally, through the medieval period and despite the Muslim conquests of the Middle East, Eastern Europe (and Spain) and parts of Asia, the local population was seldom forced to convert. Persecuted communities, like the Jews, were accorded the status of dhimmi, or protected minorities[35]. During the period of Jewish persecution in Europe, first after the reconquest of Spain, and later with the rise of Christian evangelicals, Jews frequently found asylum in Muslim territories. So much so that,

> At the end of the first Christian millennium, Germans, Nordics, Slavs, and Baltic peoples were forcibly baptised and given new names by order of their rulers. Those who resisted were murdered or driven to flight. The persecution and expulsions of Spanish and Portuguese Jews and Muslims were notable examples of Christian intolerance, including public burnings of alleged heretics and secret

---

[32]Schwartz, *The Two Faces of Islam*, p. 291.

[33]Ibid.

[34]Surah Al-Anam, Verse 6.108, https://quran.com/6

[35]Schwartz, *The Two Faces of Islam*, pp. 31–33.

> Jews and Muslims. Rage at the Jewish refusal of Jesus produced centuries of bloodshed and enduring bitterness between the two older branches of the Abrahamic tradition.[36]

This religious prejudice was in full play when the Europeans began the process of colonization, where evangelism was as much the motive as economics. Once Muslim power started to wane with the decay of the Ottoman empire and the rise of the Europeans, especially after the industrial revolution of the eighteenth century, the latter, particularly the French, started reaching out to regions like Egypt, Turkey, Iran, and gradually further south to Lebanon, Syria, and parts of Arabia. The outreach, which was premised on engagement in areas of philosophy, medicine, general sciences, infrastructure, and military technology, gradually led to the shifting of power. Avaricious and weak Muslim rulers started to increasingly depend on their European benefactors to keep their restive populations in check, and over time lost more of their control, ending up as regimes subservient to the European powers.[37]

The concept of Islamic terrorism, as it is known today, traces its origins to the pushback from oppressed Muslim people from this era, first, against their own oppressive regimes and, later, against the Europeans.

This was also the time when Indians, of whom Muslims comprised a large segment, rose up against the British. Collectively, all this brought back memories of the Crusades. Once again, it was not only convenient, but easy, too, to cast Muslims as marauding, uncivilized hordes who wanted to impose their primitive desert culture on modern civilizations. In India, this was ready-made material for the educated and 'conscious Hindu' to construct a narrative of a superior civilization that had suffered defeat and humiliation at the hands of uncouth Muslim marauders for over eight centuries.

It doesn't take much for an inflamed religious consciousness to devolve into bigotry. As Shah Waliullah had tried in the eighteenth century to rid the Indian Muslims of Hindu influences, the beginning

[36]Ibid., p. 291.

[37]Bellaigue, *The Islamic Enlightenment*, p. 355.

of the nineteenth century saw efforts by Hindu reformers, agitated by the supposed abjectness of their people's faith, to revive and reform Hinduism, and to restore its glory, and prevent ambivalent members of the flock from drifting towards Islam and Christianity.

The Brahmo Samaj movement began in Calcutta in 1828 and remained largely limited to Bengal, but a more widespread movement—the Arya Samaj—began in 1875 in Bombay to restore the pride of Hindus in their faith and prevent poaching by Christian evangelicals. With this as the guiding principle, the Arya Samaj introduced the concept of proselytization in Hinduism.[38]

To launch a project that restored pride, the Hindus first needed to be told how their pride had been hurt. By the beginning of the twentieth century, a sense of separateness—fostered by a combination of religious superiority and the effects of the cultural-political subjugation of centuries—had started to develop among Hindus in certain parts of north and west India. Muslims were increasingly being viewed not only as outsiders but also as usurpers of the rightful place of the Hindus.

The first effort to consolidate the Hindus was made in 1909 by Lala Lajpat Rai. He established the Hindu Sabha in Lahore, which metamorphosed into the Hindu Mahasabha in 1915, the credit for which goes to Madan Mohan Malviya, who also established the Banaras Hindu University the following year. Around the same time, the Muslim League was formed (in 1906), with the slogan of safeguarding the political interests of Muslims in the reformed legislative councils. In 1909, the British Indian government introduced the concept of separate electorates for the Muslims. Ostensibly, this was done to ensure that the Muslims were not overwhelmed by the Hindu majority. But, in reality, it edged the Muslims out of the freedom movement. This widened the rift that had started to form between the two communities since 1857. As mentioned earlier, the brunt of the British reprisal was borne by the Muslims, with many well-placed Hindus collaborating with the British.

World War I and the defeat of Turkey didn't help matters. A section

[38]Gyanendra Pandey, *A History of Prejudice: Race, Caste, and Difference in India and the United States*, Cambridge: CUP, 2013, p. 64.

of Indian Muslim politicians rose in defence of the Ottomans, seeing in their defeat the fall of the caliphate and consequently an attack on their faith. Even though Mahatma Gandhi co-opted the Khilafat agitation for the restoration of the caliphate into his Non-cooperation Movement of 1920, it was clear that a large section of the Muslim intelligentsia was in this for sectarian reasons (see Chapter 6: Minority Politics).

The Khilafat movement petered out because the Turks themselves had had enough of the caliphate. And the Gandhi-constructed Hindu–Muslim unity collapsed in violence, starting with the Moplah rebellion of 1921 and the Chauri Chaura incident of 1922. While the Chauri Chaura incident was an open-and-shut case where the police firing on peaceful protestors in a town in what is now Uttar Pradesh led to retaliation by mobs of rioters who set a police station on fire, killing everyone inside, the Moplah rebellion, which engulfed many parts of Kerala, was a lot more complex. It was a significant event not only in the Indian freedom struggle but also in the subsequent history of the peasant struggle in India. However, viewed through the lens of the Hindu right wing, the Moplah uprising was another piece of evidence of Muslim fanaticism, pan-Islamism, and intolerance.

The uprising of 1921 in Kerala was the culmination of a series of mini agrarian rebellions by the tillers (Muslims) against the landlords (upper-caste Hindus) over several years. In 1921, the agrarian protest coalesced with the freedom struggle, as the landlords were seen to be complicit with the British. Violence broke out in several districts, targeting both the landlords and British troops. Gradually, as the soldiers retreated in the face of the rebellion, the movement became anarchic, with the rebels running amok. Muslim religious leaders gave the rebellion a Hindu–Muslim flavour. Not only were Hindu landlords and their families killed indiscriminately, in many places they were forcibly converted to Islam. Eventually, British troops hit back hard to curb the rebellion. More violence and deaths followed. Among the grisly incidents of the rebellion was the death of over sixty Muslim prisoners caused by suffocation in a windowless train bogey en route to prison.[39]

---

[39]O. P. Ralhan, *Encyclopaedia of Political Parties: India, Pakistan, Bangladesh: National,*

Exaggerated claims of casualties were made by all sides. But the most enduring legacy of the rebellion was the massacre of the Hindus in the Malabar coastal belt in the name of establishing Khilafat. Those weeks of madness helped the Hindu leaders build their support base in all three dimensions—the intellectual, physical and emotional.

As Akshaya Mukul explains:

> The 1920s saw Hindus and Muslims slugging it out in the open through a series of communal riots 'marked by increasing violence and cruelty'—a 'casual list' puts the number of riots in this decade at twenty-nine through the length and breadth of the country, from the Moplah riots in Malabar (1921) to Ajmer and Sindh (1923), Delhi and Lucknow (1924), Allahabad, Calcutta and Sholapur (1925) to Lahore and Nagpur (1927) and Bombay (1929).[40]

The intellectual dimension was provided by Savarkar and his West-inspired treatise. The physical void was filled by RSS foot soldiers. The emotional rousing at the grassroots level was done by the magazine *Kalyan*, brought out by the Gorakhpur-based Gita Press, through exhortations: 'how the decline in religious faith had adversely affected sanatan Hindu dharma....'[41] *Kalyan* also impressed upon its readers definitions of what it deemed to be religions which were part of the larger Hindu faith. 'Buddhists, Jains, Sikhs are various branches of the giant Hindu tree. Gita Press considered religions born within India as part of the Hindu culture.'[42] This same line was also followed by the Hindu Mahasabha and the RSS, all of whom worked towards a common goal as it became increasingly clear that Independence was going to be a reality. 'In the 1940s, as the prospect of Independence and subsequently Partition became real,' explains Mukul, 'the focus of Gita Press and *Kalyan* turned entirely political, reporting and interpreting events through the communal prism.... The Gita Press took its cordial

---

Regional, Local, New Delhi: Anmol Publications, 1996, p. 297.

[40]Mukul, *Gita Press and the Making of Hindu India*, p. 228.

[41]Ibid., p. 233.

[42]Ibid.

relationship with the RSS and the Hindu Mahasabha to another level, that of open collaboration.'[43] Lending credibility to *Kalyan*'s editorials were mainstream political and intellectual heavyweights like Malaviya who provided 'ample fodder during the communally rife period between 1940–1947'.[44]

This trilateral attack—intellectual, physical, and emotional—was rather successful. Many in the country began pushing for partition of the country based on religion, while at the same time, blaming Muslims for partition. In keeping with this, the idea of a separate homeland for Muslims was first floated by Lala Lajpat Rai who, despite his association with the Hindu Mahasabha, was also a member of the Indian National Congress.

In a series of thirteen articles[45] published in *The Tribune* in 1924, Lala Lajpat Rai introduced his readers to the idea of Hindus and Muslims being different people whose unity was an artificial construct. Hence, for the attainment of Swarajya, sacrifices were required and one of these was the partition of Hindu and Muslim states. In the eleventh article, he wrote:

> Under my scheme the Muslims will have four Muslim States: (1) The Pathan Province or the North-West Frontier, (2) Western Punjab, (3) Sindh, and (4) Eastern Bengal. If there are compact Muslim communities in any other part of India, sufficiently large to form a province, they should be similarly constituted. But it should be distinctly understood that this is not a united India. It means a clear partition of India into a Muslim India and a non-Muslim India.[46]

Despite this, it seemed to me that the Hindu right wing not only successfully assumed victimhood but also convinced the Muslims that

---

[43]Ibid., p. 234.

[44]Ibid., p. 4.

[45]'The Hindu-Muslim Problem (1924): A series of thirteen newspaper articles by Lala Lajpat Rai (1865-1928)', available here: http://www.columbia.edu/itc/mealac/pritchett/00islamlinks/txt_lajpatrai_1924/txt_lajpatrai_1924.html

[46]The Hindu-Muslim Problem (1924): Some suggestions for political improvements, available here: http://www.columbia.edu/itc/mealac/pritchett/00islamlinks/txt_lajpatrai_1924/11part.html

they alone must bear the blame for dividing the country. On 16 August 1946, when the killings began in Calcutta on the call of Direct Action Day by Jinnah, once again the popular narrative was written of marauding Muslims killing helpless Hindus. While Muslims did start the violence with the tacit nod of the chief minister Huseyn Shaheed Suhrawardy, Hindu retaliation was swift and brutal.[47]

Quoting Sumit Sarkar's *Modern India, 1885–1947*, Mukul writes, 'more Muslims seem to have died than Hindus, a point made by both Wavell and Sardar Patel'.[48] But, in my view, the Hindu right wing narrative created the stereotype of the peace-loving, passive Hindu who suffered through a 'millennium' because of his passivity. Accuracy, clearly, is the first casualty of propaganda.

Through *Kalyan*'s November 1946 issue, Malaviya called for 'unity among the Hindus...due to the action of the Muslim world'. He also 'exhorted the "majority Hindus" to adopt a militant outlook: "Those who do not let Hindus live in peace do not deserve any compassion... Hindus should help each other.... If Hindus do not protect themselves they will die".'[49]

This narrative of Hindu passivity and victimhood continued right through Partition. It held that the Hindus, and, to some extent, Sikhs, were the victims while Muslims were the perpetrators, despite the fact that RSS foot soldiers were involved in concerted violence against the Muslims, not only before Partition but also after it.

Mukul recounts that in the same November 1946 issue, *Kalyan* published an anonymous letter purportedly written by a Bengali woman who was the victim of Muslim-perpetrated violence. In the hugely provocative letter, the woman narrated in graphic detail the ordeal she had suffered at the hands of Muslim marauders. The letter concluded by calling Hindu men 'impotent'. The letter writer 'appealed to Hindu women to come together and forget their dependence on men', and

---

[47]Mukul, *Gita Press and the Making of Hindu India*, p. 234.

[48]Ibid.

[49]Ibid., p. 239.

fight Muslim tyranny with the sword.[50]

The same anonymous letter was also published as a leaflet by the Hindu Mahasabha and was widely circulated. Subsequently, another right-wing publication, *Mahratta*, published out of Pune republished the letter. Given the widespread distribution of the letter and its potential to fan communal violence, the Criminal Investigation Department of Uttar Pradesh (then the United Provinces) in its weekly report to the home secretary of UP, Rajeshwar Dayal, recommended that the magazine *Kalyan*, 'which has a very wide circulation in India and the effect of the article mentioned may be extremely bad'[51] should be banned and the leaflets confiscated.

That the publication of this letter was part of a larger conspiracy wherein the RSS intended to carry out concerted attacks against the Muslims in western UP was discovered later. In his memoirs, *A Life of Our Times*, first published in 1998, Rajeshwar Dayal writes that Deputy Inspector General B. B. L. Jaitley came to him with documents that showed the plan to hit Muslim areas in UP:

> Greatly alarmed by those revelations, I immediately took the police party to the Premier's [chief minister's] house. There, in a closed room, Jaitley gave a full report of his discovery, backed by all the evidence contained in the steel trunks. Timely raids conducted on the premises of the RSS (Rashtriya Swayamsevak Sangh) had brought the massive conspiracy to light. The whole plot had been concerted under the direction and supervision of the Supremo of the organization himself. Both Jaitley and I pressed for the immediate arrest of the prime accused, Shri Golwalkar, who was still in the area.[52]

But the chief minister did not order the arrest of Golwalkar, instead asking for the Cabinet to rule on it. 'There were also other political compulsions, as RSS sympathizers, both covert and overt, were to be

[50]Ibid., p. 243.

[51]Mukul, *Gita Press and the Making of Hindu India*, p. 244.

[52]Rajeshwar Dayal, *A Life of Our Times*, New Delhi: Orient Longman, 1998, p. 93–94.

found in the Congress Party itself and even in the Cabinet....' The Cabinet issued a letter to Golwalkar demanding an explanation for the material that had been found.

Golwalkar, however, had been tipped off and he was nowhere to be found in the area.... This infructuous chase continued from place to place and weeks passed.[53]

The RSS, however, remained undeterred by any action by the authorities. On 14 March 1948, Rajendra Prasad, then president of the Congress party, and later first President of India, wrote to Home Minister Sardar Patel:

> I am told that RSS people have a plan of creating trouble. They have got a number of men dressed as Muslims and looking like Muslims who are to create trouble with the Hindus by attacking them and thus inciting the Hindus. Similarly there will be some Hindus among them who will attack Muslims and thus incite Muslims. The result of this kind of trouble amongst the Hindus and Muslims will be to create a conflagration.[54]

Despite vigilance and the positive fervour of nation-building, incidents of communal violence could not be checked. Of course, the biggest act of communal violence was the assassination of Gandhi on 30 January 1948 by Hindu extremist Nathuram Godse, who claimed to have quit the RSS, while remaining a member of the Hindu Mahasabha. A school of thought subsequently insisted, led by no less than Nathuram's brother, Gopal Godse, that Nathuram claimed to have left the RSS only to protect its leadership from prosecution.[55]

Even though the RSS was not directly blamed for the Mahatma's assassination, the organization was banned for a year. At the end of the year, Home Minister Patel listed a few conditions, which Golwalkar accepted.[56] The ban was lifted in July 1949. But sporadic violence against

---

[53]Ibid., p. 93–94.

[54]Neerja Singh (ed.), *Nehru Patel: Agreement Within Difference: Select Documents & Correspondences 1933-1950; Rajendra Prasad to Sardar Patel*, Delhi: NBT, p. 43.

[55]A. G. Noorani, 'The BJP and Nathuram Godse', *Frontline*, 8 Feb 2013.

[56]P. L. John Panicker, 'Gandhian approach to communalism in contemporary

Muslims, explained as anger fuelled by the Partition of the country, continued into the early years of the next decade. While the foot soldiers of the RSS and its cohorts were avenging their centuries-old humiliation on the streets, its ideologues were adding new nuances to the theory of Islamic/ Muslim perfidy. Given the relentlessness of these narrations, Muslims who chose to stay in India after Partition internalized the blame, weighed down by the guilt of dividing the country. This guilt has shaped their post-Independence politics in India. Not only were they made to feel unwelcome, but they also accepted this ignominy as atonement for their supposed sins. Take, for example, the views of Dr Rafiq Zakaria, a politician and author of several books, including *Sardar Patel and Indian Muslims*. According to Aakar Patel, a journalist and former executive director, Amnesty International, in the book, Zakaria discusses the deliberations of the constituent assembly on the issue of separate electorates which had been in practice since the British implemented the order in 1909. While the Sikhs demanded separate electorates in independent India, the Muslims opted for joint electorates, much to the relief and pleasure of Sardar Patel. Zakaria told Aakar Patel in an interview about his book, 'Patel understood that the Muslims, if left to themselves, would not insist on separate electorates, given Partition. He wanted Indian Muslims to come up with the proposal of joint electorates, absolving them forever of the charge of being divisive.'[57] Not only did Patel believe that Muslims were guilty of something, Zakaria condoned that belief.

The inheritance of guilt continues. Explaining a Muslim bureaucrat's diffidence in standing up for Muslim citizens, Najeeb Jung, former vice chancellor, Jamia Millia Islamia, and former Delhi Lieutenant Governor, says, 'It could be a legacy of the Partition. Some individual bureaucrats may feel a sense of insecurity born of guilt because Muslims demanded and got a separate homeland.' However, he added, this does not hold

India', *Shodhganga*, p. 100, available here: https://shodhganga.inflibnet.ac.in/handle/10603/7178

[57]Aakar Patel, 'The Case Against Joint Electorate', *Mint*, 30 Jun 2016.

true for all Muslim civil servants, certainly not for him.[58]

Mohammed Adeeb, an Uttar Pradesh-based politician and a former Member of Parliament, takes guilt to yet another level. He says, 'Muslims forfeited their rights to pursue their politics after Partition. Their only hope today is to stand with secular Hindus.'[59]

However, as Jung pointed out to me, it is evident in the manner today's Muslim youth take to the streets to assert their rights that perhaps the present generation of Muslims has shrugged off their parents' guilt. Yet, as I see frequently on my social media feed, a large number of Hindu youth, especially those aligned with the Sangh Parivar, continue to carry the burden of victimhood that their forefathers bore and then bequeathed to them. And in this, they remain victims of a skewed recording of history. As a result, the Hindu right wing's role in lobbying for Partition and, thereafter, in the violence that ensued has been whitewashed in the popular narrative.[60] The only unambiguous villain of the Partition of India is Muhammad Ali Jinnah. While the RSS frequently blames Congress leaders, starting with Jawaharlal Nehru, for Partition, hardly anyone apportions blame to the RSS.

Even today, the focus of Hindu communalism remains Partition, which is seen as the final assault by Muslims on the motherland after centuries of rapacious violations. This fuels and sustains the hatred that the foot soldiers of the Hindu right wing feel, and translates into abominable violence during communal riots decades after Partition.

Engineer attributes the growth of Hindu communalism to this distorted writing of history:

> The nature of education imparted is also quite problematic. It is far from secular and scientific as was assumed by Nehru. He was too optimistic in this regard. Education is a state subject and the Central Government could hardly influence the educational policy. Those who have [a] communal outlook control most of the educational institutions. The textbooks could not be changed

[58]Interview with the author, New Delhi, 13 February 2019.

[59]Interview with the author, Gurugram, 9 April 2019.

[60]A. G. Noorani, 'The RSS is at war with India's past', *The Hindu*, 1 May 2019.

> even after fifty years of independence. The history textbooks are still quite distorted and are written with [a] communal outlook. Thus, education has become a powerful instrument of spreading communal outlook.[61]

A measure of what Engineer writes can be seen from the reach of the RSS at all levels of society. In 2009, I interviewed Ram Madhav, then member, central executive, and spokesperson of the RSS, on increasing religiosity (and hence communalism) in society for an article I was writing.[62] He is now a general secretary of the ruling BJP and is one of their principal ideologues. According to him, the RSS ran 12,000 schools, called Vidya Bharati, as well as 100,000 projects in various tribal areas. Today, these schools cater to 3,200,000 students.[63]

'We have worked towards increasing the consciousness about the Hindu values in the country through our various organizations,' Madhav said to me, referring to the political wing, the BJP; the student body, Akhil Bharatiya Vidyarthi Parishad (ABVP); the labour organization, Bharatiya Mazdoor Sangh (BMS); an organization that focuses on global Hindus, the Vishwa Hindu Parishad (VHP), and so on. He added that RSS-run organizations have a presence in more than eighty countries throughout the world. Apart from schools, the RSS also runs several institutes of higher learning, including polytechnics and preparatory centres for admission into military institutes like the NDA.

I had also spoken to Engineer for the same article. Voicing concern about this vast network, and its impact upon the secular values of Indian society, he had said, 'By refusing government funds, it (RSS) brooks no interference in their educational curricula at all levels. Today, there are millions of people in various industries and organizations who have been trained by the RSS at some stage of their lives. And they bring their RSS-induced prejudices to their work and social sphere.'[64]

---

[61]Engineer, *Communal Riots After Independence*, p. 1.

[62]Ghazala Wahab, 'Deadly Cocktail', *FORCE*, July 2009.

[63]'PM Modi urges Vidya Bharati schools to aim for excellence', *Indian Express*, 13 Feb 2016.

[64]Wahab, 'Deadly Cocktail'.

Much before these prejudices showed up in polite society, they were rather evident on the streets, where RSS foot soldiers started to use Hedgewar's 1927 playbook to instigate communal violence. After the relative calm of the 1950s, the next decade put the idea of India to its first serious test. Starting with Jabalpur in February 1961, riots broke out with regular frequency—about six a year. The first major riot of the decade happened in Calcutta and other parts of West Bengal in 1964 in which 208 people died (unofficially, the figure is around 500) in Calcutta alone.[65]

Three years later, Ranchi convulsed with communal violence. It had started as a protest by the Bharatiya Jana Sangh against Urdu being made the second official language in the state. A total of 184 people died, of which 164 were Muslims. Of the 611 arrested for rioting, 409 were Hindus. The hand of the RSS and its affiliates was openly discernible, which led to the arrest of several of them. Also, perhaps, because of the nature of the state government, the police remained non-partisan.

Ranchi held lessons for the future, but the lessons remained unlearnt. The biggest riot of that decade took place in September 1969 in Ahmedabad. The trigger was a petty altercation between a few Hindu priests and some Muslims who had collected for the annual procession commemorating the death anniversary of one Pir Bukhari Sahib. It started with name-calling and developed into a scuffle. The scuffle spiralled into riots over the next few days, which spread to other parts of Gujarat. The official figure of deaths was 660, of which 430 were Muslims. Unofficially, the figure is somewhere between 1,000 and 2,000.[66]

As violence engulfed city after city in Gujarat, it was clear that the trigger was immaterial. What mattered was the underlying distrust bordering on hatred between the two communities. That the police force was not immune to this hatred was made clear when in their testimonies to the Justice P. Jaganmohan Reddy Commission (appointed by the government to enquire into the causes of the riots), several policemen

---

[65]Engineer, *Communal Riots After Independence*, pp. 33–34.

[66]Poorna Swami, 'A Template for Violence: The riots that changed the course of Gujarat's political history', *The Caravan*, 18 Sep 2019.

gave exaggerated versions of the riots, largely blaming the Muslims for the violence.[67]

According to Engineer, the Muslims of Ahmedabad alone suffered damages worth ₹34,738,224.[68] The biggest damage, however, was to the social fabric of not just Ahmedabad, but Gujarat itself, as insecure Muslims slunk into ghettos and the supposedly 'victorious' Hindus created borderlines within the city, dividing the Hindu areas from the Muslim ones—menacingly referred to as Hindustan–Pakistan.

The significance of the Gujarat violence lay in its experimental nature. In 1969, the RSS updated the old trope of Muslims being outsiders who could not be trusted. The two wars in quick succession that India fought with Pakistan—1965 and 1971—helped it create a new class of 'Other'—Muslim fifth columnists whose loyalties were with Pakistan. The fact that a large number of Indian Muslims had families across the border and often travelled to meet them helped. Hence, as a prelude to the actual violence, RSS-affiliated groups played on the Hindu sense of pride by repeatedly telling them how they were emasculated by foreign invaders who not only took their land, livelihood, and religion, but women too. These messages were drilled into those faithful who were susceptible to it, and many of them were, through pamphlets and speeches in select public meetings.

As a consequence, violence against Muslim women went beyond rape. 'Women were raped or stripped bare and forced to walk naked on the road. Children were beaten against stones or their legs were torn apart. Limbs were cut off dead bodies. Women's breasts were cut and sex organs were mutilated or torn apart.'[69]

The second step to riot preparation was to collect data on Muslim households and businesses (as was done in UP two decades earlier), so that they could be targeted and attacked before the police could react. As in the war of attrition, the idea was to degrade the economic standing of Muslims so they would be reduced to near penury. After the

[67]Ibid.

[68]Engineer, *Communal Riots After Independence*, pp. 31–194

[69]Swami, 'A Template for Violence'.

Ahmedabad violence, several middle- and upper-middle-class Muslim families had to live in refugee camps for months before shifting to government allotted quarters.

Many, like my great-aunt's family, never recovered from the violence of 1969. Her husband, who used to run a successful cloth shop, died in a refugee camp, leaving her with three young daughters. She used the compensation money to marry her daughters off in quick succession lest something 'unspeakable' happened to the young, unmarried, fatherless girls. In fact, one of her daughters, despite her higher secondary education, was married to a semi-literate daily wager at the refugee camp, because that was the best my great-aunt could find in a hurry. Agra was too far away, and her relatives too poor at that point to do much. The daughters who were forced to marry below their social station gradually became part of the new milieu, their children forced to join the informal workforce when they were still teenagers.

The third step was the outreach to sympathetic policemen in sensitive areas who could be relied on to look the other way when Muslims were under attack or open fire when Hindus were being attacked. This was important to ensure that the Hindutva foot soldiers did not pay too high a price for service to their cause.[70]

All subsequent riots in India followed more or less a similar pattern. In fact, in many instances of violence in later years, more Muslims died because of police firing than in the rioting. In that sense, the word riot is a bit of a misnomer. In the long history of communal violence in India, including the anti-Sikh massacre of 1984, the state has been, if not an enabler, a spectator to the viciousness of the mob. Law-enforcement agencies have been afflicted by the 'few hours' syndrome whereby Hindu rioters are allowed a free run for a few hours before the police intervenes.

According to Engineer, while communal propaganda ensured that there was always religious tension between the two communities, the riots themselves were often caused by economic or political rivalry. Hence, despite the absence of communal harmony or intercommunity social engagements in many parts of the country, violence was seldom

---

[70]Swami, 'A Template for Violence'.

spontaneous. It was always engineered by vested interests.

'Communal violence can never be explained in terms of religion alone', Engineer explains. 'The religious factor is only apparent; but not real. Religion is being exploited by vested interests to suit their own ends. Religion is emotionally appealing and thus acts as a powerful instrument of mobilisation of potential and latent elements.'[71]

For any propaganda to succeed, it is important that the friction that fuels the propaganda stays fresh. Hence, throughout the decade of the 1970s, sporadic riots continued to take place in different parts of India, with casualties of 10 to 50 in each of them.[72]

The next major conflagration happened almost a decade after the Gujarat carnage, this time in Jamshedpur in Bihar. In a throwback to Ranchi, the RSS once again did not hesitate to show its hand upfront. The run-up to the riot saw the same tactic as the one adopted by Hedgewar in 1927. The occasion was Ram Navami. For years, a particular route had been fixed for the traditional procession. However, in 1978, the devotees proceeded via Route No. 14, which went through a Muslim locality, leading to an exchange of harsh words. Before the 1979 procession, the local administration, fearing trouble, suggested an alternate route, No. 15, to the Akhara Samiti that was scheduled to take out the procession. The Samiti was offended. It approached the Patna High Court, which stood behind the local administration. The Samiti was even more offended.

India Today magazine wrote in its 15 May 1979 issue:

> Thus checkmated, the Akhara Samiti decided to launch a tougher offensive this year. The Akhara Samiti, made up of traders who are staunch Hindus, also includes some avowed RSS workers who, it has been suggested by leaders as far apart as Raj Narain and the Shahi Imam of New Delhi's Jama Masjid...took encouragement from RSS chief Balasaheb Deoras's presence in Jamshedpur on April 1 when he addressed a huge rally in the town's Regal Ground.
>
> On April 7, a provocative pamphlet was circulated all over the

[71]Engineer, *Communal Riots After Independence*, p. 8.
[72]Ibid.

> city, stating 'that despite the peaceful protests of the people against the arrests and despite their having suffered sundry oppressions, the administration's efforts in oppressing the Hindus had gone on unabated'. The morning of April 11 was mooted as the day for all the akharas to unite and carry out a combined procession following Route No. 14.[73]

The local administration did what it could. It formed a committee comprising Hindus and Muslims to ensure that the procession remained peaceful. But those taking part in the the procession had other plans. As it meandered down Route No. 14, 'it halted near the mosque.... In spite of the District Collector making the best possible efforts to get the procession moved and cleared through the new Purulia road, the procession was held up with the result that communal disturbances flared up.'[74]

According to the *India Today* article quoted above:

> No one quite knows who called the first cry, or on whose roof the first firecrackers were burst. At about midday, the loud cries of Jai Bajrang mingled with stone-throwing, and the BMP (Bihar Military Police) began to open its first rounds of fire. After that there was no end.[75]

The end was finally reached after a couple days. The result: 117 dead, of which 'more than half were Muslims'.[76] The Bihar government instituted a three-member commission to enquire into the riots. The commission submitted its report in October 1981, indicting the RSS, its leader Deoras, the Bharatiya Jana Sangh's member of the Bihar Legislative Council, Dinanath Pandey, RSS-affiliated labour organization, BMS, and the BMP. The RSS immediately went on the offensive condemning

---

[73]Sunil Sethi and Farzand Ahmed, 'More than 100 lives lost in Jamshedpur communal riots' *India Today*, 26 Feb 2014.

[74]Engineer, *Communal Riots After Independence*, p. 49.

[75]Sethi and Ahmed, 'More than 100 lives lost in Jamshedpur communal riots'.

[76]Ibid.

the commission report.[77] Despite all the mudslinging, allegations, and counter-allegations nothing happened. Jamshedpur became another footnote, for a time.

The first incident of communal violence that I became aware of was Moradabad, 1980, though I learnt of it only in 1981. It was Eid day, at the end of July 1981. As was the family tradition, all of us kids had woken up early, bathed, and got dressed in our festival finery to accompany our fathers and uncles to Eidgah (a mosque with a large open ground where Eid prayers are offered) for the Eid namaz. However, instead of leaving for namaz, I noticed that all the adult males had collected in my grandfather's room for a meeting. The women and children were kept out.

The meeting didn't last long. They had discussed whether the children should be taken along for the Eid prayer. It was finally decided that the risk was too great. That the men were risking their lives was bad enough. One of my aunts pleaded with my uncle to offer the Eid prayer at home instead of going to Eidgah. But that would have been too cowardly. 'After all,' my father declared, 'we have to send out the message that everything is normal.'

The women of the family offered their Eid namaz in a huddle, praying for peace, and the safe return of their men, even as the other children and I sat in the central courtyard, aware of the sombreness of the occasion. It did not seem like Eid at all, more like a day of reckoning. The excitement of the festival began only after the men returned home safely.

Later in the day, I pestered my father to tell me about the source of the tension that had spoilt the festival for us and discovered the horror of Moradabad, 1980. Just as 6 December 1992, the day the Babri Masjid was demolished, is carved into the psyche of every Indian Muslim as the day their illusions were shattered, Moradabad, 1980, is post-Independence India's Jallianwala Bagh. The only difference is the victims were not freedom fighters but ordinary Muslim worshippers; the perpetrators were not colonial troopers, but independent India's police force.

---

[77]'Jamshedpur riots: Commission blames RSS for outbreak of communal disturbances', *India Today*, 31 Oct 2013.

On 13 August 1980, thousands of Muslims, some say close to 40,000, had collected in the Eidgah for the annual Eid prayer. Just as the prayer concluded, a pig ran into the Eidgah. This naturally led to a commotion. The worshippers urged the personnel of the PAC deployed there for security to remove the pig. The PAC refused, saying it was not their job. An altercation ensued and the people started assaulting the PAC personnel.

Feeling threatened by the crowd, the PAC opened fire on the unarmed worshippers. And continued to fire. According to Engineer's book, officially 119 people died that day. However, locals claim casualties of over 300.[78] The tragedy gave rise to three questions.

One, given that Eid is the biggest Muslim festival worldwide, and that Muslims consider pig an unclean animal, even the touching of which requires purification, how could the animal enter a Muslim place of worship, on Eid day no less? This was even more perplexing given the security detailing and deployment of the armed PAC to prevent any untoward incident.

Two, once the pig managed to enter and it was brought to the notice of the PAC, how did they imagine they could maintain peace without immediately removing the object that was causing such distress to the worshippers? Worse, they told the devotees that removing the pig from the place of worship was not their job. Being a UP cadre force, how were they so oblivious to the sensitivities of the local Muslims?

Three, even one shot in the air is enough to deter unarmed civilians. Why didn't the PAC stop after the first or second round of firing? What could have led them to continue firing, even when they could see a stampede unfolding before them?

The UP government, then led by V. P. Singh (who was briefly prime minister of India in 1989–90), had no answers. On the advice of the UP police, which believed that questioning their motives would demoralize the men, the government cast the cold-blooded massacre as a Hindu–Muslim riot, even when it was clear that

[78]Sharjeel Imam and Saquib Salim, 'Remembering 1980 Moradabad Muslim massacre: A harsh indictment of 'secular' and Left politics', *FirstPost*, 26 Jun 2017.

> Men of the Provincial Armed Constabulary opened fire on about 40,000 Muslims while they were at Eid prayers. No one knows exactly how many people died. What is known is that the incident at Moradabad was not a Hindu–Muslim riot but a calculated cold-blooded massacre of Muslims by a rabidly communal police force which tried to cover up its genocide by making it out to be a Hindu–Muslim riot.[79]

Like the Jamshedpur killings, the Moradabad massacre also receded from public memory in time. But before that could happen, the ripples from this incident were seen across several cities of India for the next few months. Muslims held protests, some violent, in places as diverse as Jammu & Kashmir, Bihar, Gujarat, and Karnataka, in addition to several places in UP.[80] The impact on my family was that our Eid prayers shifted from the Eidgah to the Taj Mahal, where slightly more privileged devotees gathered; moreover, it was perceived to be more insulated from prejudice than the Eidgah or Jama Masjid.

The decade of the eighties was perhaps the worst in India as far as communal relations were concerned. The south of the country was not immune to the tensions. One of the most destabilizing incidents was the conversion of 558 Dalits to Islam in February 1981 in Meenakshipuram, a small village in Tamil Nadu.[81] The mass conversion came as a surprise and a jolt to the rest of the country. 'Some Arya Samaj groups screamed "foreign money".'[82]

Consequently, members of the Arya Samaj, RSS, and BJP, led by party president Atal Bihari Vajpayee, landed up in Meenakshipuram—to persuade the neo-converts to revert to Hinduism and to figure out the political dynamics of this unprecedented occurrence. What's more, overnight the 'Hindu Munnani (Hindu Front), a mutated version of the

---

[79]Ibid.

[80]Engineer, *Communal Riots After Independence*, pp. 52–54.

[81]Saeed Naqvi, *Being the Other: The Muslim in India*, New Delhi: Aleph Book Company, 2016, pp. 74–82.

[82]Ibid.

Rashtriya Swayamsewak Sangh (RSS)',[83] sprang up in Tamil Nadu. But nothing convinced the Dalits to return to the Hindu fold. In fact, more conversions followed. According to a report in *Frontline*:

> Hardly a month after the Meenakshipuram incident, 150 Dalit families in Utharakosamangai village in Ramanathapuram embraced Islam.
>
> *The Hindu* (newspaper) of January 19, 2001, carried a detailed report...on the conversion of Dalit Hindus in the cluster of villages in and around Peraiyur in Madurai district. They did so to escape the persistent persecution at the hands of caste Hindus. A group of 30 Dalits of S. Keezhapatti near Peraiyur got converted to Islam in 1994, and another batch of 26 in 2000.[84]

Intercommunity tension continued to rise. Sporadic incidents of violence started breaking out in Meenakshipuram and adjoining districts.[85] By the end of 1982, a total of 1,026 people, of which 876 were neo-Muslims, had died in different parts of Tamil Nadu.[86]

The Meenakshipuram conversions had repercussions throughout the country.[87] The RSS tweaked the Hindutva narrative to bring in a sense of insecurity. 'Hindu khatrein mein hai' (Hindus are in danger) became the new clarion call which translated into more violence. Even as Tamil Nadu was grappling with a series of riots, major conflagrations broke out in Uttar Pradesh's Meerut district in September 1982 over the ownership dispute of a temple-mazar complex. Rioting continued for three days, starting on 30 September, at the end of which 100 people were dead. Ninety of these were Muslims, 42 of whom were killed by the PAC. Clearly, the experience of Moradabad had done nothing to rein in the force.

---

[83]'The Shocker', *Frontline*, 9 Jan 2015.

[84]Ibid.

[85]Raj Chengappa, 'Ayyapuram becomes the flashpoint for one of the worst communal clashes in Tamil Nadu', *India Today*, 15 Jul 1982.

[86]Engineer, *Communal Riots After Independence*, pp. 65–66.

[87]A. G. Noorani, *The RSS and the BJP: A Division of Labour*, New Delhi: Leftword, 2000, p. 60.

For the Muslims of Uttar Pradesh, the PAC has always been an inimical force. Writing in the aftermath of the Moradabad incident, *India Today* also made mention of this:

> Maulana Siddiqui, Congress (I) MLA from Moradabad accuses the force of having killed more than 300 people in the last three years. 'Instead of quelling the riots, PAC joins the mobs,' he charges.... Abdul Mannan, a leading lawyer from Lucknow, says, 'Muslims are badly shaken these days and there are reasons for this. There is deep-rooted bias and mistrust among the police force against the Muslims. We are as much citizens of India as Hindus or Sikhs. We should be given representation in the forces according to our population.' The critics seem to have a point. Although they constitute over 17 per cent of Uttar Pradesh's 10 crore population, their share in the police force is less than 5 per cent.[88]

Despite all this, neither the state nor union government ever took any serious action against the PAC for fear of demoralizing the force. At best, small changes were enacted to make the force a little more representative. One of the reasons for this could have been Prime Minister Indira Gandhi's evolving style of politics, which was now about pitting one religious group against another. 'The deterioration was due to a large degree to Indira Gandhi's changed style of politics.... The minorities had begun to move away from the Congress (I). Indira Gandhi made a bid for the Hindu vote, to the BJP's discomfiture.'[89]

However, the biggest horror of independent India took place in the Northeast, and showed in its savagery the cruelty humans were capable of. This was in Assam in February 1983. Though the cold-blooded massacre, which killed between 1,800 and 3,000 people in the span of a few hours, was spread across several villages inhabited by Muslims of Bengali origin, the incident came to be known as Nellie massacre because the first of the relief camps was set up near that village.

---

[88]Prabhu Chawla, 'Provincial Armed Constabulary of Uttar Pradesh becomes focus of controversy', *India Today*, 15 Oct 1980.

[89]Noorani, *The RSS and the BJP*, p. 60.

The lead-up to the massacre is uncontested; there is only one version. Bengalis, both Hindu and Muslim, from East Bengal, and later Bangladesh, had been coming into Assam and settling there since Independence. This influx reached its peak just before the 1971 India–Pakistan war when atrocities by the Pakistan Army forced a large number of Bangladeshi Hindus into India. The Bengali Muslims, on the other hand, being the largest Muslim demographic group in the world after the Arabs, had been migrating to different regions of the world, including Assam.[90] The history of Bengali Muslims in Assam dates back to the time of the Bengal Sultanate (thirteenth and fourteenth centuries), which was one of the richest empires of its time. Since the seat of the sultanate was Bengal, its officers travelled and settled down in different parts of the empire. In more contemporary times, this migration was principally driven by the need for economic betterment. However, the newcomers were not welcome in Assam because the post-Independence politics of Assam, as in other northeastern states, has been driven by xenophobia. With the growth of democratic institutions, tribal warfare morphed into sectarian politics that gave rise to ethnocentric political organizations like the All Assam Students' Union (AASU), United Liberation Front of Assam (ULFA), Bodo Liberation Tigers Force (BLTF), National Democratic Front of Bodoland (NDFB), and so on.

Quoting political scientist Akhil Ranjan Dutta, journalist Rahul Karmakar writes that

> ...the main reason for conflicts is the penetration of state dynamics into mostly tribal communities used to a certain kind of living and resource-sharing.
>
> The ultimate aim is political space for every community. The state has been playing a divisive role because it cannot control or face collective resistance. This division has percolated down to ethnically different communities, among tribes that have been neighbours for years and within certain tribes....[91]

---

[90]Yoginder Sikand, Review of Rafiuddin Ahmed (ed.), *Understanding the Bengal Muslims: Interpretative Essays*, New Delhi: OUP, 2001.

[91]Rahul Karmakar, 'That Rohingya feeling: NE no stranger to xenophobia, genocides,

The seeds of the Nellie horror lay in this xenophobia, further fanned by opportunistic politics. The AASU had been spearheading a violent agitation against all outsiders in Assam since 1979. The outfit wanted outsiders, mainly the Bengali-speaking people, to be thrown out of the state. Ignoring their agitation, Prime Minister Indira Gandhi decided to hold assembly elections in the state in February 1983. In the course of campaigning in the state, BJP president Atal Bihari Vajpayee said at a public meeting, 'Foreigners have come here and the government does nothing. What if they had come into Punjab instead? People would have chopped them into pieces and thrown them away.'[92]

Meanwhile, AASU called for a boycott of the election. Bengali-speaking Muslims of Nellie and thirteen adjoining villages ignored the boycott call and voted. This marked them out for punishment. Armed militants from AASU started moving towards these villages to surround them. On 15 February 1983, Zahir-ud Din Ahmed, the officer-in-charge of the Nowgong (Nagaon) police station, which had jurisdiction over these villages, sent a telegram to the 5th battalion of Assam Police based at Marigaon. He warned them of impending violence as 'about one thousand Assamese of surrounding villages of Nellie with deadly weapons assembled at Nellie by beating of drums. Minority people are in a panic and apprehending attack at any moment. Submission for immediate action to maintain peace.'[93]

The telegram went unheeded. Three days later, armed militants descended on the villages, setting huts on fire and killing those who tried to escape the burning homes. This macabre opera of burning and killing continued for nearly six hours.

The enquiry commission, whose report was not made public, fixed the blame on the police for negligence. But none from AASU were punished, despite there being three eye-witnesses to the massacre—Hemendra Narayan from the *Indian Express*, Bedabrata Lahkar from

---

say experts', *The Hindu*, 27 Sep 2017.

[92]Available here: https://parliamentofindia.nic.in/ls/lsdeb/ls11/ses1/0528059603.htm

[93]Ratnadeep Choudhary, 'Nellie massacre and "citizenship": When 1,800 Muslims were killed in Assam in just 6 hours', *The Print*, 18 Feb 2019.

the *Assam Tribune* and an unidentified video journalist. Narayan was the only journalist to report on the massacre. In 2008, he also wrote a monograph entitled *25 Years on...Nellie Still Haunts.*

Like an ugly scar, Nellie is something most Assamese try to conceal behind euphemisms like 'misguided nationalism'. Assamese filmmaker Shahnaab Alam insists that Nellie was not about communalism. 'The violence was directed against outsiders. Religion was immaterial.'[94]

The government announced a compensation of ₹5,000 for the next of kin of the dead. One of the AASU leaders, Prafulla Kumar Mahanta, formed his own political party, Asom Gana Parishad, and eventually became chief minister in the late 1990s. When asked about Nellie in 1997, Mahanta responded that, 'The matter was over once the Congress government of the time disbursed compensation.'[95]

Even by Indian standards, 1984 was an unmatched year for deadly communal violence. The mythically passive Hindu of the right-wing imagination was on the streets most of that year, attacking and killing those from the minority communities. It started with the Hindu–Sikh riots in Amritsar in February–March that officially left 2,733 people dead. Violence soon engulfed other parts of Punjab and Haryana, where intermittent rioting continued well into May causing the deaths of 10 to 15 people in each city, mostly Sikhs.[96]

The focus briefly returned to Muslims. In May, members of the Shiv Sena[97] called for a general strike in the Maharashtrian town of Bhiwandi to protest the garlanding of its chief Bal Thackeray's portrait with slippers. It was alleged that some local Muslims were responsible. The strike didn't remain peaceful, and the ensuing violence left 226 people dead.

However, violence against Muslims was a mere sideshow in 1984. The biggest brunt of the communal hatred that year was borne by the Sikhs.

[94]Telephonic interview with the author, 10 March 2019.

[95]Choudhary, 'Nellie massacre and "citizenship"...'

[96]Engineer, *Communal Riots After Independence,* pp. 71–74.

[97]Shiv Sena is a Hindu right-wing party founded by political cartoonist-turned-politician Bal Thackeray. Since its inception, it has indulged in politics of hostility towards one community or the other. But its perennial enemy has been the Muslim.

Prime Minister Indira Gandhi was assassinated by her Sikh bodyguards on 31 October 1984 as an act of retaliation for her ordering the army into the Golden Temple to flush out militants. Rather than mourn her death, her supposed followers sought revenge. Over the next three days, about 2,800[98] Sikhs were killed in Delhi alone. Nationwide, the recorded figure was between 4,000 and 6,000.

The brutality of the Sikh massacre jolted the nation. Even some right-wing sympathizers were shocked at the way rioters had been carried away by the Congress propaganda and had indulged in mindless violence.[99] But the Hindu right wing was even more shocked by the aftermath of the 1984 massacre of the Sikhs. The Congress party won the 1984 general elections propelling Rajiv Gandhi to the Prime Minister's Office. The BJP managed only 2 seats. After the 94 seats that it won in its earlier avatar as BJS in 1977, this was an unmitigated disaster.

The way forward was provided by the RSS which gave its advice through an editorial, 'Revamping the BJP', in its publication, *Organiser*. The RSS 'opined that the remedy lay in restoration of the leadership's rapport with a sizeable section of its selfless cadres (i.e., the RSS).... The BJP's stance of positive secularism and Gandhian socialism, it argued, had alienated the party. What mattered was ideological cohesion.'[100]

This brought the Muslims back as the main enemy. But the old narrative was not enough to spur the growth of the party. It needed something new. Ironically, it was Rajiv Gandhi who provided the idea.

Within months of Gandhi taking office, an obscure court case assumed national importance and tested the novice prime minister's political acumen. In April 1985, an Indore-based advocate Mohammed Ahmed Khan divorced his wife, Shah Bano, who took him to court demanding maintenance. The court ruled in her favour. The matter reached the Supreme Court, which upheld the verdict of the lower court. The Muslim ulema protested the verdict, deeming it interference with

---

[98]Rahul Bedi, 'Indira Gandhi's death remembered' BBC, 1 Nov 2009.

[99]Ajaz Ashraf, 'RSS was silent during the 1984 riots. At places, it was implicated in the violence', *Scroll.in*, 3 Nov 2015.

[100]Noorani, *The RSS and the BJP*, p. 62.

Muslim Personal Law.[101] Gandhi, on the recommendation of his Muslim adviser (who is now in the BJP) overturned the Supreme Court order by moving the Muslim Women's Bill in Parliament on 25 February 1986.[102] This handed the RSS a new slogan on a platter—Muslim appeasement and its corollary 'pseudo-secularism'. For the next few years, until global terrorism became the whip to beat the Muslims with, appeasement was the call used incessantly by the RSS and all its affiliates.

I first came across the term 'minority appeasement' while I was still in school in Agra. The local Hindi newspapers in the late 1980s were full of the phrase, 'alpsankhyakon ka tushtikaran'. While the trigger was the Shah Bano case, the argument revolved around two issues—the hajj subsidy and the absence of a Uniform Civil Code (UCC).

The hajj subsidy, which started in 1954,[103] was designed to appeal to Muslim sentiment. Since Islam makes hajj compulsory for all able-bodied Muslims who can afford it, devout Muslims aspire to visit Mecca and Medina at least once in their lifetime. However, according to Islamic law, one can only perform hajj after one has fulfilled all worldly obligations—including the repaying of all debts and marrying off one's daughters. The total cost of hajj has to be borne by the one undertaking it; there can be no charity here. If one accepts charity, then the sawaab or religious benefit of hajj will accrue to the charity-giver and not to the one undertaking the journey. Towards the end of his life, my grandfather wanted to perform the hajj once again. But since his health did not permit it, he sponsored another person's visit to Arabia in the belief that the hajj would be listed in his account of good deeds.

As the majority of Muslims in India are poor and illiterate, and till a few decades ago the hajj involved an arduous sea journey, the Government of India, taking a leaf out of the Mughal emperors' books, decided to facilitate the process. In any case, government intervention is required for several reasons. Hajj can only be performed during the

---

[101]This issue has been dealt with in detail in Chapter 6: Minority Politics.

[102]Ibid.

[103]Zeenat Saberin, 'India ends government subsidies for hajj pilgrimage', *Al Jazeera*, 16 Jan 2018.

twelfth month of the Islamic calendar. In 2018, over two million people performed hajj, of which 175,025 went from India. Every year, Saudi Arabia, which organizes the pilgrimage, decides the number it can accommodate for that one week in a year. Accordingly, a limit is fixed for all countries with Muslim populations. Based on the numbers allocated to Indian Muslims, the Haj Committee of India selects the potential pilgrims through a lottery from all the applications received. This entire process requires bureaucratic assistance from the government.

As long as the journey was made by sea, it was affordable for a greater number of people. Once it was replaced by air travel, fewer people could afford it, especially when, in the name of convenience, the government mandated that pilgrims could only travel on the state airlines, Air India. The 'subsidy' was paid not to the pilgrims but to Air India for the hajj flights. Hence, in a roundabout way, the government was servicing Air India's debts in the name of the hajj subsidy. A few years ago, when other airlines were finally allowed to fly this route, Air India's monopoly and arbitrary pricing ended. Air travel for hajj became affordable once again, which is why there were no protests from Muslims when the Narendra Modi government announced the end of the subsidy in January 2018.

The other measure that critics castigated as Muslim appeasement was the government's acquiescence in the Muslim insistence for a personal law as opposed to the UCC. It's true that Muslims have been the most vociferous opponents of the UCC, even though several other religious communities in India, including certain sections amongst the Hindus, have been opposed to it for reasons ranging from inheritance laws to divorce laws and so on.[104] This is the reason that despite frequent discussion on this, even the current BJP government has not made any effort to bring in a UCC. Interestingly, when the Supreme Court asked the government to make a law for the enactment of a UCC, the law ministry passed the matter onto the Law Commission of India,

---

[104]Megha Ahuja, 'Challenges Faced By Endeavours To Achieve Uniform Civil Code', Legal Service India, available here: http://www.legalserviceindia.com/legal/article-91-challenges-faced-by-endeavours-to-achieve-uniform-civil-code.html

which on 31 August 2018 submitted that a UCC is 'neither necessary nor desirable at this stage'.[105]

And that's where the matter rests. Yet, frequently, someone or the other raises the bogey of Muslim appeasement. Stripped down to its bare bones, the problem is this: the Hindu Marriage Act of 1956, passed by the Nehru government, abolished polygamy amongst Hindus, but Muslim men are allowed four wives. Hence, the slogan 'hum panch, hamare pachchees' (we are five, we have twenty-five) that is frequently used in politics to demonize Muslims. Even if one were to accept the argument of Muslim appeasement because they are allowed to marry four times and divorce their wives by merely uttering 'talaq' three times, how exactly is this appeasement detrimental to other communities? It's another matter that, despite this law, the incidence of polygamy amongst Muslims, in comparison with other religious communities in India, is amongst the lowest in the country.[106]

Never mind the data, why would a Muslim man choose to bear the cost of keeping two or more wives when he can get rid of the ones that preceded them merely by uttering 'talaq' thrice, and not even pay compensation?

In any case, Indian Muslims are unnecessarily vilified for their insistence on a personal law that governs only aspects of marriage, succession, and inheritance. The truth is, across the world, including in the West, governments allow Muslims to govern their personal matters such as marriage and divorce under Shariah-inspired laws. The reason for this is simple. The scope of personal law is so limited that it does not impinge upon national life in any way. In fact, in a country like India, family courts like darul qazas[107] (dealt with in detail in the chapter on women) take the burden off the overworked civil courts. But logic is often a casualty of propaganda.

In an interview to me, in July 2009, Arun Shourie, journalist, author,

---

[105]Krishnadas Rajgopal, 'Uniform civil code neither necessary nor desirable at this stage, says Law Commission', *The Hindu*, 31 Aug 2018.

[106]S. Y. Quraishi, 'The polygamy myth', *Indian Express*, 6 Jul 2017.

[107]Though they function as grievance redressal centres, their scope is limited to domestic violence, divorce, and petty property disputes.

and former minister in the BJP's Vajpayee government (1998–2003), calling the Shah Bano case a watershed moment in Indian history, said, 'When the Rajiv Gandhi government reversed the court order on Shah Bano case, it was seen as the capitulation of the secular forces in the face of irrational religious ones.' According to him, this drove the Hindus towards religious extremism in the 1980s.[108]

In this narrative, Rajiv Gandhi having humoured the Muslim communalists by overturning the Supreme Court verdict, tried to then placate the Hindu communalists by ordering the unlocking of the gates of the Babri Masjid in Ayodhya. The rise of the Ram Janmabhoomi–Babri Masjid issue and Hindu communalism then was the direct consequence of Gandhi's capitulation on the Shah Bano case.

But the chronology of events does not bear this out. The VHP had started the Ram Janmabhoomi programme, mobilizing Hindu support for reclaiming the mosque site, in April 1984. In September–October 1984, it took out a rath yatra (similar to what BJP president Lal Krishna Advani would do four years later) from Sitamarhi in Bihar to Ayodhya. Indira Gandhi's assassination forced the VHP to suspend the movement. It was resumed in October 1985.[109] This was also the time that the Muslim agitation against the Shah Bano verdict was at its peak. On 25 January 1986, a local lawyer, Umesh Chandra Pandey, appealed to the Faizabad court (Ayodhya is in Faizabad district) to allow Hindus to worship inside the Babri Masjid premises. 'On 31 January 1986, Faizabad district judge K. M. Pandey ordered that the locks on the gates of the premises of the Babri Masjid be opened.'[110] The Muslim Women's Bill was introduced in Parliament on 25 February 1986. This sequence of events shows that Muslim communalists were placated only after Hindus communalists had been accommodated!

The Babri Masjid issue has had a massive impact on Indian politics, inter-community relations, and sociopolitical discourse. The unlocking

---

[108]Wahab, 'Deadly Cocktail'.

[109]Sarvepalli Gopal, *Anatomy of a Confrontation: Ayodhya and the Rise of Communal Politics in India*, New Delhi: Penguin Books, 1992, pp. 64–77.

[110]Noorani, *The RSS and the BJP*, p. 62.

of the gates opened the floodgates, so to speak, for a new cycle of communal violence throughout India, including J&K, Punjab, Uttar Pradesh, Gujarat, Rajasthan, and Madhya Pradesh.

While Gujarat saw several small-scale riots every few months, the biggest brunt was borne by the Muslims of UP, where communal tensions peaked in the middle of 1987, inflaming city after city. The worst hit was Meerut, where the infamous Hashimpura massacre took place. On 22 May 1987, the notorious PAC rounded up forty-five men from the Hashimpura locality of Meerut, loaded them into two trucks and sped away. Subsequently, the bodies of the men were found in and around the Hindon canal having been killed in cold blood. The *Indian Express* photographer Praveen Jain was in Hashimpura when the men were being rounded up. His photographs subsequently became the photo-feature that the newspaper carried.[111]

The Indian Police Service (IPS) officer who discovered the bodies and filed the First Information Report, Vibhuti Narain Rai, eventually resigned from the IPS and wrote the book *Hashimpura 22 May: The Forgotten Story of India's Biggest Custodial Killing.* The book opens thus:

> Searching for those who had survived among the blood-soaked bodies strewn around the canal and between ravines near Makanpur village on the Delhi-Ghaziabad border in the pitch dark, on the night of 22 May, armed only with a dim torchlight, while ensuring that we didn't trample upon the bodies—each scene still streams through my mind like a horror film....[112]

Hashimpura had huge shock value, primarily because it happened so close to the national capital. Recalls Wajahat Habibullah, who was posted in Rajiv Gandhi's Prime Minister's Office as joint secretary, 'Rajiv Gandhi insisted that the accused policemen be tried for murder. But the Vir Bahadur Singh-led state government manipulated stuff, stalling the

[111]'Hashimpura massacre: Here is what happened', *Indian Express*, 31 Oct 2018.

[112]Vibhuti Narain Rai, 'Hashimpura, May 22, 1987: The forgotten story of one of India's biggest custodial killings', *Scroll.in*, 3 Jun 2016.

enquiry. Eventually, Rajiv lost the election in 1989.'[113]

From the Muslim perspective, Hashimpura was just one of the many atrocities they suffered that year. The violence in the Maliana locality of Meerut, a day before the Hashimpura incident was worse. Here the PAC stood around while a Hindu mob indulged in arson and killing. From time to time, it was alleged, the PAC even participated in the rioting. A total of seventy-six Muslims died in Maliana, several of whom were burnt alive.[114] Finally, when the violence subsided after a few days, the total death count of Muslims in Meerut hovered between 200 and 300 depending on whom you asked.

Over the next few years, the Ram Janmabhoomi–Babri Masjid movement moved from city to city, claiming more and more lives. RSS affiliates like the VHP and the Bajrang Dal became increasingly emboldened, stirring up conflict in areas where none had existed. For instance, in 1988, members of the Bajrang Dal collected at the steps of Jama Masjid in Mathura just as devotees were leaving after prayer. They insisted on installing a Hanuman idol at the doorstep of the mosque amidst chants of Bajrang Bali and the playing of drums and cymbals. Sure enough, violence broke out.[115]

The deadly 1980s culminated with violent convulsions in Bhagalpur, Bihar, that officially consumed over 1,000 people, 93 per cent of them Muslims, according to the findings by the People's Union for Democratic Rights (PUDR). Unofficially, the count hovered at around 2,000.[116] The trigger was same. On 24 October 1989, the VHP took out a series of Ramshila processions, in which bricks collected for the construction of the Ram temple were to be paraded around the city before being taken to Ayodhya. Rumours were spread that Muslims had killed hundreds of Hindus in Bhagalpur and thrown them into a well. No one tried to find out if this was true.

---

[113]Interview with the author, New Delhi, 21 October 2018.

[114]Sandeep Rai, 'Maliyana, where 72 Muslims were killed in '87, afraid case might go Hashimpura way', *Times of India*, 30 Mar 2015.

[115]Engineer, *Communal Riots After Independence*, p. 95.

[116]Ipshita Chakravarty, 'The forgotten riot: How Bhagalpur 1989 left a memory trace in Bihar politics', *Scroll.in*, 12 Aug 2015.

The VHP once again insisted that its procession pass through a Muslim-dominated area. Armed with swords, the devotees in the procession raised slogans like 'Bachcha bachcha Ram ka, baaqi sab haraam ka' (Those who do not belong to Ram are bastards) and 'Hindi, Hindu, Hindustan, Mullah Bhago Pakistan'. As the procession progressed through the area, some started throwing stones at it. Clashes began soon after. The bloodbath continued till the end of the month. In several instances, Muslims were massacred in places they had fled to for refuge. This was made possible with the support of the administration which withdrew security. In Logain village, the mob not only had the time to kill 116 Muslims but also bury them in a mass grave and plant cauliflowers on it to hide the evidence.[117]

The N. N. Singh Commission appointed to investigate the violence and fix responsibility submitted its report in 2015. It recommended disciplinary action against 125 IAS and IPS officers for collusion with rioters and dereliction of duty.[118] One such IPS officer K. S. Dwivedi, who was the superintendent of police during the riots, and was indicted by the then chief minister Satyendra Narayan Sinha, as well as the inquiry commission, was appointed director general of the Bihar police in 2018.[119]

And Advani's rath yatra was yet to begin.

On 25 September 1990, L. K. Advani, who had succeeded Vajpayee as the BJP president, set off on a road journey through India in a Toyota truck improvised as a chariot. Called the Rath Yatra (rath means chariot)—an allusion to Lord Ram's victorious march to Ayodhya—he began his journey from Somnath and intended to finish it at Ayodhya. Explaining his objective, he said, 'The choice of Somnath as the starting point of the yatra had a powerful symbolic value, made evident by repeated references to it as the target of Muslim tyranny against the Hindus.... The intention was to contextualize Ayodhya in the historical

[117]'"Vultures" Vie for Credit', *Telegraph Online*, 19 Jul 2007.

[118]Chakravarty, 'The forgotten riot'.

[119]Tarique Anwar, 'Indicted for his Role in Bhagalpur Riots, KS Dwivedi Takes Over as New Bihar DGP', *NewsClick*, 28 Feb 2018.

lineage of Muslim aggression and then to seek legitimacy for [the] Mandir movement by drawing a parallel. The parallel the Sangh Parivar drew was with the reconstruction of the Somnath temple.'[120]

The underlying intention was to whip up a campaign for the demolition of what he called a 'disputed structure' and to mobilize kar sevaks (volunteers) for carrying out the task. Advani's rath blazed a trail of violence and fear of more to come.

A research paper from the Institute of Peace and Conflict Studies (IPCS) noted:

> The mobilization campaign for Kar Sevaks to construct the proposed Ram Janma Bhoomi Temple at Ayodhya on 30th October 1990 aggravated the communal atmosphere in the country. Communal riots occurred in the wake of L. K. Advani's Rath Yatra wherever it went.... These riots were led by RSS-BJP men to consolidate the 'Hindu' vote bank. They were widespread over almost all the states from Assam to West Bengal, Bihar, Orissa, Uttar Pradesh, Madhya Pradesh, Rajasthan, Andhra Pradesh, Karnataka, Gujarat, Maharashtra and Delhi.[121]

From April 1990 to April 1991, a total of 1,520 communal incidents took place in Gujarat alone, causing the death of 303 people. The majority of these incidents occurred in the period between September and December 1990. In the rest of India, a total of 691 people died in communal violence during the same period. Incidentally, thirty-one among these died in Agra, most of whom were Muslim, according to the IPCS compilation.[122]

In a hair-raising documentary, *Ram Ke Naam*[123] (1992), filmmaker

---

[120]Kabir Agarwal, 'L.K. Advani, the Provocateur in Chief', *The Wire,* 9 Nov 2019.

[121]B. Rajeshwari, *Communal Riots in India: A Chronology (1947-2003),* IPCS Research Paper, Marc 2004, available here: http://www.nagarikmancha.org/images/1242-Documents-Communal_Riots_in_India.pdf

[122]Ibid.

[123]*Ram Ke Naam* won the Filmfare Award for Best Documentary and National Film Award for Best investigative film. The full film is available here: https://www.youtube.com/watch?v=OO-VaJBHiik

Anand Patwardhan captured the deliberate rousing of religious passion and the deep communal polarization that led to the eventual demolition of the Babri Masjid two years later.

In his 1,000-page memoir, *My Country My Life*, Advani disclaims responsibility for the mayhem: 'As records show, there was not a single instance of communal violence along the route of my yatra. There were indeed riots in several parts of the country, but none at all along the Rath Yatra trail. I was, therefore, pained to see a section of the media carry reports that had sensational titles like "Advani's blood yatra".'[124]

Advani's yatra was marked by several pit-stops where he addressed large crowds. He sometimes appeared with a trident, sometimes a sword or bow and arrow, exhorting people to rise in the name of the Hindu religion and throw away the yoke of centuries-old subjugation. He coined several catchphrases which became the leitmotif of the BJP's subsequent campaigns, such as minority appeasement, pseudo-secularism, Babur ki aulad (offspring of Babur) etc., and inspired slogans like Jo Hindu hit ki baat karega, wohi desh pe raj karega (those who talk of Hindu rights will rule over the country).[125]

Eventually, as his rath trundled into Bihar, Chief Minister Lalu Prasad Yadav, making good on his earlier warning[126], had Advani arrested in Samastipur. But the wheel of violence continued to roll, with Gujarat once again topping the list as the worst-affected state. In fact, so frayed were communal relations that even a minor scuffle, something as innocuous as children playing cricket in a lane, could spark furious conflict, provoking the police to fire. As in a large number of earlier conflagrations, more people continued to die in police firing than in the rioting itself. And, as always, the biggest brunt of the violence was borne by the Muslims.[127]

---

[124]L. K. Advani, *My Country My Life*, New Delhi: Rupa & Co, 2008, p. 379.

[125]Aakar Patel, 'Advani the party man or Singh the economist?', Mint, 24 Apr 2009 and Jyoti Punwani, 'LK Advani led BJP's Hindu nationalism movement in 80s, 90s; espousing diversity today won't erase his past', *Firstpost*, 7 April 2019.

[126]'Lalu Yadav Firing Speech on Rath Yatra by LK Advani in Bihar', 9 Dec 2019, available here: https://www.youtube.com/watch?v=oyScQpExPgw

[127]Irfan Engineer, 'Role of Police in Communal Violence', Centre for Study of Society

Describing the mundane routineness of communal violence in India, in 1993, Urdu poet Bekal Utsahi wrote in his evocative poem, 'Fasaad Kaise Hua' (How Did the Riot Begin),

Hakim-e-shaher ne poochha yeh pehredaaro se,
Fasaad kaise hua
Kaha adab se yahi milke pehredaaron ne
Huzoor, ghaur karein—
Wahan na mandir-o-masjid na koi gurudwara
Khada beech sadak par ek purana fawwaara
Wahin pe Deen Mohammed lagata hai thela
Huzoor shaam se rehta hai bheed ka raila
Wahin sauda Bhagat Ram lene aaya tha
Phisal ke gir jo pada, shor ka dhamaka hua,
Aur mach gayi bhagdar
Kisi ne kuch bhi nahin dekha, kuch nahin poocha
Fasaad aaise hua...

(The city magistrate asked his men/ How did the riot start?/ With respect all of them said/ Sir, draw your attention here/ There was no temple, mosque, or gurudwara/ Only one old fountain in the middle of the road/ That's where Deen Mohammed used to ply his goods/ To a huge crowd that collected every evening/ And that's where Bhagat Ram came for some shopping/ He slipped and fell/ In the ensuing noise, people started running helter-skelter/ Nobody saw anything, nobody asked any question/ That's how the riot began)

In the last stanza, Utsahi comes straight to the point.

Huzoor, Babri Masjid yeh Janmabhoomi hai jo
Isi ke naam par kuch yaatra-ein hoti hain,
Sabhayein hoti hain
Dharm ke naam pe yeh saazish-e-zamana hai

---

and Secularism, Nov-Dec 2013; Also see, Asim Ali, 'UP Police didn't become anti-Muslim under Yogi. Look at secular Congress' bloody past', *The Print*, 27 Jan 2020.

Hai teer apna magar bahri nishaana hai
Huzoor ya toh siyasi koi bahana hai
Fiza banana ka, rakam kamane ka
Sadan mein jaane ka
Fasaad aaise hua

(Sir, this Babri Masjid, which is also the birthplace/ In its name people take out processions, hold public meetings/ It is a conspiracy in the name of religion/ It's our own people, but inspired by outsiders/ Or perhaps it is an excuse for politics, to create a certain atmosphere, for personal benefits or to win elections/ That's how the riot started)[128]

Finally, the two-year-long period of internal strife and fear reached its pinnacle on 6 December 1992. The VHP, which was spearheading the Ram Janmabhoomi campaign, called for a massive rally in Ayodhya. Senior leaders of the BJP, including Advani,[129] then president Murli Manohar Joshi, Uma Bharti, and Sadhvi Ritambhara etc., were among the guests at the rally, as were senior leaders from the VHP and Bajrang Dal. The purported purpose of the rally was kar seva (voluntary service) for the Ram temple. However, as it subsequently came out in several reports, the real purpose of the rally was the demolition of Babri Masjid.[130]

In a video, shot by UP state intelligence agencies, available on YouTube,[131] Vajpayee, who subsequently became the prime minister, is seen addressing the kar sevaks in Lucknow, about 135 kilometres from Ayodhya, a few days before 6 December. With his well-known oratorical flourish, Vajpayee urged the kar sevaks to level the ground at the site by removing pointed stones. Once the video surfaced, Vajpayee insisted that his speech was rhetorical in nature and he did not mean to instigate

---

[128]Dast-e-Gul: Compilation of poetry recitation from the 1993 Shankar Shaad Mushaira, New Delhi, p. 17.

[129]Advani had relinquished the office of president the previous year.

[130]'Babri Masjid demolition was planned 10 months in advance: Book', *Outlook*, 30 Jan 2005.

[131]Part of the speech is available on YouTube: https://www.youtube.com/watch?v=-EhMmJEwbTg

the mob. He did not mention the mosque directly in this speech.

The *Indian Express* photographer Praveen Jain was in Ayodhya on 5 December 1992. Joining the crowd of kar sevaks, he secretly shot them practising pulling down the mosque by use of pickaxes, ropes etc. His video, narrating what he saw on 5–6 December, along with the photographs, is in the public domain. In the video, Jain says that not only were the kar sevaks prepared with the implements for demolition, they even trained for it.[132]

On the morning of 6 December, Advani 'made a spirited speech from the Ram Katha Kunj Manch, barely 150-200 metres from the disputed site, which charged the people. He repeatedly said that the temple would be constructed at the same site', police officer Anju Gupta who was with the BJP leader, told the CBI special court. She also told the court that 'when the kar sevaks began demolishing the Babri Masjid none of the BJP leaders who were present, including Advani, made any efforts to stop them. Once the mosque was demolished, the BJP leaders distributed sweets.' Eventually, 'The CBI chargesheet had noted that Advani had said that the 6 December kar seva "would not mean only bhajan and kirtan, but would also involve construction of the Shri Ram temple".'[133]

As Noorani has recorded,[134] the BJP continued to indulge in doublespeak. In private forums it said the demolition of the Babri Masjid was a historical development and was needed to restore national pride, but in public engagements, leaders like Advani and Jaswant Singh continued to express their disappointment at the demolition. Perhaps it was necessary to do so to keep up the morale of the foot soldiers while escaping the indictment by the inquiry commission that had been ordered by the Narasimha Rao-led union government.

The M. S. Liberhan Commission eventually did indict the senior BJP leadership, including Advani, in its report,[135] submitted to the

---

[132]'Witness to Babri Masjid demolition remembers 1992 as PM Modi lays foundation stone of Ram Mandir', *The Print*, 8 Nov 2019, available here: https://www.youtube.com/watch?v=YyPV71GEC6k

[133]Agarwal, 'L.K. Advani, the Provocateur in Chief'.

[134]Noorani, *The RSS and the BJP*, pp. 73–89.

[135]Liberhan Ayodhya Commission: https://www.mha.gov.in/about-us/commissions-

Government of India in 2009, after labouring over it for seventeen years.

The late Nobel Laureate V. S. Naipaul weighed in on the debate saying that he believed Babur 'had contempt for the country he conquered. And his building of that mosque was an act of contempt for the country.... The construction of a mosque on a spot regarded as sacred by the conquered population was meant as an insult...an insult to an ancient idea, the idea of Ram.' According to Naipaul, the demolition itself was an act of passion which suggested a 'new historical awakening'.[136]

Unfortunately, for India, this historical awakening came at a high price. Violence broke out in several parts of the country immediately after the demolition. First, the jubilant kar sevaks ran amok, looting and plundering wherever they went in a sort of a victory lap. After a few days, Muslims started retaliating in places where they deemed themselves powerful, for instance, in Bombay.[137]

As I wrote in my earlier book *Dragon on Our Doorstep: Managing China Through Military Power*,[138] the communal violence that followed was not something that Indians were used to. The difference didn't lie in the level of violence. It was in the sentiment that drove the violence. It was as if a historical wrong were being righted. The accompanying rhetoric was about the resurgent Hindu staking his rightful claim to the land that historically and religiously belonged to him.

Amongst the worst-affected places was Bombay[139], where over 900 people (nearly 575 of them Muslims)[140] were killed in a relentless orgy of communal hatred that lasted over a month and half. The perpetrators fearlessly moved around the city carrying assorted home-made weapons,

---

committees/liberhan-ayodhya-commission; Also see Puneet Nicholas Yadav, 'What Liberhan Commission Had Said About Leaders Acquitted In Babri Demolition Case', *Outlook*, 30 Sept 2020.

[136]Vaibhav Purandare, 'In India, V S Naipaul was reviled by some, revered by others', *Times of India*, 13 Aug 2018.

[137]See Liberhan Ayodhya Commission.

[138]Sawhney and Wahab, *Dragon on Our Doorstep*, pp. 221–20.

[139]It was renamed Mumbai in 1995.

[140]Meena Menon, 'Scars of the Bombay Riots Remain, but for Many Victims It's a Closed Chapter Now', *The Wire*, 6 Dec 2017.

claiming political patronage, which wasn't entirely an empty boast.

The union government set up the Justice B. N. Srikrishna Committee to investigate the communal violence in Bombay between 6 December 1992 and 20 January 1993. The commission, in its report submitted in February 1998, accused the Shiv Sena and its then supremo, Bal Thackeray, of perpetrating the second phase of one-sided violence from 8 January 1993. Justice Krishna observed that: 'From 8th January at least there is no doubt that the Shiv Sena and Shiv Sainiks took the lead in organising attacks on Muslims and their properties under the guidance of several leaders of the SS from the level of the Shakha Pramukh to Shiv Sena Pramukh Bal Thackeray, who, like a veteran General, commanded his loyal Shiv Sainiks to retaliate by organized attacks against Muslims.'[141]

Once the Shiv Sena–BJP government came to power in Maharashtra, it disbanded the committee in 1996 on the plea that no purpose would be served by its findings as too many years had passed since the riots and its report might further vitiate the communal situation in the state. However, when the BJP-led government came to power at the centre for two weeks with Vajpayee as prime minister, it persuaded the Maharashtra government to revive the committee, which it did. The terms of reference, however, were enhanced to include the bomb blasts which happened on 12 March 1993. Eventually, the report was ignored by the government. Only three people, including one low-rung Shiv Sena leader, were held guilty—they were released on bail within days of their sentences being passed. Effectively, none served a prison sentence.

What 1969 did in Ahmedabad and other parts of Gujarat, 1993 did in Bombay, even though terrible violence had also broken out in the cities of Baroda and Ahmedabad. In Bombay, the feeling of dread and panic was widespread, even among upper-middle-class Muslims living in upmarket gated apartments. Irshad Khan (not his real name), who retired a few years ago as the CEO of a leading home appliances company, lives in a penthouse in South Bombay. In January 1993, he removed his nameplate from his door as well as the apartment lobby

---

[141]Srikrishna Committee Report, *Sabrang*, available here: https://www.sabrang.com/srikrish/vol1.htm

on the advice of his neighbours. However, as the situation deteriorated, he was advised to move out of his apartment. He checked into the Taj Mahal hotel with his family for two weeks.

'It wasn't that I feared my neighbours, but frankly who can argue with a mob. And I didn't want a situation where our relationships were tested,' he told me over the phone.[142] Two weeks later, when he returned home, he found the entrance to his apartment vandalized.

Unlike the riots of the past, the Bombay riots of 1993 had two far-reaching consequences. One, it led to the creation of the biggest Muslim ghetto in India on the outskirts of the city. Losing confidence in both their neighbours and the law-enforcement agencies, the Muslims of Bombay started moving to the shanty town of Mumbra, trading civic amenities for perceived security. And, two, the underworld community of Bombay (disproportionately Muslim) filled with a sense of revenge, opened a path for Pakistan into mainland India. Accessing the well-trodden sea routes through which smugglers imported contraband from the Persian Gulf states, and facilitated by the well-oiled network of compromised state government officials, from the port authority to customs and the police, in the spring of 1993, a new consignment landed in Bombay. It was not gold or drugs but bombs.

On 12 March 1993, thirteen bombs went off in different locations throughout the city, from the stock exchange to five-star hotels, commercial hubs, and the outskirts of the then international airport, killing 357 and injuring 717 people.

Terrorism had arrived on mainland India. The first terrorists were former criminals. Contacts in the Gulf emirates of Dubai had delivered. After the attack, Dawood Ibrahim (who India insists was the mastermind), and the rest of the perpetrators found asylum in Pakistan.

With Indian fugitives as state guests, Pakistan had a goldmine of information about the chinks in national security—government and police officials who could be compromised, places that could be developed as safe houses etc. In addition to this, it also had access to a network of young men who inhabited the shadowy spaces of Indian

---

[142]Telephonic conversation with the author, 12 September 2019.

society, committing occasional crimes. These part-time criminals did the groundwork, paving the way for Pakistani operatives to physically come to Bombay in an effort to influence educated but alienated Muslim youth.

'After the demolition of the Babri Masjid, things went completely out of control. The mafia and the foreign militants started approaching SIMI[143] members and were even invited to their annual convention in Bombay. Despite resistance, there were voices within the organization to declare a jihad. Gradually, by mid-1990s, the moderates started leaving the organization,' Saeed Khan, former president of the Bombay chapter of SIMI, told me in an interview.[144]

These developments coalesced with other events, both national and international. The insurgency in Kashmir was at its most violent. Following targeted killings, the majority of Kashmiri Pandits had to escape from the Valley, becoming the biggest group of internally displaced people (IDP) in the country[145]. Pakistan had mounted a fierce international campaign of human rights violations in India, putting the government on the defensive and under intense pressure. Outside India, the medievalist Taliban were on the rampage in Afghanistan, clawing their way into city after city.

As a result of all this, in the years following the Babri demolition, a section of Indian Muslim youth, mostly undereducated and unemployed,[146] had started to get influenced by radical motivators and external funding. Incidents of terrorist violence, mostly low-grade bomb blasts, started to take place in different cities of India through the late

---

[143]SIMI, or Students Islamic Movement of India, was formed as a students' union in Aligarh in 1977. Over the years, the organization became increasingly radicalized and politicized, going well beyond students' activities. Accused of being involved in various acts of terrorism through the 1990s, usually in the wake of communal riots, the organization was banned in 2001. According to security agencies, after the ban, SIMI went underground and became even more vicious, gradually morphing into the Indian Mujahideen.

[144]Ghazala Wahab, 'Jihad: Crisis in Faith', *FORCE*, November 2003.

[145]'India: conflicts have displaced at least 650,000 persons', Global IDP Project, 27 Oct 2003.

[146]In the following decades, especially with the emergence of IS, the profile of the radical Muslim youth changed—from semi-literate to technocrat.

1990s to the early 2000s.[147]

Once again, these incidents collectively enhanced the image of the Muslim being violent, primitive, and uncivilized—what was truly unfortunate was the fact that much of this criticism paid little attention to how Muslims have been victimized. Gradually, another layer was added to Muslim stereotyping in India—terrorist. Islamic terrorist or jihadi became part of the popular vocabulary.

Another major conflagration that would worsen the demonizing of Muslims and punitive attacks on them took place in 2002 in Gujarat. This was perhaps the first incident of communal violence that was covered live by both the Indian and international media. Private television channels in those days were riding the wave of independence and competitive fearlessness which gave them access to a lot of places and events. Consequently, the horror of violence was brought home to even those not directly affected by it. Every day, every wail of pain and despair, every instance of dehumanizing the Other, became part of the memory of most people.

The violence occurred in two phases. In phase I, on 27 February 2002, a train carrying kar sevaks returning from Ayodhya that had halted at the Godhra railway station, was set on fire just as it was leaving the platform. A total of fifty-seven passengers were killed. Three investigation reports were eventually submitted, all three differed from one another.

The Gujarat Forensic Science Laboratory's report, submitted within days of the incident, claimed that the fire started from inside the train, as there were no burn marks outside.[148] The Narendra Modi-led state government appointed a one-person commission in March 2002 consisting of a retired judge of the Gujarat High Court, Justice K. G. Shah, to conduct an inquiry into the incident. When it came under criticism for not being fair, a retired judge of the Supreme Court, Justice

---

[147]'Islamist Terrorist Attacks Outside J&K, Punjab And Northeast 2000-2019', SATP, available here: https://www.satp.org/satporgtp/countries/india/database/Islamist_Terrorist_Attacks_Outside_J&K_Punjab_Northeast.htm

[148]Concerned Citizens Tribunal, 'Report of Forensic Science Laboratory, State of Gujarat', *Outlook*, 22 Nov 2002.

G. T. Nanavati, was added to the commission.[149] The commission finally submitted its report in 2014 after twenty-one extensions.[150] This report blamed the fire on local Muslims who, it asserted, had carried out the act in a well-planned manner. But the main accused, Maulvi Husain Haji Ibrahim Umarji, was eventually acquitted for want of evidence.[151]

The third inquiry commission was constituted by the Railway Ministry in May 2004 under the new railway minister, Lalu Prasad Yadav. Justice Umesh Chandra Banerjee in his report ruled the fire an accident caused by the kar sevaks themselves as they were carrying cooking implements with them on the train.[152] The report was rejected by the Gujarat High Court.

But the investigation into the Godhra incident was a mere formality. The manner in which events unfolded after the incident has been extensively documented. Wrote the well-regarded political scientist Christophe Jaffrelot:

> Modi, known for his radical hostility toward Muslims, already on 27 February, orchestrated retaliation. Whereas [the] Godhra District Collector had spent the day explaining that the incident was not premeditated, Modi imposed his official version of the event that very evening, stating that it was a 'pre-planned violent act of terrorism.' In addition, Modi called together police officials at his home and gave them orders not to put down the Hindus who would inevitably react to the Godhra attack: the 'Hindu backlash' was not only foreseeable, it was legitimate.[153]

The bodies of the deceased were brought to Ahmedabad to '[inflame] the passions of the people'.[154] They were paraded through the city

[149]'Truth and the Nanavati-Shah Commission, *Sabrang*, 1 Jul 2007, available here: https://www.sabrangindia.in/article/truth-and-nanavati-shah-commission

[150]'With 21st extension, Nanavati report after LS polls', *Times of India*, 1 Jan 2014.

[151]'Godhra case: Eventually, Maulvi Umarji comes out unscathed', *DNA*, 23 Feb 2011.

[152]'Excerpts from the Justice U C Banerjee Committee report', *DNA*, 3 Mar 2006.

[153]Christophe Jaffrelot, *Communal Riots in Gujarat: The State at Risk*?, Heidelberg Papers in South Asian and Comparative Politics, July 2003, pp. 3–4.

[154]According to P. C. Pande, Police Commissioner of Ahmedabad, quoted in 'Decision

accompanied with rousing announcements.

Immediately, violence against Muslims spread throughout the state. Within a couple of days, most of the state of Gujarat was engulfed in unprecedented butchery, including in towns which had not seen communal tension before such as Gandhinagar.

Such was the barbarity of violence, referred to as a 'pogrom' by many, and such was the open complicity of the state government machinery that several members of the government were implicated, and a few faced trial. At least one minister of the Modi Cabinet served a sentence. Modi himself was banned from travelling to the United States by the US State Department.[155]

While men were killed, women were raped, mutilated, and dismembered before killing. Like the 1969 Ahmedabad riots, once again violence against women was inexplicably savage:

> Never had communal violence reached such heights of sexual cruelty. Among the Hindus, it harks back to an ancient obsession: Muslims have always appeared more virile to them, partly because of their diet (meat-eating) and their ritual animal sacrifices.[156]

Jaffrelot builds the case for calling the Gujarat riots of 2002 the first instance of ethnic cleansing in India. According to him, sexual violence was 'the desire to dishonor and destroy an entire community by raping and torturing its women, which of course also aims to destroy their reproductive capacity'.[157] According to him, that is what distinguished it from previous riots in the country. Hence, though in terms of the number of deaths, India had seen worse—the official count was 1,071

---

to bring Godhra victims' bodies taken at top level', *Hindu*, 10 Feb 2012; also see Parimal Dabhi, 'Nanavati report on Godhra: Four accounts on who decided to get bodies to Ahmedabad', *Indian Express*, 13 Dec 2019.

[155]Ibid; Also see, 'Timeline of the Riots in Modi's Gujarat', *New York Times*, 19 August 2015 and Sanjoy Majumder, 'Narendra Modi "allowed" Gujarat 2002 anti-Muslim riots', BBC News, 22 Apr 2011.

[156]Christophe Jaffrelot, *Communal Riots in Gujarat: The State at Risk*?, Heidelberg Papers *South Asian and Comparative Politics*, July 2003, p. 14.

[157]Ibid., p. 15.

(though, unofficially, the figure hovered around 2,000[158])—three things set the Gujarat violence apart.

One, the clockwork precision with which the mob proceeded from area to area suggested that it was planned well in advance and the crowd was being led by people who knew what had to be done and where;[159] two, open complicity of the government. Not only was most of the police partisan, the few good officers who tried to do their job honourably were blatantly victimized and persecuted by the state government;[160] and, three, far from rehabilitating or compensating the victims, the state government encouraged their further marginalization. Worse, in September 2002, just months after the carnage, Modi travelled through the state on a Gujarat Gaurav Yatra (Gujarat Pride Journey). In one of the public meetings during the yatra, he told his joyous audience, 'Do we go and run relief camps? Should we open child producing centres?' Then with sarcasm he added, 'We want to firmly implement family planning. Hum paanch, humare pachees (We are five, we have twenty-five [children]).'[161]

The radicalization that took place among certain sections of Muslim youth can be traced to the demolition of the Babri Masjid and the Gujarat riots. In an interview, former home secretary G. K. Pillai told me, 'If we look at triggers for radicalization, I would say that two events—Babri Masjid and the communal carnage (again with maximum Muslim casualties) in Gujarat nearly a decade later—contributed 60 per cent.'[162]

Yet, despite this sort of provocation, the majority of Indian Muslims did not react intemperately. Perhaps this was because India's own

---

[158]K. S. Subramanian, 'How Gujarat Carnage of 2002 was a Product of Institutionalised Riot Systems', *Sabrang*, 3 Mar 2018.

[159]'Overview Of The Attacks Against Muslims: State and Police Participation and Complicity', HRW.org, available here: https://www.hrw.org/reports/2002/india/India0402-03.htm

[160]Ibid.

[161]'"Should We Run Relief Camps? Open Child Producing Centres?"', *Outlook*, 30 Sep 2002.

[162]Pravin Sawhney and Ghazala Wahab, 'Alive and Present Danger: Religious polarisation creates flashpoints for terrorists to exploit', *FORCE*, December 2011.

indigenous Islam was largely inspired by the Sufis. They also did not rise up in overt support of the 'supposed' sufferings of fellow Muslims in other parts of the world, including at home in Kashmir. While Indian Muslims never raised their voice in support of Kashmiri Muslims, much to the regret of the Kashmiris, the Hindu right wing frequently uses the suffering and exodus of Kashmiri Pandits as a stick to thrash Muslims in the rest of India.

Prime Minister Manmohan Singh was able to assert in an interview with CNN in July 2005, 'I take pride in the fact that, although we have 150 million Muslims in our country as citizens, not one has been found to have joined the ranks of Al-Qaeda or participated in the activities of Taliban.'[163]

Ironically, two years earlier, in April 2002, when Gujarat was still simmering, Vajpayee, instead of expressing anguish or sympathy for the Muslims of Gujarat, said at his party's national convention in Goa:

> Wherever I went around the world, the heads of state or of elected governments complained to me that militant Islam is sowing thorns along their paths. Islam has two facets. One is that which tolerates others, which teaches its adherents to follow the path of truth, which preaches compassion and sensitivity. But these days, militancy in the name of Islam leaves no room for tolerance. It has raised the slogan of Jehad. It is dreaming of recasting the entire world in its mould....
>
> Wherever Muslims live, they don't like to live in coexistence with others, they don't like to mingle with others; and instead of propagating their ideas in a peaceful manner, they want to spread their faith by resorting to terror and threats. The world has become alert to this danger....[164]

[163]Interview of Prime Minister Dr Manmohan Singh with CNN, 20 July 2005, available here: https://www.mea.gov.in/interviews.htm?dtl/4535/Interview+of+Prime+Minister+Dr+Manmohan+Singh+with+CNN

[164]'"Wherever Muslims Live...": Text of Vajpayee's Controversial Goa Speech, April 2002', *The Wire*, 17 Aug 2018. See also A. G. Noorani, 'The man behind the image', *Frontline*, 16 Jul 2004.

Clearly there was no factual basis to these observations. They were merely yet another example of how Indian Muslims have been typecast.

Since 2014, ever since the Modi-led BJP government assumed power at the centre, there have been several disturbing developments that have deepened the fears of minorities in the country. Perhaps the most vicious of these have been the rise of vigilante mobs in certain parts of the country. Before 2014, the perpetrators of communal violence were large groups in which individual elements remained faceless and nameless. However, after 2014, the mob, confident in its invincibility, threw away the cloak of anonymity. It was led by people who were proud of leading it to kill, maim, terrorize, or vandalize at whim. Sometimes, these were small-time leaders or aspiring leaders from one of the several militant right-wing organizations under the RSS umbrella, who believed, and as the subsequent years showed, rightly so, that violence against minorities creates a shortcut to fame and upward mobility within these organizations.[165]

Three parallel narratives were built by the right-wing extremists to create conditions for violence. First off the block, which started the moment the BJP came to power, was 'love jihad', a variant of the old canard aimed at 'virile' Muslim men. Middle- and lower-rung BJP leaders started talking about a diabolical Islamic conspiracy in which Muslim men enticed Hindu women and married them for the sole purpose of procreating jihadi terrorists. Once this objective was met, the gullible Hindu women were abandoned or sold into the sex trade.[166]

The Hindu pushback against supposed 'love jihad' served two purposes. One, it encouraged the lumpen, including impromptu women's vigilante groups, to terrorize young couples in public places, even sometimes forcibly entering their homes.[167] Such was the impact of this narrative that in one incident in Kerala, a medical intern, who had

---

[165]Manoj K., 'Hate-Speech Accused 3 Times More Successful In Elections', *IndiaSpend,* 28 Mar 2106.

[166]Siddharth Vardarajan, 'Raising "Love Jihad" Bogey, Yogi Threatens Death for Men Who "Hide Identity, Disrespect Sisters"', *The Wire*, 1 Nov 2020.

[167]Annie Gowen, 'A Muslim and a Hindu thought they could be a couple. Then came the 'love jihad' hit list.', *Washington Post*, 26 Apr 2018.

first converted to Islam and then married a Muslim man, had to fight a legal battle to win her right to live with her husband. Her father had approached the Kerala High Court alleging love jihad and expressing the fear that his daughter had been brainwashed and would eventually be sent to Syria as a sex-slave for the IS. Heeding the father's concern, the high court annulled the marriage. The decision was challenged by the couple and finally the Supreme Court of India had to step in to restore the marriage.[168] In late 2020, the Uttar Pradesh government brought in a new anti-religious conversion ordinance, ostensibly to curb 'cases of love jihad'.[169] This was widely criticized. Clearly the 'love jihad' bogey will continue to be used as and when necessary to vilify Muslims.

Love jihad was also used as a catalyst to militarize unemployed Hindu youth—men and women. Young people, who now believed that the Hindu faith was in danger, were herded into training camps for basic martial arts and arms training. They were told that there would soon be a decisive battle between the Hindus and the Muslims for the future of Hindu India. Hence, they would have to be prepared.[170]

The second narrative was the religious compulsion of Muslims to eat beef, because of which cows, revered as mothers by some Hindus, were in danger. Hence, anyone even suspected of having traded in, slaughtered, or eaten beef was a legitimate target for the lynch mob. This has had an even deadlier fallout than the love jihad campaign. According to the data website *IndiaSpend*, since 2010, 86 per cent of the victims of cow-related violence were Muslims and 97 per cent of these attacks have occurred after 2014.[171] Interestingly, in most of these cases, the police also registered concurrent complaints against the victims on charges of cow-trafficking.

The third narrative is an old angst of the right-wing club—the

---

[168]Rahul Bhatia, 'The Year of Love Jihad in India', *New Yorker*, 31 Dec 2017.

[169]Alok Pandey, '"Anti-Conversion Law Brought In Hastily, Reconsider": Mayawati To UP Government', NDTV, 30 Nov 2020.

[170]'India's Hindu Fundamentalists | People and Power', *Al Jazeera*, 8 Oct 2015, available here: https://www.youtube.com/watch?v=FE8p9-rtHkY

[171]Rohit Parakh, '84% Dead In Cow-Related Violence Since 2010 Are Muslim; 97% Attacks After 2014', *IndiaSpend*, 28 Jun 2017.

evangelism of the Christians. While in the more distant past, violence was sporadic—such as the murder of the Australian missionary Graham Staines and his two pre-pubescent sons in Odisha in 1999—since 2014, violence against Christians and churches has become less sporadic and more organized.

In an interview to *The Guardian*, Dhirendra K. Jha, author of *Shadow Armies: Fringe Organizations and Foot Soldiers of Hindutva,* says that while Modi has repeatedly emphasized that his government will promote 'complete freedom of faith', his elevation has been a green light for radical Hindutva groups. 'After Modi became prime minister, these groups started thinking they have assumed power, it is their government,' he says. 'So they have gone amok. They don't fear law and order or any democratic institution. They are on a rampage.' According to him, a 'perfect parallel' is the growing boldness of white nationalist groups in the US under Donald Trump. 'Modi would never come out and openly help them,' Jha says. 'But he rarely criticizes them. Because of his silence, the message goes to the state machinery that they don't have to take action against them.'[172]

In 2016, *IndiaSpend* did a lead article on the role hate speech plays in election campaigns. According to its figures, candidates who give hate-filled or enmity-inducing speeches during their campaigns have a greater chance of success as opposed to those who don't. Not only that, even the filing of court cases against them for their conduct only helps them win their seats. In the 16th Lok Sabha (2014–19), twenty-eight members of Parliament from the BJP had cases of hate speeches filed against them.[173] In the 2019 general elections for the 17th Lok Sabha, one of the BJP candidates was under trial—out on bail on health grounds, yet campaigning for her election—in a case of terrorism in which ten people died in a bomb attack in Malegaon in 2008. She eventually won with a margin of a few hundred thousand votes, defeating the former

[172]Michael Safi, 'Christmas violence and arrests shake Indian Christians', *The Guardian*, 24 Dec 2017.

[173]Ghazala Wahab, 'The Idea of Secularism', *FORCE*, Nov 2016.

chief minister of the state.[174]

The most successful example of the rise of a politician thriving on hate speech has been Uttar Pradesh's chief minister, Yogi Adityanath. Until Prime Minister Modi nominated him as the chief minister of India's biggest state, and the one which sends the maximum number of MPs to the Lok Sabha, Yogi Adityanath (born Ajay Singh Bisht), was dismissed as a fringe element in Indian politics. According to an article in *The Hindu*, 'There are several criminal cases pending against him. He has issued bigoted and hateful statements like "if given a chance, I will install Ganesh statues in every mosque" and "if they take one Hindu girl, we will take 100 Muslim girls".'[175] But once he became a mainstream politician by becoming the chief minister, cases against him were withdrawn.[176]

Even as the mood of the country has swung right under the BJP, and deepened the insecurities of the minorities, especially Muslim, the government frequently claims that since 2014 there hasn't been any major communal conflagration in India. The truth is there have been multiple minor communal incidents at such frequency that they have created an atmosphere of perpetual fear and anxiety. By the Government of India's own statistics, there has been a 41 per cent increase in communal incidents across the country.[177] Victims have mostly been Muslims, followed by Christians.

But what has really been crippling the Muslims is the attack on their livelihoods, which will have a long-term impact on their capacity to pull themselves out of abject poverty and socio-economic backwardness. Cow politics, apart from ruining the agrarian economy, has robbed Muslim peasants of their traditional livelihood in the cattle trade. The extension of the ban on cow slaughter to buffaloes and oxen has affected

---

[174]Deeptiman Tiwary, 'Explained: The case against BJP candidate Sadhvi Pragya Thakur', *Indian Express*, 20 April 2019.

[175]Manjari Katju, 'Yogi Adityanath as UP CM: The fringe goes mainstream' *The Hindu*, 21 Mar 2017.

[176]'Yogi Adityanath govt orders withdrawal of case against Yogi Adityanath, others', *India Today*, 27 Dec 2017.

[177]Mukesh Ranjan, 'Communal violence cases up 41% in 3 years: NCRB', *Tribune*, 27 Jul 2017.

the meat and leather industry, both of which, at the small-scale level, have been the domain of Muslims.[178]

Socially, economically, politically, and in terms of security, Muslims today are already second-grade citizens in India. This affects the psyche of the community, its relationship with itself, and with others. Frightened people cannot think clearly. The walls that Muslims are building around themselves for self-preservation come in the way of free-thinking, progress, integration, and religious reforms.

Though senior fellow, Brookings Institution, and author of *Islamic Exceptionalism,* Shadi Hamid, said this about Muslims in the US under Donald Trump's regime, he could well have been talking about Indian Muslims.

> Under Trump—who famously said, 'I think Islam hates us'—Islamophobia has intensified, surpassing the paranoia of the post-9/11 period. This more palpable anti-Muslim bigotry has had a number of effects, some unintended. One is that it makes Muslims feel even more conscious of being, well, Muslim.
>
> There was a time not too long ago when Muslims in the West weren't viewed primarily as Muslims, but rather as Arabs, Moroccans, Turks, and Pakistanis. Those are also our identities, but gradually our Muslimness took over.
>
> I, like so many others, have been pushed and pressured to feel part of a group. I have been drafted into a war of representation, standing in for something bigger than myself in the perpetual fight against the forces of Trumpism, ethnonationalism, white supremacy, or whatever else.
>
> Like it or not, I've become a we.[179]

Something similar is happening in India. Although, as I have said earlier, for the most part, Muslims in India have remained quiescent even after hate-filled attacks on them in the 1990s and the early 2000s.

---

[178]Afroz Alam, '"Cow Economics' Are Killing India's Working Class', *HuffPost,* 22 Jul 2017.

[179]Shadi Hamid, 'How Donald Trump Made Us Muslims', *Medium,* 23 Apr 2019.

As a result of the attacks on them, they have now started becoming conscious of their Muslimness, and they are also becoming conscious of the plight of Muslims outside the country. They are reaching out to help fellow Muslims, something which did not happen in the past, whether financially or through the giving of their time and support by holding free coaching classes for them or simply by counselling them so they do not drift into criminality or extremism. This is a positive development (see Chapter 8). But what erodes its positivity is the force that is propelling this—fear. And 'pushed to the wall' defiance. Both these sentiments crush openness. They also make people resistant to positive change.

Today, both Indian Islam and Muslims need to embrace modernity, especially in matters of education, careers, and women's rights. But it can only happen if the community feels secure and at peace. The current atmosphere in India is the exact opposite of that. It is inducing fear, self-pity, as well as latent anger. Nothing good can emerge from this.

6

MINORITY POLITICS

Over 8–9 August 1964, a group of concerned Muslims, driven by the twin forces of rage and helplessness, met at the Islamic seminary, Darul Uloom Nadwatal Ulama, in Lucknow. The provocation was the communal violence in the states of Bihar and Orissa. The state governments were found to be complicit through acts of omission and the union government through indifference as law and order was a state subject. This motley crowd included members of the Congress party, some religious organizations, and independent citizens.

A notable inclusion was the chancellor of Darul Uloom Nadwatal Ulama, Syed Abul Hasan Ali Nadvi, reverentially called 'Ali Mian', a renowned Islamic scholar with nearly a dozen books to his credit. Though Sunni Islam does not have a formal clergy like the Shia, Ali Mian had the stature of an Ayatollah. He was known throughout the world. Several north Indian Muslim politicians frequently consulted him and asked him for favours, including of the electoral kind (as in, influencing people to vote for them), which he meted out at his discretion. It's hard to tell just how much political power he wielded. Ali Mian inaugurated this two-day meeting, which led to the formation of an umbrella organization, the All India Muslim Majlis-e-Mushawarat (AIMMM).

As the name suggested, it aimed to be a non-political pressure and advisory group that would flag Muslim issues to the government of the day. Given the backdrop of communal violence against which it was formed, the organization's immediate concern was the rehabilitation of the riot victims and the promotion of communal harmony. But equally important was the protection of Muslim institutions which were, in their perception, integral to Muslim identity in India.

To this end, the AIMMM drew up a nine-point programme which was offered to candidates contesting the Uttar Pradesh assembly elections in 1967. These points were:

- Make Urdu the second official language of UP
- Set up an Urdu University
- Teach Urdu from primary to higher classes in schools
- Restoration of minority character of Aligarh Muslim University
- Grant of licence to Muslims to enable them to purchase arms for self-defence
- Payment of suitable compensation to Muslims affected by anti-Muslim communal riots
- Employment of Muslims in government jobs in proportion to their population
- Vacation and rehabilitation of mosques and other religious places occupied by government
- Deletion of anti-Muslim articles or passages in Hindi or other books.[1]

A total of one hundred aspiring candidates, mostly non-Muslims and from different political parties, signed up for AIMMM's programme. The organization not only canvassed for these candidates, it also ensured that Muslims voted for them instead of the Congress, which, so far, had been the party of choice. Sixty-seven of these candidates won. It was the first time that a non-Congress coalition government was formed in Uttar Pradesh. Among the parties of this alliance, under the banner of Samyukta Vidhayak Dal, were the Bharatiya Jana Sangh, Bharatiya Kranti Dal, and Praja Socialist Party. Chaudhary Charan Singh of the Bharatiya Kranti Dal was elected chief minister by the coalition.

However, once elected, of the sixty-seven candidates who were supported by the AIMMM, sixty-four reneged on their commitment to work to implement the measures designed to help the Muslim community. 'They openly acknowledged that they accepted the AIMMM programme to ensure their victory by getting the Muslims to vote for them,' says Mohammed Adeeb, who was one of the members of AIMMM

[1]N. A. Ansari, 'Dr Faridi—a forgotten giant', *Milli Gazette*, available here: https://www.milligazette.com/Archives/01072002/0107200270.htm

and had attended its first meeting in 1964. An alumnus of AMU, he has been an occasional politician who has worked extensively in Uttar Pradesh. He was nominated to the Rajya Sabha by the Congress in 2008.

'Thereafter,' he laments, 'they said that there was nothing they could do to address the Muslim issues.'[2] Luckily for the Muslims, this betrayal wasn't too much of a setback as the government fell shortly after. After a year of President's Rule in the state, the Congress won the next election and formed the government. The rumblings of revolution had turned out to be a false alarm. But this did not deter one member of the AIMMM, Dr Abdul Jaleel Faridi, a practising doctor from Lucknow and an activist and philanthropist. In 1968, he established the political wing of AIMMM called Muslim Majlis. Despite its name, he envisioned it as a party for all marginalized people. Hence, for its first meeting, he invited the Dalits to join hands with the Muslims to fight their common adversary—the caste Hindu who dominated the political landscape of India and shaped its politics. The Dalits were interested, and were probably inspired by the idea of a broad Dalit–Muslim coalition, but were deterred by the name.[3]

The idea of the Muslim Majlis was a bit akin to the idea of Pakistan—confused at inception and at execution. Muhammad Ali Jinnah, a Shia who eventually became the first president of a Sunni Pakistan, expended a good part of his political career in demanding a separate homeland for Muslims, first under a broad Indian confederacy, and later as an independent sovereign nation because, he argued (as did Hindu right-wing organizations like the RSS and Hindu Mahasabha), Muslims and Hindus were too different to live together.

This argument led to the worst ever incidence of communal violence in India. Over a million people—Hindus, Muslims and Sikhs—were killed and nearly 15 million were displaced in the weeks preceding and succeeding the Partition of India into two nations[4]—Pakistan for the

[2]Interview with the author, Gurugram, 9 April 2019.

[3]Mohammed Adeeb told me that years after this, he had met Kanshi Ram, the founder of the Bahujan Samaj Party. Kanshi Ram told him that he had attended the first meeting of Muslim Majlis. It was there he got the idea of starting a party in which both Dalits and Muslims could be represented, but led by the Dalits.

[4]William Dalrymple, 'The Great Divide', *New Yorker*, 22 Jun 2015.

Muslims who wanted it; India for everybody else, including the Muslims.

But, addressing the Constituent Assembly of Pakistan on 11 August 1947, Jinnah told those who were tasked with creating a constitution for the new country:

> I cannot emphasize it too much. We should begin to work in that spirit, and in course of time all these angularities of the majority and minority communities, the Hindu community and the Muslim community...will vanish.... You are free; you are free to go to your temples, you are free to go to your mosques or to any other place of worship in this State of Pakistan. You may belong to any religion or caste or creed—that has nothing to do with the business of the State.... We are starting in the days where there is no discrimination, no distinction between one community and another, no discrimination between one caste or creed and another. We are starting with this fundamental principle: that we are all citizens, and equal citizens, of one State....
>
> ...you will find that in course of time Hindus would cease to be Hindus, and Muslims would cease to be Muslims, not in the religious sense, because that is the personal faith of each individual, but in the political sense as citizens of the State.[5]

There couldn't have been an address nobler than this. But this address was also sadly removed from reality. If Pakistan was to be a secular, multi-ethnic, multi-religious state which would ensure equal rights to all, where then was the Muslim homeland Jinnah and his Muslim League had promised? The nation for which millions of Muslims had left the land of their ancestors, left graves unattended, risking death and worse? Did they make these sacrifices for a diminutive version of India? If Muslims and Hindus could live together peacefully in Pakistan, why couldn't they do so in India?

It was as if the seventy-year-old Jinnah did not really know the

[5]Muhammad Ali Jinnah's first Presidential Address to the Constituent Assembly of Pakistan, 11 Aug 1947, available here: http://www.columbia.edu/itc/mealac/pritchett/00islamlinks/txt_jinnah_assembly_1947.html

hearts and minds of those who had followed him on the journey to Pakistan. As it turned out, Jinnah's vision died with him a year later. When the Pakistanis gave themselves their first constitution (two more followed—each more Islamic) in 1956, it incorporated not Jinnah's advice but the demands of the Jamaat-e-Islami, which was pushing for Pakistan to become a true Islamic nation, governed solely by the laws of the Shariah. Just as the RSS envisions Muslims as protected minorities in India and not equal citizens, the Jamaat-e-Islami also 'generously' offered the same to the minorities of Pakistan.

The Muslim Majlis of Dr Faridi's imagination fell in the same realm of fantasy. For all his exertions, it remained a party of the Muslims, by the Muslims, and for the Muslims. As a result, his political experiment succumbed to its contradictions a few years after the death of its founder in 1974. However, in the years that it existed, it fired up aspiring Muslim politicians with the romanticism of disruptive politics. They failed to see that 'Aagaz ke din tera, anjaam teh ho chuka' (The end was written the day you began), as the lyricist Shailendra wrote.

Was the Muslim Majlis a political party to save the Urdu language? Or save Aligarh Muslim University? Or for demanding licensed weapons for Muslims to defend themselves? Which Muslim outside the states of Uttar Pradesh and Bihar would identify with these issues? How could these be the only issues of importance for an all-India consortium of Muslim organizations? Instead of trying to protect one AMU, why didn't they demand an AMU in every state? Or more schools in Muslim-dominated areas? Forget working with the government, why couldn't an apex body of Muslim organizations directly reach out to the poorest among the Muslims—the peasants and artisans—by organizing them into a cooperative that could enhance their livelihood, lift them out of poverty and improve the quality of their lives? Why didn't they persuade their benefactors—rich Muslims—to institute scholarships or specialized coaching for backward or lower-caste Muslim students? All this would have had a beneficent cascading effect on future generations. And this would have certainly been in the spirit of Islam, which stands for equality and fraternity.

It was this myopic quality of upper-caste Muslims, or those referred to as Shurafa (gentry), that led to all their attempts at providing leadership to the Muslim community at large to fail. They simply could not look beyond their privileges. Consequently, the larger Muslim community—the backward and the lower castes—remained disenchanted, denying the Muslim politicians a support base.

My father calls organizations like AIMMM shops run by vested interests who only mislead gullible Muslims. 'Their only contribution has been negative. See the state of the Muslims today, it has progressively deteriorated over the years,' he told me over dinner one evening.

'But that is not the worst part,' he added. 'The worst part is that these exclusive organizations have periodically aligned with one political party or the other for personal benefit, further harming the interests of the larger Muslim community.'

According to him, both inside and outside the political sphere, Muslims benefitted the most from secular well-meaning individuals, irrespective of their religion. To make his point, he gives examples of victims of communal riots or innocent youth arrested on false charges of terrorism. 'Muslim organizations have been unable to help them in any substantive manner. Whether it is getting them justice or rehabilitating them. The people who have helped the most in such cases have been human rights activists or non-governmental organizations.' The biggest failing of Muslim organizations has been their inability to even form a lobby.

The reason for this is simple. Muslim political leaders, even in pre-Independence India, have seldom gone beyond the issues of religious identity, which revolve around the protection of the faith, language, and personal law. Since these are also the issues that the ulema raise, Muslim political leaders are forced to compete with the religious leaders to appear as the bona fide representatives of the people. The Muslim Majlis of the 1960s–70s was only following the historic precedent set by post-1857 Muslim leaders of India.

As mentioned earlier, after the 1857 war, the British came down very heavily on the Muslims. Even after the military reprisals ended, Muslims were edged out of key administrative positions. While the ulema were gripped with the anxiety of preserving the religion, scholars like Syed

Ahmed Khan, who founded the Muhammadan Anglo-Oriental College (which became the Aligarh Muslim University) believed that to get back in favour, Muslims needed to embrace English education and stay away from politics.

Consequently, as Maulana Abul Kalam Azad wrote about the early decades of the twentieth century:

> The leadership of Moslem politics at this time was in the hands of the Aligarh party.[6] Its members regarded themselves as the trustees of Sir Syed Ahmed's policies. Their basic tenet was that Moslems must be loyal to the British Crown and remain aloof from the freedom movement. When *al Hilal*[7] raised a different slogan and its popularity and circulation increased fast, they felt that their leadership was threatened. They therefore began to oppose *al Hilal* and even went to the extent of threatening to kill its editor.[8]

However, in 1919, they made an exception. Like-minded Muslim leaders came together to agitate against the British. The leader of this agitation, Muhammad Ali Jauhar (later addressed with the honorific maulana), even served prison time for his pains. Their cause: the restoration of the caliphate in Turkey. At this time, after the defeat of the Ottomans in World War I and the rise of Mustafa Kemal Atatürk, Turkey had turned its back on the caliphate as it began the process of secularization and modernization.

And in India, while the rest of the country was rising up against the British, protesting the monstrous Jallianwala Bagh massacre, influential Muslims (mostly from the United Provinces) were worried about the fate of the caliphate, an institution that had decayed over the centuries, held no religious significance, and was symptomatic of the atrophy that had gripped Islam after the fall of the Abbasid Caliphate (750–1517 CE).

In 1920, Gandhi saw an opportunity in the emotional Khilafat

---

[6]Those who studied at AMU and were aligned to Sir Syed Ahmed Khan's thinking.

[7]The first weekly newspaper founded by Islamic theologian and freedom fighter Maulana Abul Kalam Azad.

[8]Maulana Abul Kalam Azad, *India Wins Freedom: An Autobiographical Narrative*, London: Longmans, Green and Co., 1989, p. 266.

movement to forge a united Hindu–Muslim front against the British. He offered the agitating Muslims a compact of reciprocity. He would support their cause in return for their support to his call of non-cooperation. The Muslims were taken aback. 'Hakim Ajmal Khan said that he wanted some time to consider the program.... Maulvi Abdul Bari said that Gandhiji's suggestions raised fundamental issues....' Azad, however, had no doubts, 'I said without a moment's hesitation that I fully accepted the program.'[9]

Determined to get the support of the entire group, Gandhi attended and addressed the next Khilafat Conference held in Meerut in 1920. He urged them to participate in the Non-cooperation Movement and publicly extended his support to their cause. At the special session of Congress in September 1920, Gandhi reiterated this saying that 'the program of non-cooperation was necessary if we wished to achieve Swaraj and solve the Khilafat problem in a satisfactory manner'.[10] Eventually, Muslim leaders saw merit in the nationalist movement and worked closely with the Congress. And since part of the motivation was Khilafat, the ulema also joined in.

However, the union was short-lived. As we have seen, Gandhi called off the Non-cooperation Movement in 1922, following the violent incident of Chauri Chaura. The institution of the caliphate was formally abolished by Kemal Atatürk when he took over as president of Turkey in 1923. With no common cause holding them together any more, the Muslim leaders who had reluctantly embraced politics to save Islam drifted away from nationalistic politics towards sectarianism. Only those who were in politics for nationalist reasons, like Abul Kalam Azad, M. A. Ansari, Abbas Tyabji, and others remained with the Congress.

Here we need to rewind a bit and go to the beginning of the twentieth century to get a complete picture of Muslim participation in Indian politics. In 1906, the All-India Muslim League was founded—the natural choice for Muslims of conservative bent. This party, that was later accused of playing communal politics, did not begin with that idea. It was an offshoot of the All-India Muhammadan Educational Conference,

---

[9]Ibid.

[10]Ibid.

founded by Sir Syed as an educational and social organization that would carry the spirit of Aligarh to other parts of India.

Perhaps Sir Syed envisioned that more AMU-like institutions could be established. Or, perhaps, he just wanted educated and socially well-placed Muslims to have a forum in which to discuss and raise issues of Muslim welfare. Politics was banned in the Muhammadan Educational Conference. However, by 1901, well after the death of Sir Syed, members of the Muhammadan Educational Conference felt that Muslims needed political representation and that the largely Hindu Congress would not be able to represent their interests fairly.

The result was the All-India Muslim League. The League had its first taste of success when it got the British India government to accede to its demand for separate electorates in 1908. Even though several members of the League were also members of Congress, their paths continued to diverge over the next few decades and, by 1945, they were unable to even be civil to each other.

The members of the Muslim League from the time it was founded until the Partition of India were largely from the land-owning elite who had escaped the reprisals of 1857.[11] This was the same class that Sir Syed belonged to—the Shurafa Muslims. A majority of them effortlessly switched loyalty from the kings and nawabs to the British, for which they were suitably rewarded. Their children studied in AMU or institutions established by the British, and they went to England for higher education before entering into government service in British India.

When this class entered politics, it was driven solely by self-interest. Freedom from the British was not on its agenda. They wanted to strike a better bargain with the British for themselves and people like them. This class was neither religious nor nationalist, rather, as has been noted, it was self-centred. In Attia Hosain's novel *Sunlight on a Broken Column*, one of the characters, Saleem, argues with his taluqdar father.

> What you said, father, about the landlords' fear of abolition is the crux of the matter. This fear for their existence is the basis for the

[11]Mushirul Hasan, *Legacy of A Divided Nation: India's Muslims From Independence to Ayodhya*, Boulder: Westview Press, 1997, p. 368.

> formation of a new party which is interested in keeping the status quo intact that is favoured by the British and is fundamentally opposed to progressive, national movements....'[12]

Since self-preservation was the goal, when the two-nation theory first entered the popular discourse, through the article written by Lala Lajpat Rai, the Muslim League did not immediately warm to it. The landed gentry feared losing their estates and the power and prestige that came with it.

Even the poet Mohammed Iqbal, who later became the national poet of Pakistan, floated the idea only in 1930, though historian Tara Chand doubts if he was envisaging an independent Muslim country.

> It is, however, doubtful whether he [Iqbal] contemplated the partition of India and the establishment of a sovereign Muslim state...at Allahabad, in December 1930.... It was certainly not a scheme for the partition of India into two independent sovereign states...his plan of amalgamating Panjab, North-West Frontier Province, Sind and Baluchistan in one autonomous region.... There is no reference here to the two-nation theory and to the incompatibility of Hindu and Muslim cultures.'[13]

One of the reasons the Muslim League was reluctant to push for this could be that it had no mass following until 1940 when it adopted the Pakistan resolution and sects like the Barelvi and organizations like the Jamaat-e-Islami backed it; and Jinnah decisively assumed its leadership. Even after it started to push for an independent Pakistan through street violence (such as Direct Action Day), the Muslim League's campaign was largely driven by its desire to secure the interests of the upper-caste and class Muslims, rather than creating a true Islamic state. This explains the contradictions between the leaders of the Muslim League and its foot soldiers, who formed the cadre of the Jamaat-e-Islami.

In the years after Independence, especially after the passing

---

[12]Ibid.

[13]Tara Chand, *History of the Freedom Movement in India, Volume Three*, Publications Division, Ministry of Information and Broadcasting, 1983, pp. 252–53.

of the leaders of the freedom movement, the contours of Muslim politics changed from secular and nationalistic to largely parochial and conservative. Diverse types of leadership then emerged.

One (and this was the minority) was of 'progressive' Muslims, fired with Communist ideology. According to Congress politician, lawyer, and author Salman Khurshid, 'The "progressive" Muslims were Communists or Leftists. Though steeped in Islamic culture by way of mannerisms and attire, they were not always practising Muslims.'[14] What's more, they did not see themselves as representatives of Muslim interests alone. Their politics, though nationalistic, was aligned with the international Communist movement. A large number of 'progressive' Muslims, especially the litterateurs, identified with Communist ideology because of its emphasis on social justice. This was because they found echoes of the Islamic principles of equality and fraternity in the ideals of Communism. Hence, even though their respective parties may have viewed them as Muslims, neither they nor their constituents regarded them as Muslim politicians because they did not conform to what was expected of a Muslim—as a result, few of them won elections.

Another type comprised the conformists. For this lot, how their constituents viewed them mattered greatly because their relevance in politics depended on their ability to win elections. In their perception, religion was not just a matter of personal faith, but a qualification for practising politics. Hence, they had to not only look Muslim but also be more Muslim than others. 'We have to conform to the expectations of our constituents,' admits Khurshid. 'It helps us connect with them. Hence, issues like namaz and roza become important because these are the questions politicians like us are asked by our constituents.'[15] The dichotomy here is that many of these politicians are progressive in their outlook but are often forced to take regressive positions. Instead of inspiring their constituents to become progressive or liberal, they fuel religious conservatism.

Historically, Muslims, by and large, from the days of the caliphate

---

[14]In conversation with the author, New Delhi, 22 October 2018.

[15]Ibid.

onwards have regarded spiritual and temporal powers as unified. Even in later centuries, when hereditary dynasties took over the function of governance, the kings maintained the façade of being guided by divine law. The ulema were part of the court. When the Mughal Empire fell, the ulema effortlessly moved into the role of community leaders, as a kind of a bridge between the state and the people.

Subsequently, when non-religious Muslim politicians emerged in the beginning of the twentieth century, their focus was the political representation of their class of Muslims, which was the Shurafa, rather than the uplift of the downtrodden. To discredit them as representatives of the larger community, the 'nationalist Muslims', essentially members of the Indian National Congress, turned to the ulema, mainly from the Darul Uloom Deoband and its Delhi-based associated group, Jamiat Ulama-i-Hind, to steer the Muslim masses towards the Congress and its politics. Explaining this paradox of supposedly liberal politicians seeking Muslim support through its least liberal entity, the ulema, Khurshid says that once the educated class—the AMU crowd and the landed gentry—drifted towards the Muslim League, thereby according it legitimacy, the Congress party had to find a new class of grassroots leaders whom the masses could identify with. In their perception, the ulema had that sort of persuasive power to steer the masses towards the Congress.

'There was no choice but to pick potential leaders from the madrassas,' says Khurshid. 'I had once asked the senior Congress leader Narayan Dutt Tiwari[16] why most of the Congress leaders were Brahmin. He said that was because Brahmins could mobilize people at the grassroots level. In a similar manner, the catchment area for Muslim leadership became the madrassas.'[17]

There was another reason why the Congress party gravitated towards the ulema of Darul Uloom Deoband. Between 1913 and 1920, the ulema from Deoband ran an underground campaign which came to be known as Reshmi Rumaal Tehreek (Silk Scarf Movement) that sought

---

[16]Former Chief Minister of Uttar Pradesh and Uttarakhand, and Governor of Andhra Pradesh.

[17]Interview with the author, New Delhi, 22 October 2018.

the support of Afghan and Turkish rulers to overthrow the British. On the pretext of travelling to Mecca, the Deoband ulema travelled to Afghanistan and Turkey to garner support. Messages were relayed through silk handkerchiefs, hence the name.[18] They managed to get some support from both the Afghans and the Turks. What's more, they established communication and collaboration with the Ghadar Party[19], an underground movement formed by Punjabi peasants working in the west coast of the United States. Most of them were former soldiers of the British Indian Army who had migrated to the US after their military service and worked as labourers in parts of California.[20] The British eventually caught on after some silk letters were confiscated from Punjab. The main conspirators, the leading ulema from Deoband, were arrested and deported to Malta.

Even though the ulema were trying to wage a jihad against the British, it is not clear what kind of British-free India they sought—an Islamic India or a multi-religious and multicultural country. Nevertheless, Reshmi Rumaal Tehreek established the reputation of the Deoband ulema as nationalists, as opposed to the Barelvis who had thrown their weight behind the Muslim League. The general secretary of Jamiat Ulama-i-Hind, Maulana Mahmood Madani, says with a measure of pride, 'The ulema of Deoband participated in the freedom struggle alongside Gandhiji.'[21] In January 2013, President Pranab Mukherjee released a stamp commemorating the efforts of the ulema involved in the movement.[22]

The ulema benefitted greatly from this aspect of their historical evolution. So even when university-educated, professionally-qualified Muslims sought a political career, they felt compelled to co-opt the

[18]Maulana Muhammad Miyan, Muhammadullah Qasmi (trans.), *Silken Letters Movement: Accounts of 'Silken Handkerchief Letters Conspiracy Case' From British Records*, Shaikhul Hind Academy, Darul Uloom Deoband/ Manak Publications Pvt Ltd, 2013.

[19]Seema Sohi, 'The Ghadar Party', South Asian American Digital Archive, 8 May 2018.

[20]Tariq Hasan, *Colonialism and the Call to Jihad in British India*, New Delhi: SAGE, 2015.

[21]Interview with the author, New Delhi, 15 November 2018.

[22]Jitesh Jha, 'Commemorative Postage Stamp on Silk Letter Movement released by President', *Jagran Josh*, 12 Jan 2013.

ulema. This gave rise to the perception that to represent Muslims the leader must be, or at least appear to be, religiously conservative. A Muslim mainstream politician, therefore, started carrying a twin burden. He (it has rarely been she) would need to appear to be devout for the benefit of his Muslim constituents and flaunt his liberal credentials to his party and possible non-Muslim voters, lest he be considered illiberal or communal. A consequence of this balancing act has been that Muslim politicians are reluctant to raise issues that genuinely affect the community and call for changes in government policy or even the accountability of law-enforcement agencies. For instance, prejudice in government employment, harassment in the name of security, the blatantly partisan behaviour of state police forces, and, most importantly, the bogey of terrorism—all of which are frequently invoked to harass Muslim youth are issues that mainstream Muslim politicians rarely take up. Instead, they dabble in the same issues that the ulema do, such as the protection of Islam, Urdu language, Muslim Personal Law and so on.

Conscious of this failing of the Muslim political leadership, at an annual function at AMU in April 2018, Khurshid, in response to a question by a student, said, 'There is blood on our hands. I am also a part of the Congress, so let me say it, we have blood on our hands.... We are ready to show the blood on our hands so that you realize that you too must not get blood on your hands.... Learn something from our past. Learn from our history and don't create such situations for yourself where if you come back to Aligarh Muslim University after ten years, you find no one like yourself putting out questions.'[23]

Interestingly, a small section of these Muslim conformists has also aligned itself with the Hindu right wing. The BJP has always had a few token Muslim politicians in its ranks—these politicians are projected to seem bigger than the influence they really wield, both within the party and amongst the voters. However, these representatives of inclusiveness are so powerless that they are unable to register even a token protest when their fellow right-wing hardliners victimize Muslims.

[23]PTI, 'Cong hand stained with Muslims blood: Salman Khurshid', *India Today*, 24 Apr, 2018.

Despite the necessity for minority representation in a democracy, the truth is that Muslim politicians essentially cannot do much to better the lot of the Muslim masses. Their position and power within mainstream political parties is limited to getting a few votes. Their own self-interest, insecurity, and likely inability to connect with the Muslim masses (because of their repeated failure to deliver) have rendered most of them irrelevant within their own parties.

This leads to a few questions. Who do the Muslim politicians represent? What is it that they do which non-Muslim politicians cannot do? Are there issues that pertain to Muslims alone, which only a Muslim politician can address, or would a non-Muslim be more effective in doing so? Why can't a Muslim politician be regarded as a regular mainstream politician, shorn of his Islamic identity?

Turning the argument of minority politics around, former vice president of India, Hamid Ansari, says, 'There are three things a government must legitimately be expected to do. One, ensure [the] right to security and justice; two, ensure [the] right to practise religion; and three, ensure a fair share in the largesse of the state.'[24] All these are enshrined in the Constitution and are religion and community agnostic.

Asaduddin Owaisi, president of the All India Majlis-e-Ittehadul Muslimeen (AIMIM), has been quick to understand the emerging dynamics of Indian politics. He insists, 'There is no Muslim leadership. I am a representative of my people, not just the Muslims.'[25] Owaisi's assertions notwithstanding, his core constituency remains Muslim. He is regarded as an unapologetically courageous Muslim who minces no words while raising issues, whether it is about the illegal detention of Muslim youth as alleged terrorists, or triple talaq. What's more, in his public discourses, Owaisi always exaggerates his Muslimness, whether through his appearance, language, or parliamentary interventions.

Despite having studied law in London and being supportive of women's education at all levels, Owaisi keeps the Muslim ulema in good humour by occasionally lending his voice to ideas important to

[24]Interview with the author, New Delhi, 25 February 2019.

[25]Interview with the author, New Delhi, 17 August 2019.

them. His erudition sits comfortably with his overt Muslim identity. In this respect, Owaisi heralds a new phase of Muslim politics—combative and assertive—striking a balance between religious exclusivism and nationalism. With this combination, he is an emblem of hope for his voters.[26]

In March 2014, a few weeks before the general elections, I was in Hyderabad for an aviation show. The city, which is his stronghold, was decorated with the banners of his party. Emblazoned on them was the slogan: 'May your choices reflect your hopes, not your fears' in English. 'Is that not an unusual message for the people who you expect to vote for you?' I asked him in late 2019, when his party had broken out of Hyderabad and into places like Maharashtra and Bihar. In addition to the traditional Hyderabad parliamentary seat that Owaisi has been holding for many years, in 2019, AIMIM also won a Lok Sabha seat in Aurangabad (Maharashtra) and one Bihar assembly seat from Kishanganj.

'This statement is attributed to Nelson Mandela,' he said. 'We used it because for years Muslims have been herded around by all kinds of politicians playing on their fears; and they have plenty of them. We want to tell our people that they have to look beyond their fears; that they must assert their rights, which the Constitution of India guarantees them.'[27]

Owaisi insists that his brand of politics is positive, and doesn't depend on fear of the Other. As far as the allegation of sectarianism is concerned, he says that these are the rumours spread by his opponents, based on a speech that his younger brother, Akbaruddin Owaisi, gave in 2012. Insinuating that the police support Hindu rioters, Akbaruddin had said that if the 'police is removed for 15 minutes then Muslims can finish off the 100 crore Hindus'.[28]

'Akbar has never spoken like that again,' Owaisi clarifies, adding,

---

[26]Patrick French, 'Opportunist or rockstar? Owaisi recasting Muslim politics in India', *Hindustan Times*, 13 Oct 2013.

[27]Interview with the author, New Delhi, 17 August 2019.

[28]'Akbaruddin in trouble for hate speech', *Times of India*, 29 Dec 2012.

'but you see the kind of language the BJP and its associates use. Does that not spread hatred?'

What about the allegations that Owaisi's brand of politics helps the BJP consolidate the Hindu vote, that he cuts into the votes that mainstream secular parties would get, allowing them to win?[29]

'Why is the burden of defeating the BJP only on smaller parties like mine,' Owaisi scoffs. 'What about those who have been indulging in soft Hindutva?' he says, referring to the Congress party. Owaisi says that in its attempt to woo Hindu voters who have flocked to the BJP, the Congress party has lost Muslim support. However, instead of acknowledging its own failure to take Muslims along, the party blames parties like his.

The other successful Muslim politician in the country, Badruddin Ajmal,[30] founder-leader of the All India United Democratic Front (AIUDF) in Assam also has a tough time performing the balancing act between being overtly religious and secular. Unlike Owaisi, whose qualifications and oratorical skills lend him national heft disproportionate to his party's reach, Ajmal's background comes in the way of his rising beyond his religious origins, despite his assertion that, 'We are not just a party of Muslims. We have given tickets to our Hindu brothers in every election.'[31]

An alumnus of Darul Uloom Deoband, Ajmal's calling card is his religious background. Balancing his piety with his politics, Ajmal also runs a thriving multinational perfume business in India and the Middle East. He is also engaged in several philanthropic activities, including running hospitals and educational institutions in Assam. One of his institutes is Markazul Maarif, which offers courses in intensive English to pupils graduating from his alma mater, Darul Uloom Deoband. His support base is Muslims of southern Assam (mostly Bangla-speaking) and he nurtures it.

---

[29]Syed Ubaidur Rahman, 'The rise of Muslim polity in Indian politics?', *Sify.com,* 28 Oct 2019.

[30]For more on Badruddin Ajmal, see: https://www.oneindia.com/politicians/badruddin-ajmal-32466.html

[31]Ipsita Chakravarty, '"No bigger insult than being called Bangladeshi when you are a citizen of India," says AIUDF chief', *Scroll.in,* 23 Feb 2018.

Explaining how Ajmal keeps his hold on the people, Assamese filmmaker Shahnaab Alam says, 'Since he has successful operations in the Middle East, his network helps Assamese who go there for jobs. This support has reverberations back home.'[32] However, despite the 'All India' in its name, AIUDF's influence remains limited to a few districts of Assam, where, according to his detractors, he plays off the fears of Bangla-speaking Assamese against Assamese-speaking ones.[33]

Another kind of Muslim political leader wields influence from behind the scenes. These strongmen usually belong to organizations that have consolidated influence at the grassroots level. Leading the pack is the All-India Muslim Personal Law Board. It came into being, unsurprisingly, to protect Islam which was facing multifarious threats, both from dissenting Muslims like reformer Hamid Dalwai as well as non-Muslims.

In March 1970, Dalwai established the Muslim Satyashodhak Mandal (Muslim Truth-Seeking Society) in Pune to work towards reforming Muslim Personal Law. Two years later, in December 1972, ulema of various hues got together to establish the AIMPLB to (among other issues):

- Take effective steps to protect the Muslim Personal Law in India and for the retention, and implementation of the Shariat Act[34];
- Strive for the annulment of all such laws, passed by or on the anvil in any State Legislature or Parliament, and such judgments by courts of Law which may directly or indirectly amount to interference in or run parallel to the Muslim Personal Law or, in the alternative, to see that the Muslims are exempted from the ambit of such legislations;
- Set up an 'Action Committee' as and when needed, for

[32]Telephonic interview with the author, 10 March 2019.

[33]Chakravarty, '"No bigger insult than being called Bangladeshi when you are a citizen of India"'.

[34]The Muslim Personal Law (Shariat) Application Act 1937 was passed by the British Indian government to enable Muslims to oversee matters of marriage, succession, inheritance, and charities themselves.

safeguarding the Muslim Personal Law through which [an] organized countrywide campaign is taken up in order to implement decisions of the Board;

- Constantly keep watch, through a committee of Ulama and legists, over the state or Central legislations and Bills; or Rules framed and circulars issued by the government and semi-government bodies, to see if these, in any manner, affect the Muslim Personal Law.[35]

Although in conversation with me, the AIMPLB's spokesperson, Kamal Farooqui, listed social reforms as one of the objectives of his organization, the reforms that he spoke of were similar to the ones pursued by religious sects like Deoband, i.e. removing extraneous influences from Islam and ridding the Muslims of social evils like dowry, ostentatious weddings, and un-Islamic rituals.

The AIMPLB came into its own when it spearheaded the campaign against the Supreme Court verdict in 1985 on Shah Bano's case. This forced Prime Minister Rajiv Gandhi's government to overrule the court, and instead pass the Muslim Women (Protection of Rights on Divorce) Act in 1986.

Shah Bano's case has been a watershed moment in India's contemporary history. Ironically, it impacted Indian politics more than the lives of Muslim women. In many ways, it marked the beginning of the decline of the Congress party and the rise of the BJP. It also labelled Muslims as a pampered minority which put its parochial interests above the law of the land. It is useful to delve a little deeper into the Shah Bani case to show just how enormous its influence on Indian politics and society was.

In 1932, Shah Bano, an illiterate woman,[36] was married to an affluent lawyer of Indore, Mohammed Ahmad Khan, and bore him five children. In 1948, Khan remarried, but did not divorce Bano. After several years of living together with two wives, Khan turned Bano and their five

---

[35]Aims and Objectives, All India Muslim Personal Law Board, available here: http://www.aimplboard.in/objectives.php

[36]Saeed Khan, 'My mother was wronged, gravely wronged', *Hindustan Times*, 12 Nov 2011.

children out of his house. Shah Bano was sixty-two years old, then. He did not divorce her and paid her an allowance of ₹200 per month. In 1978, he stopped this payment.

Shah Bano approached the local court, demanding ₹500 per month as an allowance for herself and her five children, who were now adults. The court ruled in her favour. Khan promptly divorced Shah Bano, paid the maintenance for the period of iddah and no further, citing Shariah.[37] Iddah is the period of seclusion that the woman must undertake after her divorce or the death of her husband. The idea is to determine whether she is carrying her former or dead husband's child. I will go into greater detail on iddah in the next chapter on women.

The matter finally reached the Supreme Court where it was taken up under Section 125 of the Code of Criminal Procedure which pertains to the destitute seeking maintenance to keep 'body and spirit' together. The Supreme Court upheld the Madhya Pradesh High Court order asking Khan to give ₹179.20 per month as subsistence allowance to his former wife. The Muslim ulema, led by the AIMPLB and Jamiat Ulama-i-Hind, challenged the verdict which they deemed to be against Shariah. According to Shariah, a man has no obligation towards his divorced wife after paying her the mehr (bride money)[38] amount and allowance for the period of iddah, after which she is free to marry again.

It was strange that Shah Bano, who had five adult children, was destitute. No court seemed to have thought this worth exploring. Given that she was married for nearly forty-six years, it is safe to assume that her first-born would have been at least forty when she divorced. Why were her children still dependent on their father?

There are other questions that come up: Could this have been a case driven by politics? After all, it did little to help the plight of Muslim women—Shah Bano herself refused maintenance under pressure from the Muslim ulema (and managed to survive)—and only strengthened elements among the Muslim and Hindu right wing.

Arif Mohammed Khan, then a junior minister in Rajiv Gandhi's

---

[37]Wajahat Habibullah, 'Deciding issues of personal law', *The Hindu*, 18 Oct 2016.

[38]See Chapter 7: Women.

cabinet, who spiritedly defended the Supreme Court order in Parliament, dismisses these questions as irrelevant. He says, 'This was not [a] case against personal law or divorce. This was about providing subsistence allowance to a destitute who had no other means of income.'[39] Khan was not the only Muslim Rajiv Gandhi was consulting. Former journalist M. J. Akbar was another one. Wajahat Habibullah, then a director in Rajiv Gandhi's PMO, wrote in 2016:

> Then one day as I entered Prime Minister Rajiv Gandhi's chamber, I found M. J. Akbar sitting across his table. Rajiv smiled cheerily, 'Come in, come in Wajahat, you are one of us.'
>
> I found this greeting odd but was to discover the reason soon enough. Akbar had convinced Rajiv that if the government were not to contest the Shah Bano judgment, it would appear to the Muslim community that the Prime Minister did not regard them as his own. In what he perceived as the defence of their religious rights, Rajiv would show himself worthy of the support that the community had always placed in his family. This was the argument that Akbar developed in a Doordarshan debate with Minister Arif Mohammed Khan, in which Khan had argued that the Koranic provision or lack of it for maintenance was neither a compulsion nor closed to interpretation. But Akbar, more westernised, had argued that the Muslims needed the reassurance that only an amendment could bring.[40]

Gandhi ultimately heeded those advising him to contest the Shah Bano judgment, and eroded his own credibility among secularists and progressives, both Hindu and Muslim.

Senior Shia leader Maulana Kalbe Jawad minces no words when he says, 'Muslims have repeatedly been let down by those who claim to lead them, starting with Jinnah. He caused irreparable harm to Muslims, especially the Muslim politicians. Out of guilt, they wrongly started to believe that to remain relevant, they must be more loyal to the parties

[39]Interview with the author, New Delhi, 7 October 2017.

[40]Habibullah, 'Deciding issues of personal law'.

they belong to instead of the people they are supposed to represent.'

Even as the AIMPLB was fighting an old woman over Muslim Personal Law, Rajiv Gandhi's government gave the board another issue through which it could assert its power over the Muslims of India—the Ram Janmabhoomi–Babri Masjid dispute. This became an even bigger issue, with the leadership claiming that the religion of Islam in India had not faced a greater challenge in decades: an obscure medieval mosque was in danger.

The AIMPLB quickly formed the Babri Masjid Action Committee, because, 'protection of mosques, under Tahaffuz-e-Mazajid, is one of our roles,' explains Farooqui.[41] It moved into the space which ideally should have been occupied by mainstream politicians. Today, all protests by liberals that the AIMPLB, which calls itself a non-government organization, is an outdated institution which does not represent the Muslims are meaningless. In the age of instant news and instant opinions, perceptions matter. And, in the popular perception, the AIMPLB speaks for all Muslims, at least on television news channels. Theirs is the loudest voice defending Islam. Despite being accused of obscurantism and worse, the AIMPLB has never wavered from its stance. Its leaders don't care what liberals think of them, as long as the masses are behind them. Through their relentless religious haranguing, they have successfully managed to rouse Muslim passions on non-issues in the name of protecting Islam. Hence, one saw the spectacle of Muslims converging on the streets to protest the visit by George W. Bush to India in 2006 because of the war in Afghanistan.[42] Or students rioting to force the Government of India to ban Salman Rushdie's *The Satanic Verses*.[43] And, as recently as 2017, over 8,000 Muslim women converged on Azad Maidan in Mumbai to protest the bill against triple talaq.[44]

Not once has such a passionate crowd come onto the streets to protest a real issue such as the poor implementation of the constitutional

---

[41]Interview with the author, New Delhi, 6 October 2018.

[42]'Bush visit to India centers on nuclear pact', CNN.com, 1 Mar 2006.

[43]Siddharth Dube, 'Elite Muslim University in India Is Torn by Violence Over Professor's Remark', *Chronicle of Higher Education*, 30 Sep 1992.

[44]'Muslim women protest anti-triple talaq Bill', *The Hindu*, 31 Mar 2018.

Right to Education. Not once have the masses who are in thrall to the AIMPLB expressed their rage against the non-rehabilitation of riot victims. No one carries out protest marches demanding the release of innocent youth arrested on trumped-up charges of terrorism. Of course, all these activities are fraught with the danger of police retaliation. But then so are demonstrations in defence of faith.

Liberal Muslims decree that too much importance is given to fringe elements like the ulema. But since the ulema manage the numbers on the streets, how can they be ignored? And how can the fact that they do control the minds of the insecure, illiterate Muslims, who believe that saving Islam is a bigger cause than improving their own lives, be ignored?

We can understand why the ulema take this line. Islam, according to them, dictates that the purpose of a Muslim's life is obedience to Allah and to prepare for the afterlife. With this as the basis of their faith, the glory of Islam is more important than development of Muslims in this life. After all, if the world is simply the staging area for the hereafter, how does it matter if the Muslims remain at the bottom of the barrel in the here and now? In Paradise, they will rule.

Muslim intellectuals assert that ordinary Muslims don't let the clergy decide their political choices. To prove their argument, they cite the example of Imam Bukhari of the Delhi Jama Masjid. A pulpit politician, in his heyday, Imam Bukhari used to be quite flexible about his political choices. Through his Friday sermons, he had managed to create an illusion about his sway over north Indian Muslims. Consequently, he was frequently wooed and humoured by political parties, including the Congress. While in the 1980s, he would issue a call from the Jama Masjid urging Muslims to vote for the Congress party (on the assumption that Muslims were waiting for his direction), in the 2004 general elections, despite the shadow cast by the Gujarat riots of 2002, he urged Muslims to vote for the BJP, claiming that its prime ministerial aspirant, Atal Bihari Vajpayee, was a friend of the Muslims.[45] The BJP lost that election.

Be that as it may, certain ulema do wield influence in limited areas.

---

[45]'Shahi Imam asks Muslims to give BJP a chance', *Outlook*, 24 Apr 2004.

Just as some groups of rural poor or Dalits cast collective votes in their constituencies at the direction of their local leaders, some Muslims heed the advice of their community head, which in many cases is the ulema.

In the final analysis, Indian Muslims, who do not form a monolithic body and have diverse social, cultural, and religious practices, have limited choices when it comes to voting in elections. They usually vote for the political party they perceive as less inimical to them rather than by gauging the local candidate's potential for bettering their lot. It is only when the party is too distant, and the candidate local, that they vote for the person they have known for years. Once again, this choice is not determined by the candidate's religion but familiarity with the constituents.

Three very distinct aspects of Muslim politics in India at the present moment deserve mention. The foremost is the deterioration of Muslim political leadership since Independence, both qualitatively and quantitatively (with some exceptions, as mentioned earlier). Of course, this trend is more prevalent in the north than the southern part of India. This has been the direct consequence of the population profile of post-Partition north India. Since a large number of the so-called Shurafa or high-caste Muslims, which also implies better educated and professionally qualified, migrated to Pakistan, the new leadership started to emerge from those who remained behind. Even though this new leadership claimed Shurafa status to distinguish themselves from the 'low' and 'backward' castes, the people they sought to represent were poor, deprived, and low-caste Muslims. Hence, their politics became reactive and reactionary than visionary.

While this worked for a long time, in the last decade or so, as the social profile of Muslims changed, with more educated youth entering the organized workforce, their expectations from their leaders started to change. Hence, the traditional Muslim politician no longer holds the same sway over the people. The very small Muslim middle-class votes like anybody else, and often is less likely to vote for a Muslim candidate.[46]

[46]Hilal Ahmed, 'Muslims' Voting Patterns Show They do not Constitute a Vote Bank', *The Quint*, 3 Aug 2016. Also see Debu C., 'How Did Muslims Vote?', *MyIndia*, 26 May 2019.

With their increasing irrelevance, Muslim politicians also became more hyperbolic, further alienating themselves from the people. For instance, when I met Arif Mohammed Khan in October 2017, I commiserated with him for being sidelined within the party. Not taking kindly to my comment, Khan told me that he cannot be sidelined by anyone given that he is worthy of being a prime minister. According to him, there was no one else in the BJP more qualified than him. To pacify him, I agreed with him. And he calmed down.[47]

The second distinctive aspect is the rise of backward and Scheduled Caste Muslims—the Ajlafs and the Arzals. Theoretically, Islam is casteless, but in India, there are three broad castes, as we've seen. At the top of the order are the Ashrafs, the upper caste who form the Shurafa or the elite. Shurafa is a derivative of the Urdu word sharif, which loosely translates to decent and honourable. Among Indian Muslims, these qualities are not a function of education and exposure, but birth. Those who belong to this segment had their origins in the Middle East, Turkey and Central Asia or are descended from upper-caste Hindus who converted to Islam.

The Ashrafs are followed by the working castes, the Ajlafs, equivalent to Shudras in the Hindu caste hierarchy and comprise tradespeople like weavers, ironsmiths, barbers, carpenters, etc. The lowest in the pecking order are the Arzals or the Dalits—this group comprises sweepers or those who collect night soil (called halalkhor) and others who perform similar menial jobs. Both the Ajlaf and the Arzal are native Indians who converted to Islam over the centuries. They form the majority, not only because they are native, but because of the movement to Pakistan of the Shurafa Muslims, as mentioned earlier.

As among the Hindus, the Ashraf Muslims were the first to access education and political power. Since they didn't have to face problems in areas of education and employment, they engaged with issues like religion, language, and culture. But post-Independence, there has been an increasing churning among the non-Ashraf classes for a fairer representation in what is regarded as Muslim politics.

Dr Khalid Anis Ansari, senior assistant professor of sociology at

[47]In conversation with the author, New Delhi, 7 October 2017.

Glocal University, says that for a long time the Ashrafs controlled the political narrative of the Muslims. 'Hence, they articulated it only in terms of religion, language, and elite culture. Since they were a privileged class, they were far removed from the issues of livelihood and survival that Pasmanda Muslims faced,' he says.[48]

Apart from being an academic, Ansari is also an activist for the cause of non-Ashraf Muslims, who describe themselves as Pasmanda, a Persian word for those who were left behind. Describing the Shurafa class, Ansari said, 'The sharif culture uses language as a boundary maintenance mechanism. There has always been an emphasis on Persian and, increasingly, Urdu. As a child I noticed that ladies in the family would place Urdu grammar books next to the Quran. So Urdu was considered sacred.'[49]

Yet, ironically, they chose a word from the language they accuse of discriminating against them to describe their movement. By not calling their movement by a word/ phrase from their own language, they willy-nilly endorse the superiority of the Persian language.

According to Ansari, the Pasmandas are increasingly demanding representation in electoral politics. And though political parties dominated by the high castes (this is true across the religious divide) are reluctant to share power with the deprived, the push continues. 'Caste overrides religion,' he says.[50]

Referring to the Pasmanda slogan, 'Dalit-Pichhda ek samaan, Hindu ho ya Musalman (All Dalit-Backwards are equal, whether they be Hindu or Muslim)', he says that the Pasmanda Muslims, especially in the region abutting Bihar and eastern UP, would prefer voting for subjugated castes (irrespective of his religion) instead of an Ashraf Muslim. However, the future lies in creation of a party of the deprived, he insists.

'The members of the Pasmanda Muslim Mahaz, a social organization led by Ali Anwar, and other community activists, intellectuals, and

---

[48]Telephonic interview with the author, 21 November 2019.

[49]Ajaz Ashraf, 'For Indian Muslims, elections bring caste divide among Ashrafs, Pasmandas to the fore', *Firstpost*, 23 Apr 2019.

[50]Interview with the author, New Delhi, 25 February 2019.

entrepreneurs recently met in Delhi. They came to a consensus for starting a party in Bihar, Uttar Pradesh and Jharkhand, to begin with,' says Ansari.[51]

Like the earlier 'good intentions' of a well-meaning Muslim leadership, this is also an idea past its sell-by date. First, because of the huge outreach by the RSS among the Dalits, a growing number of them have started identifying as Hindu.[52] This is the reason many Dalits have started voting for the BJP—24 per cent in 2014 and 34 per cent in 2019.[53]

This brings me to the third aspect of Muslim politics that deserves mention and which I have touched upon earlier in the book—its irrelevance. Owaisi is blunt, 'The Muslim vote has been rendered meaningless today. This is the reality we must accept. No one specifically represents the Muslim interests, especially since 2014.'[54]

Just as radicalization among Hindus crept in slowly and insidiously after Independence, the political marginalization of Muslims has also been a gradual but steady process, with some exceptional disruptive moments like after the Emergency. Indira Gandhi's triumphant return to power after the failed experiment of the Janata government (1977–80), brought 49 Muslims to Parliament, 30 from the Congress party alone. This has been the highest Muslim representation ever, nearly 10 per cent,[55] though still lower than the percentage of the Indian population they constitute. However, the situation returned to 'normal', that is, poor representation, in the next election. While the 2014 elections returned 23 Muslims to the Lok Sabha (roughly 4 per cent of the House), the number increased to 27 in the 2019 elections, with 12 of them from

[51]Ibid.

[52]D. K. Singh, 'RSS rewrites history: Dalits "created" by invaders', *Hindustan Times*, 22 Sep 2014. Also see, 'RSS reaches out to Dalits', *Deccan Herald*, 25 Feb 2018.

[53]Sanjay Kumar, Pranav Gupta, 'Where did the BJP get its votes from in 2019?', *Hindustan Times*, 3 Jun 2019.

[54]Interview with the author, New Delhi, 17 August 2019.

[55]Daniel Wolfe, Dan Kopf & Aria Thaker, 'Why is Muslim political representation declining in India?', *Quartz India*, 22 May 2019.

UP and West Bengal.[56] Even with this increase, the Muslim strength in the lower house of Parliament remains under 5 per cent. The Muslim population of India, according to the 2011 Census is 17.22 crore, i. e. 14.23 per cent of the total population.[57]

Analysts say that the declining Muslim representation is a consequence of the rise of the BJP.[58] The argument goes that given its antipathy towards Muslims, the BJP does not field Muslim candidates, unless it must, as in the case of Kashmir. And since the BJP has had sweeping victories in the last two general elections (2014 and 2019), Muslim representation has fallen substantially.

However, these reasons do not tell the full story, which is more complex. There are only fifteen constituencies in India, three of which are in the union territory of J&K and one in Lakshadweep, where Muslims are in such an overwhelming majority that they alone determine the outcome of the elections.[59] It is only in these districts that Muslims are fielded by all contesting parties. With only Muslims in the fray, irrespective of which party wins, a Muslim candidate wins. For instance, in 2019, the BJP had no choice but to field Muslim candidates from the three parliamentary constituencies of Kashmir. All three lost. As a result, the ruling party does not have a single elected representative from India's largest minority. So, when it needed a Muslim minister to helm the Ministry of Minority Affairs, they had no option but to nominate a Muslim to the Rajya Sabha.

However, Muslim representation from Kashmir is mere tokenism because they do not speak for the Muslims of the rest of India just as Muslims from other parts of India do not stand up for the problems of the Kashmiris. And in the rest of the country, two factors undermine

---

[56]'2019 Lok Sabha election results: Only 27 Muslim MPs elected to Parliament, none from the BJP', *Scroll.in,* 24 May 2019.

[57]Religion Census 2011, Census 2011, available here: https://www.census2011.co.in/religion.php

[58]Christophe Jaffrelot, Gilles Verniers, 'The dwindling minority', *Indian Express,* 30 Jul 2018.

[59]Rukmini Srinivasan, 'Polls 2019: A view on 15 Muslim-majority Lok Sabha constituencies', *Economic Times,* 7 Apr 2019.

Muslim representation. One, the delimitation of constituencies over the years has divided Muslim populations in such a manner that they no longer hold a collective decisive vote in any district. This means that for a Muslim to win, he must get communities other than his own to vote for him. Of course, the fact that Muslim politicians have won from such seats suggest that non-Muslims do vote for them. And while several factors determine the outcome of elections, the most important is the candidate's ability to draw certain castes and communities to vote for him.

Consequently, Muslim candidates are fielded by the major parties for their ability to win. Over the years, for reasons I have explained, their ability to win has weakened. Deploring the creation of a Muslim vote bank by the Congress party for years, the BJP, according to Owaisi, has successfully consolidated a Hindu vote bank.[60] Such is the impact of this consolidation that even in districts with substantive Muslim populations, where till a few years ago a Muslim politician had a chance of winning, even parties in opposition to the BJP are wary of fielding a Muslim candidate. They feel that the presence of a Muslim candidate will consolidate all Hindu votes against him. The assumption behind this thinking is that today an upper-caste Hindu voter will not vote for a Muslim candidate.

Veteran Congress leader Ghulam Nabi Azad—once regarded as someone who could ensure a candidate's victory by campaigning for him—alluded to this in 2018, when in an address to students he said, 'Since Youth Congress days I have been campaigning across the country from Andaman and Nicobar to Lakshadweep. Ninety-five per cent of those who used to call me were Hindus. However, in the past four years the percentage has dipped from 95 to 20.... This means that there is something wrong. Today, people are afraid to call me because it might have an adverse effect on votes.'[61]

What has further reduced the chance of a Muslim winning elections is the double-edged role played by money in elections. In areas where

[60]Interview with the author, New Delhi, 17 August 2019.

[61]Nelanshu Shukla, 'Hindu candidates don't ask me to campaign, says Congress leader Ghulam Nabi Azad', *India Today*, 18 Oct 2018.

Muslim votes are likely to have a decisive impact because of the population distribution, the party with the most resources—and today few can compete with the BJP on this[62]—fields several dummy Muslim candidates. These come in the form of independent candidates, each of whom polls a few thousand votes. Some even forfeit their deposits. In the bargain, they split the votes that the serious Muslim contender would have got. Moreover, Hindu votes get consolidated in favour of one Hindu candidate in the fray. This experiment was so successful in the 2014 elections in UP that Muslim candidates lost even from their presumed strongholds, for instance, Deoband.[63] This also helped perpetuate the idea that Muslims were voting en masse for the BJP.

On the flip side, the absence of money holds Muslims back from electoral politics. Najeeb Jung says bluntly, 'Electoral politics in India is driven by money. The political parties help you fight the elections, but only to some extent. Beyond that, the candidate has to raise his or her own funds. A Muslim's prospects of raising funds to fight elections are quite bleak because the community as a whole is not rich.'[64]

This is the reason that several experiments of establishing exclusively Muslim political parties have failed repeatedly. The most high-profile of these was the Insaf Party floated by former foreign service officer Syed Shahabuddin in 1989. Shahabuddin was articulate and a well-known face on television, so his party was regarded as a potential disruptor. But it dissolved in 1990 without causing any ripples.[65]

Consequently, Muslims have increasingly become politically disempowered and largely irrelevant to the political process. The growth of Hindu right-wing politics has made even the centrist parties, which earlier openly espoused the cause of Muslims (seeing in them a vote bank), wary of them, lest they be viewed as being against the interests of Hindus.

---

[62]Sangeeta Tanwar, 'Indian political parties spent $8 billion on this year's elections—nearly half was by the BJP', *Quartz India*, 5 Jun 2015.

[63]Manish Chandra Pandey and Tariq Khan, 'Muslim leaders struggle to understand how BJP won in minority-dominated UP seats', *Hindustan Times*, 6 Apr 2017.

[64]Interview with the author, New Delhi, 13 February 2019.

[65]Rahman, 'The rise of Muslim polity in Indian politics?'

As has been discussed earlier, the RSS and its cohorts have successfully created the narrative of Hindus being ill-treated even in independent India. In this narrative, talking of interests other than the Hindu interest is viewed as being against the majority community and appeasement of the minorities. In the last decade, this perception has gained such traction that most political parties, except the Communists, go out of their way to appeal to Hindu voters by indulging in what is referred to as 'soft Hindutva'. This has further narrowed the political space for Muslims. 'But Muslims must continue to participate in electoral politics,' insists Owaisi. 'Otherwise, they will fall off the radar screen and get reduced to second-class citizens.'[66]

Winning elections may not be in the control of Muslims. However, a greater number of Muslims must remain politically engaged, both with political parties and the electorate, so that they are gradually able to create a non-sectarian space for themselves. No Muslim can win the battle of competitive sectarianism in today's India. Their only hope is to fight sectarianism through inclusive and progressive politics.

---

[66]In conversation with the author, New Delhi, 17 August 2019.

7

WOMEN

Two momentous events occurred in my cousin's life in 1999. She turned thirty and she got married that year. She decided to mark these milestones by cloaking herself from head to toe in the Islamic garment called the burkha, so that 'not even her nail' could be seen by the world.

This mobile tent, which she chose as her hiding place, comprised four separate pieces of clothing. Starting at the top was the headscarf, wound tightly around her head and held in place by a few safety pins. Below this was a crocheted triangular mask which covered her nose and mouth. Placing it on the bridge of her nose, she would tie the mask behind her head, with the ties concealed inside the headscarf. The mask fell well below her chin, almost touching her collar bone. This part was neatly tucked into the long, floor-sweeping, full-sleeved, closed-necked coat that she wore over her clothes. Her hands were shoved inside a pair of gloves.

This religious modesty came at a price. Not only did her expenses increase, because she had to buy a few full sets of this ensemble, she had to start dressing up well before everyone else whenever she had to go out. First, the mask had to be fitted, followed by the robe. Then the headscarf. And, finally, the gloves. The only thing that she could take off in a hurry, if required, were the gloves. The mask was the most complicated because even if she pulled it off, she couldn't throw it back without taking off her headscarf.

A few weeks after her marriage, on a pleasant, post-monsoon day in Bombay, her husband was in a romantic mood. He took his wife for a drive and a stroll by the Gateway of India. I don't think they would have held hands, but they would have looked like an Islamic couple—the man in a pair of fitted jeans and an equally fitted shirt to show off his gym-acquired body and, hobbling a few steps behind him, a shapeless apparition in black and grey.

The incident that followed has become part of family folklore. After the walk, they stopped at a street-food vendor for a plate of gol gappas. Eating gol gappas in the street is an art form. You have to match the speed of the vendor serving you. If you are too slow, you end up with several cracked gol gappas on your plate, the spiced water overflowing.

My cousin must have taken all this into account when she agreed to partake of the snack. She placed her plate on the vendor's cart, held a gol gappa in one hand and, with the other, held her crocheted mask away from her face so that she could push the snack into her mouth from above. Anyone who has eaten gol gappas knows that it is impossible to manoeuvre this particular snack into your mouth in this fashion. The gol gappa fell apart between her nose and the mask. The spicy, tangy water ran down her chin and neck, soaking the mask, and parts of her coat. That was the end of that romantic evening.

The burkha is not merely a piece of clothing. It is an integral part of a philosophy by which honourable men and women are kept chaste and away from fitna. Fitna is an Arabic word. It means a range of things from disobedience to rebellion and secession, all of which are grave crimes and must be prevented at all cost. After the death of the Prophet, the ulema came up with a strategy to keep faithful men away from fitna based on some Quranic verses and purported private conversations with the Prophet during his lifetime.

One element of the strategy was to remove women completely from public spaces; and two, if at all they must appear in public because of some unavoidable necessity, then they would have to hide their bodies from the public gaze. After all, women are the root cause of all fitna. Wasn't it a woman who brought about the downfall of Adam by colluding with Satan? Never mind that without the fall of Adam, the world as we know it wouldn't have come into being.

The burkha, in essence, combines these two injunctions. It is both a cloak of invisibility that women must wear when stepping out of their homes as well as the boundary line, the Islamic 'Lakshman Rekha', behind which women must remain. Had my cousin understood the true meaning of the Islamic veil, she wouldn't have made a public spectacle of herself.

Muslim theologists, jurists, and philosophers over the centuries have concluded that for a woman to embrace Islamic life, she must not step out of the house unless absolutely necessary, and certainly never for fun.

Muslim women and their issues are the most debated and protracted subjects in Islam, even more than jihad. The best Muslim minds, from the days of the Prophet and thereafter, have been exercised and obsessed with the subject of women—what they should wear, study, eat, how they should bathe, sleep, how long they should grow their nails, what the decibel levels of their voices should be when they speak, how they should keep themselves chaste and yet desirable for their husbands, how they should be punished for offences of commission and omission, what degree of beating is necessary for discipline, and so on.

Given the volume of instructional manuals for Muslim women, one would imagine that the religion of Islam was revealed with the sole objective of taming the wayward women of the world and to keep them from having indiscriminate sex, when the truth is, in pre-Islamic Arabia, it was the male of the species who was sexually promiscuous.

This was the reason that Islam, as revealed in the Quran, tried to give women equal standing and rights. This is all the more remarkable given the social climate of medieval Arabia. Women in pre-Islamic Arabian society were considered subhuman. On the one hand, female children were undesirable and were often killed at birth. On the other hand, adult women were hugely desirable, irrespective of whether they were wives, stepmothers, or slaves. It was a common practice for the eldest son to take as wives his father's widows inherited as property with the rest of the estate'.[1] Note the term 'wives', which puts no limit to the number. An adult woman in Arabia had a very limited role beyond her sexual function. The lucky ones managed to fulfil their sexual responsibilities as one of several wives of a rich man, while the slaves or poor had to work in brothels, vulnerable to both sexual violence and debasement.

[1]Sayed Abul Hasan Ali Nadwi, Muhammad Asif Kidwai (trans.), *Islam and the World*, Academy of Islamic Research & Publication, Nadwatul Ulama, 3rd edition 2013, p. 39.

Even today, horror stories of the sexual exploitation of women at the hands of Arab men are frequently reported in the media.[2] Clearly, the humanizing touch of Islam has not been able to penetrate the thick walls of male entitlement and old-fashioned debauchery of Arab society.

During Prophet Muhammad's time, the only women to escape this subhuman existence were the beloved daughters of tribal chieftains, especially if they survived their male siblings. Despite this, there is only one recorded woman in pre-Islamic Mecca who had any agency over her life. As we've seen, this was Khadija, a successful businesswoman who had large trading caravans going in and out of Mecca. She was the daughter of a rich merchant who inherited her father's business. Muhammad, her distant relative, came to work for her. As he gained her trust, he started to accompany the caravans. Over time, Khadija increasingly came to rely on him and proposed marriage.

Most accounts agree on these facts. Thereafter, discrepancies creep in. For instance, while everyone agrees that Khadija was older than Muhammad, the age difference varies across accounts. Some Sunni versions say that she was forty at the time of her marriage and Muhammad twenty-five. Also that she was a widow who had a few children from her previous marriage.[3] Some Shia accounts put her age at twenty-eight and refer to her as a virgin. These variations can be explained by the fact that there was no tradition of history writing during the Prophet's time; the first account of his life and times was written a century after his death.

The importance of Khadija lies in the fact that not only was she the first person to convert to Islam, but she also used her enormous wealth to support Prophet Muhammad and the early Muslims. She paid to free slaves and stood as a shield between her husband and the rest of the Meccans, who were up in arms against him for questioning their existing

---

[2]Osama Al Madania et al, 'Child physical and sexual abuse in Dammam, Saudi Arabia: A descriptive case-series analysis study', *Egyptian Journal of Forensic Sciences*, Volume 2, Issue 1, March 2012, pp. 33–37. Also see 'Torture, abuse, & harassment: ex-housemaids describe horrors of working in Saudi Arabia to RT', RT, 28 Feb 2017.

[3]Khadījah, *Encyclopedia Britannica*, available here: https://www.britannica.com/biography/Khadijah

religious beliefs. Owing to her family's stature, as long as she was alive, no harm came to Prophet Muhammad; it was only after her death that he had to escape to Medina. An Islamic proverb acknowledging her contribution says: Islam did not rise except through Ali's sword and Khadija's wealth.[4]

Moreover, her marriage to Prophet Muhammad was monogamous. She was his only wife at the time and the only one to have children with him—it was these children who carried forward the Prophet's line of succession. Hence, she is respectfully referred to as the mother of the believers. It was only well after her death that the Prophet took another wife, and then another, thereafter taking several others.[5] With a few exceptions, all his marriages were with war widows and took place after he had established the first Islamic state in Medina.

How appalling it is then that this astonishing and unparalleled story of a remarkable medieval woman has been relegated to the footnotes of Islamic history, and is remembered only for her piety and devotion to her husband. Subsequent Islamic narrations, while dwelling on Prophet Muhammad's relationship with his youngest wife, Aisha, gloss over the nature of his relationship with Khadija, which was clearly based on equality and mutual respect. When Prophet Muhammad's actions are held as Sunnah,[6] worthy of emulation, why don't Muslim men emulate the beloved Prophet when it comes to marrying older, widowed women? Where has this craving for young, virginal, stay-at-home wives come from? It is certainly not Islamic.

Coming back to Khadija, could she be the reason that the early

---

[4]Yasin T. Al-Jibouri, 'Khadijah, Daughter of Khuwaylid, Wife of Prophet Muhammad', *Islam.org*

[5]After Khadija's death, Prophet Muhammad took twelve more wives, most of whom were widows older than him. The only other wife who is as famous as Khadija is Aisha, daughter of Abu Bakr (who became the first caliph). Aisha's age at the time of marriage has been a subject of vicious debate, amongst Muslims and non-Muslims. See here: https://www.youtube.com/watch?v=YYNmCsZRV84. Moreover, since history-writing began over a century after the Prophet's death, details about his personal life have largely remained in the realm of conjecture.

[6]Sunnah are the habits and practices of the prophets starting from Adam.

Quranic verses revealed to Prophet Muhammad tried to reform Arab society, especially in its treatment of women? Of course, before the society of the time could contemplate giving equality, it had to first recognize women as fellow humans, and that is what the Quran sought to do, with limited success. As Laila Tyabji points out, 'Islam is the only religion that gave women a fixed share in the property/ estate of her father and later her husband. People now say that it treats women as inferior to men because a daughter gets less than the son, but remember this happened in the seventh century when women were treated as no more than chattel. Can you imagine what Prophet Muhammad would have done today?'[7]

Unfortunately, the patriarchy eventually triumphed over the word of Allah, a process in which women have been complicit through their silence and absence of protest. 'Allah created man and woman as equal but the men created a discriminatory system to take unfair advantage for themselves,' says founding member of the Bharatiya Muslim Mahila Andolan (BMMA), Zakia Soman. 'Religious text is open to interpretation and we see a lot of misinterpretation based on gender, local context, and mindset of the scholar. Triple talaq, halala, and polygamy are social ills that are not supported by the Quran but conservative maulvis insist that this is religion. In India, the personal law board and others have always resisted any reform in the family laws. This has led to inequality and injustice for women in family and marriage.'[8]

Injustice to women begins immediately after birth. Because of the obsession with a woman's sexuality that is directly linked to family honour, several Arab tribes, inspired by the Pharaonic practice,[9] used to mutilate the girl's genitals in the name of circumcision. Sometimes, in addition to the clitoris, even the labia used to be cut and sewed up to prevent sexual desire and pleasure. The Quran did not address any kind of circumcision—for men or women. However, the pre-existing

[7]Interview with the author, New Delhi, 22 March 2019.

[8]Email interview with the author, 20 March 2019.

[9]Debangana Chatterjee, 'Female Genital Cutting (FGC): Is it an Islamic Practice? (Part 2)', *Sahiyo*, 13 Oct 2018.

Abrahamic practice of male circumcision was endorsed by Prophet Muhammad as Sunnah. Hence, all Muslim men were obliged to get themselves circumcised. There was no such command for women.

This clearly did not please the tribal chieftains. From their perspective, while they were willing to give up the faith of their forefathers and accept a new religion, Prophet Muhammad was not even willing to accommodate a few of their concerns. According to one Hadith, quoted by both Sunni and Shia scholars, when these men urged the Prophet to allow female circumcision for the sake of their family honour, he is supposed to have said that it could be done as long as it did not cause harm or excessive pain.[10]

Based on this Hadith, it was concluded that while it was not compulsory, Islam permitted female circumcision. Gradually, fantastical stories started to be spun around the virtues of female genital cutting. But the majority of Muslims remained unconvinced. While among the Sunni Muslims, only a small section based in Yemen practises female genital mutilation (FGM) today, amongst the Shias, it is prevalent in the extremely closed Bohra community.

In a conversation recorded on the portal Café Dissensus, Mariya Taher, a Bohra Muslim woman and co-founder of Sahiyo, an online movement against FGM, says, 'I had heard from my mother that in Islam women are not supposed to be sexual, and that khatna [circumcision] is done to help curb that sexual desire. But after I did my study, I was shocked to learn that there is a certain justification used by the religious clergy that khatna allows for a kind of knowledge, an ilm, to be passed between husband and wife when they have sex.'[11]

Journalist-activist and co-founder, Sahiyo, Aarefa Johari, was given a different justification when she questioned FGM. 'When I first questioned the practice, my mother said she had me cut simply because it was something the religion (basically community) expected everyone to do. It was only about faith. Later, she must have discussed it with some friends who justified it on (pseudo) medical grounds that if male

---

[10]Ibid.

[11]Mariya Taher, Aarefa Johari, 'Just a Slice of Skin', *Café Dissensus*, 5 May 2016.

circumcision has medical benefits, then female circumcision also serves to prevent STDs or uterine cancer, or some such. An aunt of mine defended the practice because it controls women's excessive sexual urges and prevents them from becoming promiscuous.'[12]

And that, perhaps, is the most honest explanation for FGM as it is for all the other injunctions which have been imposed upon women in the name of religion—to keep them subordinate. This is in direct contravention to the spirit of Islam as revealed in the early Quranic verses.

That the Quran identified men and women as equal and hence responsible for their own conduct, instead of the former being the keepers of the latter, can be seen in the way Quranic verses addressed the believers. Take Verse 35 from the 33rd chapter, Al-Ahzab, of the Quran:

> Surely for Muslim men and women, believing men and women, devout men and women, truthful men and women, patient men and women, humble men and women, charitable men and women, fasting men and women, men and women who guard their chastity, and men and women who remember Allah often—for all of them Allah has prepared forgiveness and a great reward.[13]

Yet, judging by the way women have been treated throughout the history of Islam, Muslim men have always regarded women as inferior. In his book *Bahishti Zewar* (Heavenly Ornaments), written in the late nineteenth century, Maulana Ashraf Ali Thanvi, one of the founders of Darul Uloom Deoband, argued in favour of imparting only religious education to women on the grounds that, 'So where there is no knowledge at all, and added to this where the intellect is naturally deficient (because women are naturally deficient intellectually, meaning that where there is no intellect and no knowledge) then there will be

---

[12]Email interview with the author, 9 January 2019.

[13]Surah Al-Ahzab, Verse 33:35, translated by Dr Mustafa Khattab (https://quran.com/33).

no limit to the shortcomings mentioned in the above matters.'[14]

Bahishti Zewar is a compendium of eight smaller books that explains the ways and means of leading an Islamic life. It incorporates everything from eating and bathing and also addresses issues like masturbation, ejaculation, wet dreams, and so on, leaving absolutely nothing to an individual's discretion or judgement. It would be unfair to blame Thanvi alone for peddling regressive ideas. He was the purveyor of staunchly held beliefs handed down through the generations from the time of the Prophet. This despite the fact, as has been pointed out earlier, that Islam, in its formative years, attempted to treat women on a par with men. Not only did the verses address both men and women, the instructions about clothing and modesty were given to both. For instance, in the seventh chapter, Al-Araf, of the Quran, which was revealed in the early years of Islam and before the Hijrah to Medina, verse 26 says:

> O children of Adam! We have provided for you clothing to cover your nakedness and as an adornment. However, the best clothing is righteousness. This is one of Allah's bounties, so perhaps you will be mindful.[15]

The instructions were applicable to both men and women. The first verse that is considered to have contained a reference to the hijab (without actually using the word) was revealed five years after Hijrah, sometime before the Battle of Trench (January–February 627 CE). As part of the Surah Al-Nur, the instructions on covering up were revealed in two consecutive verses, the first of which was addressed to men. It said:

> O Prophet! Tell the believing men to lower their gaze and guard their chastity. That is purer for them. Surely Allah is All-Aware of what they do.[16]

---

[14]The English translation of the book can be downloaded for free from https://archive.org/details/BahishtiZewar/page/n3

[15]Surah Al-Araf, Verse 7:26, translated by Dr Mustafa Khattab (https://quran.com/7).

[16]Surah Al-Nur, Verse 24:30, translated by Dr Mustafa Khattab (https://quran.com/24).

The next verse addresses women:

> And tell the believing women to lower their gaze and guard their chastity, and not to reveal their adornments except what normally appears. Let them draw their veils over their chests, and not reveal their hidden adornments except to their husbands, their fathers, their fathers-in-law, their sons, their stepsons, their brothers, their brothers' sons or sisters' sons, their fellow women, those bondwomen in their possession, male attendants with no desire, or children who are still unaware of women's nakedness. Let them not stomp their feet, drawing attention to their hidden adornments. Turn to Allah in repentance all together, O believers, so that you may be successful.[17]

No matter how one interprets the above verse, even if one considers 'adornment' to refer to breasts and not jewellery, it is clear that the focus of this verse was on modesty and that it was not instructing women to cover up. That this is how the verse was understood by the Muslims is evident by the second and the last verse on clothing that was revealed after the Battle of Trench. But first, an interesting story that has been noted in the Hadith by Imam Bukhari, trusted by Muslims as the most accurate, even though, as we've seen, there's reason to be sceptical.[18]

This Hadith traces its origin to Prophet Muhammad's wife Aisha. According to her:

> The wives of the Prophet used to go to Al-Manasi, a vast open place (near Baqi at Medina) to answer the call of nature at night. Umar[19] used to say to the Prophet 'Let your wives be veiled,' but Allah's Apostle did not do so. One night, Sauda bint Zam'a the wife of the Prophet went out at 'Isha' time and she was a tall lady. Umar addressed her and said, 'I have recognized you, O Sauda.' He said so, as he desired eagerly that the verses of Al-Hijab (the observing of veils by the Muslim women) may be revealed. So Allah revealed

[17]Ibid https://quran.com/24, Verse 24:31

[18]I explain why many of the Hadiths cannot not be taken as the absolute truth in the Chapter 5.

[19]Umar succeeded Abu Bakr as caliph.

the verses of 'Al-Hijab' (a complete body cover excluding the eyes).[20]

Apparently, the reason Umar was keen that Prophet Muhammad's wives should be fully covered was because a group of bandits was known to be in the area where the women went to relieve themselves at night. Umar's argument was that if the women were known to be Muslims then the bandits, for fear of retribution, wouldn't molest them.

If indeed this was the case, then wouldn't it have been more logical to task the Muslim soldiers to take on the bandits instead of asking the women to cover up? In any case, the verse was revealed:

> O Prophet! Ask your wives, daughters, and believing women to draw their cloaks over their bodies. In this way it is more likely that they will be recognized as virtuous and not be harassed. And Allah is All-Forgiving, Most Merciful.[21]

This verse does not describe how exactly women should ensure that they are not recognized—these details were subsequently provided by those who interpreted this verse according to their social conditioning. The operative part of the verse was that it was suitable to do so to avoid harassment. Hence, if there was no fear of harassment, would there be any need for women to conceal their identity?

However, the verse was constructed in a way that suited the patriarchal male mindset of the time. And from that point onwards, throughout the Muslim world, such has been the level of misogyny that women who did not cover up were considered fair game for sexual abuse, molestation, and rape. Few Muslim men remember that the Quran asks them to 'reduce [some] of their vision', all they remember is that if a woman is not covered from head to toe, she is asking to be molested.

While Mona Eltahawy has dealt with this subject in great detail in her book *Headscarves and Hymens: Why The Middle East Needs a Sexual Revolution,*[22] people of a certain generation in the Indian subcontinent

---

[20]Sahih Bukhari, Volume 1, Book 4, available here: https://quranx.com/Hadith/Bukhari/USC-MSA/Volume-1/Book-4/Hadith-148/

[21]Surah Al-Ahzab, Verse 33:59, translated by Dr Mustafa Khattab (https://quran.com/33).

[22]Mona Eltahawy, *Headscarves and Hymens: Why the Middle East Needs a Sexual*

may remember the blatantly misogynistic jokes by Pakistani stand-up comedians like Moin Akhtar and Umar Sharif. The joke used to be that it was the birthright of young men to collect outside women's colleges and harass (quaintly referred to as eve-tease) unveiled women, because if they didn't want to be harassed, they would cover their faces!

Burkha, hijab, purdah, no matter how many names one gives it, the impact remains the same—these are all ways to disempower women. It is an entirely facetious argument that empowered women also wear the hijab, and purely out of choice. Often names of politicians like Benazir Bhutto are offered to make the case for the hijab. Bhutto drew her power from several factors and the hijab was certainly not one of them. It was something she wore in public life because she, like most women politicians of the Indian subcontinent, irrespective of their religion, believed that it would help her connect better with her voters—who were mostly male and conservative.

So, should a Muslim woman exercise her free will to wear a hijab? By all means. But while doing so she should be aware that there is no 'free will'[23] in Islam. In addition, the veil adds nothing to one's faith. It is merely an item of clothing, which has its roots in culture rather than religion. Wear it as a sign of piety, a sign of defiance, or as a tactic to win your freedom to step out of your house for education or work. Whatever be the motivation, wearing a hijab adds nothing to one's faith; and not wearing one takes nothing away from it.

The religious veil is just another means of segregation—a way of restricting women's access to public spaces; and this fits in nicely with yet another Islamic injunction that a woman's place is within the four walls of the house. The source of this injunction is the Quran, but its context needs to be understood. The Quranic verse instructing women to stay indoors was directed specifically towards the wives of Prophet Muhammad during the Battle of Trench, in which the combined forces of the Meccan and Medinan rebels laid a month-long siege to the Muslims.

Revolution, London: Weidenfeld & Nicholson, 2015, p. 238.

[23]See Chapter 5: Insecurities of Muslims in India.

The first verse in this context said:

> O wives of the Prophet! You are not like any other women: if you are mindful of Allah, then do not be overly effeminate in speech with men or those with sickness in their hearts may be tempted, but speak in a moderate tone.[24]

This was followed by:

> Settle in your homes, and do not display yourselves as women did in the days of pre-Islamic ignorance. Establish prayer, pay alms-tax, and obey Allah and His Messenger. Allah only intends to keep the causes of evil away from you and purify you completely, O members of the Prophet's family![25]

There are two issues here.

One, across cultures, women of a certain class, especially royalty are distinguished from the working class by ways of segregation or veiling. It is done not with a view of disempowering them but to reinforce their superiority. That it also disempowers them is secondary. A veiled woman is a trophy, a mark of success for the man—he is able to provide for the women under his care so that they don't have to work like the peasantry. Hence, the verses for the Prophet's wives were to distinguish them from the rest.

Two, the fledgling religion of Islam was constantly under siege and hence vulnerable to assault from known and unknown enemies—referred to as hypocrites in Islam and termed more dangerous than those who opposed the Prophet and his followers openly. Hypocrites or munafiqeen were those who pretended to be Muslims to ingratiate themselves with Prophet Muhammad only to collude with the enemy at the first opportunity. The harshest of the 'sword verses' were directed at these people who 'deserved no mercy' because of their duplicitous behaviour. Since these people could not be identified till they actually betrayed the faithful and the Prophet, it was felt that the women of the

---

[24]Surah Al-Ahzab, Verse 33:32, translated by Dr Mustafa Khattab (https://quran.com/33)
[25]Ibid., Verse 33:33.

Prophet's household should not be exposed to them.

Yet, over time, this verse was taken to be a blanket instruction for all Muslim women for all time to come, thereby ensuring that they remained out of the workforce and financially dependent on men. In response to a question by a young girl, an interactive website on Islamic issues says,

> The basic principle is that a woman should remain at home, and not go out except for necessary purposes....[26]

Then, quoting an obscure Hadith attributed to the Prophet, it says,

> Woman is awrah[27], and if she goes out, the shaytaan (devil) raises his hopes (of misguiding her). She is never closer to Allaah than when she stays in her house.

Making allowances for modern times, the website lists conditions under which women can step out of their homes.

- That she needs to work in order to acquire the money she needs.
- The work should be suited to the nature of woman, such as medicine[28], nursing, teaching, sewing, and so on.
- The work should be in a place that is only for women, and there should be no mixing with non-mahram men.
- Whilst at work she should observe complete shar'i hijab.
- Her work should not lead to her travelling without a mahram.
- Her going out to work should not involve committing any haraam action, such as being alone with the driver, or wearing perfume

---

[26]'Guidelines on women working outside the home', Islam Question and Answer, available here: https://islamqa.info/en/answers/106815/guidelines-on-women-working-outside-the-home

[27]Awrah is an Arabic word drawn from the root word 'awr' which could mean any of the following: nakedness, defectiveness, blemish, weakness, vulnerability, or imperfection.

[28]Medical education for Muslim women has been a very important subject and encouraged by even the most conservative clergy. This is because Muslim women can only be treated by female doctors, or female nurses. A pious woman cannot be treated by a male doctor. Hence, this is not an argument in favour of higher education, but out of sheer necessity.

where non-mahrams can smell it.

- That should not lead to her neglecting things that are more essential for her, such as looking after her house, husband and children.

While misinterpretation is certainly a problem, a few Quranic verses do lend themselves to problematic interpretations. For instance, the following verse from the chapter Surah An-Nisa can be understood as both misogynistic and against the spirit of justice which the Quran otherwise professes. Incidentally, this Medinan chapter (after Hijrah) was revealed over eight years and during the period when Islamic laws, including laws of inheritance, were being enunciated. The verse is often interpreted as saying men are 'the caretakers of women, as men have been provisioned by Allah over women and tasked with supporting them financially. And righteous women are devoutly obedient and, when alone, protective of what Allah has entrusted them with. And if you sense ill-conduct from your women, advise them first, if they persist, do not share their beds, but if they still persist, then discipline them gently. But if they change their ways, do not be unjust to them. Surely Allah is Most High, All-Great.'[29]

Abusive men frequently take recourse to this verse to justify their behaviour. However, over the last few decades, newer translations of the Quran, especially by women,[30] have contended that the Arabic word 'yadribuhunna' mentioned in the verse comes from the root verb 'daraba', which has multiple meanings, derived mainly from the context in which it is used. In the Quran alone, the verb daraba has been used several times,[31] with interpretations ranging from 'to turn away', 'to leave', 'to strike', to condemn', 'to explain' etc.

Pakistan-born Canada-based Sufi Islamic scholar Muhammad Tahir-ul-Qadri interprets the entire verse from the perspective of a woman in his sermons.[32] According to him, the verse does not give men control

---

[29]Surah An-Nisa, Verse 4:34, translated by Dr Mustafa Khattab (https://quran.com/4).

[30]Laleh Bakhtiar, *The Sublime Quran*, Kazi Publications, 2009 and Amina Wadud-Muhsin, *Qur'an and Woman*, Oxford Fajar Sdn Bhd (Oxford Fajar), 1992.

[31]Edip Yuksel, 'Beating Women, or Beating around the Bush, or...', True Islam, available here: http://www.quran-islam.org/articles/beating_women_(P1179).html

[32]Dr Tahir-ul-Qadri, Dawra-e-Quran: Surah Al-Imran & Surah an-Nisa (Session 2),

over women; rather, it puts the responsibility on husbands to ensure their wives' rights, safety, and well-being. He bases his arguments on the preceding and succeeding verses, which give women enormous liberties, including the freedom to pursue a career and spending their earnings as they wish. The husband has no right to his wife's earnings; though the wife may wish to give some part of it to her husband as a gift. In this perspective, Qadri argues that the word 'yadribuhunna' means striking a temporary separation after all means of reconciliation fail.

Women writers like Laleh Bakhtiar also use similar logic. 'When the Prophet had difficulty with his wives, what did he do? He didn't beat anybody, so why would any Muslim do what the Prophet did not?' she said in an interview before the publication of her book, *The Sublime Quran*.[33] According to her, the verse tells the husband 'to go away'.[34]

However, despite these feminist readings of the Quran, the most widely accepted interpretation of the verse is the husband is permitted to use some measure of physical force to discipline his wife if everything else fails. This interpretation is based on a Hadith which refers to the last sermon of the Prophet in Mecca. According to that Hadith,[35] the Prophet told the believers that husbands could hit disobedient wives to discipline them but only in such a manner that it did not cause any injury. Also, they should not be hit on their faces. Conscious of the subjectivity of the instructions, over the years, ulema have consistently condemned domestic violence, holding that it has no basis in religion.[36]

Yet, despite all kinds of contextual explanations, the fact remains that some Quranic verses must be tempered with principles of civility and justice. The absence of this, perhaps, is one of the biggest failings of Muslim men and women who cling to medieval laws in modern times

---

available here: https://www.youtube.com/watch?v=qI7QqYR0WCY

[33]Neil MacFarquhar, 'Verse in Koran on beating wife gets a new translation', *New York Times*, 25 Mar 2007.

[34]Ibid.

[35]'The Chapters on Marriage', Sunnah. com, available here: https://sunnah.com/urn/1319250

[36]'The Right to Beat Wives (Some Misconceptions)', *Al-Mawrid*, 2 Mar 2017, available here: https://www.youtube.com/watch?v=z80u77sGQfA)

because they insist on following the letter of the verses instead of its spirit.

This is not true of all Muslims, but the majority is indeed victimized by dogmatic clerics citing such verses and making them even more atrocious with their misogynistic interpretations. A consequence of this is that in India, the lot of the vast majority of Muslim women is the worst among all communities, including the traditionally victimized scheduled castes and tribes. While the latter's abjectness is attributed to marginalization by caste Hindus, in the case of Muslim women, marginalization happens at the hands of the people they trust the most—the men of their family and community.

In its 2005 report, the Sachar Committee observed the double victimization of Muslim women. They are the first to disappear from formal education and the last to join the organized workforce.[37] It is this peripheral existence that renders them helpless and at the mercy of the men in their families and the mullahs from whom they seek advice.

Shaista Amber, who started the AIMWPLB in 2005 because the existing board, the AIMPLB, which oversaw issues of Muslim Personal Law had repeatedly failed women, says, 'I was stunned by the trio of patriarchy, class consciousness, and feudalism among Muslim men who did not even consider women worthy of basic human considerations.'[38]

Zakia Soman adds, 'The old dictum that the "place of women is inside the home" needs to change. The community will remain backward if women are denied the opportunity to empower themselves. We need to look at daughters as equal to sons and enable them to avail every opportunity in life. Unfortunately, most girls are denied this despite their desire to study and to work. Social and cultural barriers come in the way of women in India and all over South Asia.'[39]

This state of powerlessness shows itself most palpably in the instances of arbitrary divorce and absence of compensation. This situation is

[37]Social, Economic and Educational Status of the Muslim Community of India: A Report, Prime Minister's High Level Committee Cabinet Secretariat, Government of India, November 2006.

[38]Interview with the author, Lucknow, 15 December 2018.

[39]Email interview with the author, 20 March 2019.

peculiar to Muslims. Marriage in Islam is a socio-legal contract, it is not a holy union. Hence, the terms and conditions of the contract are to be negotiated before signing on the nikah document or nikahnama. These terms include the bride money or mehr[40] which is the money the husband must pay his wife immediately upon marriage to give her a sense of financial security, irrespective of the fate of marriage; and the mechanism of breaking the contract, that is divorce.

Once again, there is a huge gap between theory and practice. In spirit, the mehr depends on the husband's capacity to pay. This is one of the reasons that middle- or low-income Arabs used to scout for brides among the destitute in India, Pakistan, and Bangladesh. Here, they could get young wives by paying only a token mehr! In the Indian subcontinent, men negotiate the mehr amount based on the financial strength of women and their families; the poorer the woman, the smaller the mehr. Unfortunately, poor women and their families are so desperate to marry off their daughters to the first available groom that they agree to this. Worse, several men insist on the mehr being a gesture, instead of money that will provide financial security to the bride. In such cases, they contract for the amount that Prophet Muhammad paid his wives when he got married. In one such instance in 2010, after adjusting for inflation, that amount came to the princely sum of thirty-two rupees and six paise![41]

But this is not all. A lot of men never pay the mehr, citing financial constraints, and if the marriage survives, then the women don't insist on it. Some men get their wives to formally forgo the mehr, so that there is no obligation to pay. This should be regarded as against the spirit of the Quran, because for some women, the mehr is the only thing (in cash or immovable assets) that gives them a semblance of financial security. Once a woman is divorced, then under the Muslim law, her husband is only required to pay her money for her upkeep for the mandatory waiting period of three months called iddah.

---

[40]Mehr is a negotiable sum of money or fixed asset that a husband must pay his wife the moment the nikah is contracted. This is the wife's undeniable right.

[41]Nilofer Ahmed, 'The importance of "mehr"', *Dawn*, 14 June 2012.

Iddah is the period that a woman—divorced or widowed—must spend in isolation, without any contact with a male with whom marriage is permissible. This period is three months for a divorcee and four months and ten days for a widow after the loss of the husband. The idea is to determine whether the woman is carrying her divorced or deceased husband's child. If she is found to be carrying a child, then her rights and responsibilities change.

If a woman is pregnant at the time of the divorce, the husband is required to pay for her upkeep till the child is born and as long as she breastfeeds the child. Thereafter, she is a free woman, and can remarry. The husband no longer has any contractual obligations towards her. His obligation is only towards the child. But this ability to remarry is notional for most women. In a country where destitute and desperate unmarried Muslim women are willing to marry geriatric, much-married men, why would any man choose to marry a divorcee, especially one with children, despite the recommendation in the Quran?

Curiously, despite a very explicit Islamic law on divorce, which is addressed in several verses in the Quran (first in the Surah Baqarah and thereafter in the exclusive chapter devoted to divorce called Surah Talaq), in India, it continues to be misrepresented, primarily because it was interpreted differently by different imams who codified Islamic law in the eleventh and twelfth centuries. For instance, in verses 2:29–2:30 of chapter Surah Baqarah, the Quran says,

> Divorce may be retracted twice, then the husband must retain his wife with honour or separate from her with grace. It is not lawful for husbands to take back anything of the dowry given to their wives, unless the couple fears not being able to keep within the limits of Allah...(2:229)
>
> So if a husband divorces his wife three times, then it is not lawful for him to remarry her until after she has married another man and then is divorced. Then it is permissible for them to reunite, as long as they feel they are able to maintain the limits of Allah...(2:230)[42]

[42]Surah Al-Baqarah, translated by Dr Mustafa Khattab (https://quran.com/2).

Of the four schools of Islamic jurisprudence, while three interpret this as pronouncements made over a period of time (hence the option of reconciliation even after the second pronouncement of talaq), a section of the Hanafi school interprets this as all three talaqs being given in one sitting, popularly known as triple talaq.

In the foreword to *Till Talaq Do Us Part*, Faizan Mustafa, vice chancellor, NALSAR University of Law, Hyderabad, considers triple talaq not only bad in interpretation but also bad in spirit. He writes:

> The expression 'al-talaqu marratan' in verse 229 means that divorce may be pronounced twice. Marratan (twice) implies a gap between two pronouncements, which would mean there should be sufficient gap between two pronouncements of divorce. When we say, 'I went to your office twice but you were not there,' it cannot mean that you went to the office twice in one go. It means that you went once and then again after a reasonable period of time.[43]

Fortunately, this is the interpretation of most of the Hanafi imams. In fact, some say that the gap between each pronouncement of talaq should be equal to the iddah period, i.e., three months, so that the man should know if the woman he wishes to divorce is carrying his child. The idea is that the knowledge of pregnancy may help in reconciliation.

Despite this, if a man resorts to triple talaq, quoting one interpretation of the verse based on an obscure Hadith which said while Prophet Muhammad condemned triple talaq, he did not forbid it, then, clearly, he is misusing the law. Fortunately, of all the Muslim men who divorce their wives, only a small number take recourse to triple talaq. But what makes this small number significant is the fact that most perpetrators and victims of triple talaq are people from the poorer segments of society. An arbitrary divorce means that the woman could end up homeless.

When the triple talaq debate raged in 2018, the BMMA surveyed 4,710 women from poor economic backgrounds. Of these, 525 were found to be divorced, 408 through triple talaq. This put the prevalence

[43]Ziya us Salam, *Till Talaq Do Us Part*, Gurugram: Penguin India, 2018, p. x.

of triple talaq at 78 per cent.[44]

However, the data from the AIMPLB, based on figures given by Muslim family courts from eight districts of Kerala, Maharashtra, Telangana, and Andhra Pradesh, found 1,307 instances of divorce among Muslims, none through triple talaq.[45] These discrepancies could very likely point to observer bias. In the absence of Government of India statistics, all figures are conjectures made to serve one argument or the other. The only reliable figure, as quoted by Faizan Mustafa, is based on the 2011 Census, which puts the number of divorced women at 0.49 per cent of the total number of Muslim women in India.[46]

However, once the Narendra Modi government decided to throw its weight behind the cause of victims of triple talaq in 2014, the issue assumed outsize importance, eclipsing every other issue that Muslim women face. First, in 2015, while hearing a case of a Hindu woman's right to her ancestral property, the Supreme Court asked for the setting up of a Constitutional Bench to 'examine the lack of rights of Muslim women though this was not an issue before the court'.[47] Thereafter, in 2016, Shayara Bano, a thirty-five-year-old resident of Uttarakhand approached the Supreme Court pleading that the triple talaq that her husband had pronounced against her be declared invalid. Subsequently, as two other women represented themselves in the case, BMMA joined them as a petitioner. Flavia Agnes, lawyer, women rights activist, and founder of Majlis (a legal resource centre for women), explains that since Shayara Bano had left her matrimonial home and was living with her parents to escape domestic violence, she could take recourse in the Protection of Women from Domestic Violence Act, 'but perhaps no one advised her about this....

'When her husband filed for Restitution of Conjugal Rights, she contacted a Supreme Court lawyer to transfer this case from Lucknow to

---

[44]Zeeshan Shaikh, 'No solid numbers for triple talaq, but divorce data show interesting trends', *Indian Express*, 5 May 2017.

[45]Shaikh, 'No solid numbers for triple talaq, but divorce data show interesting trends'.

[46]Salam, *Till Talaq Do Us Part*, p. x.

[47]'Indian courts had settled Triple Talaq issue decades ago: Women's rights lawyer', Ummid.com, 28 Sep 2018.

Kashipur. As a counter blast, the husband's lawyer sent her a talaqnama. Since a Constitution Bench was constituted, her lawyer advised her to file a writ petition and challenge the talaqnama though she herself consistently maintained that she does not wish to return to her husband due to domestic violence. So according to me this case does not strictly fit the formula of "instant and arbitrary triple talaq". But the writ petition gave her instant fame and she became known as a crusader for Muslim women.'[48]

In 2017, as Uttarakhand was about to go for state assembly elections, Bano's case got enmeshed in electoral politics. The BJP won the elections. In August 2017, the Supreme Court of India declared the pronouncement of triple talaq unconstitutional. This was the latest in the series of pronouncements that the Indian judiciary has been making in cases of divorce and maintenance for Muslim women since 1981, when Justice Barul Islam of the Guwahati High Court laid down the procedure for pronouncing talaq. Thereafter, citing the high court verdict, the Supreme Court of India also laid down the correct procedure for pronouncing talaq in 2002 (*Shamim Ara vs the state of Uttar Pradesh*).

Meanwhile, the issue of compensation for women was settled by the Supreme Court in 2001, when 'in another important judgement, *Danial Latifi vs Union of India*[49]...the Supreme Court held that a divorced Muslim woman is entitled to a fair and reasonable settlement for her entire life,' Agnes said in an interview in September 2018. 'But no one bothered to highlight this historic judgement and media continued to project that after divorce a Muslim woman is devoid of rights.'[50]

In pronouncing this judgment, the Supreme Court referred to the Muslim Women (Protection of Rights on Divorce) Act of 1986 which the Rajiv Gandhi government had passed after overturning the Supreme Court verdict in the infamous Shah Bano case (discussed earlier in the

---

[48]Tish Sanghera, 'Through Our Ignorance, We Are Branding Everything Concerning Islam As Anti-Women', *IndiaSpend*, 23 Sep 2018.

[49]Paushali De, *Danial Latifi v. Union of India*, Legal Service India, available here: http://www.legalserviceindia.com/article/l141-Danial-Latifi-v.-Union-of-India.html

[50]Sanghera, 'Through Our Ignorance, We Are Branding Everything Concerning Islam As Anti-Women'.

book). According to the Protection of Rights on Divorce law, a husband is liable to make a 'just and fair provision' for the maintenance of his divorced wife within the iddah period, i.e., three months. This amount, though paid within the iddah period, was meant to provide support to her through her life, effectively safeguarding Muslim women from destitution upon divorce.[51]

The media's ignorance about the existing laws was pardonable because Muslim women activists, led by the BMMA, agitated for a ban on triple talaq not only to safeguard women's rights but to ensure penal action against the errant men. This fit in well with the Modi government's strategy of using the Muslim Personal Law issue for political purposes. After all, it had worked well in the Uttarakhand elections. Hence, despite the Supreme Court verdict of 2017, the government introduced the Muslim Women (Protection of Rights on Marriage) Bill in the Lok Sabha, and it was passed in December 2018. However, the bill could not be passed in the Rajya Sabha, as the ruling party did not have adequate numbers there and it consequently lapsed.

Once the Modi government returned to power in May 2019 with greater numbers, including in the Rajya Sabha, it reintroduced the bill. On 30 July 2019, the bill was passed by both Houses; and on 1 August 2019, President Ramnath Kovind signed it into an Act.[52] Among the main features of the Act is the invalidation of triple talaq—which means that divorce given in this manner will not be considered valid—and a three-year jail term without bail for the man.

There is no doubt that the government calculated that legislation against triple talaq would please the Hindu vote bank. Indeed, in the February 2020 Delhi state elections, one of the listed achievements of the government was this very issue. Given that the BJP campaign during the elections was unprecedentedly hostile towards the Muslims,[53] listing

[51]Ajaz Ashraf, 'Arif Mohammad Khan on Shah Bano case: "Najma Heptullah was key influence on Rajiv Gandhi", *Scroll.in,* 30 May 2015.

[52]'President gives assent to triple talaq bill', *Economic Times*, 1 Aug 2019.

[53]Purnima S. Tripathy, 'BJP's Delhi election campaign: Hate and perish', *Frontline,* 28 February 2020. Also see: 'Bullets, biryani and fake exposes: A snapshot of the BJP's communal campaign for the Delhi election', *Scroll.in*, 7 February 2020.

this achievement was meant for the Hindu audience.

Interestingly, after the court verdict, both Shayara Bano and her co-petitioner, Ishrat Jahan, expressed their desire to join the BJP, but after a few preliminary meetings, nothing came of that.[54] Clearly, they had overvalued their utility. Sadly, their financial and social status remains poor. They remain dependent on their relatives. The political patronage and media attention they had received did nothing to improve that. Worse, the Muslim community support system also dissolved once their political aspirations became public.[55]

Conscious of the limitations of the law and the politics behind it, Sheeba Aslam Fehmi, writer and Muslim women rights activist, says, 'It is the obstinacy of the AIMPLB that has brought about this sword over the head of Muslim men. Had the board not behaved like the private club of the clergy and heeded the pleas of Muslim women, there was no need for this law. But they could not bring themselves to say that triple talaq is un-Islamic.'[56]

While Soman, whose BMMA was one of the petitioners to the Supreme Court against triple talaq, insists that, 'We needed a law against triple talaq in India,'[57] Shaista Amber is against criminalizing Muslim men over triple talaq. She says, 'We demand a Muslim Marriage Act which is in consonance with both the Quran and the Indian Constitution.'[58]

To the argument that the triple talaq law by criminalizing Muslim men is effectively further victimizing women, Soman counters, 'Has criminalizing dowry or domestic violence rendered women further destitute? If so, then the demand by men to dilute dowry law and domestic violence law should be accepted. A lot of people are indulging in politics over the triple talaq law but these people were silent when the Muslim woman was suffering.'[59]

---

[54]Nihi Sharma, 'Triple talaq crusader Shayara Bano set to join BJP', *Hindustan Times*, 6 Jul 2018.

[55]'Triple talaq crusaders continue to fight for survival', *Economic Times*, 14 Apr 2019.

[56]Interview with the author, 23 August 2019.

[57]Email interview with the author, 20 March 2019.

[58]Interview with the author, Lucknow, 15 December 2018.

[59]Email interview with the author, 20 March 2019.

Yet, for all the arguments in favour of or against the triple talaq law, four important aspects are lost sight of.

One, when a poor, unemployed Muslim woman is divorced, whether instantly, or following the prescribed waiting period, she is left to fend for herself. Under the Muslim Personal Law, her husband is obliged to only pay her the predetermined mehr and maintenance for the period of iddah. If she appeals to the court under the Muslim Women (Protection of Rights on Divorce) Act of 1986, then she can at best expect a one-time payment which can take care of her beyond the iddah period. Hence, the manner of divorce does not change her circumstances. 'A woman's fate is in any case sealed upon divorce,' argues Fehmi. 'This law does nothing to empower or protect her. But at least it punishes the man. And that may be a lesson to others.'[60]

That leads to the second aspect of the triple talaq law. History shows that laws have seldom been a deterrent, whether they are anti-terror, anti-rape, or even anti-murder laws.[61] Hence, it is unlikely that men who wish to instantly get rid of their wives will stop doing this just because the law now threatens them with a jail sentence. According to the BMMA, it received complaints of forty-five cases of triple talaq in different states despite the Supreme Court judgment. Given this, it is likely that men who would instantly divorce their wives earlier will now simply abandon them. In any case, under Islamic law, a man can have four wives. But an abandoned woman cannot remarry unless she is divorced.

The argument that as an abandoned wife she will still have the right to her husband's property is a hollow one. A woman from the 'weaker economic strata', probably semi-literate, is hardly likely to have married into a family that owns property. Moreover, if the husband has thrown his wife out, where will she have the means to demand her share in the property or take him to court? Besides, the man can still divorce

[60]In conversation with the author, New Delhi, 23 August 2019.

[61]'Law is no deterrent, it is the enforcement which deters: Kamini Jaiswal', *News18*, 24 December 2012. Also see 'Anti-terrorism laws in India: Distinguishing Myth & Reality', Legal Service India.com, available here: http://www.legalservicesindia.com/article/382/Anti—terrorism-laws-in-India.html

his abandoned wife through one of the approved ways of talaq, thereby availing the advantage of triple talaq without attracting penal action.

Third, of all the triple talaq cases which made the news, the majority were where the husband was leaving or had already left either town or country for employment abroad. This explains the talaq sent through text messages, emails, or over the phone. Will the long arm of the law book these offenders living in the Middle East or elsewhere? How will this law be enforced?

And, finally, what is the purpose of the law against triple talaq? Is it to ensure that men follow the Shariah in spirit and pace out each pronouncement of talaq? Or is it to make the process of divorce difficult by discouraging it and thereby forcing women to stay in unhappy, and sometimes, abusive marriages?

One of the arguments against triple talaq is that men often pronounce talaq in haste or anger and regret it later. Then, when they want to get back to their wives, they cannot because the Quran stipulates that after the third pronouncement, the nikah is broken and the wife is no longer 'lawful to him'. He will have to marry her again. But this can only be done once her second marriage breaks down or her second husband dies.

To mitigate this impediment, Indian mullahs have devised an entirely local jugaad called halala. In this, a mullah himself marries the divorced woman for money, paid by the ex-husband, has sex with her, and then divorces her. The woman once again waits out her iddah period and remarries her first husband.

The champions of triple talaq law say that making it illegal will curb the cruel halala practice. Since triple talaq will not be valid, the woman will remain married and can reconcile with the husband. However, what happens when a man, after uttering triple talaq, tells the wife that he wants to reconcile to escape the prison term? What kind of married life will this woman have? Will she not be exposing herself to abuse, living with a person who doesn't want to live with her? To escape this, if she lodges a police complaint against her husband, who will provide her with the support she might need?

If the AIMPLB was finding it difficult to declare triple talaq un-Islamic (because of its faith in Hadith), wouldn't it have been better if it had invalidated the process of halala by declaring it un-Islamic—because a divorce without witnesses is not a divorce? As the second verse of the chapter Al-Talaq makes clear:

> Then when they have almost reached the end of their waiting period, either retain them honourably or separate from them honourably. And call two of your reliable men to witness either way—and let the witnesses bear true testimony for the sake of Allah. This is enjoined on whoever has faith in Allah and the Last Day. And whoever is mindful of Allah, He will make a way out for them.[62]

Hence, a divorce pronounced in rage or in a state of inebriation should not be considered valid, thereby nullifying the need for halala. Having dragged its feet on the issues of Muslim women, the AIMPLB, which has some measure of influence in the Muslim community at the pan-India level, needs to step in for the sake of Muslim women and men, and look at matters beyond nikah and talaq. Especially given its widespread network across the country and the access it has to the poorest through its family courts, the sixty darul qazas, which, it announced in 2018, will expand to every district of India[63]. Even though critics of darul qazas point out that they have no legal validity, and push Muslim women further into the clutches of medieval forms of justice, Agnes points out the importance of these Muslim family courts: 'Today our judiciary is clogged and cases drag on for a very long time. So, actually solving disputes through alternative dispute resolution mechanisms like Lok Adalats (People's Courts), mediation centres etc. are encouraged.'[64]

According to her, darul qazas offer women an accessible and reassuring option of grievance redressal. 'I have visited around eight that are functioning and each one said more women approach them than

---

[62]Surah Al-Talaq, translated by Dr Mustafa Khattab (https://quran.com/65).

[63]See All List of Darul Quaza Established by AIMPLB, All India Muslim Personal Law Board: http://aimplboard.in/darul-qazah_All.php; and Ziya Us Salam, 'Councils of contention', *Frontline*, 17 Aug 2018.

[64]Sanghera, 'Through Our Ignorance, We Are Branding Everything Concerning Islam As Anti-Women'.

men. A few of these stated that around 95 per cent are women.' She furthers notes that 'when a Muslim woman faces domestic violence, she often prefers to go to a darul qaza to dissolve her marriage rather than the family court. In a darul qaza women feel more comfortable since they are familiar with the culture, understand the language. Also, darul qazas offer expeditious and cheaper options to resolve family disputes, than the civil courts.'

Agnes says that the AIMPLB does not have a monopoly on darul qazas; several Muslim organizations including Imarat-e-Shariah in Bihar, which was set up in 1920, as well as sects like Barelvi run a network of such quasi-courts. 'Any learned mufti who is socially conscious may set up a darul qaza to help resolve family disputes.'[65] Hence, it is at this level that the law has to make a difference, because for a majority of Muslims, this is the first level of judiciary that they encounter.

This is the reason Faizan Mustafa insists that even retrograde organizations such as the AIMPLB have their uses. 'It is silly to say that it should be dismantled. What we need are reforms in the organization so that it is more responsive to the needs of the people it is supposed to serve.'[66] The first step towards reform of the board would be to make the distinction between the divine and the human. For example, the AIMPLB has perpetuated the myth in India that the Muslim Personal Law is divine law that cannot be tampered with 'when the truth is that only the inspiration of the law is divine as it is drawn from the Quran. The law itself is the human interpretation of what the Quran says by way of Shariah. One must understand that the Quran is not the book of law. It is the source of law.'[67] Given this, Muslim Personal Law can be interpreted according to the region and circumstances. This is the reason that, throughout the Muslim world, Islamic law varies. It is responsive to the society and historical precedence of the region. For instance, in Turkey, the nikah is a cultural ceremony, which some couples chose to have while others don't. It has no legal validity. All marriages have to

[65]Ibid.

[66]Interview with the author, New Delhi, 13 September 2019.

[67]Ibid.

be registered in court.[68]

While avoiding the argument about the divine sanctity of Muslim Personal Law, Kamal Farooqui, the spokesperson of the board, insists that the organization has been evolving with the times. A measure of this evolution, according to him, is that '28 per cent of the total members of the board are women. We came up with a model nikahnama (marriage contract) twenty-five years ago, in which we clearly laid down the rights of the wife and the responsibilities of the husband. The model nikahnama also disapproved of triple talaq.'[69]

However, the limitation of the model nikahnama was that it laid down broad guidelines which are non-binding. As mentioned earlier, the AIMPLB is registered as a non-governmental organization. Hence its influence remains advisory. 'The nikah contract is drawn up by the individuals. We can't dictate terms to them. Even if we train the qazis (lower-level jurist) to conduct the nikah, he remains a mere deed writer. What has to be written in the deed is determined by the individuals.'[70]

In 2008, Amber's AIMWPLB also issued a model nikahnama invalidating triple talaq which, she claims, is being used by an increasing number of women. The AIMPLB issued yet another model nikahnama in 2018 at the peak of the triple talaq controversy. In a statement to the Press Trust of India, the AIMPLB spokesperson, Maulana Khalil-ur-Rahman Sajjad Nomani, said, 'We are making a provision in the model nikahnama in which there will be a column—I will not give triple talaq. Once during nikah (marriage), this column is ticked, one will not be able to give triple talaq.'[71]

Given the attention the triple talaq issue has commanded in the media and public discourse, it appeared that this was the only challenge before Muslim women. This is not to say that triple talaq should not be challenged, only that it should not be allowed to overpower the larger

[68]Conversation with Ayse Akalin, publisher of Turkish magazine *Defence Turkey*, Munich, 5 November 2019.

[69]Interview with the author, New Delhi, 6 October 2018.

[70]Ibid.

[71]PTI, 'Model nikahnama to be modified to deter Muslims from giving triple talaq: AIMPLB', *India Today*, 3 Feb 2018.

narrative of Muslim women in India. As discussed, their religion and gender work in tandem to disempower them. As seen earlier, no law can help a woman if she remains uninformed, ill-educated, and financially dependent on male family members—whether she is unmarried, married, divorced, or widowed.

Take, for instance, the law of inheritance. According to Islamic law, all women, irrespective of their age and relationship to a particular man, (i.e., as mother, wife, sister, daughter, or granddaughter), have a fixed share in his wealth, including his estate.[72] No Muslim man can will his estate to his chosen inheritors, denying those who, according to the Quran, have rights to the inheritance. 'If you wish to will your wealth to one inheritor, you need consent from others to do so,' says Mustafa.[73] However, during a man's lifetime, he is free to give part of his wealth/ property (and not all of it) as a gift to whoever he wishes. The restriction on not willing away one's wealth while alive is to ensure that the person does not have to depend on others, including children, for his upkeep, as well as his/ her funeral expenses.

Since the daughter is entitled to half of what the son gets, a lot of progressive Muslims use this clause to gift part of their inheritance to the daughter[74] so that eventually both the son and daughter get an equal share. However, the same provision has been misused by men who want to limit the inheritance of the women in their families. They gift their immovable properties to their male inheritors, reducing the overall value of their estate.

A crucial lacuna in the Islamic law of inheritance is that the 1937 Muslim Personal Law (Shariat) Application Act left agricultural property or zamindari out of its purview. Since zamindari was a big source of revenue for the British India government and the powerful landholders were local agents of governance, the government didn't want to dilute the holdings. After Independence, while south Indian states—Karnataka,

---

[72]Dr Abid Hussain, 'The Islamic Laws of Inheritance', Sunnah Online.com, available here: https://sunnahonline.com/library/fiqh-and-sunnah/780-the-islamic-laws-of-inheritance

[73]In conversation with the author, New Delhi, 13 September 2019.

[74]Ibid.

Andhra Pradesh, Tamil Nadu, and Kerala—made agricultural land part of the Shariat Act, in north India, it remains excluded.[75] Citing this, even today, most north Indian (including Pakistani) Muslim rural families deny property to their women.

Eventually, it all comes down to men exercising control over women in a variety of ways, and, especially, when it comes to her mind and body. Like all religions, Islam remains a patriarchal faith which, despite the early spark of equality, could not completely overcome the tribal instincts of men. And men, across cultures and religions, have always had a primordial fear of a woman's sexuality, independence, and free will. Hence, all regulations, within and outside the Quran, pertain to controlling a woman's independence and desire to exercise her choices through purdah, segregation, FGM, or denial of equal education and employment rights.

Therefore, it is even more important to focus one's efforts towards empowerment through education, which eventually leads to financial independence. Importantly, education must include religious learning too, so that women's dependence on dogmatic, semi-literate mullahs is progressively reduced and they are able to judge for themselves what is in the spirit of Islam and what is in the interest of the mullahs.

Since education and empowerment will take time to come about, the biggest landholder of this country, the Central Waqf Council[76] should

[75]Bina Agarwal, 'Women's inheritance: next steps', *Indian Express*, 17 Oct 2005.

[76]Waqf is an Islamic trust. Over the centuries, those who were able to, donated their wealth and/or property to a religious trust for the purpose of helping Muslim communities. Various Muslim rulers used to allocate land to this trust or waqf for the building of mosques, religious schools, guest houses for pilgrims, graveyards, or open spaces for religious congregations. Despite the allocation of these properties being centuries old, the waqf functionaries have been extremely diligent with the paperwork. All documents, with official seals, have been handed down from generation to generation of waqf functionaries. Since a lot of waqf land is idle, it is leased for commercial purposes and the rent earned goes into the coffers of the council. Waqf also frequently sells land to finance some of its welfare programmes. The Central Waqf Council was created by an Act of Parliament in 1954 to centrally monitor state and district waqf boards as well as advise the government on the optimum running of the waqf properties: http://centralwaqfcouncil.gov.in/

step up to help destitute Muslim women, whether divorced or widowed, through monthly stipends and vocational training, eventually helping them get employment. Given that there are thirty-two state Waqf boards under the central council, setting up destitute homes and vocational training centres on Waqf-owned land should not be a problem. Perhaps it can institute a mechanism by which part of the annual zakat that Muslims give can be directed towards the upkeep of destitute women and their children. After all, helping poor Muslim women is also service to Islam.

Knowledge is power. A well-informed woman is an empowered woman who can not only steer her life better, but also cut off her dependence on the mullah who holds the sword of religion over her and counter the politician who pretends to speak for her.

8

THE CHANGING FACE OF MUSLIM SOCIETY

On the evening of 12 December 2019, as the Indian Parliament passed the Citizenship Amendment Bill, Tarannum Begum, a widow of many years, was making rotis for her children in her home in Batla House. The news that was to change her life forever passed her by. Her priorities were her two sons, the older of whom had just started working.

Three days later, on 15 December 2019, this life-changing news finally hit home. The Delhi police had entered the Jamia Millia Islamia campus next to her house and had brutalized the students. The police also entered the library, using tear gas shells to flush out the students; they then used batons to beat them.[1]

Tarannum turned off the stove, wrapped a shawl around her shoulders, and stormed out of her house screaming, 'Ab nahin toh kab' (if not now then when). Her neighbour, who too had heard the news of the assault, joined her. And then a few more women joined them.

'I was very angry at the police for hitting our children,' she recalls. 'I wanted to protect our children. I wanted to hit back at the police. I wanted to scream. I wanted to tell the police to go away.' Then catching her breath, she says, 'I had no idea what I wanted to do.'[2]

One of her neighbour's daughters was among the students who were hurt by the police batons. As the anguished mother joined the impromptu protest, more women poured out on to the streets—for the sake of their children, and for all the children who studied in the university.

For some time, the group of screaming women moved down the road

[1]'Jamia Protesters Release Video Of Cops Attacking Students In Library', NDTV, 16 February 2020.

[2]In conversation with the author, New Delhi, 12 January 2020.

further inside the university campus without a sense of direction. Their only thought was to claim the space for the children. Then somebody mentioned the police barricade towards the southeastern end of the campus in the area called Shaheen Bagh. The marching women found direction.

'We went there. The police stopped us at the barricade, pushing us back. Some women fell back. I don't know what came over me,' says Tarannum. 'I just sat down there on the road. Two other women also sat down with me. We refused to leave.'[3]

The women spent the night of 15 December under the sky in numbing cold, kick-starting what is now known as the Shaheen Bagh protest. 'We didn't feel the cold. Our rage was keeping us warm,' says Tarannum, her face breaking into a grin for the first time since we started to talk, softening the lines on her face and her anger.

By the next morning the word had spread. More women and men came to join them, in the spirit of Majrooh Sultanpuri's couplet 'main akela hi chala tha janib-e-manzil magar/ log aate gaye, karwaan banta gaya' (alone I started towards the destination, people joined me and we became a movement). As more women started joining in, an impromptu coordination committee was formed from among the locals to give political orientation to the protest. At its inception, the movement was only about concern for the students and demanding justice for them.

Over the next few days, the women of Shaheen Bagh started making the news. Neighbours and good Samaritans started pitching in to help the protesting ladies. Mattresses, quilts, braziers, and tents were arranged. Volunteers started contributing drinking water, food, and over-the-counter medicines to the women sitting on the road. As the numbers soared and facilities improved, several similar protests started to sprout around the country. Within a week, the Muslim women of Shaheen Bagh, erstwhile homemakers, some barely literate, had found their real calling. They became both the metaphor and the anchor for the anti-Citizenship Amendment Act (CAA), anti-National Register of Citizens (NRC), and anti-National Population Register (NPR) protests in the

[3]In conversation with the author, New Delhi, 12 January 2020.

rest of the country. By February 2020, there were, according to lawyer and Muslim activist Anas Tanwir, 'sixty-eight permanent sit-in protests throughout India',[4] all led by Muslim women.

It was unprecedented and remarkable. Conservative, veiled Muslim women had never been seen or heard on the streets before. At Shaheen Bagh, not only were they seen and heard, they were expressing sound political opinions with clarity. They were giving interviews to television channels without the least bit of self-consciousness. They were articulate and consistent in their assertions.

'How did you learn about the CAA and NRC?' I asked Tarannum. It was 12 January 2020. We were sitting inside the medical tent next to the Shaheen Bagh protest site, as a havan (a Hindu prayer ritual in which offerings are burnt in consecrated fire) was underway. A woman doctor, who volunteered at the medical camp on weekends, rushed to answer my question.

'They don't have to understand everything. There are people like us who understand—'

Tarannum, her face framed by a headscarf and forehead smeared with a thick vermilion mark, raised her hand to interrupt. Though she did not utter a word, her expression told the doctor to shut up. Then turning to me, she said firmly, 'It is true that when I left my house on 15 December, I had only heard of CAA. I had no idea what it was or what it would mean for people like us. I was angered by the police action against young children. But I was also curious to know why the students were protesting. What had brought them onto the streets?'

Another woman entered the medical tent—also wearing the headscarf and the vermilion mark on her forehead. Tarannum greeted her warmly. 'She has been with me since the beginning,' she said by way of introduction.

'Do you understand what CAA–NRC is?' she asked her, and said to me, 'She is from Bihar.' The doctor tried to intervene again, but Tarannum told her gently, 'Let her speak.'

'Even if I didn't know what it was, the Home Minister has made

---

[4]Interview with the author, Noida, 16 February 2020.

sure that everyone knows what it is,' said the woman from Bihar with a confident grin. 'Amit Shah has explained everything clearly. I know what he wants to do. We came to Delhi six years ago from Jehanabad. My husband was a daily wager there. Here, he pulls a rickshaw. We don't have any papers. So, when they ask us, we cannot show anything. And then they will tell us we are not Indians. Where will we go after that?'

'Nobody is going anywhere,' Tarannum said firmly.

I pointed to the vermilion mark on her forehead. 'Oh, I sat at the havan for some time. The panditji put it.'

When Darul Uloom Deoband was trying to create a unique Muslim identity in the late nineteenth and early twentieth centuries, its biggest struggle was to dissuade Muslims, especially women, from following Hindu cultural practices and wearing 'Hindu' clothing. This was easier said than done, since recent converts were reluctant to let go of their family traditions. Hence, fanciful stories were invented about punishments that would be meted out to women in the afterlife if they wore vermilion on their foreheads. One such story that I heard as a child was that a burning rod would pierce the exact spot on the woman's forehead where she wore the bindi. As a north Indian Muslim, Tarannum would have heard these stories too.

'Do you know what they say about putting vermilion on the forehead or in the hair?'

Making a gesture of tauba or penance (touching of earlobes with her fingers) she said, 'Devotion to Allah is a debt on me. I will spend my life trying to repay this debt. Today, this is more important. This is the battle for our existence itself. As Allah tells us, survival with honour is most important. That is why I am here, sitting on the road, doing things I have never done before because I will not hear from anyone that I am not an Indian and this is not my country. I am sure Allah understands this and will forgive me.'

'You think we like all this,' interjected the lady from Bihar gesticulating to her forehead. 'You think I like spending the night guarding the "border" in this cold. I have been suffering from severe backache because of the cold. But what choice do we have?'

The border that she referred to was the edge of the protest site where the police had put up barricades. Despite the barricades, the police did not stop pedestrians from crossing over to the protest site. In the early days of the protest, some people with crude weapons entered the site and tried to create mischief. Since then, a man and a woman were deployed at the barricade to frisk all pedestrians, as the police stood by.

'Only yesterday, I found a woman carrying big stones in her backpack,' said the woman from Bihar. Then, turning towards Tarannum, she added, 'I handed her over to the police. But they did nothing. What are they sitting there for?'

'We should not criticize the police,' Tarannum told her, exchanging a glance with me, probably looking for approval. 'They are poor and helpless like us.'

'Till what level have you studied?'

'Class 10,' Tarannum replied.

'I have not been to school at all,' volunteered the woman from Bihar. 'But I can read the holy Quran,' she added with a touch of pride.

We returned to the main tent. The havan was over. The fire had been extinguished. Only embers remained and some smoke. A Sikh priest was standing on the low podium chanting verses. From time to time he would chant, 'Jo Bole So Nihal' (whoever says finds ecstasy). The audience, women in hijab, men in skullcaps and hennaed beards, replied in unison, 'Sat Sri Akal' (the Lord is eternal).

'Were you ever familiar with all this before you started to protest?'

Tarannum's smile was a mix of satisfaction and confidence.

'I have met more non-Muslims in these four weeks than I had in my entire life,' she said. 'Like everyone else, I grew up believing that they are different from us. But let me tell you, they are like us. Even those who do not speak openly support us silently. So many tell me when they come here that they never thought Muslims are like this. I tell them we are all Indians. I was born here. I will die here.'[5]

On my walk back to the main road from the protest site, I was flanked by the national flag, as well as the national colours splashed onto bunting, streamers, banners, murals, graffiti, and posters. It was

---

[5]In conversation with the author, New Delhi, 12 January 2020.

like a festival—a festival of freedom. There were slogans, music, and street theatre. There were children with painted faces. The elderly were sitting quietly on the pavement reading books borrowed from a street library created by the students of Jamia in protest against the police action inside the library.

Conspicuously absent were any Islamic symbols—Quranic calligraphy and the crescent moon. One banner that stayed with me had an image of Ashfaqullah Khan on one end and Ram Prasad Bismil on the other. Linking the two images was the line: Ashfaq–Bismil ki yaari, virasat hai hamari (Ashfaq–Bismil's friendship is our heritage). Ashfaqullah and Bismil were freedom fighters as well as friends who were hanged to death by the British in 1927 on charges of looting the government treasury. The raid came to be known as the Kakori incident.

The anti-CAA–NRC protests across India have indeed created a watershed moment for Indian Muslims. For the first time since Independence, they took to the streets, protesting peacefully, often facing violence, for a cause other than religion. Far from the calls of 'Islam is in danger in India', it appears that never before have Muslims been so secure in their Muslimness. Their confidence in their Muslim identity and the ensuing assertiveness has suffused both the physical and cyber world. From social media to the streets, Muslims are wearing their Muslimness and patriotism on their bodies and seemingly rejoicing in both.

Is this the new face of Muslim society? Self-assured and assertive? Or will the movement crumble under its own contradictions, as Naved Masood, retired secretary, Government of India, insists, because everything about it is superficial?[6] Is it hyperbolic to say that Shaheen Bagh as a metaphor is a turning point in the history of independent India?

'Mashallah, Mashallah, Mashallah,' says thirty-year-old Tanwir in a sing-song voice.[7] His exuberance is effervescent. Quoting a senior lawyer, who was appointed by the Supreme Court as one of the interlocutors to start talks with the women of Shaheen Bagh in February 2020, Tanwir

---

[6]Interview with the author, New Delhi, 13 February 2020.

[7]The literal meaning of 'Mashallah' is 'Allah willed it', but it is uttered in happiness for something wonderful having happened, and that nothing should spoil it.

says, 'This is the first time Muslims of India are having a conversation as Muslims with the rest of India.'[8] All these years, he says, 'We were advised to subsume our identities into the collective identity of the nation. We tried to merge with others, as if by standing out we would embarrass the idea of India. But today we are saying, "look at me". This is what I am—distinct, yet as much of an Indian as anybody else.'

Atika Zakir, a branch manager at Jamia Cooperative Bank's Jasola branch, which overlooks the Shaheen Bagh area, is slightly more circumspect. 'After 15 December, there was a lot of anger here. That the police is partisan is no secret, but we believed that it won't be so openly hostile in Delhi. After all, this is the capital city. But we were all proved wrong,' she says, shaking her head in dismay. With television and social media streaming the images of the police action in Jamia Millia Islamia and Aligarh Muslim University, the contrast of the conduct of the Delhi police with police behaviour in other universities was unmistakable.

'It is very clear that the police would not have dared to behave like this in any other university,' she says. 'Jamia and AMU were targeted because they are seen as Muslim universities. How can one ignore this fact or make excuses for police behaviour?'[9]

From Partition to the present day, it has been a very long journey for the Muslims of India. At least two generations of post-Partition Muslims suffered the psychological consequences of that brutal sundering. While some were weighed down by guilt (as mentioned in an earlier chapter), some, according to Masood, only felt weakly connected to India. These were the people who faced prejudice and sometimes communal violence, and continued to wonder if they had made a mistake by staying on in India.

'The sentiment was: why should we care when they don't care for us,' says Masood.[10] Having grown up with this sentiment, this group of people sought their fortunes outside India, not only because there were better opportunities there, but because they were convinced that they would have no opportunities in India. Referring to this, Irshad Khan

[8]Interview with the author, Noida, 16 February 2020.

[9]Interview with the author, New Delhi, 19 February 2020.

[10]Interview with the author, New Delhi, 13 February 2020.

(name changed), whom I have quoted earlier in the book, says, 'In my time, I frequently came across young people who didn't even want to make the effort in India.'[11]

However, this attitude of 'not making the effort' is not as simple as it sounds. Using the example of her own family, journalist Afreen Khan (not her real name) points out that people often wanted to make themselves invisible for fear of getting sucked into sectarian politics. Muslim youth were frequently mobilized by opportunistic politicians to be used, in Tanwir's words, as 'cannon-fodder'.

'My mother was an educationist. She had been a witness to both aspirational strivings of young Muslims, as well as killing by the police in bids to quell communal violence,' says Afreen. 'She was convinced that a Muslim boy in India will either be a wastrel or viewed as a rioter and be killed by the police. "Ya to woh patang udhayega ya pathar maarega (either he will fly kites or throw stones)" is what she said. She didn't want that fate for her sons. She was determined that the moment they came of age they should leave India.'[12] But neither Afreen nor her parents ever thought of leaving India for better opportunities abroad. The idea of sending the sons out of India stemmed not from lack of opportunities but from a sense of self-preservation.

The present generation that is leading the charge for change is largely unaffected by guilt and insecurity. Tanwir describes this moment as one without fear. Quoting Urdu poet Sahir Ludhianvi, he says, 'Zulm phir zulm hai, barhta hai to mit jaataa hai/ khoon phir khoon hai, tapkega to jam jaayega (It's in the nature of oppression that when it crosses the limit it ceases to oppress/ just as blood, when it spills, freezes, becoming difficult to erase).

'Today, the Muslims in India are at that point in their lives when fear has stopped being a deterrent. They have been pushed so much to the corner that they are convinced they have nothing to lose any longer,' he says.[13]

---

[11]Telephonic interview with the author, 12 September 2019.

[12]Interview with the author, Noida, 15 February 2020.

[13]Interview with the author, Noida, 16 February 2020.

Masood says roughly the same thing. 'Very few are immobilized by fear,' he says. 'Fear makes you more aggressive.'[14] The difference in their outlook is perhaps reflective of both the generational gap between the two, as well as the side of the divide they both currently occupy. Masood is a retired bureaucrat with operational experience in Kashmir and the Northeast; Tanwir is a lawyer-activist and founder-member of Indian Civil Liberties Union (a legal advocacy group) which oversees cases pertaining to human rights and civil liberties, ensuring that the accused have access to legal help, and that the law is followed to the letter.

Bridging the gap between the two extremes is Dr Shah Alam Khan, a paediatric orthopaedic surgeon by day and a writer by night, who has experienced both extremities of emotions in the last few years—from fear to anger.

'When mob-lynching in the name of cow protection started, I became afraid because I felt vulnerable. I felt that I was under the scanner, which made me make a few lifestyle changes. For instance, to strangers I started introducing myself as Dr Shah, because that did not give away my religion. I stopped bringing Eid food home, especially kebabs, from my parents' home in Aligarh whenever I returned to Delhi after the festival. As I and my family travelled by road, I felt extremely worried about their security.'

Having lived with this fear for a few years, something snapped in Khan. He attributes it to the growing virulence among educated, affluent Hindus and the manner in which he started losing friends. 'I had no idea there was so much prejudice, dating back to Partition among Hindus,' he says.[15] Worse, they expressed it in a self-righteous manner.

A consequence of this was that over time his fear turned into anger. From Dr Shah, he became Dr Khan again. And despite being a non-practising Muslim, virtually an atheist, he stridently started identifying as a Muslim. 'At the core of my resistance was the realization that I was prepared to be lynched if that was the price I had to pay for my

[14]Interview with the author, New Delhi, 13 February 2020.

[15]Interview with the author, Noida, 6 October 2019.

identity. But I will not hide,' he says.[16]

Neither hide nor conform to what is expected of an acceptable 'Indian Muslim'.

'Isn't it strange that the word "progressive" is used only for Muslims?' asks Salman Khurshid. 'One never says progressive Hindu or progressive Sikh. There is an assumption in this that a Muslim will be regressive unless proved otherwise.'[17]

As it turns out, there is a growing tribe of young Muslims today determined to prove their Muslimness and not their progressiveness, no matter the cost. 'A former colleague of mine labels the assertion of my Muslim identity as communal,' says Dr Khan. 'But he calls his bigotry the response to centuries of "supposed" oppression that Hindus suffered at the hands of Muslims, the culmination of which was the Partition of India. In the last few years, I have discovered that doctors are the most illiterate people amongst all professions. We have a very limited perspective.'[18]

'Positions have hardened among my Hindu friends,' says Irshad Khan. According to him, the purely Hindu–Muslim narrative pushed by the Narendra Modi government is only one part of it. 'The other and more damning part has been the strident nationalistic rhetoric peddled by the government in which Kashmir–Pakistan has become a nexus and a litmus test for Muslims to prove their loyalties. This never happened before. Kashmir was never an issue in mainland India. Muslims were never asked to take sides on this issue. But, today, all of this has become part of one narrative in which Muslims are always the oppressors. When I point out a case of lynching, they say, "our soldiers are dying in Kashmir", when I mention growing intolerance against Muslims in public spaces, they say, "what about the Kashmiri Pandits". Of course, Muslims are feeling insecure, and, in some places, extremely frightened. And frightened people tend to become more religious.'[19]

---

[16]Ibid.

[17]In conversation with the author, New Delhi, 22 October 2018.

[18]Interview with the author, Noida, 6 October 2019.

[19]Telephonic interview with the author, 12 September 2019.

This, however, is not entirely correct. While it is true that a large number of young Muslims are increasingly turning towards Islam (more on that later), the assertion of Muslim identity is more about the politics of religion than faith itself. For years, the markers of Muslim identity—beard, short trousers, skullcaps, burkha, hijab—were singled out for stereotyping and ridicule. Hence, a Muslim, who wanted to be absorbed into a larger socio-economic group, or become invisible as a religious minority, shunned these symbols. In better times, there was no need for the assertion of religious identity for the simple reason that Islam does not prescribe a fixed identity. A Muslim's faith depends on her deeds (amal), instead of how she looks or what she wears. But these are not those times.

Two concurrent developments changed the way a Muslim sees herself in India today. One, the rise of Narendra Modi and his brand of unapologetically provocative politics; and, two, the growth of social media. While the former pushed Muslims into a corner, the latter gave them a mechanism to amplify their voices.

When the Narendra Modi-led BJP first stormed to power in 2014, there was an inevitability to its victory. After ten years of the Congress-led United Progressive Alliance government, the closing years of which saw rampant corruption and inertia, Modi's call for a corruption-free, development-focused government appeared as the panacea that the nation needed. Even though most Muslims did not buy into these twin promises (see Chapter 6), they understood the urge of their non-Muslim friends and colleagues to overlook Modi's history with the RSS and the 2002 violence in Gujarat. So much so that many Muslim influencers, including from Gujarat, reached out to the new prime minister, offering him support, in the belief that this would mellow his position towards the community, and even accrue some personal benefits to them. The Prime Minister reciprocated by doling out rewards to these people by way of sundry government appointments. One such notable Muslim businessman from Modi's home state, Gujarat, who spoke to me informally and cannot be named, claims that he offered his support to Modi because, 'dushmani karne se apna hi nuksaan hai, isliye socha dosti karke dekhtein hain' (nursing a grudge will only harm us, so I thought why not try the friendship route). Though he claims to be disillusioned with government's open hostility towards the Muslims, having exposed himself so much, he feels that turning back will do him, and 'the community', no good.[20]

To be fair, the Modi government did not mislead anyone about its agenda, which was clearly enunciated in the BJP manifesto. Once in power, it began initiating some policies and making utterances that were inimical to Muslims—identifying terrorism as the biggest threat to the country, for example, then suggesting that all terrorists are Muslims[21]; rousing public sentiment against cow slaughter, thereby encouraging extra-constitutional vigilante groups to stalk and assault whoever they suspected of trading in cattle, leading to the lynching of Muslims[22]; and creating the bogey of love jihad[23].

While all this instilled fear in the Muslims, forcing them to fall further back into their mental and physical ghettos, despair had still not set in. At some level, there was confidence that once the people of India realized that the government had failed on all its promises—from development and employment to 'acche din' (good days)—it would be voted out of power. This faith in the idea of India and secular beliefs of fellow Indians led the Muslims to think that by keeping their heads down they would be able to ride out the 2014 storm.

Even in early 2019, the belief was that the hatred unleashed by the outfits which claim closeness to the government[24] would be checked once the BJP lost the general elections scheduled to be held in May 2019. In a conversation with me in February 2019, Najeeb Jung was quite sanguine about the future: 'Things will sort out with time. We

---

[20]Telephonic conversation with the author, 2 February 2019.

[21]Aakar Patel, 'Are Most Terrorists In India Muslims?' *Outlook*, 5 Apr 2015.

[22]Iain Marlow, 'Cow Vigilantes in India Killed at Least 44 People, Report Finds', *Bloomberg*, 21 Feb 2019.

[23]'"Love jihad' a big threat to national security: VHP', *Business Standard*, 20 November 2017; also see Rohan Venkataramakrishnan, 'How real is the threat of love jihad?', *Scroll.in*, 14 Aug 2014.

[24]'Union minister Jayant Sinha garlands 8 lynching convicts, faces opposition flak', *Times of India*, 8 July 2018.

notice enhanced majoritarianism currently when a section feel they have government patronage. These are phases in democracies and things change with time.'[25]

This faith was belied in May 2019. The government returned to power with an even greater majority following an election campaign which was openly sectarian and divisive. A sense of foreboding was created in the country—it was made to seem as if India was at war with Pakistan and threatened by divisive forces within the country—the tukde tukde gang—a group of people working to break up India. Naturally, the majority of those painted as part of this gang were Muslim and their collaborators were painted as 'self-hating Hindus'. Such was the fervour of nationalism that all this evoked that even a new genre of film emerged—stridently nationalist in which the villain was always a Muslim.

And so, to protect the motherland from such perfidies, Modi had to triumph at the hustings. This time he bested his last performance. Despite presiding over a faltering economy and other failings, Modi and the BJP still swept to power. This made many in the Muslim community feel that a large number of Hindus in India hated Muslims and supported the idea of a theocratic India in which the latter lived at the pleasure of the former.

'For people like me, this was the turning point. A betrayal of faith, so to speak,' says Tanwir, insisting that he speaks for a large number of Muslims. His argument is that the Muslims chose to stay in India in 1947 because it was going to be a multicultural, secular state with one of the world's most visionary and liberal constitutions. Those who wanted a theocratic state migrated to Pakistan. 'In his second term, the Modi government has mounted a unilateral attack at the heart of this sacred document,' he says.[26]

He evokes the supposed compact Maulana Abul Kalam Azad made with the Muslims from the steps of Delhi's Jama Masjid on 23 October 1947. Urging Muslims to forsake fear for hope in independent India, Azad said:

---

[25]In conversation with the author, New Delhi, 13 February 2019.

[26]Interview with the author, Noida, 16 February 2020.

> I want to remind you that these bright etchings which you see all around you are relics of the Qafilas of your forefathers. Do not forget them. Do not forsake them. Live like their worthy inheritors, and rest assured that if you do not wish to flee from this scene, nobody can make you flee. Come, today let us pledge that this country is ours, we belong to it and any fundamental decision about its destiny will remain incomplete without our consent.[27]

On 30 May 2019, the new BJP-led NDA government was sworn in.[28] Two months later the Triple Talaq Bill was passed.[29] On 5 August, the government abrogated Articles 370 and 35A which gave the state of Jammu & Kashmir special status in the Union of India. Going a step further, Jammu & Kashmir was stripped of its statehood and bifurcated into two union territories—Ladakh and J&K.[30] Two months later, on 9 November, the Supreme Court of India gave its verdict on the protracted Ram Janmabhoomi–Babri Masjid case, finally clearing the ground for construction of the Ram Temple.[31] The top court of India, while acknowledging the criminality of the act of demolition, refrained from apportioning any punishment. Instead, it sought closure of the issue by offering a piece of land in a different spot in Ayodhya to the Muslims to build a mosque as compensation.[32]

And on 12 December, Parliament passed the CAA. The amended citizenship law allows Hindu, Sikh, Christian, Parsi, and Buddhist immigrants from Pakistan, Bangladesh, and Afghanistan, who have been living illegally in India because of religious persecution in their home

---

[27]Saiyida Saiyidain Hameed (ed.), *India's Maulana Abul Kalam Azad*, Centenary Vol. 2, ICCR, Vikas, 1990, pp. 170–73.

[28]'Narendra Modi to be sworn in as PM for 2nd term on May 30', *Economic Times*, 26 May 2019.

[29]'History made, triple talaq bill passed by Parliament', *India Today*, 30 Jul 2019.

[30]Prabhash K. Datta, 'Article 370 has not been scrapped. What does Modi govt move on Kashmir mean?', *India Today*, 5 Aug 2019.

[31]'Ayodhya Verdict on Ram Janmabhoomi-Babri Masjid land dispute case | Full text of Supreme Court judgment', *India Today*, 9 Nov 2019.

[32]Namita Bajpai, 'Sunni Waqf Board accepts alternative five-acre land near Ayodhya', *New Indian Express*, 21 Feb 2020.

countries, to get Indian citizenship within six years of their residence. Earlier, twelve years of residence in India was necessary for anyone seeking Indian citizenship.[33]

The Act does not extend this option to illegal Muslim immigrants (who have been branded as infiltrators or ghuspaitheeye by Home Minister Amit Shah)[34], because the government argues that since Pakistan, Bangladesh, and Afghanistan are Islamic countries, Muslims cannot be the persecuted minority there. This argument ignores the Shias and Ahmadiyyas of Pakistan who have faced persecution for decades. However, what really gives away the government intent is the exclusion of other Indian neighbours like Myanmar, Sri Lanka, and Nepal from the law, at least two of which have minority groups who have faced systematic persecution and exclusion by their respective governments from time to time—the Rohingyas in Myanmar and the Tamils in Sri Lanka.

The government also tweaked the penalty amount that visitors needed to pay if they stayed in India beyond their visa stipulation.[35] For an overstay between 90 days to two years and more, visitors would have to pay a penalty of US$ 300, 400, and 500 respectively. This expensive penalty does not apply to the other communities—Hindu, Sikh, Christian, Parsi, and Buddhist—from Pakistan, Bangladesh, and Afghanistan who have to pay ₹100, 200, and 500 for the same duration.[36] Effectively, what this means is that a Muslim from any of the three neighbouring countries will have to pay US$ 300, whereas a Hindu or a Sikh will be required to pay only ₹100 for the same offence.

According to a January 2020 report in *India Today*, 'This curious tweak in regulations wasn't just an indirect encouragement to minorities

[33]'Citizenship (Amendment) Act 2019: What is it and why is it seen as a problem', *Economic Times*, 31 Dec 2019.

[34]'Amit Shah's Big Statement on NRC', *Amar Ujala*, 1 Oct 2019, available here: https://www.youtube.com/watch?reload=9&v=xmxtVJ0PimA

[35]Suvojit Bagchi, 'India's new visa penalty discriminates on religious lines, say Bangladesh officials', *The Hindu*, 10 Dec 2019.

[36]Financial Penalty for Overstay and/or non-Registration, available here: https://indianfrro.gov.in/eservices/Financial_Penalty.pdf

from these three Muslim-majority countries to migrate to India, but also a precursor to the Citizenship (Amendment) Act, or CAA, 2019.'[37]

In any case, notwithstanding who is left out of the CAA, Indian Muslim citizens aren't affected by the new law, at least technically, and that is what the government and its spokespeople have been at pains to explain. Speaking off the record, a spokesperson explained that the government's hand was forced on CAA because of the outcome of the NRC exercise in Assam where, contrary to expectation, a large number of Bengali-speaking Hindus could not furnish papers to establish their Indian citizenship. As this would have angered the Hindu voters, the government had to find a way to accommodate them. Hence, it was to absorb these people that the government had to bring in the CAA.[38] According to him, the CAA has no relevance to the rest of the country.

However, Home Minister Amit Shah is on record saying not only that both the provisions of the CAA and NRC will be enforced throughout the country, he has also explained the mechanism by which this exercise will be carried out in his infamous 'understand the chronology' speech.[39] According to him, the CAA will first grant Indian citizenship to the above-mentioned refugees who came to India before 31 December 2014. After that the NRC process will get underway to determine who the 'infiltrators' are. Once again, Amit Shah has explained that Government of India-issued documents, such as passports, ID cards such as the Aadhaar, will not be considered proof of citizenship.[40]

What will be considered proof of citizenship is subjective and depends on when the person was born. According to the government, birth certificates will be adequate proof of citizenship for anyone born before 1987. Those born after 1987 will need to prove their citizenship

[37]Kaushik Deka, 'Who is (not) a citizen?', *India Today*, 10 Jan 2020.

[38]Prabin Kalita, 'Five lakh Bengali Hindu NRC rejects will get citizenship', *Times of India*, 11 Dec 2019.

[39]'CAB will be applicable in the entire country and not just confined to West Bengal: Shri Amit Shah', BJP YouTube, available here: https://www.youtube.com/watch?v=Z__6E5hPbHg

[40]'Shri Amit Shah's interview on Times Now', BJP YouTube, available here: https://www.youtube.com/watch?v=eNd792HSl_A

as well as those of their parents. And this is where the fear comes in. The poor migrant population of India, which moves from city to city in search of seasonal work, is hardly likely to have documents that can prove its citizenship. Among those who will find themselves outside the NRC, only Muslims will not be able to get citizenship under CAA. The prospect of being sent to one of the many detention camps being built by the government is very real for these people.[41]

Conflicting statements by the government also add to suspicions. For instance, despite Home Minister Amit Shah saying unequivocally that the NRC exercise will be carried out in the entire country to identify intruders, Prime Minister Narendra Modi said on 22 December 2019, 'I want to tell 130 crore people of India that ever since my government came to power in 2014...from then until now...there has been no discussion on NRC anywhere...we only had to implement it in Assam to follow the Supreme Court's directives.'[42] Most, especially the Muslims, believe such statements are being made to both generate confusion among the people as well as to blame the Muslims for overreaction because of their antipathy towards the BJP.

'If indeed one should believe the Prime Minister that there will be no NRC in the country, why does he not tell the Home Minister...' says Atika Zakir, adding that as long as the CAA exists, fear of NRC will remain.[43] Moreover, since the CAA has followed a long line of government legislations viewed as anti-Muslim, the popular sentiment is that the CAA is another tool to further marginalize Muslims in pursuance of a Hindu rashtra.

Tarannum sums it up, 'We kept quiet when the Babri Masjid was martyred and the highest court of the land did not do justice to us. We kept quiet when innocent boys were killed on 19 September [referring to the 2008 Batla House encounter] and labelled as terrorists. We kept quiet when our livelihood was threatened by the closure of butcheries and

---

[41]Bibhudatta Pradhan, 'Millions in India Could End Up in Modi's New Detention Camps', *Bloomberg*, 26 Feb 2020.

[42]Deka, 'Who is (not) a citizen?'

[43]Interview with the author, New Delhi, 19 February 2020.

curbs on meat and leather trade. We kept quiet when the government made the law on triple talaq, turning our men into criminals. But if we keep quiet now, we may even be thrown out of our own land. This is not about me and other Muslims. This is about our Constitution, about our country. If, today, they are successful in changing the Constitution, tomorrow they will change the country and make me an outsider.'[44]

The belief that the government is hostile to Muslims transcends educational and social boundaries. In October 2019, Faizan Mustafa told me over the phone that he was sure that the government was going to bring in the UCC Bill shortly. He suspected that the bill would factor in Hindu concerns on inheritance, where there is resistance to women getting a share in the ancestral property of their husbands. 'Until 1955, even unmarried Hindu women did not have a share in their father's ancestral property,' he says. 'It was only in the 1955 Hindu Code Bill that daughters became part of the Hindu joint family and got a stake in the property. Unlike this, the Muslim law of inheritance, derived from the Shariah, has a fixed share for women, both married and unmarried, in the estate of their forefathers.'[45]

Sure enough, in the second week of February 2020, rumours were rife that the government was set to introduce the UCC Bill in the Upper House of Parliament on the last day of the budget session[46] in yet another demonstration of its 'shock and awe' style of law-making.[47] That didn't happen. But Muslims remain worried about another assault on their religious and social matters.

Ignoring the increasing assault on their status and rights, many Muslims now are determined to resist in peaceful and lawful ways. One of the arenas in which they have raised their voices is social media, a space many Muslims usually entered with trepidation, often operating anonymous accounts, dominated as it was until then by the right wing,

---

[44]In conversation with the author, New Delhi, 12 January 2020.

[45]In conversation with the author, New Delhi, 13 September 2019.

[46]'Will govt introduce Uniform Civil Code bill today? BJP's whip in Rajya Sabha triggers speculations' *Economic Times*, 11 Feb 2020.

[47]Mark Tully, 'Narendra Modi's Style Is "Shock and Awe", but That Strategy Doesn't Always Work', *The Wire*, 14 September 2019.

mostly spewing anti-Muslim propaganda.[48] But after 2014, platforms like Twitter, Facebook, Instagram, and YouTube became both the battleground and spaces for mobilization. Fearless Muslim influencers have emerged who not only combat right-wing propaganda in cyberspace but are also creating a new vocabulary for secularism—these appeal to Muslims and non-Muslims alike. Using the Constitution as a protest handbook, this new crop of Muslims—educated, articulate, and confident—has been countering the right-wing narrative on nationalism with arguments of inclusivity, equality, and justice. Knowledgeable about Islam, they liberally quote from Islamic texts to counter false propaganda about their religion.

Articulate Muslims run information series on social media like 'Talk to a Muslim' or 'Who is a Muslim?', aimed at dispelling preconceived notions about Islam and Indian Muslims. Drawing courage from the support system that social media provides, many share incidents of community profiling they face at educational institutions or workplaces. It is almost as if the restrictions in the physical world are countered in cyber space.

Another consequence of social media has been the emergence of a new kind of protest poetry. Unlike traditional Urdu poetry, particularly by poets like Faiz Ahmed Faiz, whose iconic 'Hum Dekhenge' (We Shall See) has been a protest anthem for years, YouTube has provided a platform to young poets like Hussain Haidry and Aamir Aziz who employ simpler language and a modern idiom to reach a larger audience. Aziz attained instant recognition when, at a protest gathering in London, Roger Waters, the founder-member of the iconic rock band Pink Floyd, recited the English translation of one of his verses,[49] which went thus:

---

[48]Sandeep Bhushan, 'The Power of Social Media: Emboldened Right-Wing Trolls Who are Attempting an Internet purge', *Caravan*, 28 Sept 2015 and Maya Mirchandani, 'Digital hatred, real violence: Majoritarian radicalisation and social media in India', Observer Research Foundation, 29 Aug 2018.

[49]P.J. George, 'Pink Floyd's Roger Waters recites Aamir Aziz's 'Sab Yaad Rakha Jayega', calls CAA Modi's "fascist" law', *Hindu*, 27 Feb 2020. The original is here: 'Dear Oppressors, Sab Yaad Rakha Jayega. Sab Kuch Yaad Rakha Jayega', *Quint*, 19 Feb 2020: https://www.youtube.com/watch?v=Qw9DRguBqRs

Kill us, we will become ghosts
And write of your killings, with all the evidence
You write jokes in court
We will write 'justice' on the walls
We will speak so loudly that even the deaf will hear
We will write so clearly that even the blind will read
You write injustice on earth
We will write revolution in the sky
Everything will be remembered.

The consequence of all this has been that Muslims have been able to share their insecurities and anger with a large number of people, Muslims and non-Muslims alike, finding understanding and support, both online and offline. This has been a major source of the confidence and fearlessness that Tanwir alludes to.

Echoing the sentiments of many young Muslims, Aziz, an engineer by education, who had his breakthrough moment on YouTube in early 2019, asks, 'Why should I have to make all the effort to look secular?'[50] Tanwir, who has been using social media platforms, especially Twitter, to talk about Muslim issues, and to educate people about their legal rights, says the same. According to him, for years, Muslims have pretended to be someone else so that they could be accepted as modern and liberal by the mainstream. 'They underplayed their Muslimness because they believed that their Muslimness would make others uncomfortable,' he says. 'But why should that be, why should my being a Muslim, wearing a hijab or a skullcap, make anyone uncomfortable? My Constitution guarantees equality of religion, so why shouldn't I be accepted the way I am?'[51] Tanwir argues that nobody thinks a religious Hindu may not be secular, but it is assumed that a religious Muslim will be intolerant; that to be tolerant, a Muslim has to be irreligious, at least, visibly.

Tanwir's comments took me back to my adolescent years. My father made sure that in public we carried no overt markers of our

[50]Deborah Cornelious, 'Why should I have to make all the effort to look secular? asks Aamir Aziz', *The Hindu*, 17 May 2019.
[51]Interview with the author, Noida, 16 February 2020.

religion on our bodies, especially clothes, as they would reflect our Muslim 'backwardness'. Even when 'Muslim clothes' like the gharara or wide palazzo pants worn with tunics became fashionable, my father remained uncomfortable with his family members wearing it. 'These may be fashionable for others,' he would tell my mother. 'But nobody will think that you are being fashionable. They will think that you are wearing them because you are a Muslim.' Clearly, young Muslims have come a long way since then.

But is this true for the whole community or just a handful of hot-headed, social media-inspired youth? Is it a natural progression of the Muslim experience in India or is it a flash in the pan? Will it have a long-term salutary impact on the community or will things settle down to indifference and self-preservation once the provocation is removed? Is Muslim society changing or is the change akin to running to stay in the same place?

As is usually the case, the truth lies somewhere in the middle. Just as a section of Muslims is becoming self-assured and assertive, another, probably larger section, finds itself even more vulnerable than before. Its priority is to keep its head down and hope that this moment of anti-Muslim hostility will pass. Citing her own example, journalist Afreen Khan (name changed) says, 'A Muslim today is more diffident than ever before. She is more frightened today because bigotry has entered mainstream educational institutions and workplaces. If you have to continue doing what you want to, you must not draw attention to yourself. These are not my imaginary fears. My non-Muslim friends have been telling me the same thing.'[52]

Admitting to the increased communalization of public spaces, including the bureaucracy, Masood says, 'I am aware of the overt bias in the administrative services today. Some of it is clearly because of the trickle-down effect from the government, but a large part is the personal prejudice that people are bringing to their offices. The reason for this could be the profile of the people who are joining the civil services. They come from smaller towns and villages, often from poor families

[52]Interview with the author, Noida, 15 February 2020.

and would have studied in RSS-run schools. After all, they have a huge network, especially in the hinterland.'[53]

Training and government policies can subdue prejudices. But once encouraged, they become policies. And this is what is happening in India today, compromising law enforcement and compounding the fears of the Muslims—all this is pushing some of them to take extreme measures such as the reinvention of their identity.

A few lower-caste/class Muslims, who are second- or third-generation converts, have started to revert to the identity of their Hindu forefathers, starting with a name change. One of them, Mohammed Islam (not his real name), who is engaged in the business of processing bovine hides for leather tanneries in Agra–Kanpur, says, 'My forefathers were Hindus. They converted because upper-caste Hindus did not treat them well. Islam offered both dignity and security. Now, if Islam does not give us the security, then we can become Hindus again. What will we do with dignity if we can't stay alive?'[54]

After having denounced idol worship for generations and holding the belief that there is only one God, Allah, can he prostrate before idols? And commit a grave sin, according to Islam?

Looking uncomfortable, Mohammed Islam looks around before answering. 'It is not that I am not a devout Muslim. I am a Haji [one who has undertaken hajj to Mecca],' he says, a bit indignantly. 'My younger son is studying to be a hafiz. But security is also important. It is not just about my life alone, but my family too.' After a pause, he adds, 'It is about my business also. If I have a Hindu name, no one will bother that I work with cattle skin. But as a Muslim, I worry every moment.'

'So, will he only change his name?'

Checking for the umpteenth time about what I was planning to do with this interview, and whether his name would appear anywhere, he finally stammers, 'I am talking to some people that we want to return to Hinduism. We will go through the reconversion process and change our names. Magar dil mein kya hai yeh kisi ko kya pata (but how can

[53]Interview with the author, New Delhi, 13 February 2020.

[54]Interview with the author, Agra, 28 September 2019.

anyone tell what is in our hearts)?'

For people like these, the stakes are very high. From being a daily wager in different tanneries, twenty years ago, Islam started his own business of skin-processing. Now he is a businessman, supplying to tanneries where he used to work earlier. As Professor Kundu had noted in his post Sachar report, the social mobility of urban Muslims largely pertains to people employed in small-scale industries starting their own enterprises taking advantage of the country's economic growth, increased demand and easy bank loans.[55]

My younger brother, who has inherited my father's footwear export business, recalls the time when my father used to run the factory. The profile of the workers then was equally divided between Muslims and scheduled caste Hindus. 'However, in the last two decades, the ratio has changed,' he tells me. 'Today, only 20 per cent of the labour is Muslim. The rest have started their own small factories, supplying to city-based exporters. These are the people who are threatened the most.'

While part of the threat comes from government policies, especially towards businesses that depend on cattle trading—'several factories have shut down in Agra in the last five years as they became economically unviable', says my brother—the bigger threat is the vigilante mob, which now operates with impunity. The labourers-turned-entrepreneurs worry that their former fellow labourers may target them out of professional jealousy. Given the open prejudice displayed by law-enforcement agencies, especially in a state like Uttar Pradesh, small business people are looking at imaginative ways of keeping out of sight.

Not everyone is an activist or has the desire to bring about a revolution. Many people, across religions, prefer leading a regular life without being challenged either for their beliefs or lack of them. And so it is for a large number of Indian Muslims. While they are not unaffected by the Shaheen Bagh protests, they are worried about its impact on their lives and livelihood.

Atika Zakir says, 'What the women of Shaheen Bagh are doing is really commendable. I hope it has positive consequences for the

---

[55]Kundu, Report of the Post Sachar Evaluation Committee.

entire community. But I don't see the point of aggressive assertion of identity. What good can come out of casting oneself in perpetual conflict with others?' Atika takes pride in the fact that she hails from a family that embraced modern education three generations ago. Her great-grandfather used to bring out a newspaper called *Medina* back in the 1940s. A deeply religious family that has been as particular about observing the prayers and Ramzan fasting as about education and employment, Atika says that her family never felt the need to assert its identity.

'I don't wear a hijab. No one in my family ever did or does even today,' she says. 'I had to fight no battles at home to pursue a career. Finding a job after my education was a very natural thing to do. No eyebrows were raised. The only time I faced a bit of resistance was after the birth of my son. My mother-in-law suggested that I should quit. But it was such a gentle suggestion that it was easily overcome,' she chuckles.[56]

Atika is part of the small Muslim middle class that has emerged over the last few decades. Her aspirations for herself and her family are similar to those of her peers, irrespective of religion. Two years ago, her family celebrated the fiftieth wedding anniversary of her parents in one of the city's hotels. The current challenge in her life is to get her husband and two sons to agree on a common holiday destination. Her older son, who is doing a master's programme in social work, thinks he is too old to go on holiday with his parents and Atika has been trying to overcome his objections. Muslims going on holiday is part of the change that has been underway in small measure. Earlier, apart from visiting relatives, the only other travel that most Muslims undertook was to Saudi Arabia either for hajj or umrah (pilgrimage to Mecca that can be undertaken at any time of year). So widespread is this notion that when my parents renewed their passports a few years ago, everyone, including one Muslim official at the Passport Service Centre, assumed that they were going on umrah!

This change in lifestyle has, in large part, been a consequence of

---

[56]Interview with the author, New Delhi, 19 February 2020.

the embrace of modern education by a growing number of Muslims. As mentioned before, when I was in school, for several years, I was the only Muslim in my class. Today, in most public schools, it is common to find at least a couple or more Muslims in all classes. Ironically, this is one of the reasons that one hears about more cases of Muslim children suffering communal profiling in schools. The target group has increased—instead of one you could have five Muslim students in a class! This, coupled with the desire of the aspirational Muslim middle class to be seen as part of the mainstream, has been a bit unnerving for those who have never seen a Muslim in their lives before.

During her university days in 2008–2011, my younger sister had moved into a paying guest accommodation close to her college in South Delhi. In that shared accommodation, she met a girl who had never encountered a Muslim before. Meeting and living with a Muslim was the biggest adventure of her life. She announced this to her parents in great excitement when they came to visit her. She also tried to show off my sister as an exhibit to them—this is what a Muslim looks like. Of course, they never became friends. My sister, completely unselfconscious about her Muslimness, told her off. Her confidence stemmed from her upbringing, as well as years of studying and interacting with non-Muslims in school and mixed neighbourhoods.

The small measure of assertiveness that one sees today among Muslims is a result of several factors. Feeling cornered by the policies of the Modi government is just one of them. A more important factor is the emergence of a substantive number of educated and professional Muslims for the first time in India—the Muslim middle class I have referred to earlier. Until a few years ago, Indian Muslims were either very rich or very poor. While the former (a small minority) inherited their wealth, and their 'type' of education as a family tradition—liberal arts or civil services qualifications—the poor were equally the products of their inheritance, both in the trade they plied and their ability to access modern education. A small number that managed to break through the restrictions imposed by their inheritance sought jobs outside India, especially in the Gulf countries. As a result, an educated, 'mainstream Muslim' was largely invisible in India.

However, in the last three decades, there has been a gradual improvement in the education level of Muslims and they have increasingly been seeking jobs in India. According to the National Family Health Survey (NFHS) report of 2016, the percentage of Muslim boys completing their higher secondary education had doubled over the previous year.[57] While the rate of growth is poorer for women, there has been a marginal improvement over the last decade. But even with this slight improvement, the visibility of Muslims, especially in urban areas, has improved. To a large extent, this has come from the upward push by the backward classes, the Pasmandas. The growing sight of Muslims struggling to offer Friday afternoon namaz on the footpaths or community parks during a short break from work is a consequence of this education and employment network. No, their population has not increased, but they have shrugged off their invisibility cloak. However, it must be said that visibility does not immediately translate into empowerment. The 2014 PSEC observed in its report that the 'Percentage increase in share of urban population in the case of Muslims is low, especially in smaller urban centers, reflecting social factors and possibly discrimination constraining their mobility. Wide differentials exist in the quality of employment wherein Muslims are found in a disadvantageous situation with reference to the type and sectors of employment'.[58] Consequently, even though, as Tanwir says, 'Itne padhe-likhe Musalmaan toh kabhi hue hi nahin' (there have never been so many educated Muslims before), and their urban visibility may have increased, a majority of the employed remain in underpaid, or low-income positions. In fact, a large number remain self-employed,[59] like Mohammed Aamir whom I met in Shaheen Bagh volunteering with the anti-CAA–NRC protest coordination committee. A chartered accountant by qualification, he gives private tuitions in mathematics to children in the Batla House–Shaheen Bagh area. Given the economic profile of the people who inhabit these areas, clearly Aamir

---

[57]Ashwaq Masoodi, 'Joining the India story: Rise of the Muslim middle', *Mint*, 24 Jan 2019.
[58]*Final Report of Kundu Committee*, Ministry of Minority Affairs, Government of India, 29 Sep 2014, available here: https://drive.google.com/file/d/0B9LZb7Yl BSHbME1HS05sRWxRNkE/view
[59]Ibid.

is not earning anything commensurate with his qualification or what his employed peers would be.

With the increasing visibility of Muslims, especially in urban areas, a perception has grown that economic liberalization and the growth of the Indian private sector has opened doors to educated Muslim youth. The reason for this perception, according to Hamid Ansari, is the belief that 'There is less discrimination in the private sector as opposed to the government services.'[60] Yet, the truth is that even in the private sector Muslims find themselves at a disadvantage, partly because of discrimination (which has increased since 2014) and partly because of lack of adequate qualifications.

Dr Shabista Gaffar, who has served as chairperson of the committee on girl's education instituted by the National Minorities Commission during the UPA government, says that what Muslims face is a Catch-22 situation. 'Schools that most Muslims have access to still teach [the] old curriculum. They have no concept of emerging career options. As a result, even the educated do not get the jobs they believe their education should get them. This disheartens them and discourages others from spending time and money on higher education,' she says.[61]

As a result, even in the private sector, among middle level to senior employees (from senior executives to director), only 2.67 per cent are Muslims. According to the ET Intelligence Group Analysis of 2015, of 2,324 senior executives in BSE-500 listed companies, only 62 were Muslims. Even more worrying was the finding that in places where Muslims were employed in very senior positions, their remuneration was comparatively lower than that of their peers.[62]

The situation is worse in the public sector. In a statement issued in 2016, the MoMA said that it maintains no statistics on religion-specific employment ratio. What it does have is a consolidated figure, which puts the employment ratio of all minorities (clubbed together) in government

[60]In conversation with the author, New Delhi, 25 February 2019.

[61]In conversation with the author, New Delhi, 23 August 2019.

[62]Naren Karunakaran, 'Muslims constitute 14% of India, but just 3% of India Inc', *Economic Times*, 7 Sep 2015.

jobs, public sector banks, public sector undertakings at 8.57 per cent.[63] As we've seen in Chapter 2, among all minorities, Muslims are the least capable of accessing schemes made specifically for them.

So, despite what looks like progress, Muslims seem to have been running to stay in the same place. In the early nineties, Arab-inspired religious consciousness had introduced young Muslims to audio and video cassettes of preachers like the South African Ahmed Deedat. The following decades saw the rise of television evangelists like Israr Ahmed and Zakir Naik. The current generation consumes religious sermons in a more intimate space, on their mobile phones or computers. The flavours of the present time are new-age preachers like Maulana Tariq Jamil and Mufti Menk, who engage with their consumers nearly one on one. Unlike television, they offer the possibility of two-way communication because of their social media presence. For instance, Mufti Menk has a following of 5.3 million on Twitter, 3.5 million on Facebook and 1.8 million on Instagram. This immediacy and intimacy do not give one the chance to reflect, question, or verify the information being given, a luxury afforded by reading. And often one fails to distinguish between fact and opinion.

Masood says that while there have always been all kinds of Muslims in India, from non-practising ones to those who are deeply conservative and would quit work if it came in the way of their faith, today, the numbers of the latter are increasing. 'Nothing wrong with that, except that the young generation is discovering Islam on its own, and often through dubious sources,' he says.

He compares this with the indoctrination by the Jamaat-e-Islami Hind. 'It used to fire up the youth with all kinds of ideas without showing the way forward. So, you had all these young, passionate Muslims filled with a sense of alienation from others, but they had no idea what to do with either their religious passion or social alienation.'

According to Masood, these were the kind of people most vulnerable

---

[63]'Percentage of Muslims in Government Jobs', *Punekar News*, 12 Dec 2020; also see, Abantika Ghosh, 'Muslim working proportion lowest among communities', *Indian Express*, 26 Feb 2016.

to manipulation by vested interests. This is similar to what has been happening with young Hindus associated with the RSS and its various offshoots. Of course, given their population and the reach of the RSS across India, and among the Hindu diaspora across the world, the numbers are much higher and, consequently, have greater potential for harm.

'That is how Jamaat-e-Islami's student wing, the Students' Islamic Organization (SIO), morphed into the radicalized Students' Islamic Movement of India (SIMI). But when it was found to have been involved in terrorist violence and was banned, Jamaat-e-Islami Hind distanced itself from it,' says Masood.[64]

The idea of Indian Muslim youth consuming radical ideas online was more worrisome when the Islamic State in Iraq and Syria (ISIS) mounted an online recruitment drive in 2014, claiming a support base in eighteen countries worldwide from Europe to Asia. In 2018, in a statement to Parliament, Hansraj Ahir, Minister of State for Home Affairs, said that the National Investigative Agency (NIA) and various state police had arrested seventy-five people for links with the IS.[65] Of these, twenty-one were from Kerala, sixteen from Telangana, nine from Karnataka, eight from Maharashtra, six from Madhya Pradesh, four each from Tamil Nadu and Uttarakhand, three from Uttar Pradesh, two from Rajasthan, and one each from J&K and West Bengal.

Of course, seventy-five is a very small number given the Muslim population of India. But the irony was that the majority of these were from the south Indian states, where the Muslim profile is vastly different from north India. They are better educated, economically secure, and have faced fewer incidents of communal profiling. Yet, they turned out to be more susceptible to radicalization and extremist views. One possible explanation for that could be education and access to technology. Most men who have been apprehended by the NIA had some technical education if not necessarily an engineering degree. A technical mind, trained to process formulas, prefers a simplistic religion with clear-cut tasks and goals. The discipline that conservative Islam imposes on a

---

[64]Interview with the author, New Delhi, 13 February 2020.

[65]'75 arrested for alleged links with ISIS: Govt', *Economic Times*, 13 Jul 2018.

person's life works better with such people because their education has already trained them to memorize and implement instead of thinking, questioning and drifting from idea to idea.[66]

Perhaps this also explains why originally north Indian organizations like Jamaat-e-Islami Hind today have a bigger network in south India than north. Most of the Jamaat's office-bearers also hail from the southern part of the country, as do members of its students' wing, the Students' Islamic Organization.

Commenting on what he calls greater religiosity among Muslim youth, Masood says, 'My generation of Muslims was more assertive about Indo-Islamic culture. The new generation is more assertive about their Islamic identity. It is a worldwide phenomenon, not peculiar to India.'[67]

An interesting aspect of this growing interest in celebrating their Muslim identity is a desire to showcase the Muslim as an altruistic, large-hearted citizen of the country to counter the right-wing propaganda of intolerance and extremism. Alluding to the Quranic injunction on charity, Tanwir says, 'Muslims are among the largest philanthropists in the country. Our religion requires us to perform a fixed zakat annually. Most Muslim shrines run a free kitchen for the poor daily. Yet, none of this gets noticed. Nobody realizes that a Muslim is doing charity because a Muslim doesn't look like [a stereotypical] one.'[68]

But isn't that in the spirit of Islam, which says that charity should be done in a manner that the 'left hand doesn't know what the right is doing'?[69]

Ideally, yes, says Tanwir. But these days when Muslims are being profiled as dogmatic, intolerant terrorists it is important to showcase the image of a modern, educated, empowered Muslim in India. He has

---

[66]Shashi Tharoor, 'Why some engineers become terrorists', *Times of India*, 30 Mar 2008; Henry Farrell, 'This is the group that's surprisingly prone to violent extremism', *Washington* Post, 17 Nov 2015; David Berreby, 'Engineering Terror', *New York Times*, 10 Sep 2010.

[67]Interview with the author, New Delhi, 13 February 2020.

[68]Interview with the author, Noida, 16 February 2020.

[69]'Giving Charity in Secret & Publicly', available here: https://www.zakat.org/en/giving-charity-secret-publicly/

a point. Not many non-Muslims realize that charity is one of the five pillars of Islam. In fact, such is the obligation of zakat upon Muslims that it is considered a grave sin if anyone in a Muslim's neighbourhood suffers starvation or illness and those able to help do not reach out. According to Maulana Mufti Nomani, 'Every Muslim has to take care of his neighbouring households—ten each in every direction, which makes it forty. If even one person dies of starvation in any of these households, and you don't come to know, no amount of penance can forgive your sin.'[70]

Perhaps this is the reason why, even during the worst restrictions, there are no starvation deaths in Kashmir. For instance, in 2008, when the Kashmir Valley was cut off from the mainland for a few days because of the blockade imposed by the BJP unit of Jammu (the only road that connects the Valley to the rest of the country passes through Jammu), the suffering was more fiscal and emotional rather than physical.[71] Even as apple traders lost money since they couldn't transport their crop to the markets of India on time, people continued to support one another. One Kashmiri photojournalist had explained to me then that everything is a collective in the Valley. 'People share everything, from food to grief,' he said, and this has been so always.

Hence, when Tanwir and his group of volunteers organize a community kitchen, disaster relief, or 'roza iftar for all', he shows up in his Muslim gear. 'I wear my black cap,' he says with a grin.[72] It's the same with women, young working professionals who are overnight discovering headscarves, thereby turning the stereotype on its head. The more one points to the headscarf as a symbol of Islamic patriarchy or women's oppression, the more professional women turn up in one to register their protest.

One of the anxieties that the Hindu right wing had inherited from the British India government was the possibility of Indian Muslims

---

[70]Interview with the author, Noida, 16 February 2020.

[71]'Impact of Kashmir's economic blockade to continue longer', *Economic Times*, 30 Aug 2008.

[72]Interview with the author, Noida, 16 February 2020.

identifying themselves as part of the worldwide ummah. All these years, the diversity among the Muslims, globally as well as within India, has ensured that each Muslim community remained and thought independently of the other. But by their broad-brushing of all Indian Muslims as a common adversary, the Modi government has successfully united them—in their fears and resistance. This has been one of the biggest changes in the profile of the Indian Muslims. The ummah is finding a common voice.

CONCLUSION

What Muslims Want

Back in the eighteenth century, poet Nazeer Akbarabadi summed up in an evocative nazm what disadvantaged people wanted the most in life. Nazeer, who was preceded and succeeded by two exemplary Agra poets,[1] Mir Taqi Mir and Mirza Ghalib, had successfully evolved his own distinct style of poetry. Instead of matters of the heart, he observed and wrote largely about matters pertaining to life, thereby poetically recording the social and cultural history of his times.

His nazm 'Rotiyaan' remains just as relevant today as when he wrote it, perhaps even more so for the Muslims of India. Eventually, everything comes down to just this—life and livelihood. It translates thus:

> Someone asked a learned person
> what has God made the sun and the moon of.
> He answered, 'May you live long,
> but I do not understand what the sun and the moon are.
> To me everything looks like roti.
> If you do not have food in your stomach, you can't do any work.
> All desire for entertainment and leisure ceases.
> A hungry person can't even focus on prayer.
> Even Allah is remembered only when one is hungry.[2]

Echoing similar sentiments, Mohammed Shoaib Qureshi, who was

[1]The lives of all three were intertwined in a manner. Mir was born in Delhi but lived and died in Agra. Nazeer, born in Agra, rose to prominence when Mir was past his prime. Ghalib was born in Agra when Nazeer was already a renowned poet. He moved to Delhi in his youth and died there a decade after the 1857 war. Nazeer had died in Agra a decade-and-a-half before the war.

[2]See original poem here: https://www.rekhta.org/nazms/rotiyaan-nazeer-akbarabadi-nazms

forced to sell his meat-processing business a few years ago, says, 'We don't want any favours. Just treat us as equal citizens. Don't deny us the right to make an honourable living that feeds us and our families.'[3] Mohammed Shoaib had been running a profitable meat-processing business near Ghaziabad in Uttar Pradesh since the late 1970s. His was a feeder unit to several export houses, which collectively exported meat worth US$ 4.15 billion in 2016. In 2017, the figure fell to US$ 3.32 billion.[4]

During his 2014 election campaign, Narendra Modi repeatedly flagged India's meat export industry as being against Hindu values. Playing on the Green and White revolutions (the former refers to increased agricultural production caused by high-yield seeds, and the latter to the creation of the Anand milk collective by Verghese Kurien), Modi derisively called meat exports the Pink Revolution.[5] India is among the biggest buffalo meat exporters in the world. In Uttar Pradesh alone, the industry employs roughly one in 1,000 people.[6] While at the top end of the production cycle are big exporters like Al Kabeer, Al Noor and others (most of which are not Muslim-owned[7] notwithstanding the names, and consequently unaffected by politics), the middle and downstream enterprises comprise mostly Muslims (and some Dalits)—including cattle rearers, traders, butchers, and processors, as well as small-time exporters, and waste managers.

These were the people worst affected by the divisive campaign. The Hindutva foot soldiers did not understand the difference between election rhetoric and government policies. Hence, vigilante groups mushroomed all over north India and went about harassing and beating up and, in some cases, lynching to death people believed to be engaged

---

[3]Interview with the author, New Delhi, 28 September 2019.

[4]'"Cow economics" are killing India's working class', *Conversation*, 22 Jun 2017.

[5]Shoaib Daniyal, 'How Narendra Modi helped spread anti-beef hysteria in India', *Quartz India*, 7 Oct 2015.

[6]Ibid.

[7]'Who is making millions in India out of beef export? Muslims? Think Again', *Sabrang*, 10 Apr 2017.

in dealing with beef.[8] Taking its cue from this, the BJP government in Uttar Pradesh led by the chief minister, Yogi Adityanath, passed a series of orders against abattoirs and skin-processing units all over the state, ostensibly to regularize the industry.[9]

'All this is nothing but the economic suppression of Muslims,' says Mohammed Shoaib. 'The government spoke of development for all. But essentially it was development of only the chosen few. For everybody else it was harassment. The policies have been made in such a way that small and medium enterprises like mine simply cannot survive.'

Mohammed Shoaib was caught in the pincer of new rules regarding slaughter and transportation of cattle on the one hand and corrupt bureaucrats on the other. 'Every few weeks, some department or the other used to raise objections, from hygiene to environment to waste treatment. Several times, my factory was sealed arbitrarily. I have been supplying meat to several export houses for decades now. I couldn't have done that if I didn't meet their quality standards. But once the state decides to finish you, how long can you fight? At my age, I could either humour the bureaucrats or run my business,' he says.

Convinced that he was targeted because of his religion, Shoaib felt that he would be better off selling his business to a non-Muslim and making money while he still could. 'We all know that the government has an agenda and it has to appeal to its core voter base. Magar kam se kam hamare pet par laat toh na maare (but at least don't kick us in the stomach).'[10]

The other sector that has been severely affected is the leather and footwear industry, which employs 2.5 million people throughout the country, most of them Muslim. India is among the world's top five producers of leather and leather goods. Most of the skins come

---

[8]'Violent Cow Protection in India', Human Rights Watch, 18 Feb 2019 and Sanjeev Singh, 'Enforce rule of law to end menace of cow vigilantes', *Times of India*, 12 Aug 2016.

[9]'Action only against illegal abattoirs: UP government', *Economic Times*, 27 Mar 2017; 'Slaughterhouses crackdown: Meat sellers in UP to go on indefinite strike from Monday', *Indian Express*, 26 Mar 2017.

[10]Interview with the author, New Delhi, 28 September 2019.

from cows that die of natural causes or from the legal slaughter of buffaloes.[11] However, in the last five years, several leather-processing and manufacturing units have either been forced to shut down or move out of Uttar Pradesh.[12] In Kanpur alone, which is one of the biggest centres of leather production, 400,000 people (the majority of whom are Muslim[13]) involved in trade pertaining to cattle have been temporarily rendered jobless, because of falling demand and the shutting down or relocation of several factories. The ripple effect from Uttar Pradesh has been felt in places as diverse as West Bengal and Tamil Nadu, the other two big centres of leather export.[14]

Consequently, 'Exports of India's leather industry declined more than 3% in financial year 2016–17 and 1.30% in the first quarter of 2017–18, according to the latest available figures, compared to a growth of more than 18% in 2013–14'.[15] Given this, Muslims cannot be blamed for thinking that the government deliberately wants to cripple them economically, in addition to the social prejudice that they have been facing. As mentioned earlier, for all the claims of appeasement, the employment ratio of Muslims in the organized sector remains extremely poor. And the sector that employs them in large numbers is the one that has come under attack, both through policy regulations and non-governmental vigilantism.

All of this combines to ensure that Muslims as a group have the worst overall socio-economic mobility in India. In their research paper, economists Sam Asher (World Bank), Paul Novosad (Dartmouth College), and Charlie Rafkin (MIT) write, 'Muslim boys now have considerably worse upward mobility today (rank of 29) than both Scheduled Castes (38) and Scheduled Tribes (33), a striking finding

---

[11]'INSIGHT-Cattle slaughter crackdown ripples through India's leather industry', *Reuters*, 14 Jun 2017.

[12]Ibid.

[13]Ibid.

[14]Suchetana Ray and Dhrubo Jyoti, 'Leather to meat, how BJP's beef crackdown is devastating Dalits and Muslims, *Hindustan Times*, 25 Jun 2017.

[15]Nilesh Jain, 'India's Leather Exports Decline, As Cow-Related Violence Increases', *IndiaSpend*, 31 Aug 2018.

given that STs tend to live in much more remote and low mobility areas than Muslims. The comparable figure for US black men is 34. Higher-caste groups have experienced constant and high upward mobility over time, a result that contradicts a popular notion that it is increasingly difficult for higher caste Hindus to get ahead.'[16]

According to their report, Indian Muslims today have the worst rate of inter-generational mobility. This is clearly the result of several factors, the most significant of which is socio-economic insecurity which effectively dictates all their choices from education to employment to place of residence. As mentioned in the previous chapters, communal violence plays some part in this. A bigger role is played by covert and overt prejudice against the Muslims. Or, as has been the case with the current government—deliberately exclusionary policies.

Not Like Other Minorities

Following the Sachar Committee Report, the Government of India created the Ministry of Minority Affairs from the Ministry of Social Justice & Empowerment in 2006. In terms of outreach it was similar to the National Commission for Minorities, and included several religious groups including Muslims, Christians, Sikhs, Parsis, Jains, and Buddhists. Any affirmative action aimed at minorities addresses all the above communities equally, despite the wide disparity in their social and economic conditions.

As mentioned in Chapter 2, of all the minorities, Muslims have been the least capable of availing governmental ameliorative schemes, scholarships or easy bank loans. This is one of the reasons why Muslims remain the most poor and vulnerable community in India. Clearly, neither has the government been able to help ameliorate their condition, nor have better-off community members been able to do much.

The reasons for this are obvious. Starting with the deadly blow of Partition, Indian Muslims have been victims of systematically cultivated

[16]Sam Asher, Paul Novosad, Charlie Rafkin, *Intergenerational Mobility in India: New Methods and Estimates Across Time, Space, and Communities*, Jul 2020, available here: https://www.dartmouth.edu/~novosad/anr-mobility.pdf

prejudice which sadly has only grown, both in proportion and reach. No other minority in India has faced this degree of vilification.

Clearly, Indian Muslims need multi-pronged action in order to progress. One, they need to be treated differently from other minorities. The Modi government slogan of 'Sabka Saath Sabka Vikas' (With Everyone for Everyone's Progress) is meaningless for the Muslims because it assumes all communities are equally impoverished. But a large part of the Muslim population is much worse off than many other minorities.

Perhaps the lot of the Muslims will not be improved as a result of governmental action especially in the current government's term—the reasons have been discussed in earlier chapters. Hence, it is imperative that non-governmental organizations, civil society, and well-placed Muslims reach out to the rest of the community.

Asking for reservations and quotas might be the easiest thing to do but these are also the most difficult to get, given the politicking at all levels. For instance, in January 2019, during the election campaign, Prime Minister Modi announced that his government would pass a general category reservation bill for those not covered by any reservation so far. Anybody whose family's annual income was less than ₹8 lakh per year, irrespective of religion and caste, would be eligible for 10 per cent reservation. A very large number of Muslims will meet this criterion.[17] But so would many among upper-caste Hindus and other minorities. Hence, eligibility for reservation would then have to be on merit. Competing with upper-caste Hindus, Christians, Jains, and the poor, Muslims are likely to be left out because of their poor competitive capability.

An exclusively Muslim reservation is highly unlikely to come about; nor is it desirable, for the simple reason that it will be accompanied by allegations of appeasement and ingratitude. In an already polarized Indian society, no Muslim will be able to live down these insinuations, even if some future government musters the courage to do so without

[17]Rukmini S., 'Why Muslims have the first claim on any new "backward" quota', *Livemint*, 10 Jan 2019.

worrying about alienating the majority community.

Given the realities of Indian society and the compulsions of Indian politics, the best way for Muslims to find their feet will be to help one another, without hiding behind euphemisms of 'helping all deserving people' or 'let's not communalize deprivation'. In the course of writing this book, I met many accomplished Muslims, even those who identify as social activists. A few of them, who have not been quoted in the book, objected to Muslims being identified as the sole community in need of affirmative action.

'Why are you talking of Muslims alone? Why not the Dalits, the historically marginalized people?' one of them asked me.

This is one of the biggest roadblocks to advancement and acceptance that the Muslim community faces. Many among the community are reluctant to name the problem. To prove their secular credentials, they try and combine the problems Muslims face with other social issues. To overcome these odds, able members of the community will have to find their voices and will. Not only in the interest of the community but the nation too. Here are some areas where the community can help others who need it.

Education

The level of education among Muslims is the poorest in the country in proportion to their population. Historically, Muslims have been less enthusiastic about non-Islamic education, especially for women. It was generally expected that women only needed to be Quran-literate. Even a reformer of Syed Ahmed Khan's stature held such views, as mentioned earlier. After Partition, Muslims' access to modern education continued to be restricted. Poverty is certainly one of the factors that forces them to drop out of mainstream education. Another equally important reason has been the absence of good quality schools in Muslim areas. With the unavailability of quality government schools, most people have no choice but to pay to get their children educated in substandard private schools.

Professor Talat Ahmad, vice chancellor of Jamia Millia Islamia,[18]

---

[18]Since my meeting with him, he has become vice chancellor of Kashmir University.

says, 'Muslim youth face difficulties right from the beginning. Since they do not have access to good quality school education, they are unable to compete in the mainstream for higher education.' Quoting statistics from the Ministry of Human Resource Development, he says that even though Muslims comprise 14 per cent of the population, only 4 per cent enrol for higher education.[19]

In all my conversations over the past few years, the lack of competitive ability among Muslims is cited as the main reason why a large number of young people continue to drop out of the mainstream. Even schools affiliated with institutions like Aligarh Muslim University (AMU) or Jamia are not a patch on Indian private schools. Remarks Lieutenant General Zameeruddin Shah, former vice chancellor at AMU, 'The reason Muslim kids are ill-equipped to get admission in good universities is the pathetic state of school education that they have access to.'[20]

Unfortunately, even these pathetic schools are extremely small in number, forcing a number of poor Muslim parents to send their children to madrassas. That ensures their ability to read and write languages—and they get free food. Justice Rajinder Sachar highlighted this irony in his 2006 report. In terms of basic literacy, Muslim children have been found to be on a par or sometimes better than their peers; however, beyond basic education, they start to fall behind.[21]

Conscious of the important role that madrassas have been playing in the basic education of Muslim children, the Government of India has been trying to mainstream them. This is being done in two ways. One, by regularizing their curriculum through a Madrassa Board and enabling the children to take their board examinations through the National Institute of Open Schooling; and two, through a year-long bridge course, in which intensive course material enables school dropouts as well as madrassa students to compete for admission in mainstream universities. Both AMU and Jamia offer this course, which has a capacity of 100 students per year. 'We have had a 100 per cent success rate at AMU,' says Shah,

[19]Interview with the author, New Delhi, 6 February 2018.

[20]Interview with the author, 13 February 2018.

[21]Social, Economic and Educational Status of the Muslim Community of India.

which means that all bridge students were able to get admission in universities, including at AMU.

But this is a drop in the ocean, given that the overall illiteracy rate among Muslim adults, according to 2014 figures, is 42 per cent of their population. Here is another statistic to consider. Every year Muslims donate money, especially during Ramzan, as part of their obligatory zakat. This amount adds up to ₹45,000–50,000 crore annually.[22] The bulk of this money goes to madrassas and mosques. No wonder institutions like Darul Uloom and Jamiatur Raza can assert with pride that they take no money from the government. Imagine if even half this amount was available for the establishment of modern educational institutions throughout the country!

People accuse madrassas and mosques of cornering zakat money. It is an unfair allegation. The foot soldiers of madrassas and mosques work extremely hard to collect zakat from able Muslims. They go door to door through the year, battling the elements, distances, and their own impoverished state to collect the money. This has been one of the main reasons why my family members and I, like most other Muslims, have been donating to madrassas. It is hassle-free zakat done from within the air-conditioned confines of our homes, making charity simple. What's more, the entire process is transparent. Madrassa workers carry receipt books with them along with carbon paper. Many of them even encourage cashless transactions.

A few years back I decided not to donate to the madrassa/ mosque and turned away the maulana who had come to collect the money. I told him that I wanted to use the money to sponsor the education of a poor Muslim child. For two years, I gave no zakat. Given my lifestyle, I could not find a poor Muslim child for a long time. And when I did find one, his illiterate mother left all the hard lifting to me—from getting him admitted to a school to paying his fees. I was willing to spend the money, but I didn't have the time or motivation to make the effort.

---

[22]Mohammed Wajihuddin, 'Use zakat money to promote modern education', *Times of India*, 24 Jun 2015.

So here is a short list of things that Muslims can do for the upliftment of fellow Muslims in India, instead of depending on the government.

Fund Collection: Despite the general abjectness of Indian Muslims, the community also has its millionaires, upper-middle and middle class, all of whom can contribute money, provided they feel confident that their money is for a worthwhile cause. Of course, door-to-door collection as in the case of madrassas/ mosques is not possible, but an industrialist with administrative staff at his disposal should be able to set up a foundation that willing and well-off Muslims could contribute to. Given how efficient online crowd-funding has become, why shouldn't this foundation get recurring contributions from fellow Muslims?

Take the example of Jamaat-e-Islami Hind's zakat collection system. The organization encourages people to donate money, which it invests in Islamic or Sharia-approved growth funds. This keeps the corpus growing and also finances various charitable schemes that the organization runs. The entire operation is transparent, with contributors getting receipts and periodic updates on various projects being run by the Jamaat-e-Islami.

Along similar lines, a Muslim welfare fund can create several verticals such as education, healthcare, vocational training, financial support to the destitute etc. The donors can choose the cause dear to them and transfer the money directly to that cause. If a reputable organization, let's say, Wipro or Hamdard, spearheads this, it will lend greater credibility to the fund. It may even encourage people, including non-Muslims, to contribute. It can also attract funding from abroad—institutional and individual. Thereafter, this fund can direct the money to various educational programmes, from grassroots to specialized. It is impossible for an individual to do so, no matter how well-meaning. But it can be done at an institutional level.

Incidentally, both Wipro and Hamdard have Muslims at the helm, and Azim Premji, Wipro's founder, is recognized as the biggest philanthropist in the country.[23] Yet, no one from these organizations

[23]Sanya Jain, 'Azim Premji, "Most Generous Indian", Donated 22 Crore A Day', NDTV, 13 Nov 2020.

was willing to speak on the record on Muslim issues. What's more, their philanthropic activity, including Corporate Social Responsibility (CSR) is religion-agnostic.

Smart Schools: It is true that schools are not about infrastructure alone. But infrastructure is important too. Luckily, most Muslim ghettos are not entirely short of unused land. In most cities, these ghettos have come up in areas where Muslims have historically lived for generations and hence have parcels of land owned by the Waqf board. Unused plots can be procured from the Waqf board for the establishment of schools in Muslim-dominated areas. The shortfall of teachers can be mitigated through the installation of smart classrooms. For better efficiencies, the running of these schools could be outsourced to professional educational bodies.

In the evenings, or over the weekends, these schools could be turned into coaching centres for higher/technical/competitive education. These could be free, or they could charge a nominal amount.

It is true that creating Muslim-only schools will be the opposite of integration and will foster a deeper sense of separateness. But in the circumstances, this is unavoidable, at least in the short term, because schools have to be located in places where Muslims live. Even if they are open to everyone, it is unlikely that many non-Muslim children will join if they don't live in that area. Perhaps once they have a sound school education, these children can join mainstream institutions of higher learning. And then perhaps, the sense of separateness will dissipate. Besides, good schools are likely to improve competitive ability, making the transition easier.

Affirmative Action: Not through reservations, but through scholarships. As in the case of schools, government-run colleges can only admit limited numbers, leaving the vast majority of youth at the mercy of private institutions and universities. Here, education comes at a price beyond the means of many and, in fact, beyond the imagination of a lot of Muslims. Perhaps at each such private or professional institution, a certain number of seats could be sponsored for Muslims who clear the admission criteria. Additionally, scholarships should be instituted for a certain number of youth in as many technical or research institutions as possible. Let the absence of paying capacity not come in the way of those who deserve a chance.

Leave the Madrassas Alone: Despite the proliferation of madrassas in India (often flagged as a national security concern), they actually cater to a mere 4 to 5 per cent of Muslim children.[24] Frankly, they should get much less attention than they do at the moment. Madrassas are very important institutions of learning and are necessary for every Muslim society. As the Muslim population grows, so do the mosques. Each mosque, howsoever small, requires at least one maulana to conduct the prayers, and a cluster of few mosques or a large mosque needs an imam, a person with deep knowledge of both the Quran and Hadith. After all, you wouldn't want a half-literate person advising you on religious matters, would you?

It takes ten years of intensive learning at a madrassa or a darul uloom before one earns the title of an imam. Of these ten years, the first eight qualify one as a maulvi aalim, a generalist. This is followed by two years of specialization. On specializing in Quran-Hadith, one becomes an imam; with specialization in fiqh or Islamic jurisprudence, one becomes a mufti, a person authorized to issue fatwas. With similar qualifications, but more experience, a person becomes a qazi or a judge in Muslim family courts or darul qazas, which facilitate marriage, divorce, and carry out small dispute resolutions.

Having supported the idea of madrassas, I should however say this—the proliferation of madrassas has not led to any improvement in the quality of learning that they have imparted to those who attend them. This is because the people who fill these madrassas mostly come from extremely impoverished backgrounds. They come without interest and without choice. Madrassa education offers them free boarding and lodging and the possibility of employment in some mosque. They usually supplement their meagre earnings from the mosque by teaching the Quran to the children of those who can afford to send them to the best schools. Clearly, they neither have the time nor skills to develop their

[24]Wajihuddin, 'Use zakat money to promote modern education'.

intellectual faculties, to do independent reasoning, or to put Quranic verses in context.

Hence, instead of the proliferation of madrassas, schools should proliferate, giving the poor a chance at a life of their choice. Madrassa education should be voluntary. Just as in the past people undertook religious education out of interest, they should be able to do that even now irrespective of their financial situation. After all, there is no restriction on an industrialist's son or daughter becoming an imam or a mufti. On the contrary, if a person with some amount of modern education undertakes religious studies, he/ she will be better placed to put things in context. Let not madrassas be the fate of the poor. Let it be the choice of everyone, including the rich.

All Terrorists are Not 'Terrorists'

For a religion that means peace, nothing could be more demeaning than to be constantly accused of devastating violence against fellow human beings. While average Muslims may not have had much of a hand in the creation of this fallacy, the truth is that they have not done much to set the record straight or clearly define who a terrorist is.

Worse, they have sought to counter the popular narrative through either denial or apologist explanations. This is yet another aspect where the Muslim intelligentsia has failed both their own community as well as the nation. Instead of explaining that a blanket definition of terrorism is counter-productive, as it comes in the way of resolving problems, Muslim public intellectuals have preferred to toe the official line on this, perhaps, for fear of being called an anti-national or 'terrorist-sympathizer'. Consequently, they have become complicit in their own vilification. And put the entire community on the defensive.

What sealed the Muslims' reputation as terrorists in the twentieth century was the Israel–Palestine war that started with the partition of Palestine into Israeli and Arab territories in 1948. This festering conflict has been the whirlpool that has fired up Muslims from across the world with a sense of unending persecution. This has been the single catalyst to the radicalization of at least two generations of Muslims, reinforcing their sense of oppression, and, hence, resistance. The unjustness of Israeli politics, supported by the US, has given the Palestinians, and Muslims inspired by them ('intifada'—resistance—is frequently invoked by resistance movements), the argument to justify their violent responses as the only means available to them.

Since Israel could not address the issue of injustice being meted out to the Palestinians without compromising its own religious nationalism (that borders on xenophobia), and the world would not force a resolution on the problem it created in the first place, out of guilt and self-interest, it suited everyone to label the Palestine resistance as terrorism. And just like that the Palestinians' right to resist was annulled. It also ignored the tragic inequality of the conflict—a technologically advanced nation that is one of the major exporters of sophisticated military equipment pitted against people armed with last generation's weapons of questionable quality borrowed or bought from nations with equally limited capability.

This seemingly intractable conflict has rendered the entire Middle East unstable. It has kept the western powers engaged and physically present (and not always in a constructive manner) in the region, which has perpetuated a cycle of self-destruction. It has been the crucible in which other movements were nurtured, each more extremist and violent than the one which preceded it. And those it did not nurture, it inspired.[25]

History is replete with examples of how unresolved political issues and protests lead to extremist reactions. The more the world ignores political grievances and suppresses voices of resistance, the more it gives space to violent extremism. The Palestine issue is not the only example of this. At home, we have Kashmir. Even though it did not directly affect the Muslims of the rest of India, it has had an indirect impact on them.

While on the one hand, the unresolved Kashmir issue has exposed the civilian population of the Valley to sustained violence, on the other hand, it has allowed the government to label violent resistance

[25]Richard Ben Cramer, *How Israel Lost: The Four Questions*, London: Simon & Schuster, 2005, p. 295.

as terrorism, thereby leaving unresolved the political problem that underlies it. This has perpetuated a cycle of unending violence and repression. Worse, it has helped spawn the perception of Kashmiris as anti-national. The fallout of this narrative has been that regarded either as terrorists or anti-nationals, Kashmiris often face assault at the hands of regular citizens.[26]

The unresolved Kashmir dispute has led to a continuous conflict between India and Pakistan, with the latter frequently supporting (and even perpetrating) acts of terrorism on mainland India. It often employed disgruntled or disillusioned Indian Muslims to carry out terrorist attacks, thereby reinforcing the notion that 'all terrorists are Muslims', and that Indian Muslims cannot be trusted. This also contributed to the deterioration of inter-community relations in India, and the mainstreaming of anti-Muslim sentiment.

The Sauds and Islam

In the course of writing this book, I often had discussions on the Arabization of Islam, especially in South Asia. The most common response was: 'What is wrong with that, Islam is an Arabian religion. The Arabs were the chosen people to whom the religion was revealed.' There are two problems with this argument.

One, Prophet Muhammad in his last sermon delivered in Mecca told the believers:

> All mankind is from Adam and Eve. An Arab has no superiority over a non-Arab, nor does a non-Arab have any superiority over an Arab; a white has no superiority over a black, nor does a black have any superiority over a white; (none have superiority over another) except by piety and good action.[27]

Two, according to Islamic belief, Prophet Muhammad was the last in a long line of prophets, and the prophethood ended with him. The first

---

[26]Rifat Fareed, 'Fear grips Kashmiris living in India after deadly suicide attack', *Al Jazeera*, 16 Feb 2019.

[27]'Prophet Muhammad's Last Sermon: A Final Admonition'.

prophet of Islam was the first human being, Adam, who descended from Paradise to South Asia (modern-day Sri Lanka), not Arabia. Similarly, other prophets of Islam were born in different parts of the world. While the Quran mentions twenty-eight prophets, the Hadith talks of around 124,000 prophets. According to a verse in Surah Yunus (Jonas in the Bible) of the Quran,

> And for every community there is a messenger. After their messenger has come, judgment is passed on them in all fairness, and they are not wronged.[28]

Even the Arabs were aware that their specialness only lay in the fact that the last Prophet of Islam was from among them, nothing more. That is the reason they strove to spread the religion to other parts of the world—to justify Allah's grace bestowed on them.

However, if even this evidence is not enough to show that Islam was meant to be a religion for all humankind, then one of the most revered scholars among the conservatives, Maulana Maududi, insisted that Islam was a religion for everyone, not just the Muslims, as mentioned earlier. Why then must Muslims hold Arabia as the chosen land? In any case, the caliphate itself was not limited to the Arabs and was held by the Turks for several centuries.

Hence, it is time Muslims hold Saudi Arabia accountable for what it has done or not done for the cause of Islam and the worldwide Muslim community. Today, Saudi Arabia rakes in nearly US$ 12 billion from hajj and umrah pilgrimages. This is 20 per cent of its non-oil GDP and 7 per cent of its total GDP. According to some estimates, by 2022, Saudi's total earnings from the twin pilgrimages will touch US$ 150 billion.[29] Given the uncertainty of the oil market, it won't be a surprise if the global Muslim community ended up underwriting the profligacy of the Saudi monarchy through pilgrimages.

But this is not all. 'The Saudi and other Gulf authorities maintain religious charities to which rich and poor donate, as prescribed for

[28]Surah Yunus, Verse 10.47, translated by Dr Mustafa Khattab (https://quran.com/10).

[29]'Why Haj will soon be the new oil for Saudi Arabia', *Times of India*, 21 Aug 2018.

Muslim believers.... Many of these charities were exposed after September 11 as backers and supporters of bin Laden,' writes Schwartz.[30]

He adds, 'Evidence of Saudi charitable institutions being used to advance terrorism was found in early 2002, in the offices of the Saudi High Commission for Relief to Bosnia–Herzegovina. Documents seized by the Sarajevo authorities revealed the scope of the Saudi-backed Wahhabi "jihad" in the Balkans during the previous decade.'[31]

Hence, it is only fair to ask what the kingdom of Saudi Arabia has done for the Muslims in return for the enormous contribution of the ummah towards its economy. That Saudi Arabia has, since after the time of the Prophet Muhammad, only contributed to divisiveness among Muslims through self-serving opportunistic politics is a matter of historical record. It has not merely exported extremism abroad, it is actively engaged in warring against fellow Muslims, whether in Yemen or Syria, with the support of so-called disbelievers. Clearly, there is much that is un-Islamic and ignoble about the country which exists only to feed its monarchy.

It's time now for the sake of its future that Islam is delinked from the land of its birth. And perhaps, Indian Muslims, given their role in the evolution of Islamic thinking, should take the lead in bearing responsibility for the future of the faith in partnership with the most populous Muslim country in the world, Indonesia. A pilgrimage zone comprising areas of Mecca and Medina should become an autonomous protectorate of an international organization, with proportional representation from all countries depending on their Muslim populations. A working committee could be elected from among the members, who, in turn, should elect their secretary general for fixed tenures. Pilgrimages like hajj and umrah should be organized by this global body. Given the revenue generated by the pilgrimages, it won't even need additional contributions from member countries. Issues like administration, management, logistics, and security could be outsourced to professionals.

---

[30]Schwartz, *The Two Faces of Islam*, p. 291.

[31]Ibid.

Over time, people will understand that the Arabia of Islam's past is not the Saudi Arabia of today. That ancient land will always be sacred, but the modern country needs to be treated like any other nation. Its tyranny needs to be called out. Often, new ideas sound preposterous at the time they are floated. But that should not hold us back from exploring them further. What is a mere kingdom in the face of the entire Muslim ummah? As Faiz Ahmed Faiz wrote,

Hum dekhenge, lazim hai ki ham bhi dekhenge
Vo din ke jis ka vaada hai...
...Sab taaj uchhale jaaenge
Sab takht giraae jaaenge...
...Aur raaj karegi khalq-e-Khuda
Jo main bhi huun aur tum bhi ho

(We shall see, it is incumbent upon us to see, the promised day... all the crowns will be tossed, all the thrones will be toppled. That will be our day of reckoning, we, who are the people of God).

Reclaim Religion

Islam is one of the few organized religions which gave agency to the individual, irrespective of gender, to decide her actions in relation to her faith for herself without any kind of mediation through mullahs or ulema. Wherever people are addressed in the Quran, the verses use the phrase 'Muslim men and Muslim women'. But this agency required individual Muslims to take responsibility for their actions.

Unfortunately, most Muslims, especially in the Indian subcontinent, remain uncertain and underconfident about their faith because, to them, Islam is not a matter of belief alone, but a pact that they have signed with Allah with an unforgiving set of dos and don'ts. Hence, they feel safe entrusting themselves, including their thinking faculties, to Islamic organizations or mullahs, allowing themselves to be herded by them unquestioningly, thereby putting the responsibilities of their actions on the mullahs. It is this class of unthinking Muslims who have aided the atrophy of the religion that continues to seek inspiration from the past and has shut its mind to the future.

Islam did not encourage a hierarchical clergy because Prophet Muhammad understood that power corrupts. And absolute power creates vested interests. If Islam is to be a religion for all humankind, and one for all time to come, then it is incumbent upon the Muslims of today to ensure that it does not atrophy. Prophet Muhammad told his companions that while the Quran answers all questions, when doubts arise, listen to your heart.

Times change. The world changes. And the application of faith has to keep pace. The religion of Islam was an idea which was the need of those times. Today, it is an idea that should invest people with nobility, virtuousness, and large-heartedness among other things. If Islam is to truly become a religion for all time to come, then each Muslim has to be an integral part of its positive evolution and change.

ACKNOWLEDGEMENTS

Thank God! If it wasn't for God, this book wouldn't exist. Nevertheless, although a lot of the book deals with the subject of God, that is not the only reason I am grateful to the almighty. Several times in the last two years that I was working on this book, I felt that I was being led to an idea I hadn't thought about consciously. Many a time, I felt that I was being directed towards research material I hadn't considered before to support the arguments that were forcing themselves on me but appeared too preposterous at first glance. And then there were middle-of-the-night epiphanies that would have me reaching for the notebook and pen on my bedstand. Divine intervention? Who can be sure. So, thank you, God!

The memories of my late grandfather formed the base on which I have built this book. This debt, I will never be able to repay. I just hope this is something he would have approved of. And worthy of the two rupees he used to give me whenever he was pleased with me.

The journey from an idea to conviction was long—full of self-doubt and inertia. That is where friend, colleague, and collaborator Pravin Sawhney stepped in. He repeatedly articulated what I was hesitant to think—that this was one book I must write. He motivated me, supported me and, most importantly, believed in my abilities to see this through. And once the process got underway, he kept pace with me, reading everything I wrote even though it was not a subject he had much interest in. By doing this he brought an outsider's perspective to the subject of Islam and helped me delve deeper into prejudice and preconceived biases.

My younger sister, Shahznan Wahab, threw an invisibility cloak around me, creating a cocoon in which I could work, diverting demands of the extended family to herself. Having created this workspace for me, she set a timetable for me and was unrelenting in her exertions to ensure I kept it. She read the manuscript as it was being written and raised questions that I hadn't considered, gave suggestions and shared her experiences to give me a perspective on how prejudice has been mainstreamed over the years. All this helped bring greater clarity to the book.

Starting the research was the most challenging part of the process. Finding a credible and open-minded Islamic scholar was not an easy task, especially in today's environment. It was a sheer stroke of luck that I met Professor Mohammed Ishaque. Even when he sometimes disagreed with my arguments, he engaged with me, never declined a request for a meeting, and introduced me to other scholars, in particular, Javed Ahmed Ghamidi, who I learnt is regarded as a foremost contemporary Islamic theologian. Others who were patient with me as I struggled with ideas, and were generous with their time, include Wajahat Habibullah, Salman Khurshid, Najeeb Jung, Professor Talat Ahmad, Laila Tyabji, and Maulana Mahmood Madani.

While the writing was a solitary process, the research turned into a community activity with family members often helping in getting answers from select muftis and imams whom I couldn't reach. A heartfelt thank you to my brothers, Rizwan and Rehan, and my sisters and brother by marriage, Hafiza, Bushra, and Utkarsh. Also to my cousins, Naghma, Sadaf, and Ambreen for frequently throwing questions about Islam at me as FAQs to help me understand the breadth of misconceptions among Muslims.

Several friends, mostly unknowingly, helped me get insights, sometimes through casual conversations and sometimes by just being who they were and are. Thank you, Raveen Suri, for the childhood lesson on prejudice and unquestioning friendship; Samita Bhatia, for your love and critical observations on the manuscript; Sanjari Chatterjee, for your optimism; Meenakshi Kumar, for being the anchor; and Shahnaab Alam.

Thank you, Pujitha Krishnan, for your patience and perseverance in steering the idea into a publishable manuscript; Bena Sareen for going beyond the obvious in conceptualizing and designing the cover; and David Davidar, for seeing a book in an idea, when it was nothing more than stream of consciousness.

There are a few other people who need to be acknowledged for making my life so comfortably seamless that I could travel, think, write and mope, without the daily responsibilities of office and home interrupting me. Sweety, Saroja, and Uday in the office; Shabana and Preety at home.

My last and most heartfelt acknowledgement is to *FORCE* magazine—a labour of love, which became my career.

INDEX